Searching for the Body

Searching for the Body

A Contemporary Perspective on Tibetan Buddhist Tantra

Rae Erin Dachille

Columbia University Press

New York

Columbia University Press
Publishers Since 1893
New York Chichester, West Sussex
cup.columbia.edu

Library of Congress Cataloging-in-Publication Data
Names: Dachille, Rae Erin, author.
Title: In Search of the Body: A Contemporary Perspective on Tibetan Buddhist Tantra / Rae Erin Dachille.
Description: New York : Columbia University Press, 2022. | Includes bibliographical references and index.
Identifiers: LCCN 2021061436 (print) | LCCN 2021061437 (ebook) | ISBN 9780231206082 (hardback) | ISBN 9780231206099 (trade paperback) | ISBN 9780231556316 (ebook)
Subjects: LCSH: Buddhist cosmogony—China—Tibet Autonomous Region—History and criticism. | Mandala (Buddhism)—China—Tibet Autonomous Region—History and criticism. | Dge-lugs-pa (Sect)—Doctrine—History and criticism. | Sa-skya-pa (Sect)—Doctrine—History and criticism. | Tantric Buddhism.
Classification: LCC BQ4570.C6 D33 2022 (print) | LCC BQ4570.C6 (ebook) | DDC 294.3/43709515—dc23/eng/20220608
LC record available at https://lccn.loc.gov/2021061436
LC ebook record available at https://lccn.loc.gov/2021061437

Cover design: Elliott S. Cairns
Cover image: Private collection. Himalayan Art Resources #4227. Photo by Jeff Watt. Courtesy of Himalayan Art Resources.

FOR MY MOTHER, Janice Dachille

Contents

Acknowledgments

The seams and sutures of this book are many. In each phase of assembling and disassembling the pieces, there have been countless guides, confidants, and cheerleaders. Their wisdom, questions, challenges, and love were essential in helping me to cultivate the endurance to continue to search for the body through the profound and complex sources of Tibetan Buddhist thought. Their support proved vital in the long process of rearticulating my findings and polishing the components of this book to engage with a diverse range of thinkers across the arts and humanities.

This book would not have been possible without the foresight of Khenpo Jorden, who provided an intellectual home for me at the International Buddhist Academy in Nepal and connected me with brilliant mentors. I extend my deepest gratitude to Drakpa Gyatso, whose expert advice on the Sakya tradition has sustained me throughout the many phases of this research and whose patience and insight have been essential. I am also indebted to Khenpo Tashi Dorjee, who read Ngor chen's biographical materials with me in the early stages of research and provided vital connections to leaders within the Sakya tradition. My deepest gratitude to Garshab Rinpoche for bringing the Sakya tradition to life for me and to the Forty-first Sakya Trizin Ngawang Kunga for granting me audience. My research was deeply enriched by reading the Gelukpa materials under Khenpo Choying Dorjee, Dongsung Shabdrung Rinpoche, and Khenpo Yeshe. I would also like to thank my many guides in learning the Tibetan language over the years in Madison, Berkeley, India, Tibet, and Nepal, particularly Tsetan Chonjore, Jampa Khedup, and Urgyen Palmo. Special thanks to Sarah McClintock, who introduced me to "cutting the ground" (*sa bcad*), a technique that is central to this book's approach to Tibetan intertextuality.

The book began with an interest in the artistic and ritual traditions of Ngor and the sage advice of Kurt Keutzer, a friend and mentor at Berkeley, who pointed me in the direction of the body mandala debate. Through Kurt's efforts and the support of the Group in Buddhist Studies at UC Berkeley I had the good fortune of first reading Ngorchen's body mandala writings under the guidance of Shabdrung Lama Kunga Thartse Rinpoche, an opportunity for which I am truly grateful.

I owe a great debt to my "root guru" at UC Berkeley, Alexander von Rospatt, who stoked my enthusiasm for Himalayan art and ritual. From our first meeting in the office of the late Min Bahadur Shakya in Patan, you have been drawing me into the mandala. And like any great *ācārya*, in your role as guide you have performed the various acts of inviting, binding, delighting, and subduing involved in effecting a meaningful transformation. Many thanks to Jacob Dalton for helping me to "tame my demons" by fostering my study of Tibetan tantric traditions and for exposing me to the ritual worlds of Dunhuang. Alex and Jake, I am so grateful for your continued support and willingness to field questions over the years. My deepest gratitude to Patricia Berger, whose warmth and wisdom nourished me through challenging moments and whose ability to see what I was thinking before I did was astounding. Thank you for expanding my horizons to include the visual worlds of Dunhuang and of the Qing and for providing the theoretical tools for articulating the modes of representations I encountered. Also to be thanked at Berkeley are Mark Csikszentmihalyi, who challenged me to employ context and specificity in my approach to critical theory, and Mark Blum, who asked questions about the role of Yogācāra thought in Tibet that led me to discover my hidden argument. Thanks to Robert Sharf, whose work on Buddhist ritual continues to inspire me to attempt to approach esoteric materials with clarity and broader perspective.

I deeply appreciate the generosity of the many scholars who met with me in the various exploratory phases of the project including Yael Bentor, José Cabezón, Richard Davis, John Dunne, Robert and Sally Goldman, Janet Gyatso, Jörg Heimbel, David Jackson, Christian Luczanits, Cyrus Stearns, Susan Stryker, and Kimiaki Tanaka. Many thanks to Sarah Jacoby and Rory Lindsay for providing feedback and further questions on my research on tantric embodiment and the Sakya tradition, respectively. I would like to thank Linda Lin for her incisive comments on my manuscript and for compelling me to continue to clarify and polish this work. The book was greatly improved by Linda's observations and by thought-provoking feedback from anonymous reviewers.

To my cohort at UC Berkeley and my colleagues in the Department of Religious Studies and Classics and the Department of East Asian Studies at the

University of Arizona, I am indebted to you for providing the support, camaraderie, and ambition to survive the world of academia. To my friends Dan McNamara and Chris Limburg, thank you for your encouragement through those early days of Tibetan-language study and the attendant growing pains. To the students I have had the pleasure of working with at the University of Arizona, Colorado College, and Bard College, thank you for prompting me to communicate and reexamine things I took for granted about Buddhist traditions.

I would like to thank Charles Hallisey, who early in my graduate training patiently mentored me in the art of asking good questions and in my interests in modes of representation. Thank you for accepting the role of respondent for a panel on Buddhist arts of citation that I organized for the 2018 AAR meeting in Denver. Your remarks played a key role in pushing this book forward and in shifting my focus to consider the mediating role of representation. Thanks to my fellow panelists, Justin Fifield, Kevin Buckelew, and Pamela Winfield, for generating a fruitful conversation. I would also like to pay reverence to the memory of Amchi Pema Dorjee, under whose tutelage I explored representations of the body within the Tibetan medical tradition. This work was formative for my later explorations of tantric approaches to embodiment. I am deeply appreciative of the generous feedback and insights of my colleague Max Strassfeld as well as his encouragement to join the reading group of the Trans Studies Research Cluster at the University of Arizona. To bell hooks, I am grateful for the inspiration to "be bold" in all of my intellectual pursuits and to engage Buddhist resources in current conversations around feminism and liberation.

To Conor Elliott Fitzgerald, thank you for coaxing me from the galleries of Buddhist art into the contemporary wing. You challenged me to demonstrate the relevance of the issues of representation I explore in the Buddhist context to those posed in contemporary photography and conceptual art. This challenge has been life-changing. I look forward to continuing to expand one another's worlds and to many more provocative conversations and gut-wrenching giggles. My cup runneth over, my love. And thanks to all the fabulous Fitzgeralds for welcoming me into the fold. To Nancy Lin, you have guided my heart and mind throughout our journey together. From our first meeting in Lhasa, through adventures in Dharamshala, Berkeley, and beyond, your wisdom has been unfailing. To Emily McRae, my gentle warrior and most devoted coconspirator, you lead by example. Your friendship has been one of this life's greatest gifts. I wish you and all those within your ever-widening circle of care boundless happiness, especially of course Asha. My dear friend Janet Um has provided unflinching support over the many years of graduate work and beyond, bringing warmth and constancy during especially troubled times. Janet has also kept me well-supplied with great stories. The fiction we read together stoked the fires of my passion for writing in subtle but essential ways over the final years of bringing this book to fruition.

To my mother, you deserve an honorary degree in both Buddhist studies and creative writing by now. In the midst of a pandemic lockdown as I despaired over revisions, you listened for forty-five minutes at a time while, crouched on my kitchen floor, I read aloud from the manuscript over the phone. This is just a speck in the multiverse of selfless deeds you have performed on my behalf in this lifetime alone. In my confidence and curiosity to teach and to learn, I have been powered by your love. May all you have given return to you threefold. To my father, whose pride in me seemed delusional at times: the unconditional love you gave me throughout your life has emboldened me to love, learn, and forgive myself for missteps. I only wish that we could celebrate this moment together. You are in my heart always. To my brother Neil, who has given me some of the best teaching advice I've ever received: from you I have learned to meet people where they are and to project my voice. You have taught me to how to use my compassion. No gift could be greater. To my brother Michael and my sister-in-law Carel: you have provided support and shelter at key moments in my learning process. I am so grateful to have had your love and encouragement over the years. To my niece Arielle, whose humor, honesty and loyalty have nourished me: you have been friend, niece, cheerleader, and critic all in one. I look forward to continuing to "grow up" together.

Over the many years of research and study entailed by this project, I have benefited from funding from the Fulbright IIE, the Townsend Center for the Humanities, the Group in Buddhist Studies at UC Berkeley, Title VI awards, and College of Humanities Faculty Research Grants and the Provost's Author Support Fund at the University of Arizona. The support of editors at Columbia University Press has been crucial to actualizing this project. My deepest thanks to Wendy Lochner for encouraging me to synthesize my interests in religious studies and critical theory in writing this book and to Lowell Frye and Susan Pensak for helping me to the finish line. Many thanks to Shan He and Alexander Trotter for additional manuscript support.

With deepest gratitude to all of you, I rejoice in this moment of completion and claim any errors as my own. Perhaps for a book focused on imagination and citation, the immortal words of Puck will suffice: "If we shadows have offended, / Think but this, and all is mended, / That you have but slumbered here, / While these visions did appear. / And this weak and idle theme, / No more yielding but a dream, / Gentles, do not reprehend. / If you pardon, we will mend."

A Technical Note

In this book, I phoneticize Tibetan proper names according to the Tibetan and Himalayan Library's Phonetic Transcription system. The bibliography and bibliographic references are exceptions; there the names appear in Wylie transliteration. In the appendixes, when I refer to Indian masters cited by the Tibetan authors, I generally list the Tibetan equivalent of the Sanskrit name when the Tibetan authors use it but also include the Sanskrit name in parentheses. For the names of living Tibetan masters, I conform to their own standard choices of spelling. In quoting the work of other scholars, I generally retain their choices of transliteration schema. When providing excerpts from and emendations to Tibetan sources within the notes, I use Wylie transliteration.

Tibetan technical terms appear in parentheses throughout the book. In cases where I supply a Sanskrit term in parentheses, I indicate it with "Skt." In the very rare cases where I retain a Tibetan technical term within the text rather than translate it, I spell it phonetically. The two most prominent examples are the term for "representation," literally "support," phonecticized as *ten* (Wylie equivalent: *rten*), and the term for winds, phoneticized as *lung* (Wylie equivalent: *rlung*). See the index for the Wylie equivalents of any Tibetan names or terms that have been phoneticized.

In cases where I am comparing Ngorchen's two body mandala texts, I add [N1] to refer to *Destroyer of the Proponents of Evil Through Eliminating Objections to the Hevajra Body Mandala* (abbreviated after initial occurrences as *Destroyer of the Proponents of Evil*) and [N2] to refer to *Dispelling Evil Views of the Hevajra Body Mandala* (abbreviated after initial occurrences as *Dispelling Evil Views*) in order to clarify the distinction between his shorter and longer body mandala texts respectively. Within the chapters, I translate and abbreviate the titles of Tibetan texts and translate or provide Sanskrit equivalents for the titles of Tibetan translations of Sanskrit texts. I refer to the titles of the tantras in a simplified form, ex. *Hevajra Tantra*. See the bibliography for full Tibetan titles of texts. When using Sanskrit terms, I employ diacritics. Buddhist terms that have been incorporated into the English language such as *sutra* and *samsara* appear without diacritics or italics unless they refer to a text's title.

Searching for the Body

Introduction

Why embrace representations if they are not "true?" From a broad Buddhist perspective, the mind's tendencies to generate representations in the form of images and concepts present obstacles to accessing the true nature of reality. Representations bombard, deceive, and proliferate beyond control, becoming standards of measure, objects of attachment, and incomplete and imperfect substitutes for reality. And yet the practices of Buddhist tantra suggest that within the poison lies the cure. If the mind's representational impulses are harnessed through tantric means, they can become powerful tools for liberation and transformation. This book is about a debate between two fifteenth-century scholar monks on one such tantric ritual practice known as body mandala. In mapping the maneuvers of these Buddhist authors as they interpret body mandala, I reveal the relevance of their approaches for contemporary struggles with the paradoxes of representations. In the process, I explore the search for meaning in and through bodies, texts, and images as a defining aspect of what it means to be human.

Body mandala is like the brain surgery of tantric "rites of attainment" (Skt. *sādhana*), meaning that it is a highly elaborate form of the core ritual act of imagining oneself as a Buddha. This is a practice performed only by the accomplished adept. According to the *Vajrayāna* tradition of Buddhist tantra, bodies contain hidden potential for meaning that is invisible to the novice. This potential is best described as the vajra body, a network of channels, winds, and drops that only the tantric adept has the skill to recognize and control.[1] Through performing the completion stage of *sādhana*, the tantric adept learns to access and manipulate the elements of the vajra body as tools for achieving enlightenment in this present lifetime and body. In body mandala, the adept rearticulates their reality by imagining the parts of the body as deities. Body mandala is therefore an especially powerful tantric tool for realizing meaning and for attaining the ultimate goal of becoming a buddha.

In documenting the quest to understand what is at stake in the body mandala debate, this book reveals a deep connection between ritual mechanics and interpretive practice. Many of the texts these Tibetan authors draw upon in making sense of body mandala are cryptic and contradictory and therefore demand intervention. The incomplete nature of such textual representations of body mandala, the way in which they demand commentary in accessing their meanings, attests to the importance of learned guides within the tantric tradition. The body mandala debate illuminates how two such guides lead readers through the intricacies of tantric text and ritual within a fifteenth-century context in which efficacy, authenticity, and the construction of meaning are intertwined.

Searching for the Body is the first in-depth exploration of body mandala ritual in tandem with transdisciplinary themes of imagination, creativity, embodiment, intertextuality, and representation. My use of the first-person voice throughout the text is one technique for reinforcing my own role in restaging, contextualizing, and translating Tibetan Buddhist texts within the shifting sands of academic and popular discourses.[2] In my reading of the debate, I respond to existing scholarship on the encounter using an approach that balances concerns with lineage, ritual, and exegesis. In the process, I uncover aspects of how representations work in perpetual tension between fabrication and naturalness, continuity and rupture, source and repetition. Cultivating attention to the manner in which Tibetan authors navigate and modify the boundaries of interpretation reveals the elegance of their craftsmanship. As I will show, beneath their strategies for establishing continuity lies a complex array of concerns with rupture, creativity, and determining who is qualified to interpret tantric texts.

Nuancing understandings of the body mandala debate with attention to these tensions and concerns, I introduce the figure of the Buddhist exegete as a guide who navigates the paradoxes of representation and cultivates the critical skills needed to make way through their potentialities and pitfalls. These skills empower the reader to face the challenges posed by fifteenth-century tantric texts as well as by the onslaught of representations that characterize life in the twenty-first century. The results promise to enrich future encounters with images, texts, and bodies as supports for accessing a more accurate view of reality and for transforming the boundaries of what it means to be human.

THE EXEGETE AS GUIDE

Exegete derives from Greek roots meaning "to lead or guide out of." The English word *exegete* typically describes someone who interprets texts, oftentimes biblical texts. I adapt the term here to describe Tibetan Buddhists navigating tantric texts and practices to create meaning. The Tibetan equivalent of exegete would be commentator (*'grel pa po*), one who "clarifies" and "unravels."[3] Within the Tibetan tradition, producing commentaries is among the most valued roles of a Buddhist teacher along with creating and performing rituals and fending off faulty interpretations. As the body mandala debate shows, these commitments are interconnected. To clarify the words of the Buddha and of his esteemed lineage of interpreters is linked with extending this lineage through ritual and defending it against both internal and external threats, real and imagined. Words such as *commentator* and *hermeneut* effectively convey the manner in which this book's protagonists "clarify," "unravel," and "interpret." However, in analyzing the authorial maneuvers of two fifteenth-century Tibetan authors engaged in a debate about body mandala, I choose to use the word *exegete* to emphasize their role as guides. I show the unique ways in which these authors lead the reader through the complex twists and turns of navigating the paradoxes of representations, in particular their contradictions, their lacunae, and their state of tension with their constructed nature.

Exegetes guide the reader through the process of rearticulating meaning as a way of breaking down and making sense of the world. They train the reader to make connections that have the potential to be transformative. Tantric practitioners use these skills to navigate texts and ritual practices, to access the profound meanings of bodies and texts while working within the boundaries of representations. Representations, in turn, proliferate beyond their original context. They are defined by a dynamic pull between limitation and potential. As I will show, in the hands of the skilled exegete, representations become not just fabrications, illusions, or objects of attachment, but supports for rearticulating meaning.

Understanding how Buddhist authors craft seamless bodies of meaning, the ways in which they imagine, construct, map, and align connections, diversifies the resources available for engaging with contemporary rearticulations of the body as a proxy for what it means to be human. In the wake of the postmodern turn and the movement away from the body as an object of knowledge, this book shows why the search for the body continues to be meaningful.

REPRESENTATIONS AS "SUPPORTS"

The closest Tibetan equivalent to *representation* as I am using it here is *ten* (Wylie equivalent *rten*, pronounced ten), a term that means "support." In Tibetan, the term *support* (*rten*) defines a collective category for representation inclusive of texts, images, and bodies. The support can refer, for example, to a text as the container of Buddha word, to a painting or statue consecrated to house the presence of buddhahood, and to a disciple as a receptacle of the guru's teachings.[4] Representation in the sense of support is therefore a category that extends across media, defined by the function of providing support for enlightened realization. The English term *representation* bears connotations of image and likeness and a complex relationship to presence.[5] In turn, English terms *text* and *image* bear roots that connect texts to being "woven" and images to "imitation." The roots of the word *body* remain somewhat unclear, but in its form as "corpus," it bridges the worlds of bodies and texts. In both Sanskrit and Tibetan languages, the semantic range of "image" and "body" as "support" (*rten*), "reflection" (*gzugs brnyan,* Skt. *prati-bimba*), or "something fashioned or molded" (Skt. *deha*) expresses their shared terrain.[6] While *support* does not share all of the meanings of *representation*, support in the Buddhist sense shares the key property of mediation.

Buddhist attitudes toward representations provide reminders of the gap between representation and reality. For example, when an image is consecrated, the ritual includes a kind of disclaimer in the form of verse teaching the truth of interdependent origination. This verse is ritually recited, inscribed, and inserted as a reminder of the constructed and ephemeral nature of all phenomena, including these supports. Moreover, there have been controversies around the nature of the mediation of ordinary and enlightened realities performed by supports. For example, Tibetan thinkers have asked whether representations manifest a divine presence that was previously absent, perform a pedagogical role, or reveal an already present enlightenment.[7] While they contain paradoxical elements prompting such existential questions, representations are valued for their potential to serve as tools in achieving freedom from the cycle of suffering. Like bodies, they provide a context and opportunity for regarding the true nature of things. For tantric Buddhists, exegetes provide the skills for using representations to their full potential.

In this book, I use the word *representation* to describe a diverse array of images, texts, and bodies. These include Tibetan paintings of the protagonists of the body mandala debate, polemical texts on body mandala together with the larger network of texts upon which they draw via citation, and descriptions of the vajra body, as well as mental representations, the fruits of tantric ritual acts of imagining. I also use *representation* to speak beyond the specific context of the body mandala debate to engage with broader Buddhist conceptions of body and mind and of representation and reality, conceptions that play a part in defining what it means to be human. In demonstrating the relevance of the Buddhist exegete's skills to contemporary twenty-first century debates, I use *representation* to explore the roles of texts and images in reflecting, limiting, and expanding the experience and potential of embodied individuals. I conclude each chapter with reflections on how to bridge these different senses of representation. I show that while there are significant ways in which these three senses of representation differ, they share key properties such as the ability to mediate between appearances and actualities and to serve as a basis for rearticulating meaning. Toward this end, I also provide two examples of contemporary exegetes, one a trans scholar and activist featured later in this introduction and the other a Black and queer contemporary artist whose work is the focus of the epilogue.

Introducing Two Fifteenth-Century Exegetes

In 1426, a Tibetan scholar monk and ritual expert, Ngorchen Künga Zangpo (1382–1456), defended his tradition against claims that struck at the heart of their fiercely guarded body mandala practice. In *Destroyer of the Proponents of Evil Through Eliminating Objections to the Hevajra Body Mandala* [N1] (abbreviated throughout as *Destroyer of the Proponents of Evil*) together with a partner text, *Dispelling Evil Views of the Hevajra Body Mandala* [N2] (abbreviated throughout as *Dispelling Evil Views*), Ngorchen refuted claims that threatened to destabilize the authority of the Sakya tradition to which he belonged.[8] The "proponents of evil," as they are dubbed in Ngorchen's title, charged the Sakyapas with transmitting an illegitimate version of body mandala, one that lacked grounding in Indian Buddhist canonical sources. This charge challenged the authenticity of the Sakya "Path and Fruit" (*lam 'bras*) tradition for which Hevajra body mandala is central.

Who is Ngorchen's opponent on the topic of body mandala? A few years earlier, Khédrupjé Gélek Pelzangpo (1385–1438), a champion of the emerging Gelukpa/Gandenpa tradition, wrote an epic compendium on an entirely different tantric ritual system. In that text, *Ocean of Attainment of the Guhyasamāja Generation Stage* (abbreviated throughout as *Ocean of Attainment*), Khédrup critiqued the Sakyapa transmission of the Hevajra body mandala, albeit not explicitly by name.[9] At that time, the Gelukpa tradition, set in motion by Khédrup's teacher Tsongkhapa Lozang Drakpa (1357–1419), was beginning to crystallize as a coherent entity independent of its roots in other lineages, including of its Sakya roots. This new development provoked anxieties around ruptures within the Buddhist community.

The debate is not about whether body mandala works. Both Ngorchen and Khédrup agree that body mandala is a unique and powerful tool for striving for liberation. Ngorchen, for example, distinguishes body mandala as the "profound shortcut" (*myur lam zab mo*) for transforming the body into an enlightened form, the ultimate goal of tantric practice.[10] For Khédrupjé, body mandala is superior among representations because it is "not newly fabricated" (*gsar du ma bcos pa*), placing this practice within a spectrum of authenticity determined by degrees of fabrication and naturalness to be discussed further in chapter 1.[11] While both authors laud body mandala as a transformative Vajrayāna technology, they disagree on the method of performing it and on which sources to rely upon as guides. Moreover, Ngorchen and Khédrup are negotiating concerns with the integrity, cohesiveness, and continuity of the communal body.

Portraits of Continuity

The Buddhist monastic code prohibits acts that create "schisms in the sangha," rifts among the monastic community. The pedagogical technique of debate and the literary genre of polemics both contain the possibility for inciting and aggravating contention between contingents of that community. Underlying both debate and polemics as vital practices of Buddhist scholasticism are limitations upon how far one can go in critiquing one's opponent and in deviating from the views of one's own teachers. In these texts of the body mandala debate, which I refer to as the first round of a more far-reaching intertextual and intergenerational web of controversy, lineage together with authorial and communal identity all play important roles. In this section I engage two lineage portraits of Ngorchen and Khédrup (figures 0.1 and 0.2). The portraits exemplify how visual and textual representations can be used both to reinforce continuity and to create space for new interpretations. They also reflect the values that Ngorchen and Khédrup upheld and the constraints within which they operated as they interpreted representations of body mandala.

A Portrait of Ngorchen

This image of Ngorchen depicts a chronological transmission of authority (figure 0.1). Portraits like this one enumerate and repeat the members of a lineage

FIGURE 0.1 Ngorchen Künga Zangpo (1382–1456) with Two Lineages. Tibet, 1430s–1460s. 34 1/16 x 28 3/8 in. (86.5 x 72 cm). Michael Henss Collection, Zurich. Image courtesy of Michael Henss.

as a means of establishing continuity with the past. Ngorchen appears in the center of the painting surrounded by the lineage gurus of two lines of teachings of which he is a part. On the right is the Sakya Path and Fruit Lineage, the source of the contested form of body mandala; the lineage of the tantric practice of the goddess Nairātmyā is on the left. Both lineages begin with the figure of the tantric buddha Vajradhara, the blue figure depicted above Ngorchen's head, and proceed through a series of Indian and Tibetan masters, many of them appearing more than once, ending with two images of Ngorchen himself (flanking the treasure vase in the row immediately below the throne). In each, he appears as a receptacle of the teachings and turns in deference to the guru beside him. As the central figure, he performs the gesture of turning the wheel of the dharma, signaling his status as a guru and a conduit of buddhahood qualified to transmit the teachings to his own disciples. Ngorchen therefore appears three times in total in the painting.[12] This visual representation therefore embraces repetition as a way of conveying Ngorchen's authority to receive and perpetuate multiple strands of tantric teachings.

The notion of the support (*rten*) helps to illustrate how continuity and connection between guru, disciple, and Buddha take shape in the tantric ritual context. The ritual transmission of knowledge enables a human being such as Ngorchen to become a vessel of buddhahood, one whose contents can be poured forth into a community of disciples. Just as an image is consecrated to house the presence of a deity, so too tantric practitioners undergo initiation rites to prepare themselves to realize their divine identity. This transformation allows the receptacle to become a support for devotion. Ngorchen was initiated into the Path and Fruit tradition by his guru, who introduced him to imagining his own body as a mandala, a celestial palace inhabited by buddhas. By undergoing the phases of ritual empowerment and repeating the practice of transforming the body into a mandala, Ngorchen became qualified to transmit the Hevajra body mandala. The central image of Ngorchen reinforces his buddhalike qualities as an empowered teacher. The portrait as a whole embodies his identity as a "support" for containing and transmitting the wisdom of his predecessors.

As the painting shows, Ngorchen's predecessors include buddhas, Indian tantric adepts, their Tibetan disciples, as well as the students of those Tibetan teachers. The Sakya tradition is among the Sarma (*gsar ma*) schools of Tibetan Buddhism that, beginning in the eleventh century, established new communities of practice based around lineage. They legitimated their claims to branch out in this way by reinforcing their connections to Indian teachers and thereby to the land of Buddhism's birth and to the Buddha himself. The Sakyapas describe the visionary transmission of the Path and Fruit from the goddess Nairātmyā to Virūpa, one of the Indian *mahāsiddha*, legendary tantric adepts whose antinomian attitudes and behaviors expressed their profound spiritual accomplishments

(Skt. *siddhi*). The Path and Fruit teachings were not recorded in writing for generations, until the time of the great Sakya patriarch Sachen Künga Nyingpo (1092–1158) and his sons. The validity of the teachings was therefore subjected to critical scrutiny at several points in Sakyapa history. One way of reading Ngorchen's defense of the Hevajra body mandala in the early fifteenth century is against the larger backdrop of defenses of the integrity of the lineage, the uninterrupted and unadulterated transmission of the teachings traced back to an enlightened source.

The portrait contextualizes Ngorchen as a continuation of this tradition and thereby authorizes him as a tantric exegete. Through repeating the forms of the gurus of these Sakya lineages, the portrait reinforces their authority as rooted in an unbroken transfer of the essence of the teachings. In the body mandala debate, Ngorchen invokes the words of his predecessors in a similar manner. His citational strategies display how repetition can create continuity and authority, informing a definition of canon that retains the musical sense of a series of overlapping repetitions. His citations display his expertise, and thereby contribute to his prestige, but also play a part in canon formation. Both text and image therefore exhibit the capacity of repetition within Buddhist representations to function as a powerful mechanism for bestowing the authority to interpret tantric texts. As Ngorchen himself will show, the flow of this authority is often multidirectional.

A Portrait of Khédrupjé

In another painting, Khédrup, Ngorchen's interlocutor on body mandala, makes a mandala offering to his own teacher, Tsongkhapa (figure 0.2). This offering expresses the macrocosmic dimensions of mandala as a ritual offering of both self and world that reinforces the bond between guru and disciple. In exchange for this offering, Tsongkhapa invests Khédrup with the authority to revise and interpret the tantric teachings.

Repetition and visionary experience also figure prominently in Khédrup's portrait, in which he appears three times. In the figure on the left, he is slumped over the ritual altar in despair at his teacher's absence. His despair is ultimately remedied by Tsongkhapa's appearance to Khédrup as a vision in the clouds performing the gesture of turning the wheel of the teaching. After his teacher's death, during his time at Dangchen, Khédrup is alleged by his biographers to have experienced such visions.[13] These visions solidified Khédrup's status as heir to Tsongkhapa's spiritual legacy, evoking the power of visionary experience in creating continuity and in bridging the gap between ordinary and enlightened

FIGURE 0.2 Portrait of Khédrupjé Gélek Pelzangpo (1385–1438) making a mandala offering to Tsongkhapa Lozang Drakpa (1357–1419). Tibet, nineteenth century. 16 x 27 in. (40.64 x 68.58 cm). P1994.8.4. Image courtesy of the Shelley and Donald Rubin Private Collection.

beings. The format of this portrait is repeated across several paintings in which Tsongkhapa assumes the forms of legendary *mahāsiddhas* and bodhisattvas.[14] These portraits promoted Tsongkhapa's divine identity, an identity perfected through tantric practice. In depicting the visionary connection of guru and disciple, they exhibit the mutually reinforcing nature of this relationship. Such representations also promote Khédrup as a spokesperson for Tsongkhapa's legacy as it began to take shape in the form of the Gelukpa/Gandenpa tradition in the fifteenth century.

Khédrup appears once again on the lower right of the painting, hard at work sifting through piles of ritual texts. The inscription explains that Khédrup is "clarifying interpolations" (*lhad zhugs sel*) from the tantric ritual texts for propitiating the featured deities.[15] In "clarifying interpolations," Khédrup roots out spurious incursions and restores the "original" meaning of the texts, a process to which the deities themselves bear witness. It is the continuity of his ritual connection to his teacher that invests Khédrup, renowned for his expertise in philosophical commentary and debate, with the authority to root out fabricated meanings from the tantric teachings.

Both the portraits of Khédrup and of Ngorchen convey the message that they are exegetes qualified and empowered to speak on behalf of their traditions. Yet affirming Khédrup's role as tantric exegete for Tsongkhapa's budding lineage may have demanded more finessing. Tsongkhapa had many disciples, and the notion that Khédrup is one of the primary heirs to his tradition was, as Elijah Ary has shown, constructed over time by biographers.[16] Moreover, while he was prolific in his tantric compositions, including his overview of the tantric system translated into English by Lessing and Wayman in 1968, Khédrup was primarily known for nontantric contributions associated within the domain of sutra.[17] In comparing the demeanor of these two scholar monks in their portraits, Khédrup appears to be working harder than Ngorchen to secure validation. Through a repertory of actions expressing grief, making offerings, and editing texts, the portrait concretizes Khédrup's ties to Tsongkhapa and verifies his tantric expertise. Representations such as this portrait push back against potential challenges to Khédrup's right to speak for Tsongkhapa on tantric matters.

Ngorchen and Khédrup's remarks on body mandala are framed by a shift in institutional dynamics connected with Tsongkhapa's rise to prominence. However, the degree to which these authors created or amplified a rift in the community is somewhat nebulous. Later depictions of the debate envisioned and constructed their roles in effecting these institutional shifts in ways that do not necessarily reflect the realities of the early fifteenth century. Understanding the nuances of the body mandala debate will therefore aid scholars in getting a more accurate picture of the early fifteenth-century moment, a picture less biased by the events of the decades that followed when the division between Sakyapa and Gelukpa became more pronounced.

On the surface, Tibetan Buddhist scholastic and ritual cultures valorize seamless continuity and sublimate creativity, in the sense of any independent conception or birthing of ideas. Yet just as exegetes clarify, they also unravel. If we tug at the threads binding together the sense of original, essential, and natural meanings in Buddhist texts, their highly constructed nature becomes apparent. In this book, I uncover the dynamic tension between continuity and innovation that propels a fifteenth-century debate about body mandala practice. In this encounter, the question of who has the authority to decide what a body or text can mean hangs in the balance. I encourage a deeper investigation of the threads and sutures binding Buddhist meanings together. In doing so, I also highlight the subtle forms of innovation occurring within representations of continuity.

SUTURES AND THREADS OF BUDDHIST TEXTUALITY

Every Buddhist sutra begins with the phrase "thus have I heard," deferring meaning to a previous moment, a previous transfer of the essence of the Buddha's intention. Within the Sanskrit lexicon more broadly, a sutra is a "suture" like the one threading together the folia of a manuscript, literally holding the text together. A sutra is also a rule holding together a coherent language, as in the case of Pāṇini's famous fifth-century rules of Sanskrit grammar. Sutras dictate the rules of domestic rites, as in the Gṛhya sutras, and of legal and social structures, as in the case of the Dharma sutras. In a similar way, the Buddhist sutra, a discourse attributed to the Buddha, expresses these qualities of binding and continuity as critical for constructing meaning.

The Tibetan texts I address in this book focus upon the interpretation of the tantras, a series of texts accepted by Vajrayāna Buddhists such as those in Tibet, as the word of the Buddha. The emergence of the tantras hundreds of years after the sutras along with their unexpected settings—backdrops like the womb of the consort—are among the many attributes that make them less conventional. Despite the challenges to authenticity posed by the details of their origin, adherents of the Vajrayāna, the "lightning vehicle," accept the authenticity and authority of the tantras as dictating the means for attaining enlightenment rapidly, even in a single lifetime. The tantras contain fundamental elements of soteriological practices such as body mandala in dialogue with a broader network of sources such as ritual manuals and commentaries.

A tantra is literally a "thread," one that strings together a lineage of teachers and disciples and the "warp" in the fabric of Buddhist textuality. The threads of the tantric tradition are secured by rules in the form of vows of secrecy, commitments to regular practice, and obligations to venerate the guru. These strictures contribute to the prestige of the tradition, and breaking these vows threatens karmic retributions of the gravest varieties. Therefore, *tantra*, like *sutra*, is associated with restriction, continuity, and binding and weaving together essential meanings.

A tantra often gravitates around the mandala of a central deity, such as Hevajra or Guhyasamāja, who serves as the primary focus of ritual attention and iconographic description. Khédrup's critique of the Hevajra body mandala appears within his larger treatise on the Guhyasamāja system. Although both authors touch upon the works of many tantric systems in the debate, the prevalence of citations of Guhyasamāja-related texts places the body mandala debate within a larger network of early fifteenth-century tantric polemics in which the Guhyasamāja played a central role. Tsongkhapa exploited the potential of one lineage of the Guhyasamāja teachings for synthesizing the paths of sutra and tantra. The Ārya Guhyasamāja was a conflation of the identity of the lineage of the Indian founder of the Madhyamaka philosophical tradition with a tantric Nāgārjuna and his disciples. This conflation proved useful for Tibetan exegetes seeking to reconcile the texts and practices of the paths. Ngorchen's abundant citations of Guhyasamāja sources in his 1404 and 1406 polemics as well as later in the body mandala debate reflect his awareness of his opponents' grounding in that tradition.

Polemics, ritual practice, and interpretation all factor into evolving attitudes toward the Guhyasamāja in Ngorchen and Khédrup's time. For Tsongkhapa's lineage, the Guhyasamāja assumed a central position as the core system of tantric ritual, in a manner comparable to the role Hevajra played for the Sakyapas. Tsongkhapa's relationship to the Guhyasamāja as a touchstone for both sutra and tantra therefore magnified its rhetorical power for early fifteenth-century interpreters.

Distinguishing Sutra and Tantra in Fifteenth-Century Tibet

The relationship between sutra and tantra was a point of tension in distinguishing Tsongkhapa's legacy from its Sakyapa roots as well as from other competing traditions. Tsongkhapa devoted substantial attention to elucidating the relationship between sutra and tantra, as textual systems tied to distinct modes of practice. Sutra forms the basis for the path of perfections (Skt. *pāramitānaya*) by which the practitioner cultivates the qualities of the bodhisattva over many lifetimes. Tantra is the foundation for the path of mantra (Skt. *mantranaya*), the accelerated path of Vajrayāna, in which ritual means provide a way of reaching the ultimate goal of attaining a Buddha body, potentially even in a single lifetime. At points in the body mandala debate, Khédrup can be a bit heavy-handed with the distinction between sutra and tantra. For example, he performs a philosophical exercise of evaluating the validity of the tantric technique of imagining oneself as a Buddha according to the standards of a "valid cognition" (*tshad ma,* Skt. *pramāṇa*), a field of Buddhist scholastic learning based in the sutras. By the time of the body mandala debate, Ngorchen himself was well-established as a tantric commentator. He negotiates Khédrup's insistence on bringing sutric matters to bear on tantric conversations in creative ways but remains focused overall on refuting the opponent's charge on body mandala through recourse to the tantras, their Indian commentaries and associated ritual manuals.

Distinguishing sutra and tantra in early fifteenth-century Tibet was tied to projects of disambiguating lineages. Ngor chen's earliest polemical writings, targeted at least in part at Tsongkhapa's Sakyapa teacher Rédaba Zhönü Lodrö (1348–1412), exemplify this trend.[18] In 1404, over twenty years before the body mandala debate, at the very beginning of Ngorchen's career, the young Sakyapa scholar wrote a text distinguishing the fruits of the tantric path from those of the path of perfections, *Dispelling Evil Misunderstandings of the Explanation of the Ground of Union Vajradhara*.[19] The Sakyapas maintain that the results of Vajrayāna practice are higher than those of that of the perfections, whereas thinkers such as Tsongkhapa advocated for the equivalence of the paths. This early polemical text shows how in the early fifteenth century, this divergence in perspectives became the grounds for debate among traditions. Ngorchen wrote his second polemical text in 1406. Like his body mandala debate texts, *Root and Commentary for Overcoming Objections to the Three Tantras* is a defense of the Hevajra tantric cycle.[20] Like his first polemical treatise, from 1404, it deals with the relationship of sutra and tantra. The objectionable charge to which Ngorchen responds is that the *Hevajra Tantra* is oriented from a Cittamātrin philosophical perspective whose "mentalistic" aspects are regarded in some Buddhist circles as reifying the nature of the mind in a distorting way. Taken together, Ngorchen's 1404 and 1406 texts suggest that Rédaba embodied a cross-contamination of lineages between the Sakyapa and the emerging Gelukpa. Khédrup's writings on body mandala further attest to the complexity of these relationships for, as Yael Bentor has shown, Tsongkhapa's disciples were also eager to untangle the connection to Rédaba.[21] Tantric polemics such as the texts of the body mandala debate provided one compelling avenue for distinguishing paths of practice and traditions rooted in human and textual relationships. In determining how one text can be brought to bear on the interpretation of another and how to fill in the blanks where one remains silent, the authors of the body mandala debate display the relationship between texts and between communities of practice to be equally important.

ON CITATION: REPETITION, RUPTURE, AND REARTICULATION

As I read the texts of the body mandala debate, the distinct styles of the two authors shifted my attention and began to reshape the questions I was asking of them. Khédrup impressed me with his rhetorical moves and his leaps across genres of Buddhist textuality, leaps that revealed a firm basis in the tradition of Buddhist philosophical debate. At times, I found his long-winded writing style frustrating and the polemical imperative hard to ignore. Ngorchen awed me with his skillful navigation of a vast span of the tantric corpus and the subtlety of his maneuvers. However, at times these maneuvers were almost too subtle, making it difficult to see his argument through the dense web of citations he deployed. What was Ngorchen hiding within the words of his predecessors and why? The overwhelming abundance of citations in the writings of both authors gave me pause. In response to the styles of these authors, their strategies of argumentation and interpretation, I adapted my approach to focus upon citation as a fundamental aspect of their meaning-making processes.

In this book, I define citation as an invocation of a precedent with the potential to be repeated beyond its original context. On the most basic level, citations therefore evoke both continuity and rupture. Buddhist authors frame their interpretations as clarifications of the words of their predecessors and of the enlightened essence of buddhahood rather than as innovations. The guru-disciple relationship and the demand for loyalty to lineage were especially valued within the Tibetan tradition. To create something new would be to fabricate a message out of sync with this legacy, to cut the threads linking past and present. In considering how Khédrup and Ngorchen use citation in the body mandala debate, I reveal the anxieties around rupture propelling this weaving and suturing of continuities. Khédrup's charges, for instance, amounted to a challenge to produce evidence from authoritative canonical sources to defend the legitimacy of Hevajra body mandala. In their approaches to negotiating such concerns with fabrication and rupture from tradition, these authors display citation as a tool to rearticulate meaning.

The authors also use citations to invoke or to destabilize networks of authority, to create space for new interpretations, and even to resurrect former debates. In response to the complexities of their citational practices, I devised a methodology informed by Tibetan sources to analyze them. I applied "cutting the ground" (*sa bcad*), a Tibetan scholastic tool for outlining a text, to map Ngorchen and Khédrup's citations. The results highlight the complexity and rich interpretive possibilities suggested by Buddhist intertextuality. In cutting the ground, I discovered that as Ngorchen and Khédrup present fragments of the tantric corpus for contemplation they create the potential for reshaping that corpus and the form of body mandala ritual.

Ngorchen and Khédrup use citations in their body mandala texts to negotiate the tension between tradition and innovation. In so doing, they display a form of what Judith Butler termed "citationality."[22] In response to the essentializing tendencies of contemporary approaches to the categories of sex and gender, Butler posits that citation is not just a way to repeat but also to "rearticulate" meaning. Adopting mannerisms, ornamenting the body, and modifying contours, protuberances, hollows, and growths are all ways of performing gender. However, this repetition of gender norms both reveals and conceals. A drag performance highlights the demands gender norms place upon all bodies to emulate an ideal. Such a gendered performance destabilizes the very categories it imitates. Khédrup and Ngorchen use citations to map and contour the tantric corpus and to construct a body mandala. Both are creative acts involving manifold varieties of "rearticulation."

Ngorchen and Khédrup's invocation of texts and arguments from previous contexts impacts the interpretive and socio-political dimensions of Buddhist scholasticism in their time and beyond. Scholars of religion and gender such as Amy Hollywood have added to Butler's formulation of citationality as a tool to rearticulate meaning in proposing that "iterability is always marked by similarity as well as difference."[23] In revealing the hidden acts of innovation occurring through Ngorchen and Khédrup's citational strategies, I explore how repetition contains both identity and difference and how it can even destabilize the sense of an original. In the process, I argue that Ngorchen and Khédrup are themselves aspects of that "difference." Through the particular manner in which they reiterate textual precedents, the authors impact not only the way in which interpretation is done but also the ways in which communities define and distinguish themselves.

Analyzing Ngorchen and Khédrup's citations shows how these authors also create space for new interpretations and conceal ingenuity. I argue that, rather than merely replicating precedents, encounters such as the body mandala debate are the ground upon which the boundaries of interpretation and of the body are established and modified.

IN SEARCH OF THE BODY: TANTRIC RITUAL AND THE VAJRA BODY

In reading the texts of the body mandala debate, I was bombarded by a vast array of different versions of this corporeal ritual practice. These versions of body mandala offered different pictures of the vajra body, options for imagining a body inhabited by assemblies of deities, configured in precise patterns and locations. The correlation of these deities with elements of the universe, like air, space, and water, as well as with qualities such as generosity and wisdom, extended their scope to include an intriguing microcosmic-macrocosmic nexus of theory and practice. I would diagram these variations, impressed by their intricacy and diversity. However, in the eyes of Ngorchen and Khédrup, not all versions of body mandala are equally legitimate or efficacious. Efficacy is grounded in the suitability of a version of the practice as a conduit to liberation. For them, efficacy is also tied to the legitimacy of claims to an unbroken stream of transmission of texts and experiences of Indian adepts and commentators who are regarded as faithful transmitters of the Buddha's tantric teachings. The diversity of maps of the vajra body in terms of body mandala therefore attested to a multiplicity of meanings for the body. These meanings were expressed through relationships to enlightened forms and inflected with complex notions of ritual efficacy, communal belonging, and textual authenticity.

With a stack of these maps of tantric ritual embodiment in hand, I read and reread the arguments in the manner of the Sanskrit expression, *anuloma* and *pratiloma*, "with or against the part in the hair" or "with or against the grain." As I did so, I gained an appreciation for the diversity of ways of mapping the body in relationship to divine forms as well as for the ways in which Ngorchen and Khédrup play upon or resist that diversity. Within these maps, I began to see the body as a support for contextualizing, literally weaving together the threads and sutures of the meaning-making process.

The texts themselves present various philosophical tensions around the status of the body. For example, Khédrup challenges the primordial equation of the ordinary body with the mandala. In making his point, he prompts his readers to question the relevance of practicing body mandala if the body were already a mandala. He also implicates the body within a more encompassing conflict between the paths of sutra and tantra. For example, he asks how imagining oneself as a Buddha isn't simply delusional and a grave confusion of ordinary karmic defilement with enlightenment. Ngorchen is less interested in these questions. Instead, he emphasizes the genuine nature of the hidden potentialities of the body harnessed by the tantric practitioner and opposes the suggestion that they might be delusions or fabrications. For example, he writes, "The five channel *cakras* are naturally established in the vajra body."[24] The term *vajra body* (*rdo rje'i lus,* Skt. *vajra-kāya*) itself reflects a fundamental tension between ordinary and enlightened forms underlying Buddhist tantra.[25]

In my readings of Ngorchen's texts under the mentorship of Drakpa Gyatso at the International Buddhist Academy, the Sakya college in Kathmandu, we referred to the vajra body as the "practice body." However, there are other instances in Indian and Tibetan texts in which the vajra body references the enlightened form.[26] My choice to use the term in this book to refer to the body of the Vajrayāna adept considers the ambiguity it presents alongside the virtues of the term. *Vajra body* firmly places this body within the Vajrayāna tradition of striving for enlightenment in this lifetime and this body and of emulating the form of the tantric Buddha Vajradhara. The soteriological resonance of the term is therefore appealing. I also wanted to avoid some of the pitfalls associated with alternatives. For example, while it nicely evokes the parsing of coarse and subtle elements of embodiment, a practice the body mandala debate shows to be key for both ritual and interpretation, the term *subtle body* has a problematic history.[27] The term entered currency in English largely through the interventions of the members of the Theosophical Society, who used it within a broader program of conflating Asian religious traditions and their respective attitudes toward embodiment. A translation of the term *sukṣma-śarīra* derived from the Hindu Vedanta tradition, "subtle body" came to refer to a hodgepodge of Indic attitudes toward the elusive aspects of human potentiality and even to cross-cultural, syncretic, and new age corporeal phenomena. While there are commonalities and even connections between Buddhist tantric practices oriented around the body and those of other traditions such as Hindu tantra and Hatha yoga, Ngorchen and Khédrup are firmly rooted in the Vajrayāna. The term *vajra body* reinforces the specificity of their bodily orientation together with the pronounced ambiguity of the body within Buddhist tantra as a site of contact between ordinary and enlightened realities.

The body mandala debate is embedded in a larger history of the creation and transformation of corporeal practices in dialogue with attitudes toward the mind's role in constructing or obstructing progress toward enlightenment, topics I address in greater depth in chapter 1. In contemplating the ritual dimensions of the debate, body mandala emerges as composite of a broader repertory of Buddhist and tantric ritual acts oriented around the body. These include acts, such as enumerating the parts of the body and breaking it down as a means of breaking attachment to the sense of a permanent self, as well as purifying and preparing parts of the body for transformation into an enlightened form. Body mandala is therefore just one of a broad array of Buddhist ritual technologies of disassembling, examining, and reassembling the body in working toward liberation from samsara, the cycle of suffering and rebirth.

Khédrup and Ngorchen's roles in constructing the body mandala practice are repeatedly obscured not only by the dizzying array of variations of the vajra body that they present but by the centrality of their strategies of citation. Ngorchen and Khédrup devote a great deal of attention to what was to be imagined where and how in the stages of body mandala. However, they do not present linear accounts of the practice. Rather, they repeat of bits and pieces of the texts of Indian masters as well as of the root tantras. They weave these fragments together and substitute one meaning for another, all the while guiding readers to disassemble, examine, and reassemble the tantric corpus.

REGARD THE SEAMS AND SUTURES: EXEGETES ENGAGING CRITICAL PRACTICE

Buddhist exegetes are guides in using representation as a tool in the meaning-making process. In "My Words to Victor Frankenstein Above the Village of Chamounix," transgender studies scholar and activist Susan Stryker models how the demand for the exegete's skill of rearticulation transcends the Buddhist context of fifteenth-century Tibet. Originally a performance piece, the essay embraces monstrosity as a tool for describing the alienation trans people experience not only within the larger public but within queer communities.[28] Stryker was addressing the tragic suicide of Filisa Vistima, a twenty-two-year-old trans woman whose journal professes a wish to be "anatomically 'normal'" alongside the statement, "I'm a mutant, Frankenstein's monster."[29] Stryker exposes the deep-seated fear of seeing the constructed nature of gender evident in popular reactions to transgender embodiment. In these reactions, she recognizes a stubborn denial of the creative power to modify the confines of bodies and identities. Stryker's words vibrate with the power of an aria:

> Hearken unto me, fellow creatures. I who have dwelt in a form unmatched with my desire, I whose flesh has become an assemblage of incongruous anatomical

> parts, I who achieve the similitude of a natural body only through an unnatural process, I offer you this warning: the Nature you bedevil me with is a lie. Do not trust it to protect you from what I represent, for it is a fabrication that cloaks the groundlessness of the privilege you seek to maintain for yourself at my expense. You are as constructed as me; the same anarchic womb has birthed us both. I call upon you to investigate your nature as I have been compelled to confront mine. I challenge you to risk abjection and flourish as well as have I. Heed my words, and you may well discover the seams and sutures in yourself.[30]

When Stryker calls her audience to regard the "unnatural process" by which the "similitude of a natural body" is rendered, she evokes one of the fundamental tensions underlying conversations on embodiment and representation today. The biological as source for the essence of human identity continues to be broken down. New technologies of modifying flesh emerge along with new systems for understanding the mind-body relationship. With them comes an expanded appreciation of the porous or even illusive boundary between self and world. And yet representations continue to construct a false and confining sense of the natural that troubles the very definition of what it means to be human. For trans people, and particularly trans people of color, the increased visibility of trans bodies in the media has brought not only recognition and legibility but also increased vulnerability.[31] As a contemporary exegete, Stryker reveals the ways representations operate in tension with their constructed nature. Her call to "investigate your nature" and to "discover the seams and sutures in yourself" challenges her audience to examine "nature" as fabrication and to question its constructed and "groundless" basis. Stryker urges her audience to cultivate critical practice in regarding the "seams and sutures" of the meaning-making process for themselves.

Critical practice and the imperative to see for oneself are qualities common to contemporary exegetes such as Stryker and to the fifteenth-century authors of the body mandala debate. While they are responding to different sets of constraints upon representation and embodiment, as exegetes, Stryker, Ngorchen, and Khédrup uncover the hidden potential of representations and creatively cope with their limitations. This process involves parsing different varieties of meaning and both refining and reworking the relationships between different kinds of texts and bodies. For example, in his body mandala writings, Ngorchen emphasizes the link between empiricism and efficacy in the approach to tantric texts. He taunts his opponent in wryly citing the iconic Indian philosopher Dharmakīrti: "Just because you don't see it, doesn't mean it isn't there."[32] With this citation, which I explore in chapter 4, he debunks several of his opponents' charges by challenging their knowledge of the tantric corpus. Khédrup shows how exegetes parse implicit and explicit meanings and suggests that the ability to parse coarse and subtle elements of the body is an essential skill for progressing toward enlightenment. Through such continuous acts of rearticulation, exegetes make representations malleable. In the process, they deconstruct and reassemble both the boundaries of interpretation and the sense of "natural" meanings.

Ngorchen and Khédrup display their exegetical skills by clarifying and unraveling the seams and sutures of Buddhist textuality in the body mandala debate. For Vajrayāna Buddhists, these skills are vital for liberation.

THE BODY MANDALA DEBATE: SOURCES AND PROBLEMS

The polemical and citation-rich qualities of the Ngorchen and Khédrup's texts indicates their grounding in historically specific relationships to individuals, to institutions of patronage, study and practice, as well as to a particular scholastic framework of prestige. These factors impacted not only what these authors said but how they said it. Their texts solidified connections as well as distinctions within, between, and beyond communities. In accounting for these dimensions of the production of the texts and their place within the broader careers of their authors, I consider both how Khédrup and Ngorchen envisioned themselves within communities of interpretation and practice and how they in turn were envisioned.

Polemics as Genre and Questions of Sectarianism

Ngorchen and Khédrup's body mandala writings fit best within tantric polemics, a genre that combines the methods of philosophical debate and tantric commentary.[33] Tibetan polemical literature, referred to as "answers to refutations" (*dgag lan*) evokes the dialectical and somewhat antagonistic quality of these texts.[34] The language of "destroying" or "conquering" (*'joms*) evil opponents and of "dispelling" (*sel*) evil views, familiar from the titles of Ngorchen's body mandala texts, are stock phrases in this genre. However, as in the case of monks engaging in philosophical debate in a monastic courtyard, the authors of tantric polemical texts perform exegetical maneuvers for an audience and work within a system of rules of interpretation and argumentation. The heated nature of some of these encounters and the tendency to get personal raise questions about the line between a healthy competition in the spirit of mutual inquiry and a battle for prestige. I argue that appreciating the complexity of Tibetan polemics demands attention to the ways in which their authors craft meaning within the constraints of competing concerns with patronage, prestige, and authority while also negotiating related concerns with lineage, ritual efficacy, and interpretive practice.[35]

This book responds to a larger call within the field of religious studies to critically reexamine the connection between polemics and sectarianism.[36] I build upon foundational works by scholars such as José Cabezón that explore sectarianism as a "pathological outgrowth" that obscures the perception of Tibetan polemical writings within both Tibetan and Western scholastic frameworks.[37] In both contexts, defaulting to sectarian explanations encourages reductionist readings of more complex events. In the study of religion, the predilection for sectarian readings stems from Eurocentric perspectives influenced in part by the continued resonance of antagonisms associated with the Protestant Reformation. In Buddhist studies, sectarianism also surfaces when a historical picture is incomplete. Reading earlier events through their later representations can generate teleological readings of encounters such as the body mandala debate. The results—such as polarization in later fifteenth-century Sakya-Geluk relations or the seventeenth-century consolidation of Gelukpa institutional power—come to obfuscate their causes. Every hint of competition or discord then becomes complicit in a narrative of fracture. Within Tibetan circles, sectarianism is formally denounced as a myopic and divisive mindset; moreover, explicitly nonsectarian movements have flourished in more recent history. However, as in the case of Ngorchen and Khédrup's biographies, Tibetan interpretations can also skew toward the inflammatory and partisan or, at the very least, default to later explanations to discuss earlier phenomena.

Biography as Polemics: Genealogizing Tropes and Ruptures

Beyond their specialized and esoteric aspects, sources for the body mandala debate present two significant challenges. The first is the "constructed" nature of the biographical accounts of the protagonists involved. By constructed, I mean that the traces of the biographers' acts of crafting charismatic personae are evident in the conflicting and disputed rendering of the timing of key life events and of the conditions of a protagonist's polemical compositions and encounters.

There is no simple correlation between the timing of Khédrup and Ngorchen's encounter and the content of their arguments on body mandala. For example, recent inroads in the study of this encounter reveal that some of Khédrup's charges are themselves citations of arguments Tsongkhapa made years before. Khédrup reiterates and at times strategically modifies these arguments to orchestrate a textual encounter with the Sakyapas. However, after carefully tracking the polemical precedents for the debate to comments in previous texts by Ngorchen and Tsongkhapa, Bentor contends that the math still doesn't add up. If Khédrup is indeed continuing arguments initiated by his teacher in 1405, "How then might we explain the timing of the Sa skya crisis, which took place in the mid-1420s?"[38] Jörg Heimbel uncovers similar "chronological problems" as exemplified by discrepancies in accounts of a Sakya travel ban. This ban allegedly prevented Ngorchen from accepting an invitation to visit the remote kingdom of Mustang known as Lomöntang. Ngorchen's biographer describes the ban as a prohibition created by the Sakyapa institution that prevented Buddhist scholars from leaving Sakya and presents it as a direct response to the assault on the Sakyapa body mandala tradition. However, as Heimbel shows, there is evidence that stories of the ban may be confused or hyperbolic.[39] The task of resolving such conundrums demands attention to the patterns of representation employed by the biographers.

As in the lineage portraits described earlier, Ngorchen and Khédrup's biographies emphasize the continuity of the connections between generations of teachers and disciples. In the process, they reinforce the authority of their protagonists and the integrity of the communal body. However, amidst this imperative to articulate lineage, the voices of the biographers themselves became, at points, polemical. They appear to amplify controversies, valorize their protagonists, and demonize opponents, justifying and concealing their own authorial interventions along the way. Elijah Ary locates the genre of biography "at the heart of Tibetan Buddhist sectarian formation itself."[40] I join Ary in challenging current understandings of the rift between Gelukpa and Sakyapa traditions by reevaluating tropes such as "defender of the faith" to better understand the mode of representing debates in Tibetan biographical sources. I also investigate the role of this particular debate in distinguishing two traditions of Tibetan Buddhism, Sakya and Geluk, by cultivating attention to the stitching together of continuities in the shadow of apparent ruptures and fissures. These efforts contribute to a larger conversation on Sakya-Geluk relations in the fifteenth century.

On Methods

I present this book as a bridge between the work of historians and philologists who are scholars of Tibetan Buddhism and the concerns of a broader humanistic audience interested in problems of representation. I do so in part by responding to questions posed by scholars of Tibetan Buddhism on polemics, sectarianism, and citation through Ngorchen and Khédrup's writings. In taking stock of the competing concerns informing the body mandala debate, concerns rooted in sociopolitical circumstance, the pursuit of enlightenment, and interpretive practice, I show how the dialectical nature of Tibetan sources resists the quest for origins. My approach to the historical sources is therefore genealogical and based in the recognition of patterns of representation of continuity and communal integrity alongside representations of threats to those same ideals.

The precedents for the debate continue to multiply with scholarly discoveries of versions of the arguments in previous texts. I employ the philologist's tools to cope with the citation-rich quality of Ngorchen and Khédrup's texts as well as with the precedents for their arguments within other sources. Philologists cope with the nuances of repetition and difference in tracing citations across texts and genres and comparing versions of a text. In the process, they often destabilize the boundary between text and commentary. Their work shows how "there is only commentary," in the sense that all texts are evidence of the continuous process of crafting meaning.[41] In this way, philologists avoid confusing precedents with "origins."

Mapping Khédrup and Ngorchen's citations by applying the method of cutting the ground led me to realize how citations expose the deeply intertextual nature of Buddhist textuality and the complex dynamics of imitation, influence, and appropriation they engender. The maps reveal how repetition, as a mechanism common to both citation and representation, operates to create meaning. My discoveries suggested grounds for conversation with contemporary debates on representation—which in light of the Buddhist category of support (*rten*) can be extended to includes images, texts, and bodies—and its role in constructing the category of the human.

CHAPTER OVERVIEW

Chapter 1 describes what's at stake for Ngorchen and Khédrup in ensuring that body mandala "works" and in establishing it as a unique technology for pursuing enlightenment. The chapter situates body mandala within a broader range of Buddhist and tantric practices focused on corporeality and imagination. Khédrup wrestles with the conflicting qualities of imagination as a tool for attaining buddhahood in this lifetime and this body and as a source of deception and "fabrication" (*bcos ma*). I analyze these concerns with the mind's potential to represent enlightened identity and link them to broader questions of creativity and ingenuity faced by Tibetan authors.

In chapter 2, I reveal how the body mandala debate has been constructed both in Tibetan biographical sources and in secondary scholarship. In so doing, I expose the process of crafting identities occurring through those narratives along with the anxieties around rupture they contain. This chapter addresses the demands Ngorchen and Khédrup faced to establish continuity with an uninterrupted stream of teachings from buddhas to Indian masters and on to an inviolate succession of Tibetan gurus. The problems of representations, such as their tendency to produce stereotypes that obscure and ossify identities, appear alongside their power as sites for community formation. In this chapter, I also reflect upon my own role in restaging this polemical encounter and cultivate a critical approach to the debate, one that creates space for new discoveries and interpretations but also establishes that not all readings are equally valid.

Chapter 3 explores citation as a form of "repetition with a difference" ripe with tensions between continuity and rupture.[42] In this chapter, I introduce "cutting the ground" (*sa bcad*), the method Tibetan authors use to organize their texts, as a way to trace and analyze Ngorchen and Khédrup's citations. An argument from Khédrup's text in which he maps the goddesses of the Guhyasamāja body mandala in connection with bodily winds serves as an exemplary case for applying this method. Comparisons with visual representations highlight how his citations participate in a dynamic process of representing mandala, one that is overlooked when citations are regarded as mere repetitions. Reading the body mandala texts through the shape of their citations produces compelling reasons to analyze citations as a formative element of Buddhist textuality. This approach opens up new possibilities for answering broader questions of canon, creativity, and the nature of representation relevant within and beyond the study of religion.

Ngorchen uses citation to balance polemical and commentarial methods in his defense of the Sakya Hevajra body mandala. Through citation, he forces consensus and sharpens his critique, making it more pointed, while neutralizing contradictions and diversifying interpretations. Chapter 4 unpacks one citation, "just because you don't see it, doesn't mean it isn't there," to show how Ngorchen refines the definition of authenticity. By playing upon a curious overlap of Buddhist epistemology and tantric commentary, Ngorchen distinguishes the skilled exegete as one who examines the sources for themselves to determine what is a reliable source for knowing the world. The chapter concludes by revisiting the discoveries gained by tracing citations in chapters 3 and 4 to highlight how citation exposes the inner workings of representation.

In the final chapter, I make explicit the connections between body and text to which I have gestured throughout the book to reveal a deeper connection between ritual and commentarial practice. This chapter illustrates how Ngorchen and Khédrup use the genre of the "explanatory tantra" (*bshad rgyud*/Skt. *vyākhyātantra*) to suture the essence of body mandala through a process of supplementing, filling in the blanks, and bringing one text to bear upon the other. Building upon a Sakya metaphor for the body as a commentary or "explanatory tantra" on the "root text" of the mind, I show how these authors use the challenges posed by the explanatory tantras as opportunities for making the tantric corpus malleable in their hands.

The conclusion reveals the ways in which both exegetes and tantric practitioners align connections and break down, reassemble, and supplement meanings; they hone these skills as soteriological tools. I propose "rearticulation" as an interpretive framework that highlights creativity and the malleability of boundaries while reinforcing the vital ways in which limitations and meanings are bound together.

In the epilogue, I extend the observations on Buddhist meaning-making to open up a conversation with contemporary artists, theorists, and activists dealing with the paradoxes of representations. I engage artist Glenn Ligon's installation piece, "Notes on the Margin of the Black Book," a critical reframing of a series of controversial photographs by Robert Mapplethorpe, to reveal the maneuvers of a contemporary exegete. Mapplethorpe's *Black Book* is composed of a series of photographs of Black male nudes. After Mapplethorpe's passing from AIDS in 1989, a retrospective of his work provoked virulent controversies around creative freedom, censorship, and sexual identity. Ligon uses citation to restage the debates provoked by Mapplethorpe's photographs. He unsutures the photographs from the *Black Book* and installs them together with citations of voices of cultural critics, activists, men who sat for the photos, and cultural conservatives responding to the images. Thus he reframes the images to expose the tropes they perpetuate as well as the nuances of representation they contain. Ligon is a skilled exegete who forces his audience out of the passive mode of receiving images and encourages them to think critically and to make connections for themselves. He presents possibilities for coping with the constructed nature of representations as well as the tensions between limitation and potential, source and repetition they evoke. As a contemporary exegete, he models the skills of parsing, supplementing, and rearticulating meaning familiar from the body mandala debate in an idiom that displays the direct relevance of these skills to contemporary debates around representation.

Translating the Body Mandala Debate for the Postmodern Age

Khédrup and Ngorchen's interpretive maneuvers in crafting continuity and natural meanings in the face of rupture, innovating within the limitations of tradition, and guiding their readers to locate the hidden potential for meaning reveal how the skills of the exegete transcend the boundaries of fifteenth-century Tibet. I introduce the potential for recognizing such connections across contexts to interpreting the body mandala debate.

Translation is an act of "carrying across," a movement between states. In the Tibetan language, translation is defined in terms "transformation" (*'gyur ba*). Translating the body mandala texts demanded a precise skill set, which includes familiarity with three textual cycles of tantric literature—the Guhyasamāja, Cakrasaṃvara, and Hevajra—together with their associated ritual systems, with the conventions of Tibetan scholastic debate, with philosophical approaches to describing the nature of the body and the mind, and with the mode of relating text and commentary within Buddhist exegesis. The quest to cultivate these skills inspired me to travel to temples, monasteries, and classrooms in Tibet, Nepal, and India as well as to form friendships and working relationships with international Buddhist scholars and practitioners.

Translating these texts for a transdisciplinary audience demands additional skills and capacities. These include an attunement to the challenges of reading Buddhist texts in light of contemporary phenomena and a dedication to de-essentializing representations of Buddhism.[43] In addition, translation has required me to dwell in between, moving across periods of my own intellectual trajectory. I found myself moving between the 1990s, a moment in which identity politics and critical theory were mobilized to advocate for legibility and rights for individuals, to the present moment, in which intersectionality assumes new forms.[44] Contemporary thinkers in fields such as transgender studies, disability studies, and critical race studies present evidence that the category of the human has been predicated on the designation of nonhuman "others." The "human" has been crafted through representations, and the contours of the question of what it means to be human, the foundation of the humanistic disciplines, are changing. The texts to which the humanities have turned for answers, the canon or core curriculum, now present problems best defined as problems of representation.

Postmodernism turned representation back on itself. Deconstruction, iterability, and performativity are among the approaches postmodern thinkers used to bring attention to the nature of representation, language, and embodiment.

Michel Foucault, for example, introduced a new approach to representations, one that observed the subterranean anxieties powering them. He also planted the seeds for approaching the body as constructed by social forces and meaning as constructed through our acts of reconnaissance.[45] With the postmodern turn, iterability was mobilized to question monolithic truths and stories of origin. Jacques Derrida, for example, highlighted "the possibility of extraction and citational grafting" as endemic to language itself, raising questions such as, "What would a mark be that one could not cite? And whose origin could not be lost along the way?"[46] The relationship of representations to context, consequently, came under new scrutiny. In responding to the essentializing tendencies of contemporary attitudes toward bodies, especially with regard to the categories of sex and gender, Judith Butler was inspired in part by Derrida's approach to iterability.[47] In *Bodies that Matter*, Butler describes performative agency "not as a singular or deliberate 'act,' but as the reiterative and citational practice by which discourse produces the effects that it names."[48] Origin and replica, text and context, cause and effect were reconfigured in these postmodern conversations, culminating in the proposal that representations are not just important for what they are but for what we can do with them. In postmodernism's wake, we continue to grapple to wield its tools skillfully. These tools brought to light the constructed qualities of bodies and texts, the dynamics of repetition, and the ways in which we draw upon a host of representations to make sense of any single one.

Anyone who says postmodernism is "over" isn't paying attention to the resonance of the patterns of interpretation first introduced by postmodern thinkers in debates occurring across disciplines and discourses today. The politics of representation, citation, and imagination are at the center of these debates. Amidst a global pandemic, statues of "founding fathers" were torn down as the nation seethed with an urgency to revise the criteria for whose image is set in stone, whose image is suitable to represent who the American people are. This phenomenon of a part or individual standing in for a whole or a community is one aspect of representation. Universities are revising the core curriculum to include the creative accomplishments of women, people of color, and other underrepresented groups. Students thinking critically about what the canon is and how it is made are rediscovering representation as a meaning-making process in which who we cite, and how we cite, matters. The impact of the state and the media's role in constructing and parsing bodies as threats and vulnerabilities through representations is receiving long overdue attention. Within literary circles, Afrofuturist authors employ imagination to revise the horizon of possibility and to resist oppressive tropes associated with nostalgia and the myth of "simpler times." The rapid dissemination of representations has amplified the need to develop better ways of reading texts and images and, by extension, bodies.[49] Making sense of representations remains vital to humanistic inquiry and demands intellectual alliances.

In this book, I contemplate how we make meaning of bodies and texts and the way in which representations are part of how we perceive ourselves and our realities. My sources for modeling the exegete's skill to rearticulate meaning lie in the fifteenth-century Buddhist context. However, this book speaks to thinkers across the disciplines to explore the power of representations, how they work and what they do, and the dangers and opportunities they present. With Ngorchen and Khédrup as guides, I invite the reader to harness the power of representations to mediate our relationship to reality as a resource for transformation.

I

Imagining the Body Mandala

The path of Buddhist tantra, the Vajrayāna or "lightning vehicle," is special because it is fast, dangerous, and, like lightning, if properly harnessed, it has the power to enlighten. The goal is to attain enlightenment in this very lifetime and this very body and ultimately to attain a buddha body. Imagination is central to the tantric method. The core ritual act of imagining oneself as a buddha in tantric *sādhana*, literally "rites of accomplishment," allows practitioners to transform the horizon of possibility, breaking down the boundary between ordinary and enlightened identity. Body mandala is a highly sophisticated version of this core ritual act and akin to the brain surgery of tantric technology. In body mandala, the practitioner transforms the body into the form of a mandala, a celestial palace inhabited by buddhas.

In the early fifteenth century, two Tibetan Buddhist scholar monks composed a network of texts debating body mandala practice. Khédrupjé Gélek Pelzangpo (1385–1438) was a champion of the emerging Gelukpa or Gandenpa tradition, and Ngorchen Künga Zangpo (1382–1456) a renowned tantric commentator and ritual specialist of the Sakyapa tradition. There is at least one thing Ngorchen and Khédrup agreed upon, and that is that body mandala works. They disagreed on how best to perform this practice, which texts to rely upon for instructions, and how to fill in the blanks where the texts remain silent. These concerns with ritual mechanics and exegesis are known as the body mandala debate.

In this chapter, I explore what's at stake for Ngorchen and Khédrup in ensuring that body mandala "works" and in establishing it as a unique technology for transformation. I introduce tantric conceptions of the body as a container and foundation for practice. I also contextualize body mandala within a broader range of Buddhist and tantric practices focused on corporeality and imagination.

Finally, I consider what body mandala and Ngorchen and Khédrup's interpretation of it reveal about representation.

According to Buddhist thought, imagination taps into the mind's tendency to make things up. The mind tends to fabricate a reality by imposing concepts, emotions, and assumptions upon experience and then takes that fabrication and holds it up as something real. Tantric ritual acts of imagination, like many other aspects of tantra, employ a logic of inversion. Something that ordinarily impedes the path to liberation, like the mind's habit of generating an excess of ideas and images, becomes a tool to overcome "the tyranny of ordinary appearances."[1] In tracing the use of "fabrication" (*bcos ma*) in conjunction with imagination in Khédrup's body mandala chapter, I reveal the complex role of imagination, as a form of representation to the mind, in attaining soteriological goals.

Khédrup and Ngorchen are most invested in the varieties of body mandala practice connected with the Guhyasamāja and Hevajra cycles of tantric instructions respectively. The Ārya Guhyasamāja tradition of propitiating the form of Guhysamāja as the deity Akṣobhyavajra is rooted in the *Guhysamāja Tantra* and its associated Indian ritual and commentarial texts. Many Tibetans conflate the tantric authors Nāgārjuna and his lineage members, who interpreted this form of the practice, with the nobles (*Ārya*) of the same names who established the Madhyamaka tradition.[2] In the introduction, I discussed the appeal of the Ārya tradition for Tsongkhapa and his followers, not only for its powerful ritual techniques but also for its utility as a framework for correlating sutra and tantra. The Sakya Path and Fruit (*lam 'bras*) tradition is rooted in the practice and interpretation of the *Hevajra Tantra* as transmitted by the Indian tantric adept Virūpa based on his visions of Hevajra's divine consort Nairātmyā. The portrait of Ngorchen featured in the introduction illustrates this lineage of teachings as transmitted from a divine source on to Indian and Tibetan masters, including Ngorchen himself. The literary and textual worlds of the Guhyasamāja and Hevajra tantras therefore form the backdrop for Khédrup and Ngorchen's encounter.

Both the Ārya Guhyasamāja and the Path and Fruit adhere to a two-part sādhana structure of generation and completion. The generation stage choreographs the correlation of self and buddha, and the completion stage focuses more precisely upon manipulating the elements of the vajra body. The vajra body is an instrument for liberation and contains the body's hidden potential for transformation. It is composed of "channels and winds" (*rtsa rlung*), energetic pathways and the winds that circulate through them, as well as "drops" (*thig le*), subtle essences or distillations of generative power. The vajra body is latent in ordinary beings and only accessible to the tantric adept who has been trained to recognize its qualities and to harness their potential to attain liberation in the present lifetime. In body mandala, imagining deities on the body is a way of engaging the vajra body, making it familiar and workable. Near the end of his body mandala polemics, Ngorchen reinforces the unique efficacy and immediacy of the practice in accessing hidden corporeal potential. He writes, "It is necessary for the Buddha to consecrate the channels (and) winds in the generation of the wisdom of bliss of the completion stage. Other than the body mandala, there is no profound shortcut for achieving that."[3] Ngorchen references the "channels and winds" (*rtsa rlung*) which together with the "drops" are key components of the vajra body. The buddhas must prepare these hidden corporeal capacities to become divine by consecrating (*byin gyis brlabs*) them.[4] Ngorchen identifies the "wisdom of bliss" as key to this transformative process of the completion stage.

Khédrup also emphasizes the importance of the completion stage of sādhana practice in fulfilling the transformative potential of body mandala.

> The completion stage, which arises from meditation by piercing to the pith of the body [*lus la gnad du bsnun*], is the main cause of establishing the supreme *siddhi* [*mchog gi dngos grub*]. By repeatedly cultivating the generation and consecration [*byin gyis brlabs pa*] of all the current parts as deities, the channels, winds and drops of the body become workable. By piercing to the pith of the body in meditation, the ripening of the effortless generation of realizing the completion stage becomes supreme.[5]

Both *siddhi* (*dngos grub*) and *sādhana* derive from a common Sanskrit root meaning "accomplish" (*sādh*). According to Khédrup, the completion stage is vital for accessing the supreme power or attainments, the *siddhi*, resulting from sustained tantric practice of sādhana. That power is actualized by first preparing the body to serve as a foundation for practice by correlating its parts with deities and then "piercing to the pith of the body" (*lus la gnad du bsnun*). The completion stage provides the ritual context for this realization in "piercing to the pith" of the body's hidden potential for supporting the goal of attaining enlightenment. I return to Khédrup's quotation later in this chapter to investigate how the completion stage is connected with this experience of effortless and natural realization in light of the relationship of fabrication to imagination.

The power of body mandala therefore lies in its status as a "profound shortcut" for a particular kind of transformation that makes the body malleable and as a tool for getting at the heart of what embodiment is all about. The body, from a Buddhist cosmological perspective, provides a rare opportunity to work toward the ultimate goal of realizing the true nature of reality and of the mind. From certain philosophical perspectives, everything we experience is merely a product of our mind. In such contexts, the act of harnessing mental tendencies to generate concepts and images helps to scrape away at bad habits developed over lifetimes; these approaches attempt to get at the essence of clarity and luminosity that is the true nature of the mind. Tantric practices, especially the precise mechanics of completion stage practices, focus upon the hidden potential of the body. In learning to manipulate the energies of the vajra body, the practitioner becomes capable of redirecting their disparate undulations and channeling them toward the goal of realizing enlightenment in this very body. Body mandala prepares the practitioner for the fruition of this soteriological goal, bringing bodies and representations into a unique relationship to the mind.

The precise corporeal mechanics of the vajra body found in body mandala practices operate in conversation with broader notions of the body as a vessel, as a foundation or support. Through tantric ritual acts of imagination such as cultivating oneself as a buddha or locating deities within a divinized body, one becomes accustomed to the idea that one possesses buddha potential. To locate buddhas in the world is to make them accessible for worship and supplication and ultimately, identification. Once properly prepared through ritual acts of purification and devotion, the tantric disciple becomes a vessel into which the guru pours the wisdom of the teachings and upon which the buddhas bestow their blessings.

In order to worship a god, one must become a god.[6] Initiation rituals provide the vital basis for the cultivation of self as buddha in tantric sādhana. The guru first transforms themself into a buddha, and that transformation or "deification" is generative; the guru becomes a buddha to produce more buddhas, to transform disciples. In the case of body mandala, the guru's body is also a pedagogical tool for instructing the disciple to produce a network of correlations between self and world. Through the ritual phases of initiation, the guru leads the way for the practitioner to realize their own hidden potential. Invested with the permission and confidence to ripen the seed planted in initiation, the practitioner engages in regular sādhana in which they employ vision, recitation, and gesture to cultivate buddhahood.

CORRELATION AND CONTAINMENT

Although Ngorchen and Khédrupjé both agree that body mandala is efficacious, they have different ideas of what a functional body mandala practice looks like.

Major points of dispute over ritual mechanics include the precise mechanisms for correlating self and world and the order for performing those correlations.

In Tibetan, the term *support* (*rten*) is used interchangeably to describe bodies and images. The ritual body as container and as support resonates with a broader microcosmic-macrocosmic order characterized by cycles of creation and destruction; this order exceeds the Buddhist tantric realm and encompasses Indian cosmology and the early Abhidharmic worldview. The Abhidharma texts include descriptions of the end of one world system corresponding with the dissolution of the cosmic elements and the beginning of the next world system with their emanation anew. Tantric accounts of the process of death and rebirth echo this cycle of ebb and flow. Tantric sādhana describe an analogous process of the creation and dissolution of images in the generation and completion stages. Tantric practitioners of these "rites of accomplishment" therefore exercise the power of imagination to tap into the generative and destructive forces of the universe, the mysteries of emanation and disappearance, and to master the challenges of embodiment as precious opportunity and ephemeral reality.

The form of the mandala, a celestial palace inhabited by buddhas, is a container organized hierarchically according to a structure of center and periphery. The center is inhabited by the main buddha being ritually propitiated surrounded by attendants. Progressing outward toward the margins, the forms of the cremation grounds and protective circles demarcate the mandala's boundaries.

The body mandala practices described by Khédrup and Ngorchen include the body mandala of the support and of the supported. Although the definitions of the body mandala of support and supported vary from one tantric cycle to the next, generally speaking, the "mandala of the support" (*rten pa'i dkyil 'khor*) is the body as celestial palace, in some cases also including the cremation grounds and protective circle. The support can also be associated with elements of the cosmos, like earth, air, fire, and water. The "mandala of the supported" (*brten pa'i dkyil 'khor*) consists of the deities inhabiting that bodily palace and, in some instances, the psychophysical elements of the vajra body like the channels, winds, and drops.

In a seminal passage from his body mandala chapter, Khédrup critiques a version of the mandala of the support articulated by "some Tibetans" as follows:

> Some Tibetans say in the many body mandalas of the mother tantras: "The crown is the *viśva-vajra*; the soles of the feet are the vajra foundation. The ribs are the vajra fence. The skin is the vajra tent and canopy. The body hairs are a net of

> arrows. The fingernails are the utterly blazing fire mountain." And also: "The four channels of the heart are the four gates. The eyes are the tiered walls of the palace. The nose is the jeweled beam. The teeth are the lace curtains.[7] The tongue and lips are the sense pleasures."[8]

This passage is interesting as an example of two forms of correlation appearing side by side, of the body and the mandala's protective circle and of the body and the divine architecture of the celestial palace. While many other aspects of their arguments are difficult to synchronize, this passage sits squarely at the center of Ngorchen and Khédrup's encounter. In his body mandala debate texts, Ngorchen cites this passage to identify his object of refutation as the claim of a critic of this particular mode of correlating the body with an enlightened architecture. This critic describes this mode of body mandala as one espoused by "some Tibetans" engaged in the mother tantras. In citing this passage, Ngorchen confirms that Khédrup's critique was waged against a form of body mandala near and dear to the Sakyapa. In the next chapter, I closely analyze Ngorchen's response and also indicate precedents for Khédrupjé's charged statement.[9] The passage is significant for the present chapter in highlighting the connection between ritual mechanics and soteriological efficacy.

This correlative logic of the body mandala practice described in the passage can also be found in contemporary Hevajra sādhana used by the Sakya school as a core part of daily practices for initiates in the Hevajra practice and central to the Sakya Path and Fruit tradition.[10] However, these sādhana were formulated and compiled after Ngorchen's time, primarily by the tenth abbot of Ngor, Könchok Lhündrup (1495–1557).[11] In looking to the works of the five great Sakyapa patriarchs for an earlier precedent for this version of the practice, it appears both in a work attributed to Jétsün Drakpa Gyeltsen (1147–1216), the *Lus kyi dkyil 'khor*,[12] as well as in Chögyel Pakpa's (1235–1280) Hevajra body mandala sādhana.[13] Drakpa Gyeltsen and Pakpa's texts share a threefold framework of correlations of parts of the body with parts of the protective circle, with the elements of the universe, and with parts of the celestial palace.[14] I address the textual dimensions of the passage, specifically, the connection of the passage to Indian tantric sources and their Tibetan interpretations, in chapters 3 and 4.

Contention over how best to imagine the body as a mandala, as found in Ngorchen and Khédrup's texts, suggests that not all ways of imagining are regarded as equally efficacious. From the perspective of the ritual body, establishing the rules for tantric ritual acts of imagination was essential to ensuring that body mandala "works."

SUTURING THE BODY MANDALA

The structure of body mandala practices suggests the stitching together of a vast repertory of ritual techniques for reenvisioning the relationship of self and world in setting the stage for liberation. This structure employs sound, vision, and gesture together with mnemonic techniques oriented around the body to effect a series of transformations. When closely examined, the form of body mandala practice reveals connections to diverse tantric technologies of protecting, purifying, and divinizing the body as well as to early (nontantric) Buddhist practices of de-essentializing the self.

Body mandala may be the brain surgery of tantric technologies, but it certainly is not the first variety of surgery performed. The Buddha performed a kind of "living autopsy" on the self. In his fifth-century text, the *Visuddhimagga* (The Path of Purification), the Buddhist commentator Buddhaghoṣa describes practices of "mindfulness of the body" that exemplify the Buddha's approach to using the body as a tool for deconstructing attachment to a stable and truly existent self. These practices include techniques of parsing the body and enumerating its parts as a way of disaggregating one's perception of one's own body and also eliminating desire for the bodies of others. The meditator reflects on the thirty-two parts of the human body through the sevenfold skills in learning: verbal recitation, mental recitation, color, shape, direction, location, delimitation (i.e., similarity and difference), and then tenfold skills in attention. The sevenfold skills in learning employ mnemonic techniques of breaking down and organizing information in a very similar way to those found in mandala construction.[15] The result of this type of practice is described as follows: "Then just as when a man with good sight is observing a garland of flowers of thirty-two colours knotted on a single string and all the flowers become evident to him simultaneously, so too, when the meditator observes the body thus, 'There are in this body head hairs,' then all these things become evident to him, as it were, simultaneously."[16] Through repetition of these techniques, one attains a certain kind of mental flexibility by which such parsing of the body can begin to occur automatically and even be applied as a strategy for combating attachment.

Similarly, within body mandala practice, repeated visualization develops the practitioner's ability to instantaneously generate and dissolve the visualized forms. The body mandala practitioner imagines the individual parts of the body as parts of the celestial palace of the buddhas. The body becomes a container housing deities whose true nature is understood as that of the psychophysical aggregates of personhood (form, sensation, recognition, volition, consciousness), of the elements (air, wind . . .), and so forth. In cultivating mental agility through ritual acts of imagination, the practitioner prepares to acquire a buddha body (seemingly) automatically and to ultimately abandon attachment to rebirth within samsara. Repetition is therefore key to unlocking the full potential of these representations or imaginings for accessing enlightenment.

Non-Buddhist tantric sources provide some of the most direct correlates for body mandala practice. The rite of "purification of the elements" (Skt. *bhūtaśuddhi*) provides a salient example of the combination of techniques for purifying, protecting, and deifying the body through choreographing relationships of microcosm to macrocosm and placing deities on the body. The *Jayākhya saṃhita*, a Vaiṣṇava tantric text produced in seventh- to tenth-century Kashmir, describes a fourfold ritual sequence for performing the "purification of the elements": purification of the place and body, divinization of the body, inner or mental worship, and external worship.[17] In this tradition, the process of purification involves associating each of the five elements (earth, water, fire, air, and space) with a shape, negotiating breath, and making connections with mantra and sense faculties. The main technique for divinizing the body is a process known as *nyāsa* in which the practitioner applies mantras to the body through touch and recitation focused on particular bodily locations beginning with the hands. The initial purification of the hands, often identified as *hasta-pūjā-vidhi,* can be found in many tantric rites; for example, the tantric Buddhist ritual specialist, the *vajrācārya*, often consecrates his hands as ritual implements before engaging in ritual action.[18] The *Jayākhya* details how the practitioner then redistributes the same mantras associated with the same deities "on the head, eyes, ears, mouth, shoulders, hands (again), buttocks, heart, back, navel, hips, knees and feet."[19]

The *Jayākhya*'s next ritual phase, that of inner, or, more appropriately, "mental worship" (*mānasayāga*), exemplifies a pattern of mapping structures onto the body and then associating those structures with philosophical ideals or aspects of existence or liberation. The practitioner visualizes the deities of the universe as located in the practitioner's own body in the region between the genitals and the heart.[20] These locations are stratified, ascending from a basis in earth, located at the penis, to the throne of Viṣṇu, at the heart. These strata are also correlated with the *tattvas,* the "true principles" of reality based in Sāṃkhya philosophy. This dual process of correlation is found in Buddhist tantric literature as well. The final phase of the rite described by the *Jayākhya* is termed "external worship" (Skt. *bāhyayāga*). Having appropriated the divine and soteriological structure through the medium of the body, and thereby in a sense having become a god in the *manasayāga*, the "internal or mental worship," the practitioner is now truly prepared to worship. They have purified or reconstructed both body and environment and are ready to create a mandala to house the deity.

The repeated navigation and purification of imaginary and real/material environments in the purification of the elements from the *Jayākhya* plays out in different ways in body mandala practice. Nevertheless, body mandala shares an emphasis upon prerequisite purification and deification of the body with non-Buddhist tantric ritual. The comparison also reveals a common repertoire of tools like the forms of deities, the Sanskrit letters (often transliterated) associated with those deities known as seed syllables, together with breath and sound. The logic of correlation, matching parts of the body with both divine and cosmological forms, is a powerful technology, laying the groundwork for and even catalyzing tantric transformations.

Deity yoga, the core ritual act of Buddhist tantra, partakes in this correlative logic. Even before imagining oneself as a buddha, the practitioner might begin by imagining the qualities and attributes of that buddha. Tantric deities, with their many arms and heads, challenge the visionary and mnemonic capacities of imagination. Ritual manuals typically correlate the parts of the deity and the attributes they hold with qualities of enlightened reality as well as with obstacles to be overcome. The visual forms of these deities often evoke the very poisons they promise to defeat. Many tantric deities, especially those associated with the higher yoga tantras, display fierce expressions and wield menacing weapons. The practitioner is encouraged to embrace the intensity of the wrath of these deities and to interpret its meaning in enterprises such as cutting attachment to the notion of self and overcoming ignorance. While violent forms fulfill ritual aims for overcoming hatred, sensual forms empower the practitioner to overcome desire. The iconography of deities in "union" displays a buddha and his consort engaged in intercourse, employing correlation to express various forms of nonduality, uniting male and female, compassion, and wisdom. Ultimately, occupying the mind in these complex orchestrations of relationships is a process of retraining ordinary conceptual habits, all the while destabilizing the practitioner's connection to an ordinary and unenlightened sense of self. In tantra, correlation is a vital aspect of the power of representation as a soteriological tool. To imagine oneself as a buddha, a celestial palace, or the cosmos is to create the possibility for change.

Body mandala is therefore a composite of different practices of purification, protection, divinization, and ultimately transformation oriented around the body.[21] The body functions as a foundation for producing relationships to the elements of the cosmos and associated cycles of creation and destruction, for breaking down attachment to a sense of self, for containing divine presence, and for erecting a palace of buddhahood. But the composite is not seamless. The sutures binding body mandala together as a coherent practice show themselves in the moments in which Khédrup and Ngorchen struggle to account for different iterations of the practice—often through their citations. These moments provide opportunities for scholars of tantra to trace the evolution of ritual technologies like body mandala as well as of the parameters of the vajra body within the terrain of both Buddhist and non-Buddhist sources.[22] In exploring the ritual body as a path for illuminating the meaning-making strategies within the body mandala debate texts, I touch on these questions of evolution. However, I am most concerned with imagination itself as a form of representation with the power to impede or advance the goal of liberation in this very body.

IMAGINED OR REAL?: THE USE OF THE CATEGORY OF "FABRICATION" (*BCOS MA*) IN KHÉDRUP'S BODY MANDALA CHAPTER

Khédrup writes, "So, if you ask, 'why is the body mandala superior to the two fabricated outer mandalas?' The distinction of the superior and inferior emerges based on the fabricated and unfabricated basis of establishment."[23] In his body mandala chapter in *Ocean of Attainment*, Khédrup uses "fabrication" (*bcos ma*) to articulate relationships, namely, the ontological relationship of the human body to the mandala and the relationship of the body mandala to "outer mandala." In this context, "outer mandala" refers to mandala paintings or ritual altars made of painted powders. Through his deployment of this category of "fabrication," Khédrup probes the boundaries of the *pāramitānaya*, the path of perfections, a process of perfecting the qualities of the bodhisattva like generosity and wisdom, and the *mantranaya,* the tantric path of using ritual techniques to produce a buddha body. He explores philosophical and ritual implications of "fabrication" side by side to establish the superiority of the body mandala to other mandala practices. In the process, he demonstrates how the body functions as a foundation for tantric practice.

In interrogating a defining feature of tantric practice, the act of imagining oneself as a deity, Khédrup reveals imagination to be a powerful tool for expanding the horizon of possibility for Buddhist practitioners as well as a volatile topic for testing boundaries between Buddhist discourses. For Khédrup, "fabrication" is a spectrum ranging from "mere imaginings" (*mos pa tsam*), "mere mental imputations" (*blos bcos pa tsam*), "false cognitions" (*log shes*), and even lies to more authentic imaginings facilitated by body mandala, imaginings secured by a proper basis for transformation. Khédrup's attempts to reconcile the methods and aims of tantric practice with the pāramitānaya at large through the language of Buddhist philosophical investigation reflect anxieties triggered by imagination. For imagination is a form of creativity with the potential to destabilize the categories of fabricated and natural and even ordinary and enlightened, categories vital to the interpretation of bodies and texts. As in contemporary conversations and polemics on gender, referenced in the introduction, the rhetoric around fabrication reveals an attendant discomfort with defining naturalness.

THE POSITIONS OF OTHERS: KHÉDRUP'S CHARACTERIZATION OF HIS OPPONENTS' VIEWS

Category Confusion

Khédrup begins his chapter on body mandala by challenging imagined opponents who confuse the categories of "body" and "mandala." He introduces a relevant passage from the writings of one of the great Indian tantric adepts (Skt. *mahāsiddha*), Ghantapa's *Condensed Activities of the Cakrasaṃvara Initiation* (*Dpal 'khor lo sdom pa'i dbang gi bya ba mdor bsdus pa*). Ghantapa writes, "These sentient beings are not separated from the naturally established mandala."[24] Khédrup uses his opponents' inaccurate interpretation of this citation as the point of entry for the portion of his text in which he assesses the positions of others. He argues, "They speak of the body mandala as an unfabricated mandala [*ma bcos ba'i dkyil 'khor*], [and] they don't understand in what way the bodies of sentient beings are primordially mandalas. Therefore, they say that what already existed [*sngar yod*] is cultivated through visualization."[25] Khédrup seems to be highlighting tensions inherent in the classification of the body mandala as "unfabricated": if the mandala is already formed, the necessity of performing the body mandala practice becomes less clear.

The tone of the critique resembles similar statements made in critiques of subitism, the archetypal enemy within the realm of Tibetan philosophical debate and reasoning, as well as in critiques of buddha nature: if we were already enlightened, then practice would be unnecessary. Similar critiques are reiterated throughout this section of Khédrup's text, bringing attention to the importance of the path structure of gradual practice in legitimizing tantric techniques for the Gelukpas. In the context of Gelukpa interpretations of Guhyasamāja ritual practices, the structure of Nāgārjuna's five stages was instrumental in such acts of legitimation. In articulating his own views on the practice, Khédrup is not defying the classification of the body mandala as "unfabricated," which I will discuss at length later in the chapter. Rather, he is pointing out areas of confusion for those he regards as lacking his training and clear perspective.

Khédrup repeatedly indicates ways in which proponents who accept that the body is already a mandala threaten the very basis of the Buddhist path and teachings. For example, he argues that they undermine the four noble truths, writing, "As for those who speak in this way, they are of improper understanding that is extremely uncritical. If you see things in this way, isn't it the case that the [noble] truth of suffering—[the very fact] that the body of sentient beings is generated by karma and afflictions (Skt. *kleśa*)—is eradicated?"[26] In these terms, the body is virtually equated with suffering, an accumulation of past actions and afflictions, making any view of it as divine a category confusion of the worst kind.

Khédrup then proceeds to make a number of hyperbolic statements targeting the opponent who confuses two very different forms of representation, human bodies and mandalas. Such an opponent jeopardizes the very pillars of the Buddhist tradition, particularly the path model of gradual practice, ethical conduct, and the theory of karma. For example, Khédrup writes, "One would thus be lead to conclude that the mandala of Vajradhara [i.e., the body mandala] is established by the power of karma and afflictions. [Further, the state of] actually being Vajradhara and [the state of] being a transmigrator would be inseparable. Not only that, but also, due to that perverse implication, the state of being a sentient being who experiences the suffering of samsara would be pervaded by [the state of] being Vajradhāra."[27] Mixing inalienable categories like buddha and sentient being contaminates both and may obliterate the possibility of moving beyond samsara at all. Even more dramatically, Khédrup elaborates upon his critique, asserting that by regarding all sentient beings as buddhas, one is leveling the very ground from which the path begins, the recognition of suffering and of the nature of samsara:

> From this perspective, one would have to claim that if there is defilement, it is wisdom, or [for that matter] anything at all. If all sentient beings were actually buddhas, the worldly container [of sentient beings] would have to be the celestial palace of self-appearing wisdom. By virtue of this contradiction, the [inevitable] consequence would be that samsara itself would be untenable as an object of knowledge. How could it be that a buddha who doesn't recognize himself as being buddha, not even knowing himself, would be omniscient? The result would be a buddha who does not know any object of knowledge at all. Such a foolish one is truly incredible![28]

If samsara, the cycle of suffering and rebirth, cannot be conceived of as an object of knowledge (*shes bya*), the entire imperative of liberation through reasoning as well as the necessity of working from within the bounds of conventional reality are called into question.

The Gelukpas consider these methods—recognition of suffering and of knowledge of samsara from within the unenlightened mindset—as essential for liberation. While the conventional truth is the version of reality available through this unenlightened mindset, the reality peopled by concepts, categories, names, and identities, things as they appear to be, the ultimate truth is the reality of things as they truly are. In this passage, Khédrup is therefore playing on the resonance of the rhetorical power of issues surrounding the relationship of the two truths, conventional and ultimate, grounded in Tsongkhapa's Madhyamaka perspective.

Next, Khédrup applies this critique of those who confuse sentient beings with mandala to explicitly challenge some interpretations of the logic of tantric ritual. He writes, "On the other hand, one who makes claims like that would have to [also] claim that it is totally unnecessary for one who is a buddha and recognizes oneself as such to cultivate the path. [Based on that] one would have to claim that cultivating the path after encountering [*brda 'phrod*] the body mandala one time is totally unnecessary."[29] More generally, Khédrup is alluding to the opponent's understanding of the relationship of the human body to the mandala as a threat to the very principle of the Buddhist path. The use of the term *encounter* (*brda 'phrod*) signals the phenomenological dimension of tantric ritual and initiation practice and the volatile status of sense perception and cognition as instruments or catalysts for realizing enlightened awareness.

Khédrup proceeds to address the status of the tantric approach in relation to that of the path of the perfection vehicle (*phar phyin theg pa'i lam*). In doing so, he attempts to demonstrate that those who reify the tantric path over the latter suffer from a fatal self-contradiction. Khédrup's use of hyperbole is charged and borders upon comical at times. However, he touches upon significant points of tension for Tsongkhapa's disciples in their attempts to position their teacher's tradition in relation to those of the others.

> One who claims that it's necessary to traverse the grounds and paths in stages while cultivating the path is unstable. Having asserted the "Universal Illumination," the eleventh [*bhūmi*], which is explained as the ultimate object of attainment of the path of the perfection vehicle, to moreover be inferior to tantric Vajradhara, [such a proponent] establishes all sentient beings as primordially the mandala of Vajradhara. [So matters really] become extraordinary.[30]

Vajradhara is a tantric buddha, envisioned as the source of the ritual transmission of the essence of the tantric teachings. According to the Sakyapa tradition, the tantric path, culminating in the thirteenth ground or spiritual level of Vajradhara, is superior.[31] The Gelukpa tradition understands the tantric view as equal to the view of the perfections. This fundamental disagreement is just one aspect of Khédrup's motivation for measuring tantric practice according to the standard of the path of the perfection vehicle, a concern that his teacher, Tsongkhapa, embraced with fervor.

Khédrup is not alone in invoking multiple frameworks of Buddhist thought in the polemical context. However, he strategically employs these arguments for a variety of purposes and in unique configurations. For example, in one section of his chapter on body mandala, Khédrup resurrects charged controversies surrounding buddha nature to give momentum to an argument. In another, he garners rhetorical advantage by accentuating certain aspects of the opponent's argument to make it resemble the view of a heretical tradition like the Sāṃkhya. Khédrup's writings on Madhyamaka and his encounters with other thinkers on the topic further inform his polemical writings on tantra. As I show later in this chapter, he also employs the tools provided by Buddhist logic and epistemology for explaining how human perception and conception work as well as how representations may be used to access the true state of things. Tsongkhapa's positions and the responses of *his* contemporaries to similar issues also factor into the interpretation of Khédrup's position. Highlighting these connections produces a more comprehensive view of Khédrup's literary persona, his authorial voice, and his strategies of argumentation as well as of the intellectual milieu of scholar monastics to which he contributed.

The Causal Link

Throughout Buddhist history, the principle of cause and effect has served as an important tool for breaking down essential meanings and attachment to inaccurate views of reality. Tsongkhapa and his descendants express concerns with establishing a verifiable causal link between this present human body and the buddha bodies produced through tantric practice. These concerns often took shape in discussions of the need to produce a "similar type cause" (*rigs 'dra'i rgyu*) as the necessary link between the ordinary and inherently flawed human body and the "form body" (Skt. *rūpakāya*) of a buddha. Buddha bodies can assume a form or be formless. The formless body is described as a "truth" body (Skt. *dharmakāya*) composed of the essence of the Buddha's teachings. Form bodies may materialize in flesh and blood, like the "emanation body" (Skt. *nirmāṇakaya*) of Buddha Śākyamuni, or assume the more abstract form of an "enjoyment body" (*sambhogakaya*), a body of light appearing in more ephemeral contexts such as dreams, visions, and buddhafields. Tsongkhapa describes the buddha body as a type of container for compassionate action in the world uniquely produced in the completion stage of sādhana practice.

> For those tormented by thirst their main focus will be the search for something to drink, but for that they will need a container. Likewise, for those of the Great Vehicle who are moved by a great compassion that is unable to bear living beings being tormented by suffering and deprived of happiness, their main focus will be striving for the welfare of others . . . actually appearing before sentient beings and then accomplishing their needs is to be performed by the form body [Skt. *rūpakāya*] from the two types of enlightened bodies, and not by the *dharmakāya*. Therefore the main focus of their endeavor is the form body. Because of this, a special cause that is similar in type to the form body, that is used as a method for achieving the form body, and that is a special and peerless feature not found in other vehicles, other classes of tantra, and in the generation stage has to be present in the completion stage.[32]

In this passage, Tsongkhapa copes with a perceived challenge posed by tantric practice to the Buddhist theories of causality that form the very basis for karmic law and theories of human embodiment. Resources for such theories of causality include the Abhidharma literature and Madhyamaka reformulations of the ideas presented therein.[33] If a buddha body is not the result of or equal to karma and afflictions (Skt. *kleśa*), then how does it manifest? Among the five standard categories of effect, the buddha body seems to most closely resemble the "natural outflow effect" (Skt. *niṣyanda-phala*); this is an effect that "corresponds to the nature of its cause in activity and experience" and is produced by the "homogenous cause" (Skt. *sabhāga-hetu*).[34] Within Abhidharmic literature, the "natural outflow effect" is used to describe how one's present actions can positively influence future moral tendencies.[35]

Tsongkhapa applies a similar formula of cause and effect within the tantric context and foregrounds the importance of the completion stage of sādhana practice. The series of simulations of self as buddha and manipulations of the vajra body that make up the two-stage sādhana structure produce the goal of attaining a buddha body. In accentuating the production of a form body of buddhahood and substantiating the coherence of causal logic for producing such a body,

Tsongkhapa identifies tantric practice as central to a larger pāramitānaya project of compassionate activity.[36]

As evidenced by his repeated recourse to hyperbolic category confusions, Khédrup expresses a comparable anxiety to negotiate the relationship of the human body to the buddha's form body in terms of the larger relationship of the pāramitānaya and mantranaya approaches. In the process, Khédrup interrogates a fundamental aspect of tantric meditation, visualizing oneself as a buddha, by subjecting it to the principles of Buddhist logic and epistemology. He writes, "Moreover, when cultivating oneself as a deity, some [say] that, 'I am actually divine.' In that case, that mind becomes a false cognition (*log shes*) when cultivating the self as divine even when it isn't. Thus, it becomes inadmissible as the cause of buddhahood."[37] Buddhist notions of causality interact with theories of perception and cognition here. Namely, false cognitions (*log shes,* Skt. *mithyā-jñāna* or *viparyaya-jñāna*) are insufficient bases for liberation. The passage suggests that certain canonical Gelukpa philosophical notions could be construed as irreconcilable with essential principles of tantric practice, most notably, with the practitioner's identification with a deity.

Khédrup probes the very basis of imagination itself and its potential as a tool for liberation and critically examines the logic of repeatedly imagining something that isn't, logically speaking, true. Ultimately, he begs the question as to how inculcating oneself in such delusions could possibly help to defeat ignorance and to realize enlightened awareness. In invoking the category of false cognition to describe such acts of imagination, Khédrup taps into yet another level of Buddhist discourse, the realm of valid cognition (*tshad ma,* Skt. *pramāṇa*). His remarks are a reminder that representations can be both instrumental and deceptive.

Pramāṇa: *On the Reliability of Human Perception*

Pramāṇa theorists explore questions about the reliability of human perception and the possibility of seeing things as they truly are. Pramāṇa theories of "valid cognition" provide a forum for considering how the two truths, conventional and ultimate reality, frame our processes of perceiving and conceiving objects. Building upon the suggested equivalence of tantric acts of visualization with false cognition (*log shes*), I examine Khédrup's relationship to pramāṇa theory and its impact upon his evaluation of tantric practice in the body mandala debate.

The Sakya patriarch Sakya Paṇḍita (Sapen) sparked centuries of controversy on pramāṇa, continuing into the present day. His thirteenth-century antirealist reading of Dharmakīrti's *Pramāṇavārttika* and its autocommentary, was a response to the works of the Sangpu tradition of Chaba Chökyi Sengé.[38] In the antirealist vein of interpretation set forth by Sapen and many of his Sakyapa followers, perception is inherently flawed. Khédrup is, by many accounts, part of the larger project of connecting Sapen's ideas to the more realist-oriented interpretation of Dharmakīrti's philosophy and particularly theories of "valid cognition" embraced by the Gelukpa.[39] As "moderate realists," Gelukpa thinkers like Khédrup emphasized the importance of the conventional tools of perception and intellect in working toward a more accurate view of things as they truly are, the ultimate truth. However, unlike extreme realists, they preserved a gap between reality and how we see it.[40]

George Dreyfus describes the climate that characterized writing on pramāṇa duing Khédrup's time as a charged "conflict of interpretations" between proponents of Sapen's antirealism and those who placed more emphasis upon the possibility of unmediated perception.[41] The Gelukpa perspective on valid cognition shared by Tsongkhapa's disciples, specifically Khédrup and Gyeltsap Darma Rinchen (1364–1432) (though they differ on various points), was distinct from Sapen's in significant ways. Their approach to pramāṇa allowed the possibility of perceiving without superimposing false constructs on reality. For Sapen and his Sakyapa legacy, perceptions simply appear in a "passive" manner; eliminating "superimposition" is not possible.[42] These opposing perspectives, inherited generally by the Gelukpa and Sakyapa traditions, respectively revolve around fundamental assumptions about the relationship between conventional and ultimate realities. For example, if it is not possible to perceive reality without projecting inaccurate frameworks of understanding onto it, practice within the bounds of conventional reality becomes problematic or even impossible.

Khédrup was embroiled in debates that dealt with how to properly understand the relationship of perception, cognition, and reality in Dharmakīrtī's thought.[43] Khédrup and his fellow "moderate realists" distinguish identity in terms of substance and concept, perception and conception. The driving imperative of the Gelukpa project was rooted in the instrumental approach to conceptuality. This imperative may have inspired Khédrup to attempt to reconcile the soteriological orientation of certain aspects of the philosophical and practical or meditative systems.

Leonard van der Kuijp has proposed that in the late fourteenth century Tsongkhapa may have started a trend of linking the Kadampa "stages of the path" (*lam rim*) teachings with discourses on valid cognition.[44] As a lineal descendent of Tsongkhapa, Khédrup therefore may be involved in a discourse on pramāṇa that incorporates the notion of a graded Buddhist path into the realms of Buddhist epistemology and soteriology. Determining the boundaries of perception and conception, how best to access a more accurate view of reality, and, ultimately, how to liberate oneself from samsara are the underlying problems framing these discourses. There are a plenitude of polemics on pramāṇa sparked by Sapen's writings. Khédrup's invocation of "valid cognition" here within his commentary on the Guhyasamāja practice resonates with the charged tenor of those debates.

In pursuing the full implications of Khédrup's comments, one would have to consider how such questions play out in the conflicting positions of the Gelukpa and Sakyapa on direct perception (*mngon sum*, Skt. *pratyakṣa*). Antirealists like the Sakyapas espouse a form of "representationalism, which postulates that awareness is directly in contact with only representations, what Dharmakīrti call *reflections* or *aspects*."[45] In contrast, Khédrup's view is described as a form of realism, "according to which mental episodes are in direct contact with objects."[46] Realism asserts a relationship between objects and consciousness in which "the reflection of a thing in consciousness is not a representation but the revelation of that thing itself."[47] The status of representations is at the center of these debates on the limits of the human capacity to know the world.

In his commentary, Khédrup continues to probe the boundaries between different levels of Buddhist discourse in introducing the terms of pramāṇa into the realm of tantric ritual and imagination.

> Moreover, having consecrated a thangka, a statue, and so forth, it becomes necessary to claim that it is really a buddha. One imagines all the realms of space to be filled with flowers at the time of making offerings. If this is as one imagines, there's the problem of it not being visually perceptible [*snang du rung ba*]. If it's not [i.e., if the statues are not really buddhas, the sky is not really full of flowers . . .], it becomes a false cognition [*log shes*]. [Therefore] it is rendered untenable as the cause of buddhahood.[48]

Khédrup is playing upon and bringing attention to the controversial status of acts of imagination by raising the problem of how representations can be validated and verified. The object of perception is negated here based upon the fact that the flowers offered imaginatively in sādhana practice are "not readily observable by everyone" (*snang du ma rung ba*). In this context, the false cognition is to say something like a statue is actually a buddha once it is consecrated or that an object of visualization is really there.

The categories of being "readily observable" and "not readily observable" refer to two basic categories of phenomena, those that are visible and those that are invisible to the ordinary person.[49] These are familiar tools for structuring refutation within the Prajñāpāramitā literature. Khédrup amplifies his investigation of possible contradictions underlying the logic of tantric ritual by combining pramāṇa with the force of the vinaya, the rules of monastic conduct.

> When one cultivates oneself as Vajradhara, one's own body is ornamented with the major and minor marks [of buddhahood]. One is practicing without experiencing any direct perception [*mngon sum du rtogs pa*] of omniscience whatsoever. So then the pretense of oneself [*mngon pa'i nga rgyal*] as a buddha as a direct perception is nuts. That being the case, assuming that we're not talking about the pride of conceit, then you know yourself to be totally devoid of the qualities of that [buddha] like longevity and so forth. Surely, it would be a [major] transgression to claim that, at that time, one is a buddha. Don't be careless by causing trouble with faulty doctrine.[50]

This passage refers to the logic of consecration ritual in which each empowerment purifies one of the obscurations like desire or hatred through association with one of the five buddha families. Khédrup evokes pramāṇa theory here by referring to *direct perception* (*mngon sum du rtogs pa*), a contentious topic of disagreement between realist and antirealist thought, as described earlier in this section. His use of this term indicates a tension between theory and practice articulated through a kind of tantric epistemology in the body mandala texts. The "pretense of oneself" (*mngon pa'i nga rgyal*) refers to the false conceit of oneself as an enlightened being. Namely, if you are aware that you are not actually a buddha, but still claim to be one, you are lying. The focus therefore shifts from faulty perception to flawed action. To pretend to be a buddha becomes eqivalent to claiming false accomplishments, one the four major transgressions or "defeats" (*pham*) outlined in the vinaya.

Many thinkers consider the reconciliation of tantric practice with the principles of the vinaya to be one of the major contributions of Tsongkhapa's monastic reform. Moreover, the clash of tantra and vinaya characterizes much of the early polemics of the Sarma era in Tibet. In this passage, Khédrup forces his opponent into a position of inevitably violating the rules of either Buddhist epistemology or of the vinaya, two charged levels of discourse, with the latter, in particular, invested with inalienable authority.[51]

Buddha Nature and Buddha Bodies

Buddha nature is loosely defined as the potential possessed by beings, and theoretically all beings, to realize buddhahood. In describing the positions of "others" and the attendant category confusions presented by the juxtaposition of human body and mandala, Khédrup recalls formal arguments found in controversies around buddha nature. These controversies came to a head in the buddha nature debates of fourteenth-century Tibet but continued to manifest in myriad forms in the ensuing century. Dolpopa (1292–1361), a master trained in the Sakya tradition but generally identified as a Jonangpa, provoked especially potent debate and dissent with his articulation of the "empty of other" (*gzhan stong*) view. Mathes describes the Jonangpa "empty of other" Madhyamaka position as accepting "a truly existing ultimate that is endowed with all Buddha qualities and thus not 'empty of an own-being' (*rang stong*), but 'empty of other' (*gzhan stong*) nonexisting stains."[52] The ontological implications offended many, both in challenging classic Madhyamaka fundamentals on emptiness and in resembling non-Buddhist heretical views. Dolpopa explains his position on the enduring essence of buddhahood through a Buddhist idiom of embodiment. He writes, "The dharmakāya is free from mental fabrications throughout beginningless time. Because of recognizing it as being free from mental fabrications, it is truly established."[53] The term Mathes translates as "mental fabrications" here is slightly different from the one found in Khédrup's texts (*spros ma* versus *bcos ma*) and refers to a form of mental "elaboration." This term indicates the tendency of our minds to proliferate concepts and images that obstruct our ability to experience reality accurately. However, the connotations of the two terms (*spros ma* and *bcos ma*) are similar. Both reflect negative associations with creativity. This passage attests to the established use of the category of "fabrication" within buddha nature discourses to articulate embodied liberation as freedom from crafting.

The contested status of buddhahood as immanent or transcendent and the relationship of buddha bodies to the mindstream of sentient beings were among the salient issues raised within buddha nature discourses of the fourteenth and fifteenth centuries. The broader implications of theories on buddha nature concerned relationships between descriptions of reality such as the two truths as well as between paths of practice like the pāramitānaya and mantranaya. Buddha nature debates also investigated how the stains of karma and afflictions factored into the foundation for Buddhist practice. Khédrup's tantric interpretations echo these concerns. He is especially interested in establishing the causal link between conventional and ultimate realities, a link that is needed to produce a buddha body.

Parsing the qualities of different buddha bodies provided a method for coping with tensions between the categories of the natural and the fabricated, that which is inherently present and that which must be actualized or acted upon. Dolpopa, for example, distinguishes "naturally present" potential from "fortified potential" and carefully describes the chain of causality for generating buddha bodies.[54] Khédrup follows his own vitriolic characterization of the practitioner who declares himself to be a buddha as either an idiot or a liar with the following direct reference to the buddha nature problem: "Anyone who makes claims like this, asserting that the continua of sentient beings possess a stable and permanent *svābhāvikakāya* together with all the qualities of results of separating (from obscurations) is an intolerable proponent."[55] In this statement, Khédrup opposes any notion of an unchanging essence of ready-made buddhahood or a naturally enlightened body present in ordinary beings; he identifies this very proposition as a threat to the urgency of engaging in Buddhist practice, the method demanded for eliminating obstacles to enlightenment. Khédrup reinforces "the distinction of the fabricated and unfabricated" (*bcos ma bcos kyi khyad par 'byed pa*) to separate bodies from any inherent association with the enlightened form of the mandala:

> If that is the case, many things could be said [such as]:
>
> "For us, considering the suchness [*de kho na nyid*] of the bodies of sentient beings and the suchness of the deities of the mandala to be inseparable in nature, all sentient beings are asserted to be mandalas primordially."
>
> If you say that the mandala of the Buddha is not actually accepted [to be primordially existent in sentient beings], well in that case, [one might reply], "by that reasoning, the distinction of that which is fabricated and that which is unfabricated is illogical just like the suchness of painted powders and cloth paintings being inseparable in nature from the suchness of deities."[56]

In his somewhat absurdist comparison of the "suchness" (*de kho na nyid*) of the materials used to construct mandala representations with the "suchness" of buddhas, Khédrup suggests that it is a given that the essences of representations and of divine reality are different. He uses the categories of fabricated and natural to address problems with both corporeal and mental fabrication.[57] The importance of differentiating bodies and mandala is as obvious to Khédrup as differentiating a material creation like a painting from a deity. As a materialization of karma, the ordinary body serves as an indicator that work remains to be done in progressing toward liberation. To suggest that supports (*rten*) for practice, like bodies, paintings, and statues, are not actually the enlightened forms they are imagined to be is to say that tantric practitioners are cognizant of the parameters of make-believe. In discourses on naturalness, such statements of "the obvious" themselves conceal subtle shifts in the horizon of possibility for practitioners of tantric sādhana.

As other scholars have observed, Khédrup is not deeply invested in problems of buddha nature in this text, although he does deal with the topic in some of his other writings.[58] Even if his mode of engaging with buddha nature in his body mandala chapter is more rhetorical than doctrinal, the nuances of his deployment of buddha nature betray enduring sensitivities around naturalness still raw from the buddha nature debates and resonating in new ways in the fifteenth century. While it is likely that the Jonangpa are indeed being targeted in this section of Khédrup's chapter on body mandala, there may also be an implied critique of the Sakyapa position as well. The Sakyapa system of three continua, according to which the fruit of buddhahood is present in the path, provoked a variety of critiques over time. Khédrup's charge may contain a subtle and mildly sarcastic critique of the Sakyapas, to the effect of something like, "You say that your theory is different from that of the Jonangpas, but it isn't."[59] Such a reading brings attention to the relation of the Jonangpas as a newly evolving institution to the Sakyapas, from whom they descended formally but distinguished themselves doctrinally, as well as to the role of buddha nature as a hotly debated topic in these encounters.[60]

There are aspects of the Sakyapa perspective that regard the body as, in a sense, divine. Initiation into the body mandala of Hevajra for the Sakyapa entails the crucial phase of the guru showing that each part of the disciple's body is a part of the mandala inhabited by deities. Of course, such initiation also demands a commitment to the continued practice of this embodied visualization. Therefore the centrality of the tantric vow to the practice itself counters Khédrup's concerns that seeing one's body as a mandala would obviate the motivation to practice. Ngorchen's choice not to engage with Khédrup's comments on the Ghantapa quote suggests that this portion of Khédrup's argument was not construed as a direct critique of the Sakyapas. However, recent research has revealed that while Ngorchen and Khédrup held compatible views on buddha nature, some of Ngorchen's Sakyapa forefathers, specifically Sönam Tsémo (1142–1182), interpreted bodies as naturally or inherently mandalas.[61] Bentor has suggested that while Khédrup is not necessarily challenging Ngorchen's own views on the primordial relationship of body and mandala, he is agitating a sensitive disjunction between Ngorchen's views and those of some of the Sakyapa patriarchs who

Ngorchen holds up as authorities.[62] This theory conveys the rhetorical implications that ontological claims held for authors in the fifteenth-century scholastic climate. Ngorchen and Khédrup may be relatively free of concerns with the inherent state of the body as either ordinary or enlightened in their body mandala writings. They are certainly more focused on refining ritual mechanics and exegetical methods. Yet the weight of obligations to lineage and enduring sensitivities around buddha nature discourses continued to shape their conversations.

Beyond solidifying doctrinal and philosophical allegiances, Khédrup exercises the rhetorical possibilities of buddha nature in his body mandala chapter through the language of "fabrication" and "naturalness." These two categories pivot upon carefully articulated distinctions of the relationship of enlightened and ordinary bodies and perceptions. For Khédrup, such distinctions are deeply entangled in tensions between pāramitānaya and mantranaya approaches. The compulsion to account for the role of the Buddhist path in actualizing the full extent of human potential is common to polemics on buddha nature and on body mandala. Polemical writings on body mandala may even transfer many of the issues addressed in buddha nature debates in terms of the mindstream and the "foundational consciousness" (*kun gzhi rnam par shes pa*, Skt. *ālayavijñāna*) onto a new locus, the human body.[63] The notion of "transforming the basis" (*gnas yongs su 'gyur pa*, Skt. *āśraya-parāvṛtti*) of practice is also common to both buddha nature and body mandala discourses. Transformation proves to be a defining feature of Khédrup's approach to body mandala as a technology that "works" in effecting liberation on the "lightning path."

KHÉDRUP'S OWN PERSPECTIVE

I have addressed the multivalence of fabrication in the preceding section of this chapter. This involved observing connections with the discourses of buddha nature and Buddhist logic and epistemology in the context of Khédrup's presentation of the views of his opponents. In keeping with established formulas of Buddhist scholasticism, he clarifies his own ideas and demonstrates their logical verifiability in relation to the positions of others. The second part of Khédrup's chapter on body mandala is specifically devoted to presenting and validating his own views. Khédrup applies "fabrication" not only to describe the ontological status of the body mandala but also to describe disputed aspects of ritual mechanics. In observing Khédrup's presentation of his own views on how best to approach the practice of body mandala, a more robust appreciation for what is at stake for him in properly describing this practice of choreographed acts of imagination tied to the body begins to take shape.

Khédrup's discussion of his own views is divided according to the subjects of the body mandalas of support and supported and of generating deities from seed syllables located on specific bodily sites.[64] Recall that the mandala of the support is the generation of the body as the celestial palace, and the mandala of the supported is the generation of deities therein.

The Mandalas of Support and Supported

Khédrup uses the category of fabrication as a key device for distinguishing body mandala from other tantric ritual technologies. For example, he emphasizes the difference between the process of generating deities from seed syllables characteristic of body mandala and other analogous methods. Nyāsa, the placement of deities upon the body through mantra, is among the repertoire of practices resembling body mandala, practices often classified as preparatory and/or purificatory in nature. In an especially salient section of the chapter, Khédrup writes, "The point of what's called cultivating the body mandala doesn't mean only merely cultivating a deity on each place on the body. Establishing each respective part of the body as the foundation (*bsgrub pa'i gzhir byas nas*) for each deity means cultivating the deity. Otherwise, even from the lower sections of tantra, many body mandala cultivations would be explained."[65] For Khédrup, unlike nyāsa, body mandala practice involves more than simply imaginatively imprinting deities on the body. In this passage, Khédrup's focus upon the body as a particular kind of foundation for practice is intimately tied to his account of body mandala as a unique and ultimately superior form of tantric ritual practice imbued with the power to rearticulate the body in enlightened terms.

Khédrup addresses the category of fabrication as it relates to the basis for establishing a mandala. In particular, he uses this category to differentiate the body mandala from "outer mandala" (*phyi'i dkyil 'khor*) such as paintings or altars made of painted powders.

> Moreover, painted powder and cloth and so forth are the basis of establishing [*bsgrub pa'i gzhi*] the celestial palace in the outer mandala [*phyi'i dkyil 'khor*]; the seed syllable, symbol and so forth are the basis of establishing the deity. Since the mandala has been newly fabricated by colors and by the artist [i.e., the causes], it is called the fabricated mandala. As for the body mandala, the particular parts

> of the body mandala have not been newly fabricated. [Rather] being perfected since the time of generation from the mother and father, [they] created the basis for establishing [the body mandala]. Since the [body] mandala is established from those, it is taught as the unfabricated mandala.[66]

In distinguishing different forms of representations, Khédrup is especially interested in the nature of the basis of establishment (*bsgrub pa'i gzhi*) and whether it is inherent or newly produced through causes and conditions. In qualifying fabrication in term of its "newness," he presents fabrication as a spectrum rather than a duality. He maintains a basic causal model: the union of the fluids of one's biological father and mother provided the basis for personhood in cooperation with karma and kleśa and, in turn, form the basis for establishing the body mandala. The bodily basis must, of course, be produced by causes. To say that it is primordially a mandala in any definitive sense would be to deny this. Khédrup defines the body as a different kind of basis for practice by distinguishing it from "newly fabricated" mandala such as a mandala painting.

The rhetoric of the naturally present over and against the produced is familiar from the discussions of buddha nature and Buddhist theories of cause and effect. That which is conditioned is a product of samsara, both produced by and productive of karma and therefore, in a sense, inferior. Deconstructing an entity in terms of its parts as well as the compounded causes and conditions that have contributed to its formation is a core Buddhist technique used to break down the conventional illusion of a self or of the true unchanging existence of an entity. Revealing an entity's conditioned status exposes its ties to defilement and impermanence. In the context of buddha nature debates, asserting the presence of a permanent, unchanging, and unconditioned buddha nature or an enduring dharmakāya posed serious problems for many thinkers. Khédrup therefore circumvents the ontological issues posed by the body mandala, the questions of the primordial equivalence of body and mandala raised by its "unfabricated" status, by qualifying it as "not newly fabricated" (*gsar du ma bcos pa*).

Khédrup juxtaposes the categories of intrinsic and conditioned, fabricated and unfabricated across the domains of causal logic, language, epistemology, ritual, and exegesis. In the following example, he applies the tools of Buddhist linguistic theory and logic to solidify his argument. Returning to further expound upon the correct interpretation of the Ghantapa quotation introduced at the beginning of the chapter, Khédrup asserts, "Therefore, since those foundations for establishing [*bsgrub pa'i gzhi*] the mandala are intrinsic [*rang chas su yod pa*] as soon as one's body is formed: 'These beings are not separate from the naturally established mandala.' So it is said. The basis of establishing the mandala is like using the verbal convention [*tha snyad*] 'mandala,' before it [a mandala] is drawn with painted powders and so forth."[67] Khédrup connects the Ghantapa quote with this notion of conventional designation to illustrate how the body is not a mandala from the beginning, but just the basis and a signifier. In other words, we just call it mandala for the sake of making communication about it easier within the parameters of conventional discourse. Therefore, one should not superimpose ideas about its ultimate primordial status upon it.[68] Khédrup strikes a balance, capitalizing upon the positive connotations of the term *intrinsic* (*rang chas su yod pa*) and its association with ultimate reality while also tempering any ontological consequences of permanence and true, unchanging existence. He does this with the help of the notion of "conventional designations." Buddhist linguistic theory such as that based within the tradition of Dharmakīrti emphasizes the conventional aspect of language. Buddhist thinkers like Dharmakīrti treat language as an intermediary in the thought process: "Thought, then, conceives its object through an object designated by words."[69] This view of language distinguishes Buddhists from Hindu schools of thought like the Mīmāṃsā that posited a true existential connection between words and referents.[70]

As explored in the section on pramāṇa, conceptual acts of superimposition or imputation are varieties of fabrication that hold a negative valence in the Buddhist context. The fact that the imaginative acts of sādhana are fabrications of the mind presents a problem for Khédrup. He writes, "Having established, when cultivating as a deity, regarding both, the outer and the body mandala, there is no distinction in terms of what is fabricated by the mind (*blos bcos pa*) and what is imputed by the mind (*blos btags pa*). And therefore, in all the stages of development from Vajraḍākinī and the 'drop of springtime'[71] and so forth, it is called the 'yoga of fabrication' (*bcos ma'i rnal 'byor*)."[72] Khédrup's direct correlation between the categories of "what is fabricated by the mind" (*blos bcos pa*) and what is "imputed by the mind" (*blos btags pa*) provides a prime example of the relevance of accounting for Khédrup's philosophical perspective in better understanding his approach to tantric materials. Further clarification of the ritual context referenced by the passage is required, but it is likely that the "yoga of fabrication" (*bcos ma'i rnal 'byor*) refers to the generation stage of sādhana practice. Bentor has observed the dichotomy of "similitude" versus "true transformation" in Gelukpa presentations of the generation versus completion stages of the Guhysamāja practice.[73] The language of "similitudes," "fabrications," "imputations," and the "contrived" pervades descriptions of the generation stage as the requisite "practice run" for the actual realization found in the completion stage.

It is clear that Tsongkhapa, like Khédrup, regards fabrication as an inferior quality. For example, Tsongkhapa extols the quality of nonfabrication quoting the *Sampuṭa Tantra*: "That with the nature of nonfabrication is known as wisdom."[74] Tsongkhapa, for his part, uses the two-stage sādhana framework to cope with the notion of fabrication in tantric practice. He neutralizes the potentially problematic status of tantric acts of imagination by relegating the qualities of fabrication to the generation versus completion stage and by stressing their value as skillful means.[75] Tsongkhapa associates the completion stage with the genuine automatic response produced by the repeated imaginings of the generation stage, writing, "Therefore, just as you can discard the boat when you arrive at the far bank of the river but have to rely upon it to get you there, likewise the attainments of the natural and uncontrived completion stage will mean the discarding of the generation stage, but to attain them you will need the contrived generation stage. Thus, for the beginner, the generation stage is worthy of great praise and very important."[76] In other words, though not ultimately viable, acts of imagination are indeed necessary. Although their "fabricated" aspects as associated with the generation stage are ultimately discarded, these fabrications are instrumental in attaining a "natural" or "uncontrived" result. This is a familiar Buddhist mode for relating different phases of meditative practice; only by forfeiting attachment to one level of experience may one progress to the next. Without the make-believe buddhas of the generation stage, no actual buddha bodies could come about. Representations—including those appearing to or generated by the mind—are crucial for tantric approaches to expanding the horizon of possibility.

Both Tsongkhapa and Khédrup agree that the body mandala is unique in its avoidance of fabrication. For example, in his own commentary upon the much-disputed Ghantapa quote, Tsongkhapa remarks, "As the mandala which pierces to the pith in the body (*lus la gnad du bsnun*), the body mandala which refrains from (*mi bya*) the two fabrications is essential."[77] The two fabrications Tsongkhapa speaks of are mandala paintings and altars of painted powders. In the next section of this chapter, I will show how Khédrup uses "piercing to the pith" (*gnad du bsnun*) to further distinguish the body mandala as unfabricated and superior. In the process, I will consider what kind of "basis" the body forms for tantric practice as well as what "true" bodily transformation entails, bearing in mind questions of how best to approach representations as tools for facilitating change.

Piercing to the Pith and the Superior Body Mandala

During our readings of Khédrup's body mandala text at UC Berkeley, Khenpo Choying Dorjee, an accomplished Tibetan Buddhist scholar and teacher of

Dzongsar Institute in Bir, India, described "piercing to the pith" through the metaphor of an arrow hitting its target, getting to the essential point or heart of the matter.[78] It is a phrase used by Tibetan exegetes to distinguish the pāramitānaya, which "pierces to the pith of the mind" (*sems la gnad du bsnun*), from the mantranaya, which pierces to the pith of the body (*lus la gnad du bsnun*). In the following passage, Khédrup proclaims the superiority of the body mandala resulting from the "unfabricated basis of establishment" previously discussed. He then uses the concept of "piercing to the pith of the body" to identify a crucial transition from the repeated imaginings or mental "fabrications" of the generation stage to the natural appearances of the completion stage.

> So, if you ask, "why is the body mandala superior to the two fabricated external mandala?" [I would reply that] the distinction of the superior and inferior emerges based on the fabricated and unfabricated basis of establishment. The completion stage, which arises from meditation by piercing to the pith of the body, is the main cause of establishing the supreme siddhi. By repeatedly cultivating the generation and consecration of all the current parts as deities, the channels, winds and drops of the body become workable [*las rung du gyur*]. By piercing to the pith of the body in meditation, the ripening of the effortless generation of realizing the completion stage becomes supreme.[79]

In tapping into embodiment's utmost potential and meaning, the tantric practitioner experiences the fruition of ritual goals. By this account, the imperative to make the components of the vajra body "workable" (*las rung du gyur*) is a key aspect of bodily transformation. In correlating body parts with divine forms, tantric practitioners exert the feats of imagination required to set the stage for "effortless generation."

Khédrup presents another comparison between the body mandala and outer mandala to emphasize the limitations of the latter, writing, "One generates the painted powders and cloth and so forth as the deity [/deities] and consecrates [them]. As in the case of the body mandala, the accumulation of merit and initiation and so forth are possible to achieve. However, there is no way to generate wisdom by meditatively piercing to the pith in colored powders and cloth."[80] Without body mandala, it is not possible to pierce to the pith of the body, to make the body "workable" as a basis for transformation, and to attain wisdom. How do ritual acts of imagination, representations as acts of mental fabrication, transform the basis for ritual action? I conclude this chapter by exploring the intersection of fabrication, imagination, and transformation in Khédrup's treatment of a few specific points of body mandala practice and reflecting upon what they reveal about Buddhist attitudes toward representation.

TRANSFORMING THE BASIS

For Khédrup, not all imaginative activities are regarded as equally transformative. Moreover, multiple phases of transformation occur within body mandala practice, as visualizations are created, dissolved, and recreated. In describing the method of generating deities from seed syllables located at various sites on the body, Khédrup explains,

> One makes each part of the aggregates, skandhas, elements and sense spheres and so forth into the foundation for establishing the deity. Once they are transformed, they must be generated as each deity. . . . For example, one's eye organ is changed into the syllable THLIM. Having been changed, that then is visualized as changing into Kṣitigarbha. First, with your mind, generate THLIM without a foundation. Having generated Kṣitigarbha from that, afterwards, it's not enough to simply imagine [*mos pa tsam*] the inseparability of own's own eye organ and Kṣitigarbha. Having finished arraying the deities on the body, there is the basic meditation upon [those deities] as essentially inseparable from one's skandhas and so on. Even though imaginative activity [*lhag mos*][81] is the repeated dissolution [of those deities] in the body, that itself is not like cultivating the body mandala.[82]

Bentor has interpreted this passage as evidence that the nature of transformation was at the heart of discrepancies involving versions of the Guhysamāja body mandala practice within the Geluk tradition; in so doing, she has highlighted the tension between "the limitations that general Buddhist theoretical considerations put on the transformative power of the mind and the point of view of meditators who were seeking a more substantial transformation than visualization alone can provide."[83] She shows how Khédrup propounds a different approach to the mechanics of the practice than Tsongkhapa himself did, an illuminating example of ritual exegesis supplanting lineage obligations. Bentor explains,

> Apparently Mkhas grub rje offers his divergent suggestion because for him a significant transformation of all the psycho-physical elements of one's body into the seed syllables of the deities is crucial. For him merely visualizing that the essence of the psycho-physical element abides in the appearance of the seed syllable, as instructed by Tsong kha pa, is an insufficient initial step for the transformation of the impure body into the pure divine mansion. Therefore he requires a complete transformation of each psycho-physical element into the respective

> seed syllable within the visualization, before the seed syllable transforms into a deity. At the same time Mkhas grub rje never regards the creation stage as capable of producing true transformations.[84]

Bentor's observations complement the themes of imagination, fabrication, and transformation explored in this chapter. It is clear that Khédrup wishes to distinguish "mere imagining" (*mos pa tsam*) from body mandala. Furthermore, he connects the term I translate here as "imaginative activity" (*lhag mos*, a term associated with generation rather than completion stage practice), with the imaginative act of dissolving deities into the body and distinguishes that particular activity from body mandala proper. It is therefore possible to interpret this passage in terms of the juxtaposition of varieties of transformation realized through generation and completion stage practice. It can be read as a modification of Tsongkhapa's approach to the mechanics of body mandala. Or, it can be read as an assertion of the distinction of body mandala from related preparatory practices oriented around the body. All of these possibilities affirm ways in which Khédrup nuances the language of imagination to negotiate a profound network of anxieties around the transformative potential of both body and mind.

Within tantric studies, the role of the consort in ritual practice has been one of the most volatile topics related to imagination.[85] The assumption has often been that concerns with the preservation of vows of celibacy provoked censure of practice with a "real" female practitioner in Tibetan monastic institutions, leading to practices in which imagined proxies replace them. And yet there is evidence that key Buddhist figures regarded the consort as essential for liberation. Khédrup makes a salient point about the connection between imagination and fabrication in the context of practice with a consort, parsing the "real" karma *mudrā* from the imagined wisdom mudrā. In doing so, he juxtaposes the aspects of pramāṇa and tantric visualization discussed above as a variety of tantric epistemology in a more practical fashion, one focused more upon ritual mechanics and questions of efficacy:

> Therefore, afterwards, in the context of union with the mudrā (consort), if one arrays the deities on the body of a karma mudrā, then it becomes the body mandala of the consort. There is the generation of seed [syllables] of the deity from that transformation of the individual aggregates and so forth of the body. For the wisdom mudrā, [on the other hand] one doesn't establish [them] in actual sites that are not the mere fabrication by the mind [*blos bcos pa rtsam*]. Therefore, the body that is the basis of establishment does not become the body mandala even though one arranges the deities in a similar way.[86]

In other words, actual transformation into the body mandala can only occur with an actual human consort (i.e., the karma mudrā), not an imagined one. The wisdom mudrā, the imagined consort, is regarded as a mere mental fabrication (*blos bcos pa rtsam*) and therefore an insufficient basis for transformation. So not only is it necessary to do more than merely locate deities on the body, one must transform the bodily basis. And in order for that transformation to be possible, that basis must be at least in some sense valid, real, or verifiable.

In the final portion of his chapter, dedicated to his views on issues surrounding the generation of deities from seed syllables, Khédrup solidifies the connection between the practitioner's own body and the generation of the body mandala. Again, the emphasis is upon establishing an unfabricated basis for practice through reliance upon an empirically verifiable body:

> Moreover, though there are six eyes that are cultivated when cultivating oneself with three faces and six arms, it's not necessary to cultivate the Kṣitigarbha from the right and left faces. Cultivating [him] as the two eyes of the main face will suffice.... Why? It is the basis of purification or the basis for establishing the deity. [As for] those limbs of the body, if there are many, it's necessary to generate many deities [on them]. It's like cultivating two Kṣitigarbhas on account of there being two eyes.... Like generating Kṣitigarbha from the right and left faces without there being an actual entity [there], the basis for practice becomes fabricated. As a result, the manner of generating deities of the unfabricated mandala does not happen.[87]

Despite the very technical nature of this passage, the general point is clear. It is not possible to achieve the body mandala just by imagining an abstract correlation between imagined deities and imagined body parts. Even though one might imagine oneself (or one's consort) as a deity with multiple pairs of eyes, only the eyes that are "really there" can be the basis or point of departure for imagining deities. True transformation necessitates a stable ground for practice and adherence to the rules of conventional reality. Representations, functioning always in tension with their constructed nature, simultaneously demand conformity with precise standards of authenticity.

Whether discussing fabrication in the context of buddha nature, "valid cognition" (pramāṇa), the Madhyamaka, or on the more general level of determining textual authority, Khédrup treats it a volatile category. Fabrication is often used to identify flawed human tendencies to superimpose false concepts upon reality, obstructing our ability to access a clear vision of things as they really are. Yet tantric acts of imagination—in particular, the act of identifying oneself with a deity—shed new light on fabrication, revealing tensions that lay at the root of Buddhist practice.

In this chapter, I have explored the ways in which Tibetan writers like Khédrup developed strategies for coping with the contradictions fabrication presents, specifically, the tension between its power to liberate or transform samsaric suffering and its deep entanglement with distortion and deception. These means of coping are productive, revealing how and why ritual, and, more precisely, tantric ritual acts of imagination like body mandala, are deemed necessary or efficacious. Consistent practice of deity yoga, the "fabrication" of a link with enlightened forms, generates a "natural" assumption of a buddha body. For some ritual exegetes, the "similitudes" of the generation stage bear fruit in the natural realization of wisdom and bliss during the completion stage. Body mandala renders the hidden potential of the vajra body accessible and malleable for the experienced tantric practitioner. It is a sophisticated means of harnessing the mind's problematic habits of "elaboration" and "proliferation" in accord with the tantric philosophy of the antidote, incorporating the poison as part of the cure. Furthermore, body mandala, like tantra itself, is unique in "piercing to the pith" of embodiment and providing the exclusive "profound shortcut" for enlightenment in this lifetime and this body.

ON IMAGINING AND REPRESENTATION

Khédrup's statements on fabrication in the context of imaginative practice enrich the study of Buddhist approaches to representation and also suggest themes that connect with contemporary controversies on representation. Khédrup uses the category of fabrication to negotiate the transformative potential of the body and mind. He also employs fabrication as a rhetorical device in distinguishing and classifying representations. Finally, the complexities of Khédrup's treatment of representation raises the question: what's the point of using representations if they are not "true?" The tantric approach to the mind's creative capacity, its tendency to elaborate, is to embrace that very quality. In tantra, representations function as part of the logic of the antidote: the cure includes a little bit of the poison.

Khédrup shows how the value of representations is weighed according to diverse standards of measure, many of which conflict with one another. Logic, epistemology, philosophy, and ritual practice present distinct senses of the value of representations as well as the dangers that attend them, especially if misused. Many of the conflicts within Khédrup's argument are part of a larger tension between the paramītānaya and mantranaya, the path of perfecting the qualities of the bodhisattva and that of employing tantric ritual means to advance toward liberation in this lifetime and this body. For example, according to some discourses in the path of perfections, a mental representation is only valid if it can be empirically verified by others. Following this line of reasoning, for Khédrup, those imagined flower offerings—hovering in space and intended to evoke a divine presence—may hold a limited value. In granting a view of his interpretive process at the confluence of these discourses, Khédrup reveals how individuals struggle to interpret representations in terms of the tools available to them.

Khédrup explores the intricacies of correlating oneself with a representation. He also demonstrates how the process of correlation can play a part in a liberatory project. The practitioner of body mandala generates representations through a correlative process to break down a confining sense of self and establish a connection to the desired result, an enlightened form. For Khédrup, the precision of body mandala's mode of correlations operates as a way of "transforming the basis" of practice. Representations can therefore be used to prepare the body as a foundation for practice, to tap into its hidden potential by harnessing the power of the channels, winds, and drops of the vajra body, and to make that potential workable in advancing toward liberation.

The ritual use of representations emphasizes how repetition is essential to their usefulness. For Tsongkhapa and others in his lineage, mental representations such as those performed in body mandala provide a vital causal link (the "similar in type cause") between ordinary and enlightened realities. In the Guhyasamāja sādhana practice that is the primary focus of Khédrup's text, the practitioner generates a host of progressively more subtle simulations of the enlightened form to facilitate the leap to buddhahood, a moment, according to Tsongkhapa, akin to a fish leaping out of water. In tantric practice, the repeated generation and dissolution of forms prepares the tantric practitioner to recognize critical moments in which the potential for liberation lies.

Representations are a way of thinking. Khédrup's philosophical orientation inclines him to regard the problematic aspect of representation in the phenomenon of superimposition, the process of imputing false concepts upon reality. From the "moderate realist" perspective of Khédrup's emerging Geluk tradition, these concepts play a vital role in realizing the ways things truly are. In this view, superimposition is a bad habit that can be unlearned. From the antirealist perspective aligned with Ngorchen's Sakya tradition, it is not possible to eradicate superimpositions. For the Sakyapa, phenomena persist in the mode of "appearing." The goal is then to regard representations in a new way, one that accounts for their deceptive nature.

Representations create the possibility for change and expand the horizon of possibility. Like ritual, representations reframe our realities and in so doing juxtapose elements of that reality that might appear to be unconnected and even contradictory. Body mandala juxtaposes things in a way that prompts Khédrup, for example, to attempt to reconcile the more traditional Buddhist notion of the body as a conglomerate formed by the "power of karma and afflictions" with the more optimistic perspective offered by tantric deity yoga, a vision of the body as the form of the buddha Vajradhara. In such attempts, Khédrup illustrates how representations are often evidence that work still remains to be done and specifically that the project of liberation is not complete.

Khédrup concludes his chapter on body mandala by critiquing yet another aspect of fabrication, the invention of spurious Tibetan body mandala practices. He identifies such practices as "baseless mental imputations (*rgyu med pa'i blos btags*) masquerading as the oral instructions and the profound dharma."[88] This climactic statement confirms mounting suspicions about the negative valences of the category of fabrication, valences I have explored within multiple levels of Buddhist discourse. In the context of questions of textual authority, fabrication is decidedly negative. Though Tibetan authors were great innovators, innovation in and of itself was regarded as a transgression rather than a virtue. The authorial ideal was to seamlessly transmit the teachings of the Tibetan masters and in particular, the Indian masters of the tradition, without superimposing one's own ideas. In order to be appreciated, innovations needed to be presented as elucidations of the teachings of the past. Building upon my exploration of fabrication, in the next chapter I shift to explore a different permutation of constructing representations. I will show how the historical sources for the body mandala debate construct Ngorchen and Khédrup's personae and craft institutional identities in alignment with lineages of continuity. I address why Ngorchen and Khédrup's claims to clarifying the essence of the meaning of the Buddhist teachings are both creative and polemical, revealing further ways in which representations operate in tension with their constructed nature.

2

Constructing the Body Mandala Debate

The quest for meaning within Buddhist texts and practices is predicated upon establishing continuity, an uninterrupted stream of transmission leading back to the intention of the Buddha and flowing through his disciples and later interpreters. The basic distinction between root text and commentary reifies that essential meaning by separating it from the texts that clarify or complete it. This distinction constructs an essence accessible only through the mediation of authentic interpreters.

Continuity is a central problem for the authors and interpreters of the body mandala debate. Can the particular version of a tantric ritual practice, the Hevajra body mandala, embraced and transmitted by Ngorchen's Tibetan Buddhist community, the Sakya, be traced without interruption to an authoritative Indian precedent? In responding to this challenge to the authenticity of his tradition, Ngorchen begins *Destroyer of the Proponents of Evil Through Eliminating Objections to the Hevajra Body Mandala* with verses of praise for his guru. This act of veneration is the quintessential expression of continuity, emphasizing the uninterrupted flow of the transmission of wisdom from guru to disciple. In these verses, he writes, "I bow my head with reverence to the feet of the excellent guru. I venerate the guru Yéshé Gyeltsen who, having eliminated all darkness of wrong views through the sunrays of omniscience, propagates the illumination of the supreme path."[1] Invoking the guru is a common way of initiating any textual or ritual act of creation along with enumerating the names of all the lineage holders. These acts of submission and recollection bind together past and present and construct an essence of the teachings, an essence that the author or ritual actor is charged to perpetuate.

The tantric tradition prioritizes continuity through the sanctity of the relationship of guru and disciple, protected by vows of secrecy and commitment to sustain and protect the teachings. The personal guidance of this teacher is a vital extension of commentarial practice, supplementing and making sense of texts and rituals. When Buddhism entered Tibet, a process of assimilation beginning in the seventh to eighth century, the tantric emphasis upon the guru-disciple relationship came to permeate all aspects of the tradition. From the eleventh century on, in the Sarma era, with the birth of new lineages like the Sakya, Tibetans showed the utmost concern to avoid the impression of breaking with the "authentic" Indian tradition. In establishing their authority to interpret the Buddha's word and thereby establish a uniquely Tibetan Buddhist identity, Tibetans accentuated connections to Indian masters while elevating the Tibetan guru to a buddhalike status.[2]

Tibetan lineage portraits attest to the power of images to craft continuity between the lineage holders of the present and their predecessors, most importantly the Indian masters and the Buddha himself.[3] One such portrait of Ngorchen, familiar from the introduction of this book, shows him surrounded by the Sakya lineage gurus for two of their tantric practices (figure 2.1).[4] The patchwork pattern of Ngorchen's upper robes, crafted in conformity with the Indian vinaya, the rules of monastic conduct, distinguish him as a disciplined upholder of the Buddhist tradition.[5] Simultaneously, the painting, inscribed "Homage to the great Vajradhara, Künga Zangpo," establishes him as an authentic heir to that Buddha's enlightened legacy.[6] The lineage of the Sakya Path and Fruit (*lam 'bras*) to which the Hevajra body mandala at issue belongs consumes the right side of the painting. Both the lineages depicted derive from a common source, the tantric Buddha Vajradhara, inhabiting the position directly above Ngorchen's head in the middle of the upper register of the painting. The Path and Fruit lineage proceeds to the right with the tantric goddess Nairātmyā, consort of Hevajra, and on to the Indian mahāsiddha Virūpa to whom she appeared in a vision and transmitted the tantric teachings. The transfer from divine source to Indian masters and further on to a line of Tibetan Sakya spiritual heirs culminates in the figure of Ngorchen himself. Like this painting, commentarial practice and polemics, both fundamental to the body mandala debate, reinforce the value of continuity in the mission to clarify the essence of the Buddha's teachings.

Ngorchen's humble tribute to the guru's abilities to illuminate the path to liberation contains pronounced polemical implications. Through his words of praise, Ngorchen solidifies his connection to an authoritative teacher who "eliminated all darkness of wrong views." The guru's acts of illumination typify the

FIGURE 2.1 Ngorchen Künga Zangpo (1382–1456) with Two Lineages. Tibet, 1430s–1460s. 34 1/16 x 28 3/8 in. (86.5 x 72 cm). Michael Henss Collection, Zurich. Image courtesy of Michael Henss.

ambitions of Buddhist commentary to eradicate misunderstanding, to bring the essential intention of the Buddha and his legacy of liberation to light. When those wrong views are connected with particular texts and communities, the mode of engagement becomes "polemical." Ngorchen's tone quickly shifts to identify his motivation for composing the text. Ngorchen writes, "How could there be the mere stain of manifesting delusions in the explanation by the supreme venerable Sakyapa which established through flawless instructions in scripture and logic, the supreme essence of speech of the mighty lord Virūpa?"[7] Ngorchen expresses alarm and disbelief at the apparent challenge to the integrity of the lineage holders of the Sakya tradition.

What makes the opponent's claim so outrageous? According to Ngorchen, it is well-established that the Sakyapas have performed their obligation to use all the tools offered by intensive monastic training to transmit the "supreme essence" (*snying po mchog*) of the teachings of the Indian masters, in this case Virūpa, the source of one of their most cherished tantric traditions. Defining the essence in question and determining who is qualified to transmit it is at the heart of tantric polemics, like those of the body mandala debate.

I am responding to the challenges posed by the texts themselves, challenges recent scholarship has highlighted. These include the difficulties of attempting to reconcile hagiographical accounts of Ngorchen and Khédrup's lives with their own claims from their body mandala debate texts, as well as the historical events and changes of the early fifteenth century. The lack of a precise match among these sources disrupts any attempt to produce a coherent narrative of the debate or to identify its causes and consequences. In chapter 1, I introduced Khédrup's critique of the approach to correlating the body with the mandala practiced by "some Tibetans" in the context of "the many body mandalas of the mother tantras." I also located this method of correlation in the writings of the early Sakyapa masters of the Path and Fruit. I will pursue Khédrup's critique in further depth in chapter 3 and show how it is linked to citational practice. I remind the reader of those remarks from the last chapter here to demonstrate how even a brief sketch of Khédrup's body mandala chapter suggests that the Sakyapa Path and Fruit tradition is at least one of the targets of his critical statements. And yet years after his writings on body mandala, in a different text, Khédrup writes: "Which Path and Fruit exactly do I refute? How, before whom, and in which text do I refute it?"[8] As I will demonstrate, there are multiple possible readings of Khédrup's apparent denial of his part in the controversy after the fact. None absolve scholars of the hard work of cultivating more sophisticated tools for approaching the meaning-making processes found in these Buddhist texts. This work demands bringing nuance to the reading of

FIGURE 2.2 Tshongkhapa amid Refuge Field. Mongolia, nineteenth century. Pigments, gilding on sized cloth, 4 1/8 x 3 ¾ in. (10.48 x 9.53 cm). 2014.23.366.1.A-C. Courtesy of Kruizega Art Museum, Hope College; gift of David Kamansky and Gerald Wheaton.

the body mandala debate using the methods of philology and history and also extending the reach of these methods to address incommensurabilty among representations more broadly. In striving to understand what is at stake for these Tibetan authors, I thereby reveal how representations operate in tension with their constructed nature.

Tibetan Buddhists have used lineage portraits as a tool for branding distinct traditions. A painting of Khédrup's teacher Tsongkhapa implanted within a "refuge field" presents an elaborate visual arrangement summoning all the gurus of the lineage, clouds full of buddhas, and enlightened human masters (figure 2.2). The Buddha appears at Tsongkhapa's heart center, and delicate threads connect Tsongkhapa to the various assemblies of enlightened entities. In the lower right, a monk, a prototype likely modeled after an image of Khédrup himself, performs offerings to the lineage. The painting envisions a mode of invocation in which ritual practitioners use sound, gesture, and imagination to express devotion and establish themselves as members of this lineage. Through these means, they solidify their identities as legitimate heirs to the Buddha's enlightened legacy and as members of a distinct Buddhist community.

ESSENCES, RUPTURES, AND UNSTABLE ORIGINS: PROBLEMS IN APPROACHING THE BODY MANDALA DEBATE

Institutions of belonging, power, and prestige set the stage for the body mandala writings. The vexing question troubling the interpretation of this debate is this: When did the emerging Gandenpa/Gelukpa tradition, claiming Tsongkhapa as founder, definitively split from the Sakyapa tradition? Tsongkhapa himself was a Sakyapa lineage holder. At some point, his status changed, and the emerging rift with the Sakya tradition became irreparable. There is a distinct possibility that Ngorchen and Khédrup played a part in creating or exacerbating this split. However, the degree of their responsibility or complicity in forging this distinction is hard to determine. Textuality is vital to creating these distinctions, but also to how they are retroactively mapped onto the identities of these authors in hagiographical materials in the form of archetypes like "defender of the faith" or qualities like "remaining faithful." Reading Tibetan texts with attention to the push and pull of continuity and innovation produces a clearer view of the constructed nature of these histories.

Another key challenge posed by the body mandala debate texts is the infinite regress of the sources encountered. Each time a previous iteration of the debate is located, the sense of "origin" of the dispute and an "exact essence" of the debate becomes less stable. This instability calls for a recalibration of approaches to the archive. Michel Foucault challenged the paradigm for conducting historical inquiry by evaluating how meaning is constructed by the very act of reconnaissance. He allied his approach with a particular quality he saw in Friedrich Nietzsche's work, a critique of essences, writing, "Why does Nietzsche challenge the pursuit of the origin (*Ursprung*), at least on those occasions when he truly is a genealogist? First, because it is an attempt to capture the exact essence of things, their purest possibilities, and their carefully protected identities, because this search assumes the existence of immobile forms that precede the external world of accident and succession."[9] In Foucault's hands, Nietzsche's ideas clarify the manner in which the search for meaning within representations plays a part in constructing essences. This movement toward critical reflection on the constructed nature of history is useful to keep in mind while searching for meaning within the body mandala debate.

In this chapter, I illuminate the ways in which Buddhist authors craft charismatic identities, a sense of continuity with a lineage of enlightened masters leading back to the Buddha, communities of belonging, as well as a sense of history. In examining the "constructed" qualities of the debate as well as of Ngorchen and Khédrup's identities, I reveal the creativity of the authors, their biographers, and of Buddhologists in producing these representations. I also present tools for making sense of the network of fifteenth-century texts that form the basis of this study by showing how naturalness, continuity, and essential meanings are constructed in Buddhist texts and the different shapes these constructions assume in polemics, hagiography, and textual exegesis. In the process, I present the possibility that the search for the essence of the body mandala debate in a single cause or origin immune to the craftsmanship of human interpreters may be a distraction from some of the more radical acts of meaning-making involved. Attending exclusively to the sociopolitical circumstances and institutional intrigues surrounding the debate, for example, obscures the mini revolutions occurring in Ngorchen and Khédrup's styles of navigating the rules of interpretation or of determining what makes a body mandala authentic and ritually efficacious. I therefore encourage a wariness of "essences" of representations by repeatedly revealing the many layers of construction of this debate by the authors themselves, by their biographers, and by scholars of Tibetan Buddhism.

Essences pose problems for Buddhist thinkers, problems connected with the practical and symbolic role of bodies and language. The Buddha distinguished his project from those of other philosophers and renunciants of his time by promoting teachings on "no-self" (Skt. *anātman*). According to the doctrine of no-self, the search for the true, divine inherent essence or nature of the self is a futile distraction from life's most crucial challenge and opportunity: realizing the way things really are. No-self was not an existential statement but rather a call to action, a call to divest the self as unchanging essence of its dominion over the quest for meaning. Over time, Buddhists have used ritual, metaphysics, philosophy, and exegesis to chip away at the sense of an essence of selfhood, one that is static and independent of realities like cause and effect and the conceptual fabrication of reality by the mind. Yet despite the perpetual denial of essences, Buddhist textual and ritual traditions suggest that essential meanings are deeply valued.

I investigate how historical genres and methods have been vital in constructing essences and reveal the power of genealogy to expose these creative acts. Critical attention to the bubbling up of the repressed transgressions of cultural norms reveals a perpetual tension between the integrity of a unified Buddhist communal body and the inevitable rifts and ruptures that appear on its surface. Polemical texts like those of the body mandala debate establish the prestige of their authors and, by extension, of the lineages they represent. This prestige translates into resources of patronage and devotion needed to sustain this community. Like Ngorchen's patchwork robe, the social body of early fifteenth-century Buddhist monasticism is sutured to hold together the past and the present. From certain angles, at least, they even appear to be seamless.

THE SOCIAL BODY OF FIFTEENTH-CENTURY TIBET

Reducing the body mandala debate to sectarian differences between Geluk and Sakya traditions misses the dynamics of patronage and power shaping religious and political life in the fifteenth century. This is a period that has been somewhat neglected in historical scholarship on Tibet, perhaps in part because it marks a time of intensive growth and change in the relationship of political, monastic, and intellectual institutions.[10] As a result of its transitional nature, the fifteenth century has generally been characterized by the more easily defined periods it follows and precedes. The previous century and a half is understood in terms of the reform of the monastic system, the fall of the Mongol-Yuan Dynasty, and the solidification of the Tibetan Buddhist canon.[11] The seventeenth century is regarded as a time in which political might was centralized, the Gelukpas rose to power, and encyclopedic projects in all domains of Tibetan life were initiated by the Fifth Dalai Lama.

The Sakya tradition of Tibetan Buddhism was on somewhat shaky ground in the fifteenth century relative to its previous flourishing in alliance with the Mongol-Yuan Dynasty (1271–1381). In the mid-fourteenth-century, the ascent of Pakmo Drupa Tai Situ disrupted the political hegemony of the Sakyapa.[12] In 1434, the successors to the Pakmo Dru legacy began challenging one another, destabilizing power relations in Ü and Tsang for the next century, with the gradual rise of the Rinpung family.[13]

This instability disrupted the institutional life of Buddhist monasteries and modified the climate of competition for patronage among traditions. While they retained some influence, the Sakyapas in particular encountered uncertainty and change in the fifteenth and sixteenth centuries. During this time, the internal organization of their institutions transformed and expanded and the dynamics of their relationship to other traditions shifted. In the midst of these changes, Tsongkhapa initiated the formation of a new tradition, the Gelukpa or Gandenpa. Modeled upon the teachings of the eleventh-century Indian reformer Atiśa, Tsongkhapa's teachings gradually gained momentum, aided by the efforts of disciples including, notably, one of this book's protagonists, Khédrupjé. Tsongkhapa's roots within the Sakya lineage created challenges for disciples seeking to establish the integrity of his project and to promote an independent Gelukpa institutional identity. These developments participated in broader tensions between continuity and change within fifteenth-century Tibetan Buddhism.

Foreign relations significantly impacted Tibetan religious life in the fifteenth century. Indian masters continued to travel to Tibet, although certainly with less regularity than in the time of the "later dissemination" of Buddhism in Tibet, at its peak from the approximately the late tenth through the twelfth centuries.[14] Moreover, although the nature of Tibetan and Chinese relations shifted during the Ming Dynasty (1368–1644), important diplomatic connections between religious masters and the court continued to be forged. For example, the Fifth Karmapa visited the court of the Ming emperor Ch'eng-tsu in 1407–1408 to perform funerary rites for the emperor's parents.[15] The domain of scholasticism was deeply entrenched in these institutional intrigues and exchanges.

One way to read the body mandala debate is to look at these texts as inscriptions that reveal elements of the social, economic, and doctrinal anxieties and desires of their authors. Approached in this way, the debate reveals how patronage, lineage, and abbatial succession factored in the creation and interpretation of Tibetan texts. Accounting for the dynamics of "sectarian differentiation" and apologetics in Khédrup and Ngorchen's writings on body mandala demands continuous balancing of these concerns with ritual and exegetical imperatives.

Over the course of this chapter, I introduce critical tools for evaluating representations of Khédrup and Ngorchen and their polemical activities as "constructed." I begin by reflecting upon the complexities of framing this network of texts as a "debate" and then situate the debate within Khédrup and Ngorchen's respective careers, furnishing a more intimate portrait of their lives and accomplishments. I also suggest broader institutional and sociopolitical dynamics at play in fifteenth-century Tibetan monastic life that will prove useful for interpreting the significance of the body mandala debate.

THE VIRTUES AND LIMITATIONS OF THE CATEGORY OF DEBATE AS A TOOL FOR INTERPRETATION

In Tibetan monastic education, debate functions as a pedagogical tool for clarifying ideas and forming convictions.[16] The spirit of debate in the courtyard of the monastery is dramatic, accompanied by bravado and the competitive edge of a sporting event. The syncopated physical gestures and raised voices might easily distract an observer from the common quest for clarity that lies at the root of this tradition. The form of debate challenges assumptions by forcing participants out of their comfort zones; it requires them to think from the perspectives of opposing positions, to exchange subjectivities as a means of arriving at certainty.[17]

Not all Tibetan debates occur in the courtyard. Some debates are initiated through written correspondence, through a series of questions and replies. Others, perhaps like Khédrup and Ngorchen's body mandala texts, qualify as "debate" in a more general sense and present themselves as efforts to dispel mistaken views of texts and practices. However, the "unnamed opponents" they target occupy a substantial presence within the texts as the proverbial elephants in the room. The heated critical nature of tone, the playful and sometimes not so playful sarcasm, remind the reader of their presence. The vibrant genre of polemical literature, "answers to refutations" (*dgag lan*), expresses the dialectical and somewhat antagonistic spirit of intellectual engagement engendered by texts like those of the body mandala debate.[18]

The category of debate in Tibetan Buddhism is charged not merely with doctrinal significance but also with the sociopolitical aspects of the invention, preservation, revision, and revival of tradition. The Samye Debate, the alleged historical encounter between Kamalaśīla and Mohoyen, is a prime example of the iconic status of debate in constructing tradition.[19] That debate functions as the origin story of sorts for Tibetan scholasticism; it is Tibetan Buddhism's testament to its transmission of the Indian "gradualist" versus the Chinese "subitist" approach to enlightenment. However, the actual contents of the debate at Samye and its historical veracity remain unclear.

Tibetan biographers and historians have used such iconic aspects of debate to craft the personae of charismatic individuals and institutions, such as Khédrup as "defender of the faith." They have used debate to reinforce allegiances and distinctions between traditions. Building upon the work of Elijah Ary, I critically examine debate as a trope in Khédrup and Ngorchen's biographies. In the process, I foreground the "constructive" dimension of history and resist a reductionist approach to representations of the body mandala writings.

ROUND ONE

The life and import of the body mandala debate exceeds the lives and also likely the expectations of Khédrup and Ngorchen. It is a debate more likely to have occurred in a metaphorical rather than an actual courtyard.[20] Disciples of these thinkers and their disciples return to points from the debate in later texts. Even today, monks are still discussing it, including conversations between the Fourteenth Dalai Lama and prominent Sakyapa teachers.

In this book, I focus only upon what I call round one of the body mandala debate, composed of two main parts. The first is Khédrup's chapter on body mandala, consuming about thirty of the approximately four hundred total folia sides of his *Ocean of Attainment of the Guhyasamāja Generation Stage* (abbreviated hereafter as *Ocean of Attainment*), a commentary on the generation stage of the Guhyasamāja sādhana in which he wages his critique of a particular form of body mandala practice.[21] Although Khédrup's text specifies the place of composition, no date is recorded. Round one also includes two "versions" of Ngorchen's response to Khédrup's charges, *Destroyer of the Proponents of Evil Through Eliminating Objections to the Hevajra Body Mandala* (abbreviated hereafter as *Destroyer of the Proponents of Evil*) or [N1] and *Dispelling Evil Views of the Hevajra Body Mandala* (abbreviated hereafter as *Dispelling Evil Views*) or [N2], about thirty-five and forty folia sides respectively.[22] The colophons of Ngorchen's two texts both date to 1426 (*zil gnon*), three years before Ngorchen founded Ngor Monastery (Éwam Chöden). The period of composition of this network of texts coincides with institution-building activities for both Khédrup and Ngorchen at Gyantsé and Ngor Monastery, respectively.

Khédrup and Ngorchen strategically engage with teachings from centuries past. Moreover, the issues they dispute have continued to be taken up in debates for generations. Recently, for example, Yael Bentor has identified arguments within Tsongkhapa's writings that Khédrup resurrects and reiterates in *Ocean of Attainment*.[23] Her findings have led her to conclude that Khédrup's arguments in *Ocean of Attainment* "did not initiate the debate as such, but contains responses to one argument and gives rise to another."[24] A generation later, Ngorchen's student Gorampa Sönam Sengé (1429–1489) was still defending, clarifying, and elaborating upon Ngorchen's views on visualization practice within the Hevajra mandala system.[25] The reverberations of the issues and dynamics initiated in round one found (and yet to be discovered) in other texts by Ngorchen and Khédrup, their disciples, and later members of their traditions as well as by their predecessors reinforce the importance of the body mandala debate and its relevance to broader concerns with Tibetan Buddhist history, ritual practice, and textual exegesis. I have chosen to focus on this limited range of texts in order to address these concerns and to lay the foundation for scholarship of other body mandala debate texts.

KHÉDRUP AND NGORCHEN'S UNNAMED OPPONENTS

Traditionally Tibetan authors of polemical texts do not name their opponents. There is often a strong implication, however, that "you know who you are." Upon occasion, authors test the limits of this culture of anonymity with comments that lie somewhere between teasing and accusation. Such comments often assume a form like "You yourself said so in your text on . . ." Ngorchen, the less strictly polemical of our protagonists, peppers versions of his body mandala writings with such comments. Reductionist approaches to both identifying unnamed opponents and to the relationships implied by these exchanges have often limited the scope of appreciation of polemical texts. Even within round one of the body mandala debate, there are potentially many more interlocutors or "unnamed opponents" than Khédrup and Ngorchen. Ronald Davidson cautions against the tendency to assume that Gelukpas are always attacking Sakyapas or that there is only a single opponent in a given exchange.[26] The hyperbolic tone of scholastic debate has lent itself to such misunderstandings, prompting the impression that "refutation of a facet of a practice indicates a wholesale condemnation of the tradition."[27] Davidson attributes these trends to "modern Tibetan religious folklore" as well as to the monastic community, and certainly Buddhologists are equally culpable. These trends are fueled by a combination of factors including the conventions of the polemical genre together with a familiar impulse to construct coherent and relatable narratives.[28]

Bentor provides insights into the identity of the "unnamed opponents" in Khédrup's body mandala writings. In a 2006 article, she introduced the manner in which Khédrup's readings of the Guhyasamāja sādhana together with its associated body mandala practices relate to those of his teacher, Tsongkhapa. She contextualized both in conversation with the writings of Butön Rinchen Drup (1290–1364) as well as Tsongkhapa's own teacher, Rédaba Zhönü Lodrö (1348–1412).[29] As more of the latter's texts have become widely available, Bentor has come to focus more prominently upon Tsongkhapa and Khédrup's participation in a joint project of distinguishing their interpretations from those of Rédaba.[30]

It is likely that Ngorchen, too, has other unnamed opponents. There is some evidence to suggest that these may be proponents of the Kagyu tradition. Ngorchen's body mandala debate texts are dedicated to defending the integrity of the transmission of the Hevajra-based practices within the Sakya tradition.

As I have established, the lineage of transmitting the Path and Fruit as based upon the Hevajra tantric teachings was integral to the tantric tradition of the Sakyapas. However, theirs was not the only lineage through which these teachings were passed. There are two systems of pith instructions on Hevajra practice. The teachings Virūpa passed to "Nagpo of the East" (Kanha) are followed by the Sakyapas;[31] those that Nāropā passed to Marpa are followed by the Kagyupas. In his 2008 study of Amézhap's (1597–1659) *Notes on How to Enter Into the Writings of the Sakyapas* (*Notes*), a text primarily composed by Chöpel Zangpo (fifteenth century) based on Ngorchen's own teachings, Jan-Ulrich Sobisch unveils evidence of Ngorchen's participation in mutual critiques between Sakyapas and Kagyupas of the validity of the other's Path and Fruit lineage.[32] For example, in the *Notes* text, Ngorchen quotes a couple of polemical comments by Kagyupa authors that elevate Marpa's transmission and even critique the efficacy of the Sakyapas' received transmission. There, in *Notes*, Ngorchen (as rendered by Amézhap) proceeds to expose the weaknesses of the Marpa transmission. In particular, he problematizes the absence of the transmission of the *Sampuṭa Tantra* and the commentaries on the Hevajra and Vajrapañjara tantras within Marpa's version. As will become increasingly apparent in the later chapters of this book, the triad of the Hevajra root tantra accompanied by the Sampuṭa and Vajrapañjara tantras is vital to the ritual and exegesis of the Sakyapa Path and Fruit.

Tropes and genres play a part in framing representations and set up certain expectations about what a representation means. Remaining open to the possibility of multiple simultaneous interlocutors, both within and across traditions, allows for a more nuanced approach to this network of texts within the framework of a debate.

"SECTARIAN DIFFERENTIATION" VERSUS SECTARIANISM

Within the field of religious studies, there has been a tendency to transpose the doctrinal approach to sectarian division born from the Reformation onto the study of other religious contexts. Buddhist studies and Tibetan studies have both suffered from such faulty projections.[33] In response to this problem, José Ignacio Cabezón introduces an important distinction between "sectarian differentiation" and "sectarianism" in his study of philosophical exchanges involving Ngorchen's student Gorampa. He distinguishes the two phenomena as oriented around "belonging" and "pathology" respectively:

> The former is simply an inevitable historical development that arises out of human beings' desire to create and nurture social and institutional structures of belonging—intellectual and spiritual homes, places where we share common goals and a common language—in a word, traditions. Sectarianism, by contrast, is a pathological outgrowth of sectarian differentiation wherein traditions become static and reified, and wherein dogmatism prevails.[34]

In reducing the body mandala debate to a sectarian conflict between two opposing factions, there is the risk of missing some of the more informative dynamics it suggests for describing the fifteenth-century monastic context. These include dynamics of patronage, prestige, and identity construction as well as previously neglected dimensions of exegetical and polemical practice. Yet while Ngorchen and Khédrup's engagement is not just about Gelukpas versus Sakyapas, these identity categories have influenced the creation and interpretation of their body mandala debate text. Moreover, there is evidence that tradition formation is one, albeit not the only, factor motivating these authors.

READING "SECTARIAN DIFFERENTIATION" OVER TIME IN BIOGRAPHICAL WRITINGS

The incommensurability of events with biographical accounts and other historical sources for the body mandala debate raises questions as to whether the debate was a sectarian issue or rather later interpreted as one.[35] Ary locates the biographical genre "at the heart of Tibetan Buddhist sectarian formation itself."[36] Some of the "sectarian distinctions" of Gelukpa from Sakyapa traditions may have been retroactively projected and even created by biographers in ensuing generations as the divide between Sakyapas and Gelukpas became more pronounced.

In situating the body mandala debate within both Khédrup and Ngorchen's careers, ruptures in the social body of Tibetan Buddhism become part of the story. Over time, ruptures appeared in connection with the acts of "sectarian differentiation" happening between the Gelukpas and Sakyapas of the fifteenth century. One challenge in approaching Ngorchen and Khédrup's writings on body mandala is figuring out what role their engagement played in producing these ruptures while resisting the temptations of teleology to read all engagements as an inevitable progression toward sectarian schism.[37] It becomes equally important to devise tools for detecting minuscule cracks beginning to form in the social body, tools that are useful in evaluating how these cracks were produced over time. In his work on Khédrup's biographical writings, Ary highlights the use of salient tropes to describe Khédrup, such as "defender of the faith"; he unpacks the manner in which these tropes reflect anxieties surrounding betrayal of lineage and creating schisms within the monastic community.[38] Tracing these tropes and related anxieties within representations of the body mandala debate is an effective way of discerning how these ruptures were produced over time.

I share Ary's concern with establishing whether there was a precise historical moment when defending Tsongkhapa's views became formally distinguished from defending the Sakya tradition and when that moment would be. Both Tsongkhapa and Khédrup possessed strong ties to the Sakya tradition; both were students of great Sakya masters like Rédaba. Before ever studying with Tsongkhapa, Khédrup indeed received the Hevajra initiation and Path and Fruit teachings from Yéshé Pel and studied with esteemed Sakya teachers like Sönam Gyeltsen and Nazawa. Two years after his full ordination, Rédaba sent him to study with Tsongkhapa.[39] This aspect of Khédrup's biography reinforces his identification as a Sakyapa, inculcated in the primary tantric ritual tradition of the Path and Fruit including the Hevajra body mandala practice. The body mandala debate texts and their later interpretations are resources for developing a more nuanced understanding of how this distinction was realized.

I am also making a somewhat stronger claim for Khédrup's culpability in authoring his fate than found in recent more charitable interpretations of his polemics as "passionate" or merely "hyperbolic."[40] While he may have not intended to burn his bridges with the Sakyapas and their patrons and allies through his polemical writings, I argue that Khédrup's actions aggravated already existing tensions to produce some irreversible effects. His nebulous departure from Gyantsé provides clues while also raising questions of method for approaching conflicting representations of a "debate."

KHÉDRUP AND THE CONTROVERSY AT GYANTSÉ

Questions and Sources

Around the same time that Khédrup composed his body mandala writings, he was involved in an alleged, by some accounts even scandalous, encounter at Gyantsé. The diversity of conflicting accounts of Khédrup's role in that encounter illuminates the constructed nature of records of debates, their sometimes tenuous historical foundation, and the sensitive nature of patronage in fifteenth-century

Tibet. These accounts raise questions about how best to interpret depictions of debates within biographical materials. Khédrup's alleged encounter at and ensuing departure from Gyantsé demonstrates the complexities of reading biographical sources and, in particular, the portrayal of debates therein. These biographies, when situated in a particular religious and sociopolitical context, destabilize and marginalize the search for a singular true history. Instead, the constructed character of these narratives and what they accomplished assumes center stage.

Beyond the illustrative nature of the Gyantsé accounts for interpreting debates in Tibetan sources, there is also a concrete connection between Khédrup's first body mandala debate text, *Ocean of Attainment*, and Gyantsé. The colophon for that text reveals that it was written "at the Great Temple of Pelkhor Déchen, the place which is the source of reasoning [in] upper Nyang [*nyang stod*], in Tsang."[41] Pelkhor Déchen is one of several monasteries Khédrup was involved in founding within the region, such as Nyangtö Changra and Dangchen.[42] In 1424, at age thirty-nine, five years after the death of his master, he founded Pelkhor Déchen in Gyantsé.[43] He is alleged to have spent four years there.[44] Like many of Khédrup's texts, *Ocean of Attainment* does not provide a date of composition. As Ngorchen composed his reply in 1426, the precise timing for Khédrup's composition is likely around 1425.[45] During this period, Khédrup also composed the polemical work referred to as the "Thousand Topics" (*Stong thun chen mo*) as a defense of Tsongkhapa's interpretation of the Madhyamaka philosophical perspective.[46] Therefore, Khédrup composed at least two significant polemical works during his time at Gyantsé, based in the tantric and philosophical genres respectively.

The conflicting accounts of the circumstances of his departure from Gyantsé in 1428 invite further investigation. While several primary and secondary sources suggest that Khédrup left his seat at Gyantsé as a result of a scheduled debate between himself and the Sakyapa Rongtön Shākya Gyeltsen (1367–1449), the conditions of the debate and of his departure remain unclear. Cabezón has observed that while many accounts devote minimal attention to Khédrup's activities in establishing a monastery at Gyantsé, two biographies, Jétsün Chökyi Gyaltsen's (1469–1544/46) *Secret Biography* (*Gsang ba'i rnam thar*) and Nénying Jamyang Künga Gélek Rinchen Gyeltsen's (1446–1496) *Rnam mthar mkhas pa'i yid 'phrog* (KYP), are quite concerned with depicting his departure, albeit in different ways.[47]

Patronage

The disparity between accounts of the departure raise questions about the nature and potential transformation of Khédrup's relationship to his patron, local ruler,

Rapten Künzang (1389–1442).[48] Khédrup's involvement at Pelkhor Déchen may be read within a larger pattern of patronage in the early to mid-fifteenth century. Local rulers put in place by the Pakmo Dru supported emerging Gelukpas, and specifically figures new to monastic stewardship; these new Gelukpa leaders presided over monasteries established in close proximity to the patron's political stronghold.[49] Portrayals of Khédrup's patron vary widely within the accounts of the events at Gyantsé, ranging from ally to antagonist or at least enabler of his opponent. For example, Jackson suggests that Khédrup initiated the encounter and that his patron obstructed his attempts: "(I)n 1427, Khedrubje tried to engineer a public doctrinal confrontation with Rongtön Sheja Kunrik (1367–1449), another preeminent Sakyapa luminary. . . . When at the last minute the Prince of Gyantse stepped in and prevented a planned public debate, the disappointed Khedrubje resigned the abbacy of Gyantse monastery."[50] According to Jackson, Khédrup's resignation was a direct result of his patron's intervention. Conflicting accounts of Khédrup's departure from Gyantsé exemplify some of the difficulties of constructing a coherent historical narrative of a debate and therefore support this book's approach to de-essentializing the body mandala debate. The Gyantsé case is also valuable on another level, for Khédrup's involvement there may have played a part in alienating the Sakyapas and therefore contributed to the conditions for the body mandala debate.

Cabezón describes how one biography of Khédrup (the KYP referenced earlier) as well as the monastery's "oral tradition" depicts the conflict between Khédrup and his patron as sparked by Rapten's desire to arrange a debate with Rongtön. According to the KYP, Khédrup accepted the challenge and the details were arranged, including the summoning of erudite scholars to arbitrate the encounter. The KYP's author claims that Rongtön evaded the encounter, leaving Gyantsé together with his patron. Khédrup was thus provoked, according to this account, to post a letter to Rongtön on the door to the monastery in retaliation.[51] Khédrup's letter paints Rongtön as a coward seeking the protection of his "benefactor:" "Finding a refuge in the words of your benefactor who has said that in this district conferences of scholars are not allowed, you tell him what a great kindness he has done you."[52] Yet, by Khédrup's account, Rapten's offense is ultimately even more detrimental to the progress of Buddhist learning. The letter emphasizes this critique of Rapten, "the protector":

> Though many hooded *nāgas,* the scholars,
> Have come together in this place as judges,
> From their respective oceans, the great seats of learning . . .
> The word has come from him who is your protector

That, having returned to their respective abodes,
The oceans, which are the treasuries of water,
The mandala of disputation will not take place.[53]

Khédrup suggests that by preventing the "mandala of disputation," Rapten has overstepped the bounds of the patron's role as a lay supporter of the Buddhist community and encroached upon the territory of monastic specialists. In banning "district conferences of scholars," Rapten has become a ruler blind to the fruitful nature of debate for advancing intellectual discourse. Inhibiting the gathering of the great minds for this contest, Rapten's interests are, by this account, out of synch with collective advancement of the Buddhist scholastic community.

There is no explicit mention of how the encounter impacted Khédrup's relationship with his patron in the *Secret Biography*. Yet, based on this account, Ary identifies the "debate" between Khédrup and Rongtön as the cause for the deterioration of that patronage relationship.[54] Leonard van der Kuijp even links Khédrup's departure to his patron's disapproval of his manner of engaging Ngorchen and other Sakyapas.[55] This theory emphasizes the political dimension of patronage and also suggests more far-ranging consequences for polemical activities than might be expected. It also implies that Khédrup's mode of engaging the Sakyapas was especially extreme and produces a possible link between the body mandala debate and Khédrup's departure.

The disparities in the accounts regarding Rapten's role provoke a series of questions such as the following: Was it Khédrup or his patron who initiated the debate with Rongtön? Why would the patron cancel a gathering that he himself had orchestrated? The prospect that the patron was balancing a host of interests, relationships, and allegiances further complicates matters. Such problems suggest that patronage played an important part in the construction of this debate at Gyantsé in Khédrup's biographies and even in his eventual departure.

Fragmenting the Social Body: Schisms in the Sangha

While the KYP depicts Rongtön as a coward hiding behind a meddling patron, Khédrup's *Secret Biography* (SNT) tells another story. It paints Rongtön as a provocative Sakyapa opponent, baiting Khédrup into a debate to exacerbate existing tensions with the Sakyapas: "While at Nyang stod, Rong ston continuously nagged Mkhas grub rje, saying 'Come, let us debate together.'"[56] The *Secret Biography* identifies Rongtön specifically with a group of ill-intentioned

Sakyapas bent on the destruction of Tsongkhapa's lineage. These malevolent Sakyapas are rendered as crafty and rumor-mongering magicians. Threatened by Tsongkhapa and his followers, they falsely accuse the latter of violating the code of respect for spiritual ancestors: "At that time, all the fools at Sakya who were skilled in magical incantations, blind to what are dharma activities and what are not, spread the rumor out of competitiveness, attachment and aversion, that Tsongkhapa and his followers had criticized the tenets of the Sakya school. They even performed rituals such as casting out ritual cakes to send evil their way."[57] Buddhist monastic law prohibits inciting divides in the Buddhist community. Such divisions are termed "schisms in the sangha" (Skt. *sangha-bheda*) and are literally rifts in the social body of the Buddhist community. Therefore, in suggesting that Sakyapas like Rongtön generated spurious rifts in the community, the text brands these Sakyapas as un-Buddhist. The irony is that the account is a defense against the claim that Tsongkhapa and his disciples did that very thing to the Sakyapas. Statements from Ngorchen's biographical materials to be discussed later in the chapter suggest that the he too found himself to be the target of sorcery and spells cast by rivals triggered by his composition of "answers to refutations."

The *Secret Biography* frees Khédrup of blame, guarding him against charges of causing schisms in the sangha or of betraying his lineage of Sakyapa ancestors. Moreover, the biographer implies that Rongtön is creating the schism in his refusal to properly credit Tsongkhapa's contribution to the Sakya legacy, namely, the faithful transmission of Nāgārjuna's spiritual lineage. By investing Khédrup with the duty to fend off attacks of traitors who have disrupted the integrity of lineage, the biographer endows Khédrup's polemics with a noble purpose: to restore the integrity of the body of the community. This body relies upon the continuity of relationships between masters and disciples, a continuity that rumors, betrayals, and even magical onslaughts could jeopardize. In absolving Khédrup in this way, the biographer uses representation as a tool to justify Khédrup's polemical activities and potentially, his own.

Defender of the Faith: Biography as Polemics

Learning to see the human hand at work in constructing history calls for reevaluation of authorial contributions. In considering how Khédrup's biographers crafted and augmented his identity as a "defender of the faith," the constructed nature of historical sources becomes increasingly apparent. Jétsünpa, the author of Khédrup's *Secret Biography*, elevates Khédrup's persona as a "great debater" and "defender of Tsongkhapa's tradition;" some other biographies of Khédrup apparently completely neglect these dimensions of his persona.[58] This disparity between sources suggests that Khédrup may not have envisioned himself as a defender of the faith to the same degree that his descendants did. These observations open up the possibility for reading biography as polemics.

Jétsünpa himself is also famed for some of his intellectual encounters with Sakyapa scholars, including two of Ngorchen's students, Shākya Chokden (1428–1507) and Gorampa.[59] In discrediting the Sakyapas as traitors, Jétsünpa ennobles Tsongkhapa and his disciples. He also craftily disentangles the ties between the Sakyapa and emerging Gelukpa traditions. In the process he inscribes or even incises a rift between these traditions. By defaming the character of prominent Sakyapas as guilty of creating schisms, the biographer conceals Khédrup's role in differentiating traditions. Moreover, Jétsünpa conceals his own craftsmanship, obfuscating the polemical imperative informing his own creative acts of shaping Khédrup's persona in relation to a hostile socioreligious terrain.

The Departure from Gyantsé

Jétsünpa's *Secret Biography* of Khédrup claims a debate did indeed take place after all. In this source, Khédrup initiates the debate, and there is an elaborate portrayal of Rongtön's agitation in his various attempts to circumvent the encounter. Khédrup challenges him: "If you truly cannot debate [me], then you must cease denigrating Tsong kha pa and the tenets of Nāgārjuna and his disciples!"[60] The contents of the debate are mysteriously omitted. Instead, the biographer emphasizes Rongtön's resulting acute humiliation, so profound that he was rumored to have been driven to take a vow of silence. Therefore, the *Secret Biography* paints Khédrup as the victor and upholder of the integrity of Tsongkhapa's legacy while Rongtön is made the fool.

There is another layer to the story of Khédrup's departure from Gyantsé. The politics of institution building coupled with the complex dynamics of patronage may have threatened to resist Khédrup's efforts to establish dominance for Tsongkhapa's tradition there. Competing for both patronage and prestige is vital for new traditions in particular. The Gelukpa colleges at Pelkhor Déchen in Gyantsé did not exist in isolation. For Khédrup, "sectarian differentiation" may have been an survival strategy in the service of promoting Tsongkhapa's legacy within a more diverse scholastic context.[61]

Jackson depicts Rongtön's involvement in a "multisectarian" approach to institution building at Gyantsé in collaboration with the Rinpung lords, with the Sakyapas as a substantial presence within that new framework; he suggests that this approach impeded Khédrup's quest for dominance at Gyantsé and that Khédrup "had little patience with prominent representatives of the other schools or broad-minded patrons."[62] Rongtön was one such "prominent representative" and Rapten one such "broad-minded patron." Diversity and open-mindedness allowed space for the Gelukpas to stand alongside other traditions, but these same conditions could easily lead a new tradition to get lost in the shuffle. The institutional dynamics at Gyantsé and Khédrup's relationship to his patron did not secure a dominant position for Tsongkhapa's tradition among the others represented there. Furthermore, the dense web of patronage dynamics involved both the Rinpung and Pakmo Dru lords. Therefore, accounts of Khédrup's debate with Rongtön and his dramatic departure from Gyantsé may be read alongside his writings on body mandala as attempts to secure the dominance of the emerging Gelukpa tradition within an increasingly diverse socioreligious context with complex patronage relations.

After departing from Gyantsé, Khédrup returned to Dangchen, where he allegedly had encountered visions of his deceased master. The variety in these accounts of the debate with Rongtön, in terms of how and by whom the debate was initiated and interrupted or completed, exemplify how the phenomenon of "debate" served as a platform for both real and imagined encounters in the Tibetan context. It played a vital role in the construction of identities, traditions, bodies, and histories. Regardless of who initiated these alleged encounters and exchanges, one thing is clear: the competition for prestige and patronage in fifteenth-century Tibet was real. Polemics provided both a narrative construct and a dialectical forum for participating in and justifying this competition.

THE THUNDERBOLT WHEEL OF REPLY TO NGOR

In 1431, Khédrup proceeded to Ganden where he assumed the throne together with the responsibilities of the newly formed order. Between his arrival at Ganden in 1431 and his death in 1438, Khédrup composed another body mandala debate text. In this text, *The Thunderbolt Wheel of Reply to Ngor* (*Ngor lan gnam lcags 'khor lo*) (*Thunderbolt Wheel*), Khédrup replies to Ngorchen's rebuttal to the charges he leveled in *Ocean of Attainment*.[63] Khédrup thereby initiates "round two" of the body mandala debate. Citations from round one, including both Khédrup and Ngorchen's contributions, form a major component of the text.

The *Secret Biography* frames Khédrup's *Thunderbolt Wheel* as a response to Ngorchen's attack against Tsongkhapa's legacy: "Around that time, Ngorpa Kunsang was the bearer of the Sakya tenets, and he sent a letter to both Rongtön and Chöjé Sönam Lo[drö] saying, 'Since Khedrup Jé has criticized the Sakya tenets, I will debate him on Mantra! Rongtön, you are known for debating Prajñāpāramitā, and Sönam Lo for debating Pramāṇa. It is not good that you were ineffective [against him]!"[64] This passage is important, for it links Ngorchen's engagement with Khédrup on tantric subject matter with the alleged encounter of Khédrup and Rongtön at Gyantsé; it even presents an additional figure, Chöjé Sönam Lodrö, involved in similar contentious interchanges with Khédrup.[65]

Read against the grain, this passage reveals a great deal about its protagonists as well as about the scholastic climate of the day. It affirms Ngorchen's expertise in tantra and also suggests that any comprehensive "defense" of a tradition required a multidisciplinary team of specialists in tantra, philosophy, and epistemology. Evidence of this concern with division of areas of expertise appears in Ngorchen's biography as well. There, Ngorchen's biographer, Sangyé Püntsok, quotes Rongtön saying: "Here in my monastery Nalendra, there is the din and roaring [of] the explanation of scripture and reasoning. If you strive for the meaning of the mantric perspective, one goes to the new Ngor monastery."[66] The passage from Khédrup's *Secret Biography* also admits that the Sakyapas were indeed reacting to Khédrup as a perceived threat to their tradition.

The author of Khédrup's *Secret Biography* continues by pitting a reactive Ngorchen against the "defender" Khédrup:

> Then, relying on the Sakya tenets, Ngorpa composed a critique of the views of Tsongkhapa and his followers and had it delivered to Khedrup Jé. In this text, he misunderstood the teachings, writing that, "Earth, water, fire, and wind are the *five* types of form"! Furthermore, having misunderstood Jñānagarbha's discussion of the two truths, he [misquoted the texts] saying, (18a) "According to the self-commentary of Śāntarakṣita on the two truths," and so on. In short, he did not even understand the general language of the texts and succeeded only in shaming himself. Nevertheless, to refute this nonsensical argument, Khedrup Jé composed a rejoinder entitled *Wheel of Thunderbolts* and disproved all his erroneous views.[67]

Ngorchen is depicted as lashing out against Tsongkhapa and his disciples in an attempt to compensate for the unsuccessful attempts of his fellow Sakyapas to fend off Khédrup's critiques. Khédrup is once again depicted as "defender of the faith," and specifically of Tsongkhapa's tradition. Despite the supposedly "nonsensical" nature of Ngorchen's own critique, Khédrup endeavors to correct his views by composing *The Thunderbolt Wheel*. The quotations from Ngorchen's own critique cited within the passage do not appear in his main body mandala debate text, suggesting a larger web of interchange and lost correspondence existed beyond the present sources.[68]

Another passage from the *Secret Biography* harshly critiques Ngorchen together with Rongtön as representatives of a menacing group of traitorous and strategic Sakyapas. This critique goes so far as to suggest that these Sakyapas are not only ignorant but also un-Buddhist in their disruption of the continuity of lineage and of the body of the community:

> Also, Ngorpa Kunsangpa, who was treated like Vajradhara himself by the Sakyapas, out of attachment to worldly fame and riches and disregarding his precepts and promises, slandered Tsongkhapa a despite having received Vajrayāna teachings from Tsongkhapa himself. The scathing rejoinders to the self-damaging argument texts [*rtsod yig*] composed by the so-called Kunting Gushri geshé of Sakya are clearly given in Tsongkhapa's collected works (8a). Thus, indeed, how could the Sakyapas be anything but idiots who had never heard the essence of the teachings?[69]

The reference to Ngorchen's connection to Tsongkhapa and his violation of that bond is an especially potent aspect of the critique. Ngorchen's polemics are depicted as his undoing, a betrayal of the bonds of lineage. Furthermore, the biographer rallies sentiment to conceal and justify his own interventions and polemics, his own acts of construction and harsh critique of the Sakyapas as "idiots" oblivious to the "essence of the teachings." Jörg Heimbel suggests that "it would be unjust to think that rJe btsun pa simply fabricated his portrayal of Ngorchen. He actually drew on a slanderous passage that mKhas grub rJe himself included in one of his writings originating within the body mandala controversy."[70] Heimbel's remark provides an excellent example of the manner in which the language of fabrication haunts not only Tibetan accounts of the debate but also Buddhological ones.

No work fitting Jétsünpa's description of such an "argument text" (*rtsod yig*) has turned up in a preliminary scan of Tsongkhapa's collected works. Moreover, the identity of "Kunting Gushri géshé" is a puzzling issue to which I return in the next section of this chapter. However, the problem of absences and disjunctures in the historical record exemplifies larger challenges presented by the body mandala debate materials. By attuning readers to the particular dynamics of round one and its representation in biographies, this book lays the groundwork for the study of later iterations of the body mandala debate like *The Thunderbolt Wheel*.[71] Yet questions of absence and identity are not the only problems posed by *The Thunderbolt Wheel*. The sheer density of citations demands a way of interpreting the particular brand of intertextuality and reiteration found there. The methodological tools I introduce and apply in later chapters for navigating citational practice are a necessary complement to the revelations of constructed histories in this chapter. Together with attention to the soteriological concerns powering Ngorchen and Khédrup's encounter, they form a cluster of approaches necessary for making sense of the body mandala debate.

A RETRACTION?: THE QUESTION OF "REMAINING FAITHFUL" IN *REPLY TO THE QUESTIONS OF THE KALYĀNAMĪTRA KÖNTING GUSHRĪBA*

To read representations against the grain is to become attuned to the anxieties and concerns hidden within historical inscriptions. Whether enacted in the courtyard or in writing, there were repercussions for failing to defend one's tradition or for too harshly criticizing one's opponent in Tibetan polemics. Anxieties surrounding violating the code of lineage and producing schisms in the sangha gave rise to the narrative construct of "defender of the faith." Identifying these tropes exposes the hand of the biographer, historian, and Buddhologist as participating in and recreating the parameters of tradition formation and competition.

One final text by Khédrup describes his motivations and regrets for engaging in the body mandala debate. Although Khédrup's tone denies a reading of this text as an outright retraction, the apologetic impulse in parts of the text is undeniable. *Reply to the Questions of the Kalyānamītra Kon ting gug śrī ba* (*Reply to the Questions)* appears in a collection of Khédrup's miscellaneous writings (*thor bu*).[72] The colophon emphasizes Khédrup's polemical prowess with epithets like "venerable dispeller" and "learned and fearless before scholars." It identifies Nyangtö as its site of composition; therefore, Khédrup likely composed it after leaving Gyantsé.[73] The introduction to the text identifies it as a summary of Khédrup's reply to a message from the "spiritual friend" (Skt. *kalyānamītra*) Könting Gushrība, a message he received when he was at Gyantsé.

Who is Könting Gushrība? The phrase itself is a Tibetan transliteration of a Chinese title *guanding guóshī* or "anointed national preceptor."[74] In the Yuan period, this title conferred actual power upon Tibetan masters as part of the "patron-priest" alliance of the Yuan with the Sakyapas in particular. However, by the Ming this power was more symbolic than actual, and "these titles functioned more like gifts offered to visitors to the Chinese court to assure Tibetan allegiance than as an actual political position."[75] The passage from the *Secret Biography* described a "Kunting Gushri geshé of Sakya" in connection with Ngorchen's polemics and Gelukpa responses: "The scathing rejoinders to the self-damaging argument texts (*rtsod yig*) composed by the so-called Kunting Gushri geshé of Sakya are clearly given in Tsongkhapa's collected works."[76] However, the identity of this "anointed national preceptor" of Sakya remains somewhat unclear. While it is tempting to conflate him with Ngorchen, they may be two different figures, albeit figures with a substantial relationship. Heimbel posits the figure to be a Namkha Zangpo[77] while van der Kuijp suggests Tekchen Chöjé.[78] Even without definitively identifying Könting Gushrība, the passage suggests a connection between Khédrup and Ngorchen's body mandala debate and an earlier exchange between Tsongkhapa and a Sakyapa géshé.

In *Reply to the Questions,* Khédrup reacts to public opinion of his body mandala writings and a general sense that he went too far in his critique of the Sakyapas and their Path and Fruit tradition. Davidson interprets Khédrup's apparent change in attitude in this text with more than a hint of skepticism: "(H) e had generally refuted the *Lam-'bras* ideas of the physical mandala (*lus-dkyil*) and the reception of consecration during meditation (*lam dus kyi dbang*), without citing the system by name. He complains that everyone jumped to conclusions. Given the inflammatory language mKhas-grub was wont to use, it is easy to see how such an impression developed."[79] Of course, in Khédrup's case, his inherently polemical style as expressed by this "inflammatory language" makes a wholesale retraction impossible. However, even his claim that it was all a big misunderstanding suggests that there were real consequences for his writings on body mandala. These consequences may have impacted his reputation as well as his relationships to his contemporaries (patrons and other superiors as well as peers) and reflected poorly upon the public image of Tsongkhapa's followers.

Khédrup insinuates that his audience overreacted to the "little bit of affirming and negating" standard in polemical discourse. He attempts to correct the mistaken impressions his writings on body mandala have produced: "Some have mistakenly assumed that the little bit of affirming and negating I've done on body mandala is a refutation of the Path and Fruit and empowerment at the time of the path."[80] He also expresses frustration at being called to once again justify his position on the Hevajra tantras and Path and Fruit materials. His remarks raise questions about the boundaries of polemical tactics and the degree of tolerance for polemical flair to be expected of an audience.

Khédrup describes the circumstances that inspired *Reply to the Questions* as follows: "Könting Gushrība, the *kalyāṇamitra* of the great monastic seat, hoarded up a few choice comments I made in the context of body mandala in my commentary on the Guhyasamāja sādhana. A request to expand upon them arrived before my eyes at Gyantsé."[81] Khédrup's description of his motivation for creating this text is more extreme than that for the *Thunderbolt Wheel*. Unlike in both the *Ocean of Attainment* and *Thunderbolt Wheel*, Khédrup explicitly mentions the Sakyapas in setting the stage for his statements here.

Khédrup justifies his choice to once again belabor his views on body mandala through deference to the Sakya masters and their tradition. Khédrup begins by denying the accusation that he had denounced the Path and Fruit tradition, the core tantric tradition of the Sakyapas, in his writings on body mandala:

> Which Path and Fruit exactly do I refute? How, before whom, and in which text do I refute it? Having carefully sought the answer to these questions, seek the unchanging source resembling the speech of the rainbow in the sky of the ultimate. Remaining faithful [*yid ches kyi gnas su*] to the *Vajra Verses* of the Path and Fruit and the three tantras without distinction, though I've already explained this material more than once, I will do it again. There is no reason to think otherwise. The venerable great Sakya fathers and sons, the *dharmarājas* and *mahāpanditas* expand the knowledge of all the Buddha's scriptures, sutra and tantra, without obstacles.[82]

Khédrup affirms that he is "remaining faithful" (*yid ches kyi gnas su*) to the primary texts of the Path and Fruit, the *Vajra Verses* transmitted by the mahāsiddha Virūpa together with the three Hevajra tantras, the root tantra and two explanatory tantras (*Sampuṭa* and *Vajrapañjara*). In doing so, he performs the requisite respect for his Sakya forefathers. He then proceeds to praise the Sakyapas as "lords of yoga" with mastery of the generation and completion stages of sādhana. He assures his interlocutor of the genuine nature of his praise of the Sakya tradition as "firm faith, not merely words" (*tshig tsam ma yin pa'i dad pa brtan po*). Khédrup uses terms that express a concern with asserting "faith" (such as *yid ches* and *dad pa*), terms belying anxiety around perceptions that he has betrayed his lineage.

What begins as apologetics rapidly transforms into a diatribe accusing his interlocutor of being a liar obsessed with his own opinions. He critiques the interlocutor's shortcomings in argumentation, as evidenced by an inability to establish proof according to the standards of philosophical debate. Khédrup also challenges his opponent's ability to classify teachings in their appropriate categories. This concern with categorizing texts is an enduring one in Khédrup's writings. His remarks here indicate that skill in executing doxography was a requirement for establishing one's position within the fifteenth-century scholastic context:

> You've told me lots of things I already know about practicing mantra, like the necessity of empowerment and vows. When it comes to the main issue, you totally lack any proof regarding body mandala. You work so hard to articulate an attitude while lacking familiarity with [the principles of] affirmation and negation. All scholars can see that you are a fool. Yet with little hope of classifying the general teachings, you diminish your own reputation [by writing as you have].[83]

Khédrup then challenges the way in which his interlocutor has used the classification of four philosophical schools. He explains the goals of the *śrāvakas* and *pratyeka-buddhas* as inferior to ultimate buddhahood. His other critiques range from the wrongful denigration of Sapen's astrological calculations in favor of the Kālacakra[84] to the confusion of *śamatha* with *vipaśyana* meditation. Khédrup's enduring concern with articulating the relationship of sutra and tantra, which I addressed in chapter 1 in the context of issues of "fabrication" in ritual acts of imagination, also appears here.

When Khédrup turns to addressing his tantric perspectives, his tone flips the critique on his opponent, suggesting it is this "spiritual friend" who is being polemical in making much ado about nothing.[85] After describing a few particular points of contention on the consecration within the Path and Fruit tradition, about halfway into the text Khédrup begins to specifically engage with the interpretation of his own writings on body mandala within the *Ocean of Attainment*:

> Now, I must address the main topic. These few things I say below are a response to the distortion of the relevant explanation of Guhyasamāja body mandala. I was afraid of saying too much; I did not arrange an extensive account since it was not the appropriate time to get into the establishment and refutation of the classification of other body mandala. I did not realize there would be any proponent who would probe to the depths, analyzing closely, clinging to what little I've said. Because of the utterance in the courtyard, first I will ascertain my reply to those objections.[86]

In these remarks, Khédrup portrays his opponent as unattuned to the proper time and place for engaging in rigorous tantric polemics. He implies that the opponent brought unnecessary scrutiny to bear on a few choice comments he made in the *Ocean of Attainment* and furthermore "distorted his explanation." Khédrup's reference to the courtyard suggests that an actual debate took place in the monastic compound or that rumors were circulating among the monks. He may also be referring to the courtyard as a metaphorical space of contestation. At the very least, his statement confirms that Khédrup's writings on body mandala were a source of controversy.

Whether regarded as a retraction, apologetic, or self-reflection of sorts, this text from Khédrup's miscellaneous writings provides a glimpse of how the body mandala debate continued to evolve. It suggests a series of possibilities that need not be construed as mutually exclusive. For example, it is possible that Khédrup changed his mind about some of his more extreme critiques. He may also have genuinely regarded the genre of polemical writing, like debate in the courtyard, as a liminal zone, a kind of safe space in which stronger, harsher declarations were allowed without long-lasting consequences. It is also possible that the expectations readers brought to their encounters with polemical texts changed with shifts in the sociopolitical and economic climate of monastic life, inspiring Khédrup to reformulate his approach. Of course readers may have been "overreacting" to what scholars have identified as his "passionate" tone and his penchant for "exaggeration." However, while it is possible that Khédrup has been "slightly mischaracterized" as a result of the nature of his authorial voice,[87] it is equally possible that Khédrup was attempting to produce precisely the response that he did.

"GRINDING THE AXE" AND RAKING UP THE PAST: KHÉDRUP'S APPROACH TO SUTRA AND TANTRA

Some of the most mysterious aspects of the body mandala debate are the disparities found in the biographical sources as well as the seemingly arbitrary nature of some of the points of dispute, topics that seem like they have been at least provisionally resolved in the past. For example, Bentor has located specific instances in which Khédrup reproduces arguments made by Tsongkhapa about twenty years earlier almost verbatim.[88] Chapter 3 addresses one of these reiterations to locate the fulcrum of Ngorchen and Khédrup's encounter and its basis in citational practice.

There is also evidence that Khédrup himself was instrumental in creating the faulty impression that a hard boundary existed between pāramitānaya and mantranaya during Tsongkhapa's time. In his biography of Tsongkhapa, Khédrup claimed that Rédaba disapproved of Tsongkhapa's enthusiasm for tantra.[89] Van der Kuijp disputes the accuracy of this assessment, stating, "A mere glance at the oeuvre of the most famous masters of the fourteenth century would indeed strongly testify that in fact the opposite was the case. Future research may very well establish my hunch that, with this assessment, Khédrup was grinding his own axe."[90] He speculates further that the biography may have been written in the midst of friction with prominent Sakyapas.[91] The colophon of that biography indicates that, like *Ocean of Attainment*, it was composed at Nyangtö. Therefore it is possible that both texts were written during a period when Khédrup was "grinding his own axe," emphasizing the distinction of the paths of sutra and tantra rather than their complementarity. Khédrup may therefore have been creating an artificial conflict between these two domains of Buddhist learning to bring attention to the claims of his tradition over and against that of others, a conflict that he might then skillfully resolve for his audience.

The gradual solidification of a "Gelukpa philosophical stance," based in Madhyamaka values, may have influenced Khédrup's approach to the tantric path in *Ocean of Attainment*. For example, the relationship between the two truths, the importance of working toward enlightenment from within the boundaries of conventional reality, the definition of existence, and the status of the flawed tendencies of our cognitive impulses are issues of the Madhyamaka that take on a different flavor in the tantric context. They are key issues that must be accounted for if the two paths of pāramitānaya and mantranaya, or, more loosely, of sutra and tantra, are to be reconciled.

Thus far I have investigated the contours of representations of Khédrup as a debater and "defender of the faith." This trope is construed specifically as a defense of the teachings of Tsongkhapa and his disciples. Yet some of the excerpts from Khédrup's biographical materials also reflect a sense of self-consciousness to distinguish Tsongkhapa's views from those of his teachers. Such passages betray a struggle to avoid overt divergence from or betrayal of one's predecessors. One solution was to depict the Sakyapas who chose to challenge Khédrup's views as ignorant of and therefore themselves divorced from the true tradition.

Even this preliminary engagement with Khédrup's writings on body mandala beyond *Ocean of Attainment* demonstrates that Khédrup passed the point of no return in his writings on body mandala. Whether he intentionally set out to divorce his tradition from its Sakyapa roots or not, once he had set the wheel in motion, there was no turning back. Khédrup's polemics played a formative role in distinguishing the project of defending Tsongkhapa's tradition from "remaining faithful" to its Sakyapa roots.

Having considered some of the dynamics informing Khédrup's polemics and his relationship to an emerging Gelukpa identity, I turn to Ngorchen Künga Zangpo, the monk who replied to Khédrup's charges in round one of the body mandala debate. In the following sections of chapter 2 I evaluate Ngorchen's role as a Sakyapa, how that role is understood from both an institutional and intellectual perspective, and the ways in which it characterizes his engagement in the debate. I will also revisit the trope of defender of the faith to determine how it may impact representations of Ngorchen's accomplishments and, in particular, of his polemics.

REVERSING MISTAKEN VIEWS: NGORCHEN'S CONTRIBUTIONS TO THE BODY MANDALA DEBATE

The Sarma schools of Tibetan Buddhism, such as the Sakya, relied heavily upon an inviolable connection between Indian masters and their Tibetan disciples to secure the legitimacy of their traditions. These bonds provided the license to establish contemporary relevance by innovating while remaining firmly rooted in a true Indian Buddhism ultimately tied to the words of the Buddha himself. The mahāsiddha Virūpa transmitted the primary tantric tradition of the Sakyapas, the Path and Fruit, inspired by his visions of the goddess Nairātmyā and based in the three Hevajra tantras.[92] Many critiques of the Sakyapas were founded in suspicions surrounding a tradition based in visions and passed down orally for generations before being committed to writing. Scholars have highlighted instances, as early as the twelfth century, in which the validity of the Sakya *Hevajra Tantra*–based teachings was called into question.[93] Tantric polemics provided a platform for defending against such charges.

Davidson interprets Ngorchen's polemical writings within the framework of fifteenth-century "Sakyapa apologetics."[94] This framework of interpretation helps to elucidate the significance of Ngorchen and Khédrup's exchanges as public intellectuals within the context of fifteenth-century Tibet. The nature of the critiques of Sakyapa tantric practices is familiar from previous eras, but the Sakyapas inhabited a changing socioreligious climate. Finding themselves on somewhat shaky ground relative to their previous flourishing in alliance with the Mongol-Yuan Dynasty, the Sakyapas faced increased pressure to defend the integrity of their tradition. The rise of the Gelukpa, renewed competition for patronage, and intensified political nuances to those patron relationships informed the building and reconfiguration of Sakya institutions alongside the polemical projects of Sakyapa authors.

During his time as abbot of Ngor Éwam Chöden, Sangyé Püntsok (1649–1705) composed a biography of Ngor's founder.[95] The biographer contextualizes Ngorchen's contributions to the body mandala debate within a series of polemical writings intended to "reverse mistaken views." Sangyé Püntsok's description conforms with Davidson's notion of "Sakyapa apologetics" as a genre arising in response to accusations threatening the authenticity of the transmission of the tradition from Indian to Tibetan masters. In this biographical account, debate functions as a means of preserving the integrity of the tradition, maintaining clarity, and reversing degeneration.

Overcoming Objections to the Three Tantras: The Troubled Boundaries of Philosophy and Tantra

Buddhologists have typically regarded the domains of sutra and tantra as discrete approaches to liberation, framed by distinct standards of authority, modes of practice, and textual frameworks. Only more recently has the simple divide of these discourses been questioned. Yet Ngorchen's biographer Sangyé Püntsok suggests that the boundary between the traditions of sutra and tantra in fifteenth-century Tibet is somewhat porous. In the first section of his description of Ngorchen's polemics, the biographer introduces a very particular variety of authenticity at stake for the Sakyapas. The concern here is not whether Virūpa transmitted the tantric teachings but rather what kind of philosophical view he held. In this vein, the biographer writes,

> Through debate, he [Ngorchen] reversed mistaken views. At an earlier time, some said that the great Dharma protector [Virūpa] was a Cittamātrin pandit and that the intention of his three tantras together with oral instructions was to spread the Cittamātrin perspective. [In response,] Ngorchen composed the great treatise that defends through scripture and reasoning, the *Root and Commentary for Overcoming Objections to the Three Tantras*.[96]

The term *Cittamātrin* refers to a philosophical view—overlapping in Tibet to a degree with the Yogācāra view—that centralizes the power of the mind.[97] By many accounts, for the Cittamātrin, the mind is ultimately real, rather than "empty" as it would commonly be described in Madhyamaka parlance. The notion that Virūpa, the progenitor of the Sakya Path and Fruit tradition, was a Cittamātrin apparently cast a shadow upon the legitimacy of the Sakya tradition at large.[98] However, the notion that the Hevajra literary tradition might itself be tainted with a Cittamātrin approach posed an even greater threat.

The nature of these threats reveals a great deal about the standards of authority in fifteenth-century Tibetan scholasticism and in particular the volatile status of the Cittamātrin view. Tibetan scholastics typically devalued this particular philosophical approach in favor of the Madhyamaka and encouraged charismatic individuals (and the institutions they belonged to) to seek prestige (and power) through the skillful performance of the Prasaṅgika Madhyamaka method. This translated into the composition of polemical texts like Ngor chen's *Overcoming Objections to the Three Tantras* and the practice of philosophical debate.

The alleged critique described by Ngorchen's biographer is therefore twofold. It implied that the Sakyapa interpretation of the tantric texts was imperfect. Further, it suggested that the particular tantric canonical texts upon which the Sakya ritual tradition was based were not regarded as the ultimate means for accessing soteriological truth. Of course, this critique was not so radical as to claim that the *Hevajra Tantra* was not the word of the Buddha. Instead, the critique operated on the basis of established frameworks of Buddhist doxography, such as the "three turnings of the wheel." This classificatory schema plays upon the assumption that the Buddha taught in accord with the needs and capacities of his disciples. One version of this schema popular in Tibet propounds the Madhyamaka as the pinnacle of all the Buddha's teachings. According to this standard, the Madhyamaka is a more profound and accurate teaching than the Cittamātrin view and is accessible only to the most adept disciples. In *Root and Commentary for Overcoming Objections to the Three Tantras*, Ngorchen pushes back against the denigrating implications of the opponent's characterization of Virūpa and of the Hevajra system as Cittamātrin. He does so by demonstrating how the Sakyapa tantric perspective, so heavily steeped in Virūpa's formulation of the *Hevajra Tantra*, accords with a Madhymaka view of the mind and all phenomena as empty, completely free from grasping and conceptualization.

Ngorchen composed *Root and Commentary for Overcoming Objections to the Three Tantras* in 1406, twenty years before his body mandala debate texts.[99] In describing Ngorchen's composition of these texts in terms of "defense through scripture and reasoning" (*lung rigs kyis sun 'byin par byed pa*), his biographer reinforces the trope of "defender of the faith" explored earlier. In so doing, he constructs Ngorchen as a Sakyapa champion, rising to the call to fend off the onslaught of erroneous threats, misunderstandings of the true philosophical and tantric orientations of the tradition. Sangyé Püntsok reiterates this trope in his description of Ngorchen's polemical writings on body mandala.

Destroyer of the Proponents of Evil: Defending the Hevajra Body Mandala

Twenty years after tackling the relationship of sutra and tantra in *Overcoming Objections to the Three Tantras*, Ngorchen composed his tantric polemics on body mandala. Sangyé Püntsok describes Ngorchen's inspiration as follows:

> Later on, there was a terrible misconception of imagining the Hevajra body mandala not to be explained anywhere in the Indian tantric system. Through scripture and reasoning and the oral instructions, he [Ngorchen] thoroughly refuted that circumstance of the Hevajra initiate admitting wrong [*lam dus blangs pa mthol bshags byed pa'i skabs byung ba*]. He composed the great treatise that establishes the unsurpassable intention of the tantric system called *Destroyer of the Proponents of Evil through Eliminating Objections to the Body Mandala* and *Dispelling Evil View[s]*.[100]

The two texts named in this passage are Ngorchen's contributions to round one of the body mandala debate, the focus of this book. This biographical account identifies the context for their creation as a quest to secure the basis of the Sakyapa transmission of Hevajra body mandala practice firmly within Indian sources. This motivation aligns with broader concerns among the Sarma traditions to project an image of authenticity through definitively linking their texts and practices with Indian sources. Anxieties surrounding a perceived betrayal of lineage or creation of schisms in the sangha were prominent in the biographical descriptions of Khédrup addressed earlier. Both of these tensions surrounding ruptures in the social body of Tibetan Buddhism color the accounts of Ngorchen as well. The implications of the phrase roughly translated here as "that circumstance of the Hevajra initiate admitting wrong" (*lam dus blangs pa mthol bshags byed pa'i skabs byung ba*) are compelling, yet difficult to pin down. This remark suggests that Ngorchen's unnamed opponent in the body mandala debate is a Sakyapa who has turned his back on his own tradition, someone who received the Path and Fruit initiation, but later critiqued the legitimacy of its transmission.[101]

In these passages, Sangyé Püntsok undeniably portrays Ngorchen as a defender of the Sakya tradition. The section of the biography on Ngorchen's polemical writings concludes with a verse extolling Ngorchen's polemics as the benevolent acts of a tantric expert intent on securing the endurance of the Buddhist teachings: "The master of scripture and reasoning, the glorious one beloved by all [*kun dga'*] expels the demigods' misconceptions with the vajra. The excellent [*bzang po*] author bestows wonders through increasing the three conditions of the Buddha's teachings."[102] This eloquent verse, punning on Ngorchen's name, fuses Ngorchen's prowess as commentator and polemicist with his role as a tantric ritual expert. Ngorchen quells the demons of ignorance by wielding his vajra, the quintessential tantric ritual implement. His tantric polemics are shown to be nothing short of miraculous.

CANCEL YOUR TRAVEL PLANS

Cryptic circumstances surround Ngorchen's alleged refusal of an invitation to travel to the remote region of Mustang, or, more properly, Lomöntang, around the time of his body mandala writings. While it is not clear that his physical safety was at issue, the incident raises questions about the reliability of biographical accounts in determining the degree and nature of the threats posed by tantric polemics. In an earlier section of the biography, Sangyé Püntsok collapses the two polemical charges leveled against the Sakyapas: "It was said that 'the view of the three tantras of the former Sakyapa hierarchs is Cittamātrin' and the refutation arose saying, 'the Sakyapa body mandala is not explained from the tantric [textual] system."[103] The authors of these claims are not identified. Sangyé Püntsok states that Ngorchen was obliged to decline an invitation from the ruler Amapel to come to teach in Lomöntang as a result of these ideological attacks.

Sangyé Püntsok provides an interesting if enigmatic detail here. The monastic authorities made a rule (*bca' khrims*) preventing Sakyapa géshés from traveling outside of Sakya as a direct response to the threats.[104] The biographer presents this rule as the reason Ngorchen was unable to accept his first invitation to Lomöntang. It is unclear how Ngorchen was elected to rise to the challenge of fending off these charges, or, for that matter, if there was any precedent for such rules to be made in response to offensive views. The comment does, however, imply that the critique of Sakyapa body mandala attributed to Khédrup was perceived as a serious threat to the tradition, a threat demanding a reply. However, as with the mystery of Khédrup's departure from Gyantsé and the Rongtön debate, the connection between Ngorchen's travels to Lomöntang and his body mandala polemics is not straightforward.

The disjuncture between the accounts of a connection between Lomöntang and the body mandala debate suggests that the craftsmanship of Sakyapa authors is at play. Sangyé Püntsok refers to additional details surrounding Ngorchen's invitation to Lomöntang to be found in Lobo Khenchen's (1456–1532) biography.[105] Kramer's critical edition and translation of Lobo's autobiography features the relevant section.[106]

> Later, [A-med-dpal] thought to invite [Ngor-chen] for a second time. After he had [6b] sent one petition [*zhu yig*] after another, he received [this] reply in a first answering letter: "Although I was planning to come this time, due to a letter written by lCang-ra bKa'-bcu-pa which says that the Hevajra-body-*maṇḍala* is not a correct teaching, all the monks of the monastic seat [*gdan sa pa*] got angry, and therefore an order has been enacted for the religious scholars [*dge bshes*] not to go anywhere as long as this [matter] has not been resolved. So I, too, have no possibility of going."[107]

Lobo's description of the source of the polemical charges is more precise than Sangyé Püntsok's. This passage names Ngorchen's "unnamed opponent" as Changra Kachupa; this is an epithet for Khédrup, "the scholar of Changra." Changra is among the monasteries founded by Khédrup; the title Kachu (*bka' bcu*) is equivalent to Géshé.[108] Heimbel has recently unearthed yet another layer of the history of Ngorchen's travel to Lomöntang, illuminating the disjuncture between Sangyé Püntsok's and Lobo's accounts. For while the former frames the travel ban in connection with Ngorchen's first visit to the region in 1427–1428, the latter describes it in relation to the second, in 1436–1437, after Ngorchen wrote his body mandala debate texts.[109]

According to Lobo's account, Ngorchen responded to Amapel by requesting that he cushion his invitation with some assurances "for the confidence of those here." Ngorchen asked Amapel to write a letter to the Sakya authorities guaranteeing that his stay would be brief and unhampered by visits to lots of neighboring monasteries. Ngorchen therefore negotiates a shorter, less involved visit with Amapel to reassure the Sakyapas that he would be by their side when he was needed. Lobo frames Ngorchen's negotiations as a response to a sensitive climate among the monastic community at Sakya for whom the polemical charges had provoked anger and demanded resolution.

Forms of prohibition on the movement of Sakyapa géshés are attested both in Sangyé Püntsok's account of a rule banning travel as well as in Lobo's depiction of Ngorchen's careful negotiation between a king and monastic authorities. The anxieties behind a "travel ban" include the demand to have a learned scholar present to fend off a perceived external threat, a scholar who would be prepared to speak for the Sakyapa community. Additional anxieties might even include a potential security threat to more prominent members of their sangha.[110] Heimbel reads the travel ban as the "direct outcome" of Khédrup and Ngorchen's encounter on body mandala.[111] However, it is equally possible that biographers and historians retroactively inflated their depictions of the events to create a sense of urgency that served to justify Ngorchen's body mandala polemics.[112]

BARMAIDS, SECTARIAN CONFLICTS, AND CHARISMA: NGORCHEN AS DIPLOMAT AND INSTITUTION BUILDER

Learning to read biographical accounts against the grain, to cultivate an awareness of their constructed nature, fosters attunement to the manner in which biographers employ tools for justifying debates, polemics, and "sectarian conflicts." Having analyzed the trope of "defender of the faith," it is clear that Ngorchen's biographers represented his polemical activities as necessary to preserving the integrity of the Sakya tradition. Ngorchen's obligation to fulfill this role may have even restricted his movements at times, as in the case of his trip to Lomöntang. Descriptions of the climate at Sakya monastery help to explain Ngorchen's aptitude in the eyes of his Sakya contemporaries for responding to Khédrup's polemical charges. Such descriptions also suggest a way of connecting Ngorchen's body mandala writings to his ensuing full-blown transformation into an institutional leader.

By 1426, the year in which Ngorchen completed his body mandala debate texts, he was already on his way to becoming a leader in multiple aspects of monastic life. One of the most prominent members of the Sakya Khön family, Tekchen Chöjé, also known as Künga Trashi, passed away in 1425. Jackson suggests that this figure's death prompted Ngorchen "to assume much responsibility" and dates Khédrup's "anti-Sakya tantric polemics" to the same year, suggesting that Ngorchen's response was part of this newfound responsibility.[113] In the time leading up to this change in Ngorchen's status in the community at Sakya, he was engaged in various intensive ritual programs.[114] By some accounts, in 1426, he fell ill and after recuperating bestowed the Path and Fruit initiation over four months, beginning in the summer of that same year.[115] Around this time, Ngorchen went into retreat in response to the urging of his fellow monks, who had experienced ominous dreams portending a threat to his safety.[116] The threat of sorcery here exemplifies yet another tool available to biographers for justifying polemical projects.[117] Ngorchen's biographer gives voice to Ngorchen's freedom from blame: "Apart from performing a few refutations and proofs of our doctrine, [I] have not done anything that turned out to be harmful to anybody. Nevertheless, some have performed a kind of sorcery [to magically cause harm] by the Six-armed one."[118] Recall that Khédrup encountered similar obstacles, as relayed in his own biographies. Indeed, if these accounts were all taken at face value, it would seem that tantric deities such as the "Six-armed one," presumably the wrathful tantric deity Mahākāla, were working around the clock in the 1420s.

In 1429, three years after composing his body mandala debate texts, Ngorchen proceeded to found Ngor Monastery, one of the official branches of Sakya. What was the role of the debate in motivating Ngorchen to strike out on his own, to concentrate his energies on institution building? Heimbel frames Ngorchen's project as a return to the roots of the tradition through moving away from the institutional center; he also suggests that "sectarian conflicts" together with an inhospitable learning environment at Sakya motivated Ngorchen's institution building: "Withdrawing from sectarian conflicts with the Dge lugs school on one hand, and from the worldly distractions of the bustling town of Sa skya on the other hand, Ngor chen founded E waṃ chos ldan in the remote Ngor valley, located around 20 km southwest of Gzhis ka rtse, hoping to go back to traditional Sa skya teaching and practice in a more supportive environment."[119] In Heimbel's interpretation, based on biographical sources, Ngorchen's urge to return to tradition was prompted by the atmosphere at Sakya at the time. He describes this climate as contentious, amplified by Sakya-Geluk tensions, and also hampered by "worldly distractions." The precise nature of these "distractions" allegedly plaguing Sakya and making it less than an ideally "supportive" environment for engaging in Buddhist practice is surprising, to say the least: barmaids. According to Sangyé Püntsok, Ngorchen was concerned by distractions (*g.yeng ba*) at the monastic seat and the abundance of drinking places (*chang sa*) there. Apparently, the level of distraction was so acute that some monks even disrobed. "For the greater benefit of the teachings and the monks," Ngorchen sought to establish a quiet place for study, "free of barmaids" (*chang ma med pa*).[120] He performed offerings to Mahākāla and undertook the project of locating the perfect site for a new monastery.

Both Ngorchen and Khédrup's biographers mention the overabundance of barmaids at Sakya at the time, employing a similar trope of "degeneration."

One of Khédrup's biographers describes how Mahākāla of the Tent appears to Khédrup, imploring him to remain at Sakya. Khédrup replies, "If there is one person here with pure views and conduct, I may stay. However, the tenets of the spiritual forefathers no longer exist, and their descendants have gone too. The temples are filled with women, donkeys, cows and barmaids." Mahākāla actually commiserates with Khédrup as to the state of the place. However, he attempts to order Khédrup to stay, on the grounds that he too would have gone to study with Tsongkhapa were it not for the tragic state of affairs.[121]

Depictions of Sakya as morally degenerate and chaotic justified both Ngorchen and Khédrup's institution-building activities. In both cases, such depictions justify a kind of break or fissure in the social body of the Sakya tradition. For Ngorchen, this fissure takes shape in a new monastery. For Khédrup, the break is a move toward "sectarian differentiation" of Tsongkhapa's legacy from that of his Sakyapa teachers and ultimately of Gelukpa from Sakyapa. Examined in this light, the body mandala debate becomes one instance of a broader conflict used and potentially amplified in textual sources in order to validate these projects.

Through various diplomatic, scholastic, and ritual means, Ngorchen solidified the connection between religious and political institutions. He was revered for spreading the Sakya tradition to Ngari in Western Tibet and east to Dégé. Over the course of Ngorchen's three journeys to Lomöntang, he was instrumental in establishing and perpetuating the Sakya tradition there by bringing the Tibetan compilation of the Buddha's teachings, the Kangyur, establishing and consecrating monasteries and temples, and conferring teachings, ordinations, and tantric initiations.[122] During his time in Lomöntang, he allegedly increased the number of monks there from less than four to one thousand.[123] Historical and biographical sources detail the extensive support the royals of Lomöntang, Amapel and his sons, pledged to the sangha there.[124] Ngorchen ordained the ruler of Lomöntang, Amapel, as well as the king of Gugé.[125] Lobo Khenchen's autobiography describes many examples of important institutional relationships forged by Ngorchen at Lomöntang. For example: "[Ngor-chen] erected the great Cakrasaṃvara palace . . . and consecrated it extensively. In connection with a ceremony on that occasion, the granting from the great Bla-brang of the title (*las ka*) of "chief" (*chen po*) to the religious king [A- ma-dpal]."[126] Ngorchen's relationship to his royal patrons was framed as mutually beneficial. For example, after conferring a tantric empowerment upon Amapel's sons, Ngorchen declared, "If we all, donors and teachers, manage to remain in this commitment without contradicting it, then [here], in the region of Glo-bo, all religious and worldly deeds will be increased."[127] Ngorchen also ensured the continued political and religious relationship of Lomöntang and Sakya by instituting a practice of sending monks from Lomöntang to Sakya and its affiliated monasteries in Ü and Tsang for training.

When Ngorchen returned from his first trip to Lomöntang, he conferred Path and Fruit instructions to select disciples over a period of seven months into 1429; in that same year he founded Ngor Monastery.[128] In addition to his role as ambassador of the Sakya tradition afar, Ngorchen was an accomplished ritual master, tantric commentator, and esteemed interpreter of the vinaya. Ngorchen's charisma within the domains of ritual and scholasticism and his integrity in upholding monastic law combined to assure the success of his pilot monastery.

Ngorchen was not the only charismatic Sakyapa leader of his time striking out on his own. Others, like the famous cataloguer Butön, Tsongkhapa's own teacher Rédaba, Bodongpa (Bodong Penchen Choklé Namgyel,) 1375–1451),[129] and the very same Rongtön involved in the Gyantsé controversy have also been described as creators of their own lineages (*rang rkang bzo pa*).[130] Every act of innovation required an accompanying justification of intent and a demonstrated commitment to perpetuating and clarifying the teachings inherited from generations past. Within his biography, attempts to establish relationships to these predecessors and to establish Ngorchen's superior efficacy suggest competition among such charismatic individuals. For example, Sangyé Püntsok makes a significant effort to explain Rongtön's respect for Ngorchen and to substantiate a kind of "melding of minds" (*thugs yid gcig tu 'dres pa*) between them.[131] On the other hand, in describing Amapel's invitation of Ngorchen to Lomöntang, the biographer states that initially Bodong Penchen had been invited; however, Bodongpa's teachings were ultimately deemed less efficacious.[132] Charisma was vital to flourishing in the face of this kind of competition and central to the success of fifteenth-century institution builders, impacting reputation among patrons, monastics, and the lay community.[133] Composed just three years before he founded Ngor Éwam Chöden, Ngorchen's writings on body mandala increased his prestige in the eyes of prospective donors and adherents. These texts established his command both in the realm of commentary and in the strategies of philosophical debate and displayed his commitment to perpetuating the Sakya legacy.

The patterns of patronage supporting Ngorchen and Khédrup's activities, in particular as monastic founders, differed. For example, while much of Khédrup's support was based in the sociopolitical network of the Pakmo Dru, Ngorchen's main source of patronage stemmed from a familial affiliation. The question of Ngorchen's patriliny is somewhat fraught. Although Pöntsang Drupa Yönten, a layman, was popularly regarded as his father, Ngor's true father was known to be the chief lama at Sakya, Tawen Künga Rinchen (1339–1399) of the Zhitok Labrang. The members of this monastic household and especially those living on the

Chumik estate, provided Ngorchen with invaluable support in founding Ngor as well as in ensuring financial security for the continuation of its abbacy and executing additional projects.[134] The land on which Ngorchen built Éwam Chöden was even part of the Chumik estate and virtually gifted to him by his half-brother, though Ngorchen was determined to make the transaction official with a "formal payment" in the form of a crystal bowl.[135]

Decades after round one of the body mandala debate and the events at Gyantsé, Ngorchen too is alleged to have resisted multisectarian patronage projects and challenged the perspectives of their "broadminded patrons." According to Sönam Drakpa (1478–1554), Ngorchen demanded a more exclusive allegiance from the Rinpung lord Norbu Zangpo (d.1466). Not only were this patron's devotions divided. or at least distributed between Sakyapas and Kagyupas, but he "also looked kindly upon the dGe ldan pas."[136] As a preconditon for conferring teachings upon the ruler, Ngorchen allegedly made the demands: that "all the dGe ldan pas under his [Nor bzang pa's] rule were converted to Sa skya pas" and the prevention of "bKa' bcu pa dGe 'dun 'grub from building his monastery."[137] He also demanded the ruler's patronage of Ngor Monastery.[138] Ngorchen was unsuccessful is this attempt to monopolize Norzangpa's support. Much like the events at Gyantsé involving Khédrup and Rongtön and the body mandala polemics of Khédrup and Ngorchen, the parameters of this exchange between Ngorchen and Norzangpa have been contested.[139] Yet, while the precise circumstances of the encounters are not always clear, a palpable quest for sectarian differentiation was indeed part of the world Ngorchen and Khédrup participated in. Moreover, within the socioreligious landscape they inhabited, securing exclusive patronage had tangible benefits, but also came with the risk of provoking that patron's political opponents.[140]

NGORCHEN'S POLEMICAL HISTORY WITH THE GELUKPAS

Ngorchen had a history of polemical exchanges with the Gelukpas on issues of tantric ritual. For example, according to some accounts, he critiqued Gelukpa interpretations of other tantric ritual practices not at issue in his body mandala writings, such as practices associated with Yamāntaka or Vajrabhairava.[141] Ngorchen also participated in a polemical exchange interrogating the fundamental tantric ritual act of imagining oneself as a buddha linked with the classification of bodies and texts. This exchange called into question whether the practice of generating oneself as a deity (*bdag bskyed*) had a place in the lower classificatory ranks of tantra, the *kriyā* and *caryā*.[142] Ngorchen supported the use of the lower tantras for promoting the ethical and devotional qualities conducive to monasticism.[143] He regarded kriyā and caryā as suitable for monastic discipline because they lack the sexualized content of the higher yoga tantras (often identified as the yoga and *niruttara* yoga) and promote an "emphasis on personal purification, ritual endeavor, and devotion."[144]

Ngorchen did not acknowledge the existence of the practice of generating oneself as the deity within the kriyā system; moreover, he regarded its implementation within the next tantric class, the caryā, as useful exclusively for its role in promoting monastic discipline. This was an important issue for Tsongkhapa and, following his lead, for Khédrup.[145] Khédrup (in what became the standard Gelukpa position) included meditation upon oneself as a deity within all divisions of tantra, including kriyā.[146] Sangyé Püntsok describes this controversy within the larger context of Ngorchen's polemical writings:

> He [Ngorchen] disputed the sādhana of self-generation in the dharma terminology of kriyā tantra itself; thus, he clearly taught the intention of the various manner of commentary, increasing the teaching of the kriyā tantras. [Therefore] it is called the *Ocean of Excellent Explanation of the Establishment of Kriyā Tantra*. Likewise, he refuted the entrance of the wisdom beings in the caryā tantra; he clarified the teachings of caryā tantra.[147]

In describing how Ngorchen "clearly taught the intention" (*dgongs pa gsal bar ston*) of the kriyā and caryā tantras, his biographer reinforces Ngorchen's continuity with tradition. The passage identifies two specific ritual acts of tantric sādhana at issue: the generation of oneself as a deity and the merging of wisdom and pledge beings, a ritual moment in which the actual deities enter into their simulated or imagined counterparts. These controversies were rooted in schema of classifying representations, including both texts and ritual imaginings. The advanced initiations of Buddhist tantra are ritual prerequisites for training in the texts and practices of the more profound teachings of the higher yoga tantras. Ngorchen's polemical writings on the mechanics of the lower tantras fit within a broader history of Tibetan Buddhism in which the sexualized content of the higher initiations often sparked conflicts between tantra and the vows of celibate monasticism.

Ngorchen wrote his treatises on the lower tantras in 1420, six years before his body mandala debate writings.[148] These treatises also follow Tsongkhapa's apparent refusal of Ngorchen's request for teachings during Ngorchen's visit to Ganden in 1413.[149] By some accounts, Ngorchen was attempting to collaborate with

Tsongkhapa to promote the kriyā and caryā tantras, an attempt that Tsongkhapa gently rebuffed.[150] Yet there are records of Ngorchen receiving teachings from Tsongkhapa, in particular his stages of the path treatises as well as tantric teachings including the Guhyasamāja system.[151]

This controversy over the nature of ritual practice based in the lower classes of tantra highlights the ways in which concerns with the mechanics of visualization practice, doctrine, and monastic discipline intermingle in tantric polemics. It also presents another example of a "debate" within the careers of these authors in which the practice of generating oneself as a deity, a practice so central to definitions of tantra as a fast track to attaining buddhahood in this lifetime and in this body, assumes a primary position.

ON CONSTRUCTING AND REPRESENTATION

In this chapter, I emphasized the constructed nature of biographical materials. In the process, I established one model for making sense of the body mandala debate and for challenging the quest for "exact essences" and "origins" by drawing attention to the crafting of identity and continuity within historical sources. Uncovering complex dynamics of patronage and lineage in fifteenth-century Tibetan Buddhism has involved revealing anxieties surrounding the norms of allegiance to lineage as well as to the corporate identity of the Buddhist sangha at large. Normative expectations contained in evolving dynamics of institution building, in the "multisectarianism" endorsed by "broadminded patrons," threatened to thwart Ngorchen and Khédrup's creative attempts to innovate and even distinguish traditions.

Tracing the seemingly invisible ways in which biographers craft personae is key to making sense of the body mandala debate. Debate and polemics together with associated tropes like "defender of the faith," "remaining faithful," and the myth of degeneration justify invention and allow authors to conceal their own participation in these projects. By amplifying rifts rent by polemical opponents, biographers divert attention from the ways in which their own authorial acts create and/or exacerbate ruptures in the monastic body. In some cases, Buddhologists are vulnerable to these very same tendencies, defaulting to sectarian readings of more complex intellectual exchanges. For Tibetologists, the body mandala debate is interesting because it promises to provide insight into when and where the rift between the Geluk and Sakya traditions occurred. In restaging the debate, I am contributing to an answer but also encouraging different ways of formulating the question that show flexibility in not seeking only for a single source or origin. I therefore approach sectarian differentiation and tradition formation as processes rather than teleologies.

The results of these discoveries connect to broader themes of what representations are, how they work, and the problems they pose. Representations are constructed. How do the creators of representations legitimate their constructive acts? In this chapter, I have provided two answers to this question: as defenses of tradition and as clarifications of an essence. Who resists seeing this constructed quality of representations and why? In the case of the body mandala debate, the answer is individuals invested in homogeneous narratives of what (fifteenth-century) Buddhism is about. As I have shown, there are tools available for exposing the constructed qualities of representations. For example, genealogy provides a method for tracing tropes, and philology suggests ways of interpreting instances of reiteration, of navigating lacunae, and of coping with the incommensurability of representations. Reading representations therefore demands bringing multiple lenses to bear upon them. In the case of the body mandala debate, I cultivate a balance between concerns with lineage, ritual. and exegesis.

Representations reveal anxieties. They play a role in crafting identities and communities. Representations can produce and reproduce stereotypes that ossify. Representations reverberate and are retroactively projected. In restaging the body mandala debate, I am participating in this legacy of representation. This project requires me to take stock of the risks of restaging the debate, including the risk of reinforcing stereotypes and homogeneous narratives. It compels me to be aware of the ways in which I choose to frame the encounter, including the complex role of debate as dialectical tool and narrative construct. I have referred to other debates, real and imagined, such as the iconic Samye debate and Khédrup's debate at Gyantsé, as a strategy for encouraging the reader to think critically about my framing choices. In this way, I suggest particular connections and interpretations while creating space for alternative assessments as well as for new philological and historical discoveries.

To what degree is the body mandala debate an iteration of previous encounters? Does repetition diminish, intensify, or distort its significance? The connection of Khédrup and Ngorchen's engagement on body mandala to previous encounters and critiques and its birthing of future confrontations, both real and imagined, is significant. For example, before composing his body mandala debate texts, Ngorchen had already critiqued Tsongkhapa's tantric interpretations in writings on both the Cakrasaṃvara and Guhyasamāja cycles.[152] Yet each new discovery of a previous iteration of the debate, or a later recollection or reproduction of it, contributes to the impression of Buddhist polemics as a virtual echo chamber. The challenge to balance lineage and identity, ritual practice, and exegesis as bases for making sense of Khédrup and Ngorchen's claims is amplified in this chamber.

I address this challenge in the next chapter by examining the phenomenon of iteration as it takes shape in Ngorchen and Khédrup's citational practices. Practitioners engaging in body mandala map their bodies to correspond with enlightened forms, establishing vital correlations and connections. They repeat these practices over time to attain buddha bodies. In a similar way, tantric exegetes map the Buddhist corpus by repeating the words of their enlightened predecessors. The complexity of their citational practices has inspired me to map citations as a way of mapping the landscape of the body mandala debate. In tracing citation within the debate, I reveal how representations produce tensions between "original" and repetition.

3

"Cutting the Ground"

Citations Revealing Mandala Iconography in the Making

"Thus have I heard," the iconic phrase beginning every Buddhist sutra, marks the text as a powerful form of hearsay. The phrase connotes the sense of a testament or witness arriving in the present moment from a previous one, from another context to the present. The task of defining hearsay in our contemporary context is plagued by questions about what is admissible or reliable for arbitrating meaning; rumor and testimony vie for supremacy in the act of bearing witness. For Buddhists, "Thus have I heard" signals that the words that follow are a citation of the word of the Buddha as related in a teaching encounter. To cite is to invoke a precedent with the potential to be repeated beyond its original context. The basic rules of Buddhist exegesis establish the word of the Buddha (Skt. *buddha-vacana*) as the most authoritative precedent to draw upon in making sense of a text. The Tibetan term for "citation" (*lung 'dren*) conveys the "drawing out" (*'dren*) of the transmission of a scriptural precedent (*lung*). For Buddhist authors, citations provide a way of "clarifying" the intent of their predecessors, of linking the words of the present with those of the past. There is an unspoken rule that the meaning of the citation is always located in a previous time, that it can't be entirely broken or divorced from its context.

Yet citations continuously violate the rules. While citations may claim to derive their authority from an original, their sheer density in Tibetan texts produces a tension between source and repetition. The closer you look at patterns of citation, the more tenuous the bond to original context becomes. In repeating a fragment of a text and grafting that fragment onto a new context, authors expand that text's range to such a degree that they often tip the balance between rootedness and proliferation. The English term *citation* shares the Tibetan concern with invoking a precedent as a basis for moving forward; the Latin root *citare* expresses a mechanism of exciting and setting in motion that relates equally to contexts like evoking emotion and digesting food. Investigating Ngorchen's and Khédrup's citational strategies suggests that citations may be the long-underestimated fire in the bowels of Buddhist textuality.[1]

In their writings on body mandala, Ngorchen and Khédrup cite such a volume and variety of sources that at moments citation seems to be a diversion tactic. Ngorchen, in particular, relies so heavily upon citation that I initially struggled to hear his authorial voice and to apprehend the pathways of his argument in contrast to the "hoarse screaming of the logicians" (as at one point he describes the words of his opponents).[2] One consequence of emphasizing the voices of one's predecessors is to erase one's own. As discussed in chapter 2, Buddhist authors in Tibet prioritized lineage and continuity of the past over individualized claims to innovation. Yet if Buddhist citations were "mere" repetitions, how could they occupy such an expansive terrain? In this chapter, I illuminate remarkable varieties of creativity at play by reading the body mandala texts through the shape of their citations. I present a method for mapping the landscape of these citations and observe how Ngorchen and Khédrup navigate that landscape. I continue to refine my analysis of the category of citation in chapter 4, in which I focus more specifically upon Ngorchen's use of citations to defend the Hevajra body mandala. I argue that Khédrup and Ngorchen carefully select their citations, and, in so doing, they construct and modify the boundaries of the Buddhist corpus. As I reveal in these two chapters, recognizing the variety of ways citation works proves pivotal for appreciating how Buddhist authors use representation both to construct and dismantle what Susan Stryker described, in the context of gender, as "the similitude of a natural body of meaning."[3]

"REPETITION WITH A DIFFERENCE"

Citations operate through a logic of repetition, but there is nothing trivial about the way they repeat. Citations present the reader with a form of "repetition with a difference." John Felstiner coined this phrase to describe the ways in which poet and translator Paul Celan used repetition to expand and transform the potential of words to suggest meaning. Felstiner writes of Celan's use of repetition as a way of "holding up something—both displaying and delaying it—for our attention." In the translation process, these acts of repetition "anticipate an act of renaming."[4]

For the translator, citations are evasive and present an explicit challenge to resolve the relationship between text and context. The way in which citations repeat often produces a clash of contexts, one that threatens to render them untranslatable. Derrida was among the postmodern theorists who addressed the "iterability" of language and connected repetition to the potential of words to rupture from context.[5] If using language demands a repeated rupture from context, what is the relationship between the varied contexts in which words occur? In mapping and analyzing Ngorchen and Khédrup's citations, it becomes evident that citation reveals something profound about the workings of representation and its connection to repetition and rupture.

A reader or translator may be tempted to skip over citations as mere invocations of a canonical authority intended to confer a stamp of authenticity upon a new context. The first step in appreciating how Ngorchen and Khédrup "anticipate" their own distinct "act(s) of renaming" is debunking the myth that authority and meaning flow only in one direction, from canon to citation.

CANON: BODIES OF TRANSFORMATION AND OVERLAPPING REPETITIONS

In contemporary academia, citation has become a measure of a text's and an author's relevance and claim to authority. This practice exemplifies how the flow of value and authenticity attached to canon is often reversed. Among the varied functions of citation, the conferral and the derivation of authority coexist.

Where does a canon live? In what manner are its boundaries established or extended? A canon thrives in the tensions between tradition and innovation, restriction and inclusion, described by Jonathan Z. Smith as "a basic cultural process of limitation and of overcoming that limitation through ingenuity."[6] Certainly canons struggle to articulate their meaning and integrity as they absorb new elements while attempting to maintain some sense of boundary. The meaning of canon relies on this boundary, in setting apart a set as meaningful, and yet without the ability to expand, a canon may petrify and become irrelevant. Canons provoke questions about representation, identity, and a sense of belonging. In the musical sense, a canon is a "series of overlapping repetitions."

There are many Buddhist canons and many stories around their origins.[7] For example, the Buddha's disciples are said to have gathered in the generations after his passing to recite his teachings, to transmit them through an unbroken mnemonic chain. According to legend, the Mahāyāna sutras were revealed after being carefully guarded by serpent deities for hundreds of years. In the Tibetan sense, the Buddhist canon is a body of transformations. Tibetan commentators divided the canon into two such bodies: the Kangyur (*bka' 'gyur*), "the transformation of speech," which includes translations of the word of the Buddha, and the Tengyur (*bstan 'gyur*), "the transformation of treatise," which includes translations of the commentaries of the Indian masters. The normative Tibetan canon therefore does not contain any explicitly Tibetan compositions. There were collections of Buddhist texts compiled during the first dissemination of Buddhism in Tibet (seventh to ninth centuries), generated during the dark age (mid-ninth to late tenth centuries), and further organized during the Sarma era (beginning in the late tenth/eleventh century). The earliest Tibetan canon was printed under the Yongle emperor in 1410, but by the late thirteenth century Tibetan canons were circulating, and they were not closed.[8] This is the period in which the distinction of the Kangyur and the Tengyur was created. In the fourteenth century, Butön undertook vast projects to compile a large component of the Tibetan canon, including the Indian commentaries on the root texts of the tantras. As I will show, Butön's extensive knowledge of works of the Indian tantric masters, authors of commentaries as well as of tantric sādhana, is at the center of Ngorchen and Khédrup's encounter on body mandala.

The canon lives in the material volumes that contain it, long rectangular block-printed pages sandwiched between wooden covers and carefully wrapped in colorful silks stowed away above altars and in monastic libraries. It abides and circulates in digital forms through the web.[9] The canon lives in the minds of Buddhist practitioners who inculcate its contents through rigorous mnemonic practices. The canon lives in their bodies and their speech as they deploy citations in philosophical debates in the monastic courtyard, with raised voices punctuated by an almost martial language of gestures. But the canon also lives in the bits and pieces severed off and grafted elsewhere through citational practices. In interpretive practice, these reiterations confer power upon their source through a dance of "sacred persistence."[10] The intricacy of this dance as enacted in Buddhist exegesis, polemics, and debate escapes readers intent on reducing citations to trivial parroting of the canonical.

Most of Khédrup and Ngorchen's citations in the body mandala debate are from the tantras, which they regard as the word of the Buddha, or from the commentaries of Indian masters. Both categories of texts are typically regarded as "canonical" in the Tibetan Buddhist context. On rare occasions, these two authors refer to the work of Tibetan masters. In this book, I approach canon as a body of transformations powered by a generative tension between tradition and innovation and manifesting in a series of overlapping repetitions. I am especially interested in the hidden ways in which Khédrup and Ngorchen craft and reconfigure networks of authority and meaning by citing "canonical" texts.

A LONG GAME OF TELEPHONE?: NGORCHEN CITES THE PROBLEMATIC VIEW

Ngorchen formally launches his defense of the Hevajra body mandala in a manner typical of Buddhist scholastics, laying out the objections of his opponent. While he does not name the opponent, Ngorchen refers to them as a "logician" (*rtog ge pa*) who is "inexperienced in applying the Vajrayāna corpus."[11] Describing this opponent's words as "hoarse screaming" (*skad' dzer*), Ngorchen cites the charges that Khédrup articulated in the *Ocean of Attainment*. Therefore, the reader is able to guess the identity of the "logician" to be Khédrup. However, as will become apparent in this chapter, Khédrup was not the first to introduce certain aspects of these interpretations of body mandala. The Tibetan convention of not openly naming one's opponents therefore lends itself to preserving the possibility of multiple interlocutors, some of whom may even be repeating one another and in some cases modifying words and meanings through those repetitions. Here I break Ngorchen's citation of the "logician" down in three parts: on correlation, scriptural precedents, and ritual logic and authenticity.

The context for this critique within Khédrup's text is familiar from chapter 1. Early in Khédrup's chapter on body mandala in *Ocean of Attainment*, the excerpt appears in the section in which he asserts his own tradition with regard to the mandalas of support and supported and the placement of seed syllables on the body.[12] In the first two folia of this portion of the text, Khédrup addresses the Ghantapa quote on bodies naturally being mandalas and distinguishes unfabricated from fabricated mandalas.[13] This is followed by a more detailed discussion of how this notion of fabrication plays out in the actual mechanics of the body mandala practice, all familiar from my discussion of imagination in chapter 1.[14] In particular, Khédrup describes the transformation of the psychophysical components of a person (form, feeling, perception, formations, consciousness) and their subsequent generation as deities through the use of seed syllables and a consort. Khédrup then grapples with the relationship of the body mandalas of support and supported; he also attempts to resolve the relationship of the multiple varieties of celestial palace generated and dissolved over the course of the body mandala practice.[15] Having addressed these relationships and, moreover, endorsed the teachings of the Indian tantric adept Luipa as well as his own Tibet teacher Tsongkhapa[16] as authorities on practices connected with the Cakrasaṃvara system,[17] Khédrup hones in on the object of his critique.

Correlation

I introduced correlation (*sbyor tshul*) in chapter 1 to describe the tantric technique of imagining relationships between the parts of the body and enlightened forms as central to Ngorchen and Khédrup's concerns with body mandala. Ngorchen cites Khédrup's critique of an unnamed group of opponents who explain the body mandala of the support in a problematic way. According to Khédrup, these opponents map a series of correlations of the parts of the body with the parts of the mandala's protective circle and the parts of the celestial palace as follows,

> Some Tibetans say, "In the many body mandalas of the mother tantras: 'The crown of the head is the *viśvavajra*. The soles of the feet are the vajra foundation. The ribs are the vajra fence. The skin is the vajra tent and canopy. The body hairs are a net of arrows. The fingernails are the utterly blazing mountains of flames.' And also: 'The four channels of the heart are the four gates. The eyes are the tiered walls of the palace. The nose is the jeweled beam. The teeth are the lace curtains. The tongue and the lips are the corridors of the desire goddesses.'"[18]

The reference to "some Tibetans" reinforces the convention of not explicitly identifying one's opponent. Khédrup is infamous for walking the line on conventions like this one. For example, years later, in his *Reply to the Questions of the Kalyānamītra Kon ting gug śrī ba*, introduced in chapter 2, Khédrup relies upon the thin veil of ambiguity of his initial critique to claim that he never criticized the Sakyapa Path and Fruit lineage holders.[19] The target of the logician's critique is what "some Tibetans" have to say about the body mandala traditions of the mother tantras. The modes of classifying the tantras vary, but typically the mother tantras describe the profound practices of the goddess-rich and sometimes sexually charged ritual systems of the Cakrasaṃvara and Hevajra tantras.[20] This version of body mandala described by "some Tibetans" resembles many Hevajra sādhanas such as those composed by the patriarchs Drakpa Gyeltsen and Pakpa, described in chapter 1.[21]

As I read through Ngorchen and Khédrup's writings on body mandala and consulted the texts they were citing, I drew diagrams to keep track of the different approaches to correlating the body with the form of the mandala. These diagrams suggested maps of the vajra body, the elements of profound corporeal transformation accessible only to the tantric adept. However, it was not always clear how to sequence and connect the ritual acts of imagination they describe. For example, how can the body assume both the form of a protective circle and of a celestial palace? What is the order and transition between these corporeal transformations? I turned to Ngorchen and Khédrup again to better understand their concerns with properly imagining the order and structure of body mandala practice, issues on which the tantric texts they refer to often remain silent or conflict. Over time, it became clear that ritual mechanics are accompanied by a host of issues around textual authenticity that are equally, if not more important for these authors.

Scriptural Precedents

The next section of Ngorchen's citation of his opponent's critique exemplifies how some citations contain a sophisticated series of deferrals to previous contexts. In this passage, the logician invokes the authority of Butön, the fourteenth-century compiler of the canon, a scholar esteemed for his command of the tantric corpus. Butön, in turn, cites Nagpopa, one of the great Indian tantric mahāsiddhas. More specifically, Butön is citing and interpreting Nagpopa's Cakrasaṃvara-oriented text, the *Saṃvara-vyākhyā*, to comment on the disputed variety of body mandala. Ngorchen cites the logician's objectionable claim, with its nested layers of citation, as follows:

> With regard to that writing [i.e., the mother tantras body mandala practice], the omniscient Butön says, "In the *Saṃvara-vyākhyā*[22] [it says]: 'Having generated the body in stages, there is the spontaneous generation of Vajrakīla. Together with binding the boundaries and laying the lines, make it completely stable. As for the tent, it is the very garland of bones.' Except for this, there is no explanation like that one anywhere in any Indian system."[23]

Ngorchen represents the logician citing Butön as saying that a precedent for this variety of body mandala doesn't exist (*mi 'dug*) anywhere in the Indian system. Ngorchen will ultimately correct his opponent to show how Butön merely states that he hasn't seen (*ma mthong*) that precedent. As I will show over the course of this chapter and the next, Ngorchen exploits this subtle difference between not seeing something and its nonexistence to critique his opponent's expertise, grip on reality, and just plain common sense.

Ritual Logic and Authenticity

The final portion of Ngorchen's citation of his opponent's critique provides a salient example of how anxieties around fabricating buddha bodies in tantric ritual acts of imagination translate into concerns with scriptural authenticity. In chapter 1, I described how, for Khédrup, body mandala is superior to outer mandala forms, mandala representations like paintings or altars of painted sand, because it is unique in providing an "unfabricated" (*ma bcos*) basis for practice or, at the very least, one that is "not newly fabricated" (*gsar du ma bcos pa*). In the final part of Ngorchen's citation of his opponent, the logician enumerates the points of ritual mechanics at issue in terms of the relationship of outer mandala and body mandala and connects them to issues of authenticity. Ngorchen continues the citation of his opponent as follows,

> "This [i.e., Butön's statement] is correct. That method of generating the body as a celestial mansion like that and arranging the one hundred and fifty-seven deities of the body mandala and so forth in the outer mandala of only [or without] the nine deities,[24] and arranging the deities of the outer mandala in the inner mandala, and an absence of deities common to the two [inner and outer], [such methods] are not explained in the tantra or any authentic Indian system. Moreover, although in actuality it is not the case that they are separate, in investigating with a mind that doesn't even distinguish between a body mandala [*lus dkyil*] and establishing deities on the body [*lus la lha dgod pa*], many lies masquerading [*ming brtag*] as the superior instructions appear in the Tibetan methods of establishing the body mandala. Here the affirmation and negation is not elaborated at length." So it was written.[25]

Distinguishing between these two approaches to correlating the body with mandala deities—body mandala (*lus dkyil*) and "establishing deities on the body" (*lus la lha dgod pa*, Skt. *nyāsa*)—is, for Ngorchen's opponent, a vital component of an accurate and authentic approach to body mandala. The ability to parse these different kinds of representations is key to producing a reliable account of the practice, despite the fact that ultimately there is no existential difference between these representations. This is a familiar mode of argument in both Buddhist philosophical and ritual logic. For example, the ability to parse the two truths of reality, the conventional and ultimate, to distinguish the world of forms and concepts from the way things truly are, is an important step in the realization process. This distinction is significant despite the fact that ultimately these dual components are regarded as identical. In consecration ritual, when one transforms a vessel into a home for an enlightened presence, actual and imagined components (referred to as the "wisdom beings" and "pledge beings" respectively) are created, only to be united.[26] In chapter 5, I will explore parsing in greater depth as a vital skill used by the tantric exegete to make sense of body and text. As this passage demonstrates, according to Ngorchen's opponent, the failure to parse tantric formulations obstructs knowledge and leads to "lies masquerading [*ming brtag*] as the superior instructions," in other words, to fabrications.

The phrase "So it was written" (*zhes bya ba bris*) marks the conclusion of the quote from the logician. It is a convention, somewhat akin to the modern quotation mark, for indicating a citation, often a precise one but sometimes a paraphrase. "So it was written" marks one aspect of the "difference" produced by repetition, raising questions about how setting apart fragments of grafted text indicates shifts in the relationship of writer, reader, and text. "So it was written" therefore challenges readers to read between the lines.

The logician concurs with a statement they allege Butön to have made. While there is no explicit reference to the Hevajra system here, a learned tantric reader would recognize the enumeration of 157 deities for the body mandala versus 9 for the outer mandala as that of the Hevajra system. The latter is often represented, as in the fifteenth-century painting shown as figure 3.1, as a palace whose inner sanctum is inhabited by Hevajra and his consort Nairātmyā surrounded by a retinue of eight goddesses. In the periphery of the palace, there are 8 cremation grounds and protective deities guarding the far reaches of the canvas. The body mandala translates the model of the celestial palace onto the body, mapping a vajra body of 5 *cakras* (at least according to the Path and Fruit system), energetic hubs along the central channel, inhabited by an expanded assembly of deities. The practitioner imagines the goddesses as the channels of this vajra body or as the petals of lotuses that give form to these *cakras*. The number of goddesses/petals/channels vary according to their location within the vajra body. The Sakya Path and Fruit system describes the container of these elaborate inhabitants known as the mandala of the support in a similar manner to the account of body mandala attributed by Ngor chen's opponent to "some Tibetans."

Citation is a form of repetition that often destabilizes a sense of origin even as it reinforces it. Attending to how repetition works in the case of citation bears the potential to expose the significance of repetition for understanding

FIGURE 3.1 Hevajra Mandala. Tibet, fifteenth century. Distemper on cloth, 21 ½ x 17 ½ in (54.6 x 44.5 cm) unframed. 2015.551. The Metropolitan Museum of Art, New York. Gift of Stephen and Sharon Davies Collection, 2015.

representations more broadly. The first specific problem Ngorchen's citation of his opponent poses for interpreting round one of the body mandala debate is the difficulty of even demarcating a round one, a problem I introduced in chapter 2. As Bentor has shown, Khédrup's charges are themselves extracted from a text by his teacher Tsongkhapa on Cakrasaṃvara practice; they also diverge from that "original" in a significant way.[27] The next section of this chapter attends to the "difference" in Khédrup's repetition of Butön via Tsongkhapa's text as well as to Ngorchen's response to it.

Ngorchen constructs his entire defense around Khédrup's remarks in the form of three topics:

- Rejecting the argument with regard to the body mandala of the support
- Rejecting the argument with regard to the body mandala of the supported
- Rejecting the argument that the Hevajra body mandala is not explained in the tantras or Indian systems

In the first section, he deals with the mandala of the support, the correlations of the parts of the body with the container of the body mandala in the form of components like the protective circle, celestial palace, and cosmic elements. As Ngorchen hones in on the errors he finds in his opponent's claims, he identifies these errors as both the mis-citation and misinterpretation of Butön's statement.

"JUST BECAUSE YOU DON'T SEE IT DOESN'T MEAN IT ISN'T THERE": NGORCHEN ON THE MANDALA OF THE SUPPORT

Ngorchen begins his defense by clarifying Butön's position for the opponent who has misread it. He characterizes this error in two primary senses, as both a "literal flaw" (*tshig la skyon*) and as a misapprehension of context:

> Although omniscient Butön explained most of the verses like that [i.e., like you said] in *The Activities of the Yoginīs* and the commentary on Nagpopa's sādhana, "As for the tent, it is the very garland of bones,' except for just that quote, it is not seen to be anywhere in the Cakrasaṃvara cycle of teachings." [Butön] never said "it is not anywhere in the Indian system." In the absence of such a statement, what's the point of setting forth this lie in the face of direct perception (*mngon sum*)?[28]

Ngorchen posits that even if Butön may have disputed this form of body mandala in the context of the Cakrasaṃvara teachings, he never wrote that it wasn't explained anywhere in the Indian system. Ngorchen's critique is therefore based on the relationship between citation and context, an issue to which I will return later in the chapter.

Bentor has shown that Tsongkhapa also maintained the more modest scope for Butön's remarks, confining them to the Cakrasaṃvara context. Bentor interprets Khédrup's mis-citation as a rare example of "distorting" or taking liberties within *Ocean of Attainment* on account of his "hyperbolic" and "passionate" style.[29] Ngorchen is, however, critiquing more than Khédrup's tendency to exaggerate or even fabricate a precedent. He is actually challenging the opponent's qualifications to even wage this claim. The "lie" (*rdzun*) Khédrup is attempting to pass off as a "mere" repetition is, for Ngorchen, a testament to the fact that the logician himself did not carefully examine Butön's text. Citations often reveal which version of a text an author is working with, and in many cases these citations are secondhand. It was common for Tibetan authors to access "root" texts through their commentaries, and increasingly so through genres like monastic textbooks.[30] It would not be unusual for Khédrup to have picked up where Tsongkhapa left off without taking the time to reread Butön's work.

Therefore, in critiquing the "literal flaw," Ngorchen distinguishes himself as a superior variety of tantric exegete who goes back to the source to verify and reconsider a citation rather than taking someone else's word for it. In *Dispelling Evil Views*, the longer version of his text, Ngorchen voices his concern with philological and philosophical rigor even more potently, writing, "One who says that Butön negates the explanation of the manner of generating the body as the celestial palace in [the case of] Hevajra, does not investigate [the situation] completely (*rnam par ma brtags*)."[31] This careful attitude and emphasis upon the direct experience of a text resonates with conversations around meditative realization. You certainly don't want to take someone else's word for something you must experience yourself if you hope to attain liberation.

The "lie" Khédrup is attempting to pull off concerns "direct perception" (*mngon sum*), a term that, for him, refers to a particular form of valid cognition. In chapter 1, I described how Khédrup uses the standards of valid cognition (*tshad ma*, Skt. *pramāṇa*) to interrogate the value of tantric ritual acts of imagination in light of the fact that they are not, strictly speaking true or empirically verifiable. "Direct perception" describes a kind of direct contact with phenomena, but Sakyapas and Gelukpas often disagree on whether or not it counts as a valid cognition. For Sakyapa thinkers like Ngorchen, all perception is mediated; empirical observation cannot account for all phenomena, and therefore direct perception is not an accepted means of valid cognition. In contrast, many thinkers in Tsongkhapa's lineage insist that such unmediated contact with things as they really are is possible. In referencing direct perception, Ngorchen plays upon this philosophical tension. He also artfully responds in his own way to Khédrup's use of *pramāṇa* in his tantric polemics while remaining focused upon textual exegesis for his defense. For Ngorchen, citation is a more important tool for defending the Hevajra body mandala transmitted by his Sakya forefathers than pointed rhetoric, logic, and other strategies of philosophical debate. And yet he gestures, sometimes in a playful display of wit and at other points with pronounced critical fervor, toward multiple Buddhist approaches to ascertaining the true nature of reality.

In addition to correcting his opponent on what Butön actually said, Ngorchen also emends the context in which Butön made this statement. Ngorchen returns to the source for the description of the body mandala by "some Tibetans," writing,

> Moreover, in the writings, "the tongue and the lips are the corridors of the desire goddesses." If we go further in citing [it says]: "The soles of the feet, the *lung*. The abdomen, fire. The stomach, water. The heart center, earth. The vertebra, Mount Meru. The head, the summit. The armspan, the four- cornered celestial palace. The eight bones, the pillars." If you deny that, you contradict the tantra as it's explained in the explanation from the *Samputa*. What's the point of [debating] denial or proof when other than that quote [of] the previous position, [Butön] made no [such] claim.[32]

Ngorchen shows that Khédrup still elided a crucial component from his citation. Over the course of his argument, Ngorchen slowly builds a case for the *Sampuṭa Tantra* as the linchpin holding together these different impressions of the mandala of the support. In the final chapter of this book, I closely examine the role of the *Sampuṭa Tantra* and the genre of explanatory tantra to which it belongs within the meaning-making strategies of the body mandala debate to unveil how Ngorchen and Khédrup use this genre to make the tantric corpus "malleable."

In this passage, Ngorchen shows that the length and scope of citations have deeper implications. Ngorchen is digging deeper, going "further in citing" (*zhes pa'i sogs khong nas*) a passage correlating the parts of the body with the elements as well as with the celestial palace. That passage, elided in the opponent's citation, emerged in some part from Hevajra sādhana and their addenda within the work of the Sakya patriarchs such as Drakpa Gyeltsen and Pakpa; in those texts, it formed part of a threefold method of correlating the body with the protective circle, cosmic elements, and celestial palace of the mandala. For Ngorchen, there no point spending time disputing something Butön never even said, at least not in the terms of the logician. Ngor chen shows the way in which the form of body mandala described by "some Tibetans" through a series of correlations has a firm textual basis. This basis lies in the Hevajra tantras as composed of the Hevajra root tantra, the *Vajrapañjara*, and most important, in this case, the *Sampuṭa Tantra*.

Before unleashing the full force of the tantric corpus, Ngorchen considers what he identifies as his opponent's misunderstanding of Nagpopa's text. These apparent "flaws in meaning" (*don la kyon*) regard both the mechanics of relating body and mandala as well the context for Butön's remarks. He begins by illustrating how competing descriptions (and the lack thereof) of the placement of one element of the body mandala of the support threatens to unhinge the entire celestial structure.

CONFUSING THE ORDER OF THINGS: THE PROBLEM OF THE *VIŚVAVAJRA*

Tantric texts often lack clear transitions between ritual phases and clear relationships between different versions of imaginative action. These absences contribute to the cryptic nature of tantric texts and secure the necessity of the guru as the guide in ritual practice and as an authority on tantric meanings.[33] These absences also produce a demand for commentary by ritual exegetes like Ngorchen and Khédrup, as well as by their Indian tantric forefathers.

Ngorchen and Khédrup use citation as a tool in navigating these gaps, transitions, and points of confusion. They map the landscape of body mandala through texts to align the structure and sequence of images of correlating the body with enlightened forms. In the process, they craft a body mandala practice and a tantric corpus. Sorting out "confusion in the order of things" is crucial to ensuring that body mandala "works"—ritual coherence and soteriological efficacy are intimately connected.

The Vajrayāna, the lightening path of tantra, of striving for enlightenment in this very body, is literally the "vajra vehicle." The vajra, a ritual implement imbued with associations with profound and impregnable elements like lightening, the thunderbolt, and the diamond, is a core symbol of tantric practice. The *viśvavajra* (figure 3.2) is a more elaborate form of vajra composed of two crossed vajras and is popular within tantric iconography. In this section, I discuss the way in which Ngorchen addresses his opponents' charges in connection with the order and manner of correlating the viśvavajra with other forms in body mandala. In the process, I lay the groundwork for revealing the deep entanglement of practices of correlating and aligning bodies and texts that unfolds over these next few chapters.

FIGURE 3.2 Viśvavajra. Private collection. Himalayan Art Resources #81863. Photo by Jeff Watt. Courtesy of Himalayan Art Resources.

In our readings on body mandala, Dongsung Shabdrung Rinpoche, one of the monastic experts I worked with, identified "confusion of the order of things" (*go rims 'khrugs*) as a pressing concern for Tibetan ritual exegetes.[34] It is not surprising that "confusion of the order of things" would arise in attempting to navigate complex practices like body mandala, in which multiple approaches to correlating the body with divine forms exist side by side. These concerns echo the anxieties around the confusion of ordinary and enlightened bodies described in chapter 1.

In some cases, there are historical factors underlying the composite form of the structure of body mandala. One of the challenges facing Tibetan exegetes was how to navigate varying systems of correlation developed over time, as well as the interpenetration of sources of root tantras, commentaries, and ritual manuals within the Indian context. Both Khédrup and Ngorchen work to relate the different structural components of body mandala and the transitions between the phases of the ritual practice in coherent ways. Ngorchen's opponent accentuates the importance of properly determining the relationship among various phases of the body mandala practice, among the various components of the mandala of the support (the protective circle, the "container" built of cosmological elements, and the detailed formation of the celestial palace), as well as of the mandalas of support to the supported.[35]

Ngorchen clarifies that the correlation of the "tent" and the "garland" of bones in Nagpopa's text is a reference to the protective circle of the body mandala.[36] Ngorchen, moreover, presents the Indian commentator Abhayākāragupta's descriptions as evidence. A key detail in this host of correlations is the connection of the viśvavajra with the crown of the head. Ngorchen writes, "Then, 'The bone at the crown of the head, the viśvavajra. The bones at the sole of the feet, the vajra foundation. The rib bones, the vajra tent . . .' because this transmission [*lung 'dis*] establishes it undeniably, the protective circle body mandala is never not taught in the context of the Cakrasaṃvara."[37] Ngorchen's use of the double negative here accentuates the validity of this particular way of imagining the body as a layer of the mandala: the protective circle.

Hierarchy is a structuring principle of mandala form and ritual. Two-dimensional mandala representations like paintings are organized according to a logic of center and periphery. The primary deities of the mandala inhabit the center while their attendant deities surround them, protector deities guard the gates, and accomplished tantric masters, mahāsiddhas, dwell in the quintessential marginal space of the cremation grounds (see figure 3.1). A protective circle encompasses the entire space.[38] Practitioners translate this two-dimensional form into three dimensions through choreographed ritual acts of imagination. In mapping the form of the mandala onto the human body, they introduce a vertical hierarchy oriented around the crown of the head and the soles of the feet as analogues to the pinnacle of the central chamber of the celestial palace and its base.

The position of the viśvavajra rekindles questions of the relationship between the outer mandala and inner or body mandala and of the relationship between representations. The viśvavajra appears at the base of the mandala in many ritual descriptions of the protective circle. In the fifteenth-century painting of the Hevajra mandala previously described (figure 3.1), the form of the gates of the celestial palace even evokes the form of the viśvavajra. Sakyapa commentators such as Ngorchen position this viśvavajra at the crown of the head in body mandala, although in outer mandala it appears as a structural basis.

In the body mandala debate, ritual context and textual context are equally important. According to Dongsung Shabdrung Rinpoche, some of Khédrup's problems with the relationship of inner and outer mandala can be attributed to the ritual context, the dissolution of inner into outer mandala.[39] "Gathering/Dissolution" (*bsdus pa*) is a vital ritual act that blurs the boundaries between emptiness and form and calls into question the relationship between different stages of the practice. Khédrup's concerns with the connections between the components of inner and outer mandala, as exemplified in the problem of the viśvavajra, highlight the significance of both establishing a proper basis for generating the body mandala and for maintaining order in the relationship of different types of mandala and of their parts. Bentor suggests that Khédrup even revises Tsongkhapa's understanding of the connection between earlier and later ritual acts of imagining the celestial palace in body mandala.[40] Bentor cites Tsongkhapa's *Wish-Granting Extensive Explanation of the Cakrasaṃvara Abhisamaya* to clarify this distinction: "From now on, the continuum of your earlier visualization of the stacked up physical elements, Mt. Meru and the celestial palace proceeds without being dissolved. Therefore when you begin your meditation on your body as the celestial mansion, on the basis of each former similar moment and each part of the body, a subsequent similar moment arises."[41] Alternatively, for Khédrup, it is essential to dissolve the earlier visualization of the celestial palace before generating the palace anew. Several sources suggest that the location of the viśvavajra in this version of body mandala practice provoked Khédrup by turning the practice on its head, so to speak.[42] These differences in interpretation nicely exemplify the very challenges faced by ritual exegetes as they attempt to connect different versions of a visualization or phases of a ritual practice.

For Ngorchen, the issue is not the ontological status of the varieties of mandala or their aptness to serve as a basis for tantric practice. Rather, the problem is how to relate them through the mechanics of body mandala practice. Ngorchen demonstrates how the challenge to establish a ritual chronology for relating the various imaginative acts entailed by body mandala is connected to concerns with textual authority.

Up until this point in his critique of the logician's statement, Ngorchen has remained within the purview of the Cakrasaṃvara ritual system. His next move is to use citation to substantiate the authoritative basis of this form of body mandala in the Hevajra corpus. Ngorchen summarizes this portion of his argument with a critique of the opponent's failure to understand the context for this practice. He writes,

> In short, with regard to the venerable [Sakyapa] ancestors, Butön didn't refute the container body mandala of the support of Cakrasaṃvara since they didn't accept this quote: "The ribs are the vajra fence" [in the context of Cakrasaṃvara]. Though it is accepted [by the Sakya ancestors] in the case of Hevajra, there is no error because it is explained in the transmission [*lung*] according to what arises from the oral instructions [*man ngag*]. Therefore, the one who says "the method

> of generating the body as the celestial palace like that is unacceptable," fails to comprehend the meaning.[43]

Context is key to Ngorchen's interpretation of the opponent's citation of Butön. First, the Sakya forefathers correlate the body with the mandala of the support in this way in Hevajra body mandala practice but potentially not with Cakrasaṃvara.[44] Second, they establish its validity for Hevajra practice by appealing to the oral instructions (*man ngag*) of the gurus to better ascertain the meaning of the "scripture" or "transmission" (*lung*). Over the remainder of his defense of the Sakya version of Hevajra body mandala, Ngorchen grounds his argument in an intricate web of citations. He draws upon diverse genres of tantric sources, including root tantras and commentaries of oral and textual varieties as well as sources that cross categories. In chapter 4, I will address the importance of the oral instructions to Ngorchen's map of the tantric corpus.

Making sense of how Ngorchen's web of citations constitutes his defense, and apprehending why the contexts of Hevajra and Cakrasaṃvara would be confused in the first place, demands a more sophisticated tool for navigating the landscape of body mandala. Before turning to these tasks in the final chapters, I propose a method for mapping the citations of the body mandala debate. This method provides a basis for me to consider the different approaches Ngorchen and Khédrup take to textual lacunae, to contradictions, and ultimately to parsing bodies and texts. I then apply this method in order to model how it works. In mapping Khédrup's citations in his description of the process of correlating goddesses with winds (*rlung*) in the Guhyasamāja body mandala practice, I show how citations support a dynamic process of mandala iconography in the making.

"CUTTING THE GROUND": A NEW METHODOLOGY

When ritual specialists create a mandala altar of colored sand, they begin by preparing and purifying the ground and then "cutting it" with geometric lines. These lines become the template for elaborate patterns and vibrant detail. In a similar way, Tibetan authors lay the groundwork for a new text by using a form of outlining known as "cutting the ground" to provide the basic structure or skeleton of the text. In cutting the ground, they prepare the foundation and also create basic outlines that will be filled in with elaborate detail. This convention provides a general form to which the reader can refer back as a point of orientation. Many Tibetan texts begin with or incorporate this structure to organize complex arguments and counterarguments, as well as to facilitate intricate connections between ideas. A basic attempt at cutting the ground of Ngorchen's shorter body mandala text [N1] looks like this:

MAP OF NGORCHEN'S *DESTROYER OF THE PROPONENTS OF EVIL THROUGH ELIMINATING OBJECTIONS TO THE HEVAJRA BODY MANDALA* (*KYE'I RDO RJE'I LUS KYI DKYIL 'KHOR LA RTSOD SPONG SMRA BA NGAN 'JOMS*) [N1]

Part I. Explaining the objections [to the Hevajra body mandala] (548.2)
Part II. Ascertaining their rejection (549.1)

1. Rejecting the argument concerning the body mandala of the support (*rten gyi lus dkyil*) (549.2)
    - 1A. developing flaws in word (549.2)
    - 1B. entering into flaws in meaning (549.6)
2. Rejecting the argument concerning the body mandala of the supported (*brten pa lus dkyil*) (552.3)
    - 2A. rejecting the argument of the disjunction of the number of gods of the outer circle (*phyi dkyil*) and the body mandala (*lus dkyil*) (552.4)
    - 2B. rejecting the argument of the absence of deities common to inner and outer (555.3)
    - 2C. rejecting the argument of not distinguishing the body mandala and the arraying of deities on the body (*lus la dgod pa*, Skt. *nyāsa*) (559.3)
3. Rejecting the argument that it [the body mandala] is not contained in the tantras or Indian sources (560.6)
    - 3A. method of explaining from Hevajra commentaries
        - 3Ai. Explaining from the tantra and oral instructions (561.2)
        - 3Aii. The commentarial method by the other *mahāsiddha*s (565.6)
            - 3Aiia. Nagpopa's position
            - 3Aiib. Dralé Namgyel's (Jetari's) position
                - 3Aiib1. the scriptural explanation (568.1)
                - 3Aiib2. uncovering doubts in relation to that (570.1)
            - 3Aiic. Indrabhūti's position (572.2)
            - 3Aiid. Dorjé Nyingpo's (Vajragarbha's) position (573.4)
    - 3B. Method of explaining from other tantric commentaries (576.1)

The structure of Khédrup's body mandala chapter from *Ocean of Attainment* upon which Ngorchen bases his response is even simpler:

CHAPTER 3 OF KHÉDRUPJÉ'S *OCEAN OF ATTAINMENT OF THE GENERATION STAGE OF THE GUHYSAMAJA* (*GSANG 'DUS BSKYED RIM DNGOS GRUB RGYA MTSHO*) 233.6–262

The detailed explanation of the manner of generating the body mandala (233.6)

I. Refuting the tradition of others (234.1)
II. Establishing my own tradition (250.4)
   A. the general explanation of the manner of establishing the body mandala of the support and the supported (*lus rten dang brten pa'i dkyil 'khor*) (250.5)
   B. the detailed explanation of generating any deity from any seed syllable on any place on the body (255.5)

I suggest an analogous method of mapping citations by incorporating them within the topical outline of the text. Mapping a text through its citations in this way guides the reader in locating previously invisible connections and acts of innovation occurring within the perceived boundaries of meaning-making. This method also illuminates key dimensions of representation.

In appendixes 1 and 2, I map Ngorchen and Khédrup's texts by incorporating citations into the outline generated by cutting the ground, revealing the density of these citations. In the case of Ngorchen's text, I traced a number of the citations, particularly those related to the Hevajra cycle, back to their source texts; in these cases, in the notes, I provide their location and, on occasion, suggest alternate editions to check. For especially perplexing citations, I considered the context in which they appear in these sources along with variant readings and incorporated that information into my translation and interpretation of Ngorchen's writings. What I lay out in these appendixes is a method that could be further enhanced by using digital tools such as OCR. The appendixes therefore serve as a starting point for further exploration rather than as a comprehensive map.

These attempts at cutting the ground attest to the breadth of Ngorchen and Khédrup's training in tantric texts. In some cases, these authors recalled these texts from memory. In others, they may have consulted editions or located them through their commentaries. For a reader keen to immerse themselves in the waters of tantric textuality in which these exegetes swam, cutting the ground provides a syllabus.

Mapping citation in conjunction with cutting the ground is different from statistical approaches. It illuminates context, granting a view not just of how often an author cites a text but also of how they use it. Cutting the ground reveals key dynamics of Buddhist textuality in which citation participates, including

- creating and reworking lineage;
- establishing authenticity;
- diversifying commentarial strategies;
- synthesizing sources;
- underlying practices of pedagogy and performance;
- "practical canon" in the making.

"Cutting the ground" also provides a way of comparing texts by different authors as well as by the same author. The density and variety of citations is especially obvious in mapping Ngorchen's body mandala text in this way. Ngorchen's shorter body mandala text, *Destroyer of the Proponents of Evil* [N1], and Khédrup's chapter are both about thirty to thirty-five folia in length, making comparison of the density and proportion of their citations simpler. While one may strain at times to hear Ngorchen's voice among his dense citations, Khédrup presents quite a different situation. In his body mandala chapter, Khédrup tends to enhance his citations more robustly than Ngorchen does with rhetorical and polemical statements informed by the tactics of philosophical debate. At moments, the vehemence of these comments can distract from the more subtle maneuvers he orchestrates in drawing upon a plethora of sources to construct the Guhyasamāja body mandala. To ensure that the ingenuity of Khédrup's maneuvers is not overlooked, in the next section I cut the ground of a portion of his argument.

KHÉDRUP MAPS THE GUHYASAMĀJA BODY MANDALA: LOCATING AND CORRELATING THE GODDESSES WITH WINDS (*RLUNG*)

In this section, I analyze Khédrup's strategies of citing tantric texts from one section of his body mandala chapter from *Ocean of Attainment* to reveal a form of iconography in the making. In the process, I highlight his distinct approaches to addressing the issues of textual lacunae, contradiction, and even the task of parsing which I raised earlier in this chapter. Through these citations, he correlates the goddesses of the mandala with particular winds (*rlung*) associated with the five elements and locates them within the landscape of body mandala. As his map of body mandala differs significantly from some key authorities, he is compelled to explain these discrepancies.

Khédrup uses citations to construct a ritually coherent body mandala practice in the face of normative expectations to adhere to the standards of textual authority; at the same time, he struggles to account for discrepancies among authoritative texts. He is negotiating different versions of the practice presented in various Indian texts accepted as authoritative within the Ārya tradition, texts linked with Nāgārjuna and his disciples. Recall that contemporary scholars and some traditional Tibetan experts dispute the idea that a singular figure named Nāgārjuna composed both the seminal texts of the Madhyamaka philosophical tradition and of Guhyasamāja tantric exegesis. Nonetheless, Tsongkhapa's lineage holders wielded this link as a powerful tool to construct a cohesive tradition reconciling both the path of perfections and of secret mantra, the pāramitānaya and mantranaya respectively.

Khédrup's citational strategies contribute to a portrait of his own identity as a writer, but they also contribute to the formation and distinction of a tradition of descent from Tsongkhapa that over time became identified as the Gandenpa or Gelukpa tradition. This tradition prided itself on a seamless synthesis of these two paths to liberation, those of the perfections and of secret mantra. In the case study I am presenting, Khédrup reinforces the authority of Nāgārjuna and his disciples as well as their bond with Tsongkhapa's tradition through his citation of particular sources by lineage gurus of the Ārya Guhyasamāja. He simultaneously creates a "practical canon" for Tsongkhapa's emerging tradition.

Khédrup constructs and transforms the Guhyasamāja body mandala practice through his citations. He uses citation to modify the way of locating goddesses and correlating them with winds and, in the process, to negotiate lacunae. Furthermore, in order to reconcile discrepancies between the accounts of mapping the body presented in multiple authoritative tantric sources, he uses citation to address contradictions. Khédrup also uses citations to synthesize different Buddhist ways of knowing, defining, and categorizing. His citations of competing systems of correlating and locating winds and goddesses within the body allow him to display his expertise in logic and philosophical debate in exploring what contradiction (*'gal ba*) really means in the case of tantric sādhana. In the process, he reveals the skills to parse both the ritual body and the tantric corpus—unique skills of the exegete I will explore more deeply in chapter 5—to be parallel and essential aspects of tantric practice.

Mandala Iconography In-the-Making

Like other forms of representation, mandala are constructed. The impression that mandala iconography comes into being fully formed and remains unchanged is an illusion. Art historians and philologists have been diligently dismantling this illusion by seriously evaluating noncanonical representations of mandala in both texts and images, representations that previously were dismissed as incomplete or one-offs.[45] They have shown the myriad ways in which these representations have informed the creation of what are now considered canonical or standardized mandala. For example, the basic definition of mandala as a "sacred circle" is based on a faulty assumption. Christian Luczanits evaluates a multitude of counterexamples to propose a new definition of mandala as an assembly of deities connected by a relationship of central deity and retinue.[46] The task of enumerating mandala deities, positioning them within the broader structure of the celestial palace, cosmos, and body, and correlating them with respective colors and qualities, inspired diverse mandala representations over time.

The transition from a three- to five-buddha family system that develops within Indian tantra, along with the rise of the yoga tantras in the seventh century, results in creative methods and some awkward attempts to expand the core structure of the mandala.[47] For example, esoteric drawings and paintings from the Dunhuang caves of Northwest China (under Tibetan occupation from the mid-eighth to mid-ninth centuries) attest to the vibrant experimental approach to establishing the mandala's form (figure 3.3).[48] This frequently referenced tenth-century scroll painting from Dunhuang depicts an atypical version of the Vajradhātu mandala with the five-buddha family format; in it, a yellow Vairocana (usually white) is surrounded by four buddhas/*jinas* in the corners. The colors, attributes, and positions of these budhhas all contain nonstandard elements. In comparison, a later rendition of a Vairocana mandala, from around the fourteenth century in Tibet, appears to be more complete and codified (figure 3.4). The five buddhas appear in distinct quadrants of the mandala palace with members of their retinues arrayed on lotus petals surrounding them. Their colors and alignment with the directions correspond with the more expected formulas. For example, Vairocana, white in color, appears in the central square; in this instance, all the other main deities face inward toward him, reinforcing his primacy. Akṣobhya, blue in color, appears in the square below him, inhabiting the eastern direction; unlike the orientation of a compass, in mandala paintings, the lower portion refers to the eastern direction and functions as the point of entry into the mandala. The vajra family, the buddha family over which Akṣobhya presides, is associated with the eastern

FIGURE 3.3 Mandala of the Five Buddhas. Dunhuang, second half of the tenth century. Ink, colors, and gold on silk, 105.5 x 61 cm. MG17780. Photo by Richard Lambert. Musée des Arts Asiatiques- Guimet, Paris, France. © RMN-Grand Palais / Art Resource, New York.

FIGURE 3.4 Vairocana mandala. Tibet, ca. fourteenth century. 68.5 x 60 cm. Formerly in the Collection of Anna Maria Rossi and Fabio Rossi. Himalayan Art Resources #88558. Photo courtesy of Rossi and Rossi and Himalayan Art Resources.

direction. Despite the apparent codification of the form of the mandala in this painting, artists and exegetes alike continue to effect transformations over time. They produce templates of mandala by drawing upon precedents and also modify those precedents in subtle ways. Mandala therefore provide an especially potent example of a larger tension between innovation and tradition fueling Tibetan Buddhist visual and textual representations.

As a sophisticated form of mandala technology, body mandala exhibits many of the same conundrums around mapping the cosmos and divine forms found in early mandala images. Controversies within the body mandala debate over how to correlate the goddesses or how to locate the viśvavajra are evidence that the spirit of creativity and experimentation did not end at some arbitrary historical moment of concretization—after the vibrant generation of tantric systems during the "Dark Age" of mid-ninth- to late tenth-century Tibet, for example or with the sealing of the Dunhuang library cave in the eleventh century. Over time, more rules were indeed created to determine the representation and imagination of mandala. Ritual compendia like the Indian commentator Abhayākāragupta's *Vajrāvalī* and Butön's canonical projects are just two attempts at standardizing mandala. In the Sarma era, gaining momentum from the eleventh century on, Tibetan masters work to relate different transmissions of mandala from Indian sādhana and commentaries, to explain discrepancies between them, to address lacunae in their descriptions, and to canonize particular variations. In this vein, Khédrup employs citation as a subtle tactic for manipulating the form of the mandala while consciously maintaining the mandala's integrity as a soteriological tool; he simultaneously reinforces the integrity of Tsongkhapa's legacy through his citations of key Ārya Guhyasamāja authors. Khédrup uses citations to correlate goddesses with elemental winds (*rlung*) as a form of iconography on the making.

On Lung (rlung)

Lung (*rlung*), like wind, is always in motion. Over time and across Buddhist traditions, there are various typologies of *lung*; the relationships between the various contexts for understanding them are not always clear. Both the Tibetan medical practitioners and Buddhist monastic scholars I have spoken with acknowledged the difficulties of translating the term, as well as the importance of distinguishing these different contexts for *lung*. For this reason, as I highlight the clash of different contexts for defining *lung*, I have chosen to primarily retain the Tibetan term here.

The most basic understanding of *lung* is as one of five elements: earth, water, fire, *lung*, and space. Abhidharma cosmology describes how winds play a vital role in the creation and destruction of the universe.[49] In completion stage practices of Buddhist tantric sādhana, winds are a powerful tool for navigating liberation at the moment of death. In our discussion of *lung*, one of my mentors, Khenpo Choying Dorjee, translating *lung* provisionally as "energy," explained the

Vajrayāna view of *lung* as the horse and the mind as the rider. Everything that is moving, everything in the physical world has *lung*.[50]

Within the Tibetan medical tradition, derived in part from Indian Ayurveda, *lung* is one of three humors or "faults" (*nyes pa,* Skt. *doṣa*), *lung*, bile, and phlegm, that make up a person.[51] *Lung* also comes to be subdivided into elemental varieties such as earth *lung*, fire *lung*, and so forth. Systems of five root and five branch winds describe the role of *lung* in bodily functions like swallowing and digesting. Therefore, even without the problem of associating it with goddesses, the category of *lung* is already ripe with correlative puzzles and clashing systems of correspondence.[52]

Tibetan commentators such as Khédrup responded to the particular dynamics within the Buddhist ritual and scholastic cultures of their times. Other authoritative knowledge systems such as medicine intermingled with Buddhist concerns as well. A burgeoning interest in the systems of bodily winds within both Buddhist and medical circles in relation to the formation of the body and the cosmos, the nature of consciousness, and the boundaries of life and death arose in fifteenth-century Tibet.[53] Khédrup's approach to correlating the goddesses of the Guhyasamāja body mandala with a set of bodily winds touches upon all of these contexts for understanding *lung*, some underdetermined and others overrun with possibilities. The polysemy of *lung*, its capacity to mean different things in different contexts, is a testament to the complexities of representation as powered by the tension between the limitation and cultivation of potential meanings.

Locating and Correlating Goddesses and Lung

In this portion of his argument, corresponding with section 1, "refuting the tradition of others" (see appendix 2, section 1 at 240.2), Khédrup modifies an existing correlation of these goddesses with the elements to posit and solidify their relationship to bodily winds. His efforts to correlate the set of four goddesses, Locanā, Māmakī, Pāṇḍaravāsinī, and Tārā, with a system of five *lung* within the Guhyasamāja body mandala reflect these complexities of *lung*'s multiple meanings as well as of mapping the body in connection with divine forms.

These four goddesses appear in the intermediary directions of both the Sarvadurgati-pariśodhana and Guhyasamāja outer mandala. Within Indian tantric and commentarial literature, the history of their connections with the buddha families and correlations with symbols, elements, and locales of the mandala is intricate, especially in the cases of Locanā and Māmakī.[54] In introducing the template of the body, a form charged with its own hierarchies, including its own points of power and vulnerability, the body mandala practice presents an even more elaborate challenge.

As for many other tantras of the "unsurpassed" (*niruttara*) class, the ritual system of the Guhyasamāja includes sexual practices mirroring the union of a main deity with a consort. In the case of the Akṣobhyavajra mandala of the Ārya Guhyasamāja tradition, practitioners are enacting the roles of the buddha Akṣobhya and his consort who inhabit the center of the mandala palace in outer

FIGURE 3.5 Mandala of Guhyasamāja-Akṣobhyavajra. Tibet, fourteenth century. Pigments on cloth, 14 x 13.63 in (35.56 x 34.61 cm). F1997.43.1. Rubin Museum of Art, gift of Shelley and Donald Rubin Foundation. Himalayan Art Resources #575.

mandala representations like this fourteenth-century example (figure 3.5). The incorporation of the body mandala of the consort, or "mother deity," in relation to that of the male practitioner or "father deity" is one reason for the added complexity of the argument surrounding the goddesses in this instance.

Another challenge Khédrup encounters is of lacunae within the sources on the Guhyasamāja body mandala. Earlier in this chapter, I unpacked the example of the viśvavajra to highlight how the absence of transitions between ritual moments and the underdetermined quality of the correlations with divine forms prompted controversies among interpreters. In addition to dealing with the cryptic nature of tantric texts, Khédrup is also navigating contradictions between authoritative accounts of the practice. The precise manner in which he defines and negotiates contradiction sets him apart.

Systems of Matching Goddesses with Elements and Incorrect Maps

Khédrup begins the relevant section by challenging an opponent's way of mapping the goddesses and by referencing the arrangement of the goddesses according to two authoritative texts of the Ārya Guhysamāja tradition. Khédrup asserts: "The *Samāja-sādhana-vyavasthole* (*sthāli*) intends for one to arrange the goddesses who are the five mothers (*yum*) on the bodies of both the father and mother deity. It's unreasonable (*mi rigs*) to arrange the four, Locanā and so forth on the navel, heart center, throat, and crown."[55] When Khédrup critiques the practice of mapping these goddesses onto the navel, heart, throat, and crown as unreasonable (*mi rigs*), he is taking a definitive stance against this technique, although he does not cite its source.

The *Samāja-sādhana-vyavasthole* (*sthāli*) (*Rnam gzhag rim pa*) is an Ārya cycle text attributed to Nāgabodhi dealing with the generation stage practice of the Guhysamāja.[56] Curious to understand the context better, I turned to the *Samāja-sādhana-vyavasthole* to have a closer look. The text solidifies the relationship of these four goddesses to the elements through citation of the Guhyasamāja root tantra; it also provides alternate names for the goddesses: Moharatī Locanā, Dveśaratī Māmakī, Rāgaratī Pāṇḍaravāsinī, and Vajraratī Tārā.[57] These alternate names for the goddesses appear in the *Samāja-sādhana-vyavasthole*'s description of the body mandala of the father deity, while the names Locanā and so forth appear for the goddesses of the body mandala of the consort.

Khédrup continues by citing the *Piṇḍīkṛta* (*Mdor byas*), a text attributed to Nāgārjuna that also deals with the generation stage practice of the Guhyasamāja.[58]

This text became the basis for Tsongkhapa's Guhyasamāja sādhana, a practice widely used within Geluk communities today.[59] This text is a counterpart to the more well-known *Pañcakrama*, by the same author, which focuses upon the completion stage practice.[60] Khédrup cites the *Piṇḍīkṛta* as follows:

> In the *Piṇḍīkṛta* [it says]: "As for Locanā and Māmakī, likewise Pāṇḍaravāsinī and Tārā, they are arranged by the *mantrika* on the earth [element] and so forth." And in terms of the explanation of arranging the four goddesses in the sites of the four elements: "It is proper to arrange Locanā in [the area of] the genitalia, the abode of earth *lung*, Tārā at the navel, the abode of *lung lung*, Māmakī at the heart center, in the abode of water *lung*, and Pāṇḍaravāsinī at the throat, in the abode of fire *lung*." So it is said.[61]

The first citation, from the *Piṇḍīkṛta* ("As for Locanā and Māmakī . . ."), connects these four goddesses with the elements. It appears in the *mahāsadhana* section of that text in the context of arranging the body mandala of the consort.[62] In the *Piṇḍīkṛta*, the goddesses appear in the body mandalas of both father deity and consort, albeit with different names (Locanā versus Moharatī and so forth). The buddhas of the five families are positioned upon the bodies of both the father deity and the consort at the crown, throat, heart, navel, and feet.[63] Mapping the consorts onto those points according to their ties to the buddhas of the respective families would produce a similar layout to that critiqued by Khédrup, with the addition of the feet.

The source of Khédrup's next citation, "it is proper to arrange Locanā in the [area of the] genitalia," is unclear.[64] The passage locates the goddesses Locanā, Tārā, Māmakī, and Pāṇḍaravāsinī on four specific sites on the body (genitalia, navel, heart, and throat), which are, in turn, defined as the abodes of elemental *lung* (earth, *lung*, water, and fire *lung*). These sites differ from the set critiqued by Khédrup in that the genitalia (*'doms*) replace the crown. Neither the crown nor the feet, for that matter, are included.

Khédrup has laid out the objectionable map of body mandala and cited passages from two key authoritative texts of the Ārya Guhysamāja tradition, the *Piṇḍīkṛta* and *Samāja-sādhana-vyavasthole*, both of which, like the root tantra itself, connect the goddesses with the elements but don't explicitly state their locations. Khédrup proceeds to introduce his own way of mapping these goddesses more precisely in connection with elemental *lung*. While at first glance, the citations he uses in this process appear to merely affirm tradition, I show how Khédrup modifies tradition in subtle ways while grappling with two alternative systems of correlating the goddesses with aspects of the body.

Khédrup's System of Elemental Lung

Khédrup is grappling with two alternative systems of correlation for the goddesses, as he shows as his argument on *lung* unfolds. A few pages after the excerpt interpreted in the previous section, he unleashes his polemical flair to nail down his critique and lay out his own correlative map : "There is the claim that it is necessary to arrange [deities] on sites such as the secret place based upon the explanation for arranging deities such as Locanā on [elements such as] earth. For you who lack discerning minds when it comes to the meaning of the tantra, of course you have doubts."[65] He then introduce his own position by connecting two sets of five *lung* and locating them within the body: "Nevertheless, as far as I'm concerned, this is how it is: Within the classification of five root *lung*, the abode of the earth *lung*, downward-clearing *lung*, is the secret place. The abode of balancing, the *lung lung*, is the navel. The abode of life-sustaining, water *lung*, is the heart center. The abode of the upward moving, fire *lung*, is the throat. The abode of the all-pervading, space *lung*, is the whole body."[66] The list of five primary or root winds matches a common set.[67] Here Khédrup is identifying each of the five root winds as an elemental wind and locating it within the body, at the secret place, navel, heart, throat, and bodily totality. There is, however, no mention of the goddesses, and the winds are presented as a set of five rather than four. Khédrup continues displaying the clash of systems by explaining that there are "many systems for correlating" (*sbyor ba'i skabs mang*) winds and goddesses:

> In light of this explanation, as for the one who explains the four [goddesses], Locanā and so forth, as the four elements here [this may be said]: Generally speaking, there are many contexts for correlating the four elemental winds to the four such as Locanā. However, having construed the four goddesses as the elements such as earth, here one generates the four goddesses as the aspects of bodily solidity, moisture, heat, and motility. If one arranges them like that, having condensed all five root *lung* into just the element of *lung*, it is necessary to make all of those as the basis of accomplishing Tārā. So then it would not be fitting to apply the generation of Locanā from the earth *lung* and so on, on account of the absence of the characteristics of solidity in the downward-clearing *lung*.[68]

Unfortunately, mapping the goddesses onto the body through association with the elemental *lung* contradicts the already existing system of correlating them with the (unlocated) elements in both the root tantra and the *Piṇḍīkṛta*. The dominant mode of correlation for the goddesses in the *Piṇḍīkṛta* is with the elements and the defining characteristics of those elements, like the association of earth with solidity. That text does not refer to the locations of the elements or to elemental *lung*. Likewise, the root tantra itself clearly correlates these goddesses with the elements, though there is no mention there of their locations, elemental qualities (e.g., solidity), or elemental *lung*. Khédrup copes with a clash between a system based in elements and one based in *lung* by introducing the principle of contradiction.

Of Lung *and Logic: Clashing Correlations*

Khédrup uses citation to redefine what constitutes a contradiction (*'gal ba*) between systems of meaning, drawing jointly upon philosophical and tantric exegetical techniques. In attempting to make sense of the relationship between two networks of correlation, Khédrup writes:

> For that reason, conflating earth and earth *lung* is mistaken. If it is otherwise, do you claim the pervasive *lung* is that of space? If the downward-clearing *lung* has the characteristic of solidity, then you have to say that the four, earth, water, fire, and *lung* are non-contradictory. [You are] like a child who's never mastered the signs of related and contradictory [phenomena]. Go ahead and exert your minimal effort commenting on the meaning of the sutras and tantras![69]

Khédrup invokes the terms of Buddhist logic and epistemology to deliver his critique. In referring to "the signs of related and contradictory [phenomena]" (*'gal 'brel gyi brda*), Khédrup challenges the relationship of the elements to the elemental *lung* and the five-root *lung* through the authority of firmly established categories of Buddhist logic and debate.[70] He implies that the essential properties of the elements are mutually exclusive; therefore, fusing them onto the elemental *lung* conflates contradictory phenomena. He attempts to show how earth *lung* is not simply composed of both *lung* and earth; rather, it resembles earth in certain aspects. So, for example, solidity is a property that can't exist together with nonsolidity; it is an exclusive property essential to the definition of earth.[71] Therefore, the simple conflation of correlation of the goddesses to varieties of *lung* and correlation of elements presents a potential clash of systems of meaning. Khédrup thus uses contradiction as a tool for establishing where the polysemy of *lung* hits its limit.

As an exegete, Khédrup uses citation simultaneously to promote his own version of body mandala practice, an "act of renaming" goddesses as elemental winds, and to mask his ingenuity lest it raise red flags as a threat to continuity. He also shows us how citation plays a role in constructing canon.

Creating the "Practical Canon" of the Ārya Guhyasamāja Tradition

Like the *Piṇḍīkṛta* and the *Samāja-sādhana-vyavasthole,* the *Vajrasattva-sādhana* is another text of the Ārya Guhyasamāja tradition that focuses upon generation versus completion stage practice.[72] Scholars suggest that it was authored by the same Candrakīrti who wrote the *Pradīpoddyotana* (although not the Madhyamika Candrakīrti).[73] The *Vajrasattva-sādhana* becomes canonical for Tsongkhapa's tradition because scholars like Khédrup cite it, making it part of the "practical canon" of that tradition.[74]

In responding to the clash between the systems of elements and of elemental winds, Khédrup invokes the *Vajrasattva-sādhana* to ask how earth is related to solidity and not to the elemental wind of earth (or to the downward-clearing root *lung*). He writes:

> If so, in this case, if you ask how do I know it is related to setting forth the component of solidity in earth, you can look at the *Vajrasattva-sādhana* in which Candrakīrti wrote: "When arranging the four, Locanā and so forth, on the body, the so-called Moharatī is Locanā and has the nature of the earth element." Up until: "The thus-called Vajraratī is Tārā and has the nature of the *lung* element. Having arranged [them thus], thoroughly envision solidity and moisture and heat and motility." Thus, it is clearly taught.[75]

The *Vajrasattva-sādhana* locates the goddesses upon the body through reference to the elements and their defining elemental qualities, such as earth's solidity and fire's heat; however, no specific bodily sites are named. This passage from the *Vajrasattva-sādhana* occurs within the *atiyoga* portion of the text in which the practitioner manifests as the emanation (Skt. *nirmāṇakāya*) buddha body; the passage appears alongside the description for placing Buddhas on the psycho-physical aggregates (Skt. *skandhas*), bodhisattvas on the sense faculties, and wrathful deities (Skt. *krodha*) on the limbs.[76]

Tibetan exegetes disagreed on the degree of authority that the *Vajrasattva-sādhana* held. Ngorchen as well as Tsongkhapa's Sakya guru Rédaba were among the Sakyapa scholars who rejected its credibility together with the claim that it was authored by the Madhyamaka Candrakīrti; in contrast, Tsongkhapa and Butön accepted it.[77] In citing the *Vajrasattva-sādhana*, Khédrup reiterates its authority, exemplifying how the logic of citation can reverse traditional expectations that canon is always the origin of authority.

Shifting Portraits of the Vajra Body: Citations from the Vajramālā

Khédrup proceeds to cite a different variety of tantric text to establish the absurdity of systems of correlating *lung* that disagree with his own. He provides an example of how the correlation of goddesses and elements might be extended to include not only elemental qualities but also bodily substances: "In the *Vajramālā Explanatory Tantra* [it says]: 'Moreover, the Bhagavatī Locanā abides in the earth element, in the fat and so forth of this one. The Bhagavatī Māmakī abides in the water element, the blood and so forth. The Bhagavatī Pāṇḍaravāsinī abides in the fire element, heat and so forth. The Bhagavatī Tārā abides in the *lung* element, trembling and so forth.' Thus it is clearly explained."[78] Based upon these correlations, Khédrup asks, "How could anyone in their right mind claim that the flesh of the body [is endowed with/made up of] the earth *lung* and the blood [with/of] fire *lung*?"[79] The relevant section of the *Vajramālā* describes five root winds, associates them with the five Buddhas, and locates them within the body. In invoking the *Vajramālā*, Khédrup can be more precise about what the goddesses and elements look like in a body. This heightened precision speaks to the unique qualities of this explanatory tantra in synthesizing different formulations of the vajra body derived from different classes of tantric texts.

Some of the clashes of systems that Khédrup encounters are evidence he is coping with the evolution of tantric ritual and textuality, including a complex history of influence between tantric cycles and genres. For example, some of the commentarial traditions of the Guhyasamāja coincide with the composition of the *yoginī* tantras. This set of tantras, part of a special category introduced by Indian commentators, contain sophisticated formulations of the inner workings of the vajra body. The yoginī tantras uncover the body's hidden potentialities, those accessible only to the tantric adept trained to recognize and manipulate the channels (*rtsa*), winds (*rlung*), and drops (*thig le*). These pathways, energies, and essences distinguish the vajra body as a valuable soteriological instrument. The yoginī tantras also focus upon the ritual propitiation of female deities. Both the Hevajra and Cakrasaṃvara tantras are yoginī tantras.[80] There are multiple ways of classifying the Guhysamāja over time in India and Tibet. For example, it has been classed as a *mahāyoga* tantra, and it also comes to inhabit the classification of *niruttara* tantra together with the Hevajra and Cakrasaṃvara tantras (albeit generally in distinct subcategories).[81] However, the *Guhysamāja Tantra* does not qualify as a yoginī tantra. Khédrup's citation of the Vajramālā explanatory tantra invokes an Indian text that itself synthesizes multiple tantric systems and includes vital elements from the yoginī tantras. Therefore Khédrup uses citation to synthesize sources and ritual systems in a manner akin to the Indian sources themselves.

Khédrup cites two explanatory tantras, the *Vajramālā* as well as the *Sampuṭa,* to introduce sophisticated descriptions of the vajra body as well as to experiment with synthesizing different tantric systems, much as those sources themselves do. In chapter 5, I will reveal the centrality of both these "explanatory tantras" to shed light on what is at stake for Ngorchen and Khédrup in parsing bodies and texts in the body mandala debate. As I will explain, the citation of these explanatory tantras within the body mandala debate highlights the delicate network of relations between root and explanatory tantras as well as between different tantric textual cycles. First, in chapter 4, I build on the theories and methods of citations I have presented here to offer a chapter analyzing Ngorchen's use of citations. I show how he provides additional approaches to contradictions and lacunae, as well as how he uses citations to defend and delineate the Hevajra body mandala.

ON CITATION AND REPRESENTATION

Tracing Ngorchen and Khédrup's varied citational practices grants a view of how representations produce tension between source and repetition. For example, Butön's remarks on the form of body mandala that Khédrup attributes to "some Tibetans" are themselves a commentary on the writings of the Indian master Nagpopa. Khédrup's critique is derived from that of Tsongkhapa. The task of resolving the way in which these citations function in the debate involves looking at these previous contexts. Ngorchen is quick to do just that, tracing Butön's comments and correcting both Khédrup's iteration and interpretation of them. The task of attempting to trace the manifold citations appearing in the debate back to their "original" sources highlights the infinite potential of representations to rupture from context.

Lacunae in representations are generative. The body mandala debate draws attention to the silences in tantric texts, and especially in the root tantras on crucial details of ritual mechanics. These silences include inexplicit references to locating deities in the body (such as placing goddesses in relation to the elements) and the failure of texts to elaborate upon transitions between ritual acts of imagination (one of several issues at play in mapping the body as protective circle, celestial palace, and cosmos). Lacunae demand commentarial interventions. Exegetes teach us how to navigate lacunae in representations. In the case of correlating the goddesses with bodily *lung*, Khédrup intervenes in the lacunae of the Guhyasamāja root tantra as well as the commentaries of Nāgārjuna and his disciples to introduce a new way of correlating the parts of the body with divine forms.

Representations raise questions about how to navigate relationships between bodies and texts, experience and aspiration, self and world. Khédrup and Ngorchen debate the mechanics of correlating the form of the body with the form of the mandala, as in the example of the viśvavajra. In the process, they reveal tensions surrounding the role of tantric practice in bridging the gap between ordinary and enlightened realities as well as between the approaches suggested by different tantric texts. As will become increasingly apparent in chapters 4 and 5, for Khédrup and Ngorchen, issues of ritual mechanics and textual authority are deeply intertwined.

Citations expose the role of representations in canon making. In some instances, by citing a source, Khédrup and Ngorchen contribute to its authority. For example, by citing the *Vajrasattva-sādhana*, a source whose authenticity is somewhat disputed, Khédrup creates and reinforces a "practical canon" of the Ārya Guhyasamāja practice. In learning to see how the flow of authority between citation and canon is not unidirectional, repetition unfolds as a complex and often unpredictable mechanism of representation.

Once again, representations are constructed. I first made this observation in chapter 1 in considering the relation of imagination and fabrication. In chapter 2, I highlighted the construction of personae, identities, and communities through tropes in biographical sources. In this chapter, I have introduced the ways in which art historians and philologists approach how the traditions and rules for depicting mandala in visual form, as well as in ritual manuals, changed over time. I have built upon this work to reveal how, in the body mandala debate, citation models a form of iconography in the making. Khédrup's attempts to rework the system for correlating and locating the goddesses of the Guhyasamāja body mandala are just one example of the ongoing process of constructing mandala.

Ngorchen and Khédrup use citations to cobble together a body mandala practice. In so doing, they mold and contour a tantric corpus. In the next chapter, I analyze Ngorchen's citational strategies as intricate manipulations of the Hevajra corpus. By continuing to explore the permutations of his citation, "just because you don't see it, doesn't mean it isn't there," I reveal why direct experience of representations matter in establishing authenticity and authority in fifteenth-century Tibet.

4
Ngorchen's Armor of Citations

Defending and Delineating the Hevajra Corpus

Ngorchen delineates and contours the Hevajra corpus to build an armor of citations. The most threatening charge waged by his opponent is the claim that the Hevajra body mandala of the Sakya Path and Fruit (*lam 'bras*) tradition is spurious, fabricated by Tibetan experts rather than based in the Buddha's tantric teachings or in the words of the Indian masters. The challenge posed by the body mandala debate is a challenge to cite, to invoke a precedent in order to authenticate the tradition. In response to this challenge, Ngorchen uses citation to establish continuity with an uninterrupted transmission, a lineage of spiritual descent, which he describes as the "flow of a river from the Lord of the sixth *bhūmi*, Virūpa, up until the current *vajrācāryas*."[1] The lineage portrait of Ngorchen, referenced in the introduction and in chapter 2, is one example of the ways in which representation and its mechanism of repetition construct and simulate this "flow," this continuity of transmission of tantric teachings (figure 2.1). Citation is another technique for establishing continuity, one that lends itself to both polemical and commentarial methods. Analyzing Ngorchen's citations reveals both the fusion of genres distinguishing tantric polemics as well as Ngorchen's unique approach to this genre in his body mandala writings.

The stakes of interpreting an "authentic" body mandala practice are charged with demands for the kind of experience only a skilled exegete possesses to invoke and contour the tantric corpus. Through his citations, Ngorchen demonstrates a vast experiential knowledge of this corpus, displaying his expertise as an exegete who has apprehended the texts for himself. He identifies his opponents as "a few logicians who have developed bad habits across infinite lifetimes and have failed to train in this life in the Vajrayāna" and as those who "take up sharp weapons" in the form of harsh polemical tactics.[2] For Ngorchen, these opponents are unskilled, lacking a basis in experience, and overly aggressive. He warns against the grave soteriological consequences of bad exegesis. In such warnings, the division between social realities of power, patronage, and prestige and the interpretive and ritual domains begins to break down.

In this chapter, I analyze Ngorchen's citational strategies to reveal the unique ways in which he uses citations to craft continuity and tradition as well as to balance polemical and commentarial methods in defense of the Hevajra body mandala. Having cut the ground of the body mandala debate to better understand Ngorchen and Khédrup's authorial maneuvers in chapters 3 and 4, I conclude this chapter by reflecting more deeply upon how citation speaks to broader dynamics of representation. I argue that citation models how representation produces tension between "original" and repetition and presents unique problems of context and authenticity.

NGORCHEN DELINEATES THE HEVAJRA CORPUS

The lineage portrait of Ngorchen embeds him within two lineages of teaching originating with the tantric Buddha Vajradhara, the blue buddha appearing above his head (figure 2.1).[3] To review, Ngorchen himself appears three times in the painting, once as the ultimate receptor of each lineage represented (on either side of the treasure vase just below the throne) and again as the primary object of veneration. The painting details the transmission of two lineages, of the Path and Fruit and of the Nairātmyā teachings, tracing the transmission through the figures of great Indian tantric adepts (mahāsiddhas), the five Sakya venerables (*gong ma lnga*)—Tibetan masters who received and recorded and the teachings—and the lineage of masters who studied and taught these teachings after them. This Path and Fruit lineage, depicted predominantly on the right side of the canvas, is at the very center of Ngorchen's defense in the body mandala debate.

The mahāsiddha Virūpa received the Path and Fruit teachings of the *Hevajra Tantra* in a vision from the goddess Nairātmyā, consort of Hevajra, an exchange suggested in the painting by the goddess and the yogi just to the right of Vajradhara. Virūpa transmitted the essence of these teachings in a pithy text, the "Vajra Verses" *(Rdo rje tshig rkang)*, to a series of Indian disciples, the last of whom, Gayādhara, who appears on the right as the final figure in the top row of the painting, transmitted them to Tibet. About a century later, Sachen Künga Nyingpo (1092–1158), one of the five Sakya venerables, all of whom appear across rows three through five of the painting, finally committed them to writing. After Virūpa visited him in a vision, initiating him into the Path and Fruit, Sachen composed eleven commentaries unpacking the meaning of these pithy verses. His sons, Sönam Tsémo and Drakpa Gyeltsen, perpetuated their father's legacy by organizing and clarifying these teachings.[4] In rows three and four of the painting, Sachen and his sons model the white cloth robes of the Buddhist layman, emphasizing their role as tantric practitioners and noncelibate, nonmonastic lineage holders. The painting reveals how these Sakya venerables amplified the power of this transmission in the Sakya imaginaire by archiving in written form the oral transmission of the Hevajra teachings from Virūpa on to Indian and Tibetan disciples.

Despite this chain of transmission, from as early as the twelfth century in Tibet, opponents questioned the validity of the Sakya *Hevajra Tantra*–based teachings of the Path and Fruit.[5] The long-term oral transmission of the tradition became grounds to challenge its legitimate basis in Indian sources. One way in which Sakyapa authors resisted such claims was by locating references to these teachings within the works of Indian authors.[6] Citation equaled survival in the competitive climate of the period of the "later dissemination" (*phyi dar*) of Buddhism in Tibet. Among multiple traditions claiming to be the sole inheritors of "authentic" Indian legacies, citation was a powerful tool for validating a community of transmission and practice.

In his defense of the validity of the Hevajra body mandala practice in the second part of his text, Ngorchen demonstrates the intrinsic worth of the genre of oral instruction (*man ngag*). As a skilled exegete, he relies upon an ability to distinguish the different components of the Path and Fruit to demonstrate their complementarity. In the first half of his text, Ngorchen builds momentum for his defense. He directly responds to the form and content of Khédrup's argument. In so doing, he leads his reader to a space in which he reformulates the debate on his own terms.

The Sakya tradition distinguishes between the transmission of the teachings according to the "explanatory system" (*'grel lugs*) of scriptural exegesis based in the *Hevajra Tantra* and the "oral instructions system" (*man ngag lugs*) whereby the practices themselves are explained.[7] Demonstrating his skill in tantric exegesis, Ngorchen synthesizes the tantras, their Indian commentaries, and the oral instructions of the great Indian realized tantric masters. He depicts the relationship of these genres as composite, forming a total system for interpreting the rites of the Hevajra cycle, one in which both oral and written transmission of the teachings are deeply valued.[8]

In the second half of his text, Ngorchen's citations shift to focus upon sources running the full gamut of the Hevajra cycle in defending the textual origins of the Hevajra body mandala practice. Section 3 (560.6) of appendix 1 outlines Ngorchen's response to the claim that the body mandala described by "some Tibetans," namely, the Sakyapas, is not contained in the tantras or Indian sources. His focus on Hevajra sources stands out from his choices earlier in the text where he tends to cite his opponent and to respond to the offensive charges through recourse to the Cakrasaṃvara cycle.

Through his citations from the Hevajra cycle, Ngorchen navigates the genres of tantric textuality, of oral and written instructions, text and commentary, root tantra and explanatory tantra, and establishes connections between them. Ngorchen includes the three tantras (*rgyud gsum*) of Hevajra: the Hevajra root tantra; the *Sampuṭa Tantra*, the common explanatory tantra; and the *Vajapañjara*, the uncommon explanatory tantra. The role of the *Sampuṭa Tantra* as an explanatory tantra common to both Cakrasaṃvara and Hevajra systems proves especially important. Explanatory tantras of the "uncommon" variety like the *Vajapañjara* are used exclusively to interpret a single root tantra such as the *Hevajra Tantra*; "common" explanatory tantras like the *Sampuṭa* are used to interpret multiple "roots." The inclusion of these two explanatory tantras to form a complete Hevajra system is a unique feature of the Sakya transmission of Hevajra. The explanatory tantra teeters on the boundary between tantra and commentary and challenges the rules of exegesis, a phenomenon I will explore in further depth in chapter 5.

Ngorchen's defense is divided into two parts. The first part is based in the Hevajra commentarial tradition. In addition to the three Hevajra tantras, the oral instructions and commentaries of the great Indian tantric masters, the mahāsiddhas (in this instance Jetari, Darikapa, Indrabhūti, and Vajragarbha) are also essential components of the tradition. Ngorchen claims that the second part of his defense is based in "other tantric commentaries," but, in actuality, it refers exclusively to the *Vajramālā*, the explanatory tantra attributed to the Ārya tradition of the Guhysamāja touched upon in chapter 3.

Here I closely examine how Ngorchen navigates the complexities of tantric literature to reveal what is not immediately apparent about his sources and how they support the validity of Hevajra body mandala practice. Later in the chapter, I briefly discuss how these strategies compare with those he uses in other sections of his text in which he cites the two other tantric cycles relevant to the body mandala debate: the Guhyasamāja and Cakrasaṃvara. I even consider a few key points of divergence between the two versions of Ngorchen's text to reinforce how he uses citation to strike a subtle balance between polemical and commentarial methods.

In analyzing Ngorchen's citational strategies in delineating the Hevajra corpus, I illuminate a unique connection between empiricism and authenticity. For

Ngorchen, to be an exegete, a skilled interpreter of representations, requires direct experience.

On the Hevajra Tantras and Oral Instructions

In the lineage portrait, Ngorchen wears a red paṇḍita hat, a marker of scholarly accomplishment (figure 2.1). The only other master represented wearing this kind of hat in the painting is the great Sakya scholar Sakya Paṇḍita (Sapen). One of the five Sakya "venerables," this erudite teacher appears in rows four and five of the lineage portrait. Sapen is especially esteemed for his mastery and interpretation of the texts on "valid cognition" (*tshad ma,* Skt. *pramāṇa*), as well as for his treatment of the Buddhist path as apprehended through three approaches, those of the renunciant, bodhisattva, and tantric practitioner.[9] The visual parallel in the painting between these two masters suggests that Ngorchen reiterates and emulates the Sakyapa polymath's example. In chapter 1 I referred to Sapen's role as an influential interpreter of Dharmakīrti's writings on how we perceive and conceive of the world. Ngorchen builds upon this legacy to wage a multilayered critique of his opponent through the language of valid cognition.

I introduced valid cognition in chapters 1 and 3 to describe its complex role as a competing standard for authenticating representations within the body mandala debate, especially in Khédrup's rhetorical strategies for authenticating ritual imaginings. Here I illuminate a different aspect of valid cognition, one that takes shape in Ngorchen's authorial maneuvers: its potential for determining textual validity. Ngorchen writes,

> The third main point is to refute the mistaken view of "not explaining based upon the Indian tradition of transmission." For that, you say, "[it is] not explained anywhere in the tantra or authentic [*tshad ldan*] Indian scriptures and moreover not in the implicit meaning." Your words show that you don't apprehend even a portion much less the entirety of the vast scriptural tradition. Rikpé Wangchuk says, "Just because you don't see it, doesn't mean it isn't there." I will explain excellently in accord with that explanation. You who lack extensive study, listen carefully![10]

Invoking the expertise of Dharmakīrti, here referred to as Rikpé Wangchuk (Skt. Vidyeśvara), the "lord of reasoning" or the "lord of knowledge," Ngorchen playfully alludes to his opponent's inability to see what is right before their eyes. He links this oversight to the opponent's lack of experience with the tantric teachings. In so doing so, Ngorchen echoes his earlier critique of the opponent's mis-citation and misinterpretation of Butön's remarks on the textual basis for body mandala in the Indian sources, a critique I discussed in chapter 3. In that instance, Ngorchen exposed the opponent's error of conflating not seeing something with its nonexistence. In this passage, Ngorchen brings what is "authentic" (*tshad ldan*), a reliable teaching based in an unbroken connection to the words of the Buddha and the Indian masters, into dialogue with what is a "valid cognition," a reliable perception of reality. In connecting authenticity with valid cognition, Ngorchen sets the stage for a citation-based argument in support of the authority of the Sakya tradition. He simultaneously promotes his own authority to interpret as an exegete well-versed in tantric sources and practices and capable of accessing both explicit and implicit meanings.

In this portion of his argument, dedicated to the Hevajra tantras and oral instructions, Ngorchen achieves three goals. He solidifies the basis of the practice in all three tantras of the Hevajra cycle, both root and explanatory tantras. He also provides justification from within the tantras themselves for using the "inviolate oral instructions" to clarify the meaning of the teachings. Furthermore, he forges connections between inner and outer forms of mandala practice. Utilizing the full range of exegetical potential of the resources at his disposal, Ngorchen navigates the reader through a series of relationships. These include the relationships between root and explanatory tantras and their commentaries, between scriptural and oral instructions, between extensive and pithy explanations as well as between explicit and implicit meanings.

THE ROOT TANTRA

Ngorchen begins, appropriately, at the root, with a quote from the *Hevajra Tantra* that correlates the four goddesses beginning with Locanā with the seed syllables E WAM MA YA.[11] In chapter 3, I explored how Khédrup used citations to correlate these goddesses with elemental winds within the Guhyasamāja body mandala practice. Ngorchen builds upon the *Hevajra Tantra*'s correlation of the goddesses with seed syllables as follows:

> As for the first [i.e., the topic of the tantra and the oral instructions], in the [Hevajra] root tantra [it says]:
>
> "In the aspect of E, called the goddess Locanā. In the aspect of WAM, called *bdag ma*.[12] In the aspect of MA, called Paṇḍaravāsinī. In the aspect of YA, called

> Tārā." The four cakras which are in the form of the four syllables are taught to be in the nature of the four goddesses. The additional meanings arise clearly in the implicit meaning within the full extent of the tantra [although] the words are not literally explained clearly.[13]

Ngorchen's goal here is to show how what is not readily apparent in the text of the Hevajra root tantra can be accessed, a process he refers to as "attaining the meaning" (*don thob*).

THE EXPLANATORY TANTRAS

For Ngorchen, the explanatory tantras play an important role in "attaining the meaning" of the root tantra. In particular, he frequently invokes the Sampuṭa explanatory tantra in his defense of the Sakya body mandala. Yet the *Sampuṭa*'s potential to be applied to the interpretation of both the Hevajra and Cakrasaṃvara tantras can be a source of concern. This ambiguity became apparent in sorting through the "confusion of the order of things" in the case of the placement of the viśvavajra within the mandala of the support discussed in chapter 3. The classification and relationship among texts, such as the explanatory and root tantras, and among the different ritual phases of imagining body mandala are equally contentious in such incidents of "confusion." As I argue in the final chapter, the patterns of citation of explanatory tantras within the body mandala debate suggest that tantric polemics such as those that make up this debate play an important role in establishing classifications and relationships within both textual and ritual domains.

First, Ngorchen cites the description of the mandala of the support of cosmic elements, discussed in chapter 3, as a prototype shared by both the Hevajra and Cakrasaṃvara systems:

> For the sake of clarifying that very meaning, the manner of generating the body mandala of the support and supported is clearly explained in the *Śrī Sampuṭa Explanatory Tantra*. In the third part of the sixth [chapter] it says "The deities, Heruka and so forth, arise beautifully in the form of the channels. The body abides pleasantly as the mandala." And then, "As for that, the mandala abides completely. The *lung* [*rlung*] of creation resides in the soles of the feet in the shape of a bow. Likewise, the flaming triangle resides in the abdomen. Water resides in the stomach in the form of a circle. Earth resides in the heart as a square. The spine is Mount Meru in the form of a stick." Thus the body mandala of the support is taught as common to both Hevajra and Cakrasaṃvara.[14]

Ngorchen therefore provides an example for understanding the scope of exegesis of the *Samputa* as an explanatory tantra common to both systems.[15] Then, Ngorchen proceeds to the mandala of the supported with a few verses correlating each of the four goddesses with a seed syllable (E WAM MA YA), a mudrā, a buddha family, qualities such as the perfections of the bodhisattva and the immeasurables, and with a cosmic element (earth, water, fire, *lung*).[16] The verses also locate each of the goddesses in a cakra (*nirmāṇa*, *dharma*, *sambhoga*, *mahāsukha*) at a specific bodily site (navel, heart, throat, lotus). The locations resemble the configuration proposed by Khédrup in the case of the Guhyasamāja body mandala; Khédrup even paraphrased this passage from the *Samputa* in that discussion.[17] In his passage, Ngorchen shows how the *Samputa* is also a source for understanding the mandala of the supported, the deities inhabiting the celestial palace of the body mandala, with enhanced precision, as manifesting the channels, winds, and drops of the vajra body.

Ngorchen further expands upon the correlation of the goddesses with "cakras and so forth" by referring to the fourth "cluster" (*snye ma*) (562.6–563.2), one of several references to the "cluster." This elusive term, this *cluster*, refers to a commentary on the *Samputa Tantra*, the Indian master Abhayākāragupta's *Āmnāyamañjarī*.[18] Ngorchen cites the *Āmnāyamañjarī* to reinforce the *Samputa*'s identification of the goddesses with the cakras and particular mudrās, elements and so forth and to correlate them with qualities such as emptiness and compassion, method and wisdom.[19] The passage explains that while, on some occasions, the practitioner might focus on letters associated with the deities, in others, they might focus on the mudrās.[20] Ngorchen uses this built-in flexibility within the Indian sources, the provision for different possibilities for approaching body mandala practice, to address variation among sādhanas. In doing so, Ngorchen assumes an exegetical stance of neutralizing contradictions that will become even more apparent in analyzing his citations of the Cakrasaṃvara system.

Ngorchen manipulates systems of correlation and reconciles conflicting accounts in a manner typical of Indian and Tibetan mandala iconography and exegesis. The *Saṃputa* and the *Āmnāyamañjarī* enumerate only four cakras in the vajra body, at the navel, heart, throat, and lotus, the latter often referred to as the "secret place" in the genital region. The Path and Fruit system adds the crown of the head, teaching five cakras, or palaces, within the body of the tantric practitioner. Ngorchen affirms the coherence of the Path and Fruit version by reconciling the two accounts as follows:

> Allow me to clarify. Well then, if you think only four cakras are taught here, it isn't so. The quote "resides in the great bliss cakra" means the support of bliss, the main (part) of bodhicitta, resides in the crown. Thus, there is great bliss in

> the crown. The bodhicitta which arises from that descends to the secret cakra. Because great bliss is produced there, the secret place is also labeled "great bliss." Therefore, the teaching of both cakras of top and bottom by one term emerges from the commentaries.[21]

By his reckoning, the great bliss cakra refers to both the crown and secret place. He claims that the commentaries support this reading on the grounds that bodhicitta travels between these two bodily sites.[22] In chapter 5, I will discuss Ngorchen's further citations from the *Sampuṭa* in this section of his text to more fully flesh out their relevance for mapping and classifying both bodies and texts.

Ngorchen completes his elucidation of body mandala practice within all three of the Hevajra tantras with two citations from the "uncommon" explanatory tantra of the Hevajra cycle, the *Vajrapañjara*.[23] With these citations, he places the final pieces of the puzzle into his argument on the tantras, sealing the authority of the three tantras of the Sakya Hevajra system of the Path and Fruit. Ngorchen's citations reveal canon to be a series of overlapping repetitions. In reiterating the power of the core Sakyapa texts while validating his own argument, Ngorchen shows the flow of authority to be multidirectional.

ON THE COMMENTARIES OF THE OTHER MAHĀSIDDHAS

Ngorchen illuminates the collaborative and multivalent nature of authorship within the Path and Fruit traditions, with its fusion of both oral and written dimensions and of the efforts of Tibetan and Indian tantric masters. To review, the Sakyapa understand the Path and Fruit teachings as the essence of Virūpa's experience of the visitation by the goddess Nairātmyā. Virūpa transmitted these teachings to other great Indian tantric adepts or mahāsiddhas. Sachen, in turn received them through both guru-disciple teaching and visionary experience. The Sakyapa Path and Fruit is therefore Sachen's clarification of Virūpa's experience as well as the work of Sachen's sons, who recorded, organized, and further clarified these revelations. Ngorchen solidifies the link between the Tibetan and Indian masters of the Sakya transmission of Hevajra body mandala in writing:

> Thus, the manner of cultivating the body mandala is clearly taught from the three Hevajra tantras. In the pith instructions of the glorious Virūpa, the great being who inhabits the sixth ground [Skt. *bhumī*], [it says] "Having observed the body

> mandala, the signs are manifest." And in the *Condensed Path* [it says]: "restrained and produced in the five mandala."[24] So it is taught from the condensed meaning and ascertained in the whispered lineage by the mahāsiddhas as the inviolate oral instructions.[25]

In this passage, Ngorchen displays the diversity of sources within the collaborative landscape of the Path and Fruit in the form of tantras taught by the buddhas and revelations of their meaning by great Indian tantric adepts. These sources also include "whispered lineages" and oral instructions, teachings received in intimate transmissions and those passed on and recorded in written form by the Tibetan inheritors of this enlightened legacy.[26] In forging these connections, Ngorchen reenacts a trend that began in the eleventh to twelfth centuries. The Sarma traditions of Tibetan Buddhism invoked the mahāsiddhas in visual form through lineage portraits as well as through a host of textual strategies to emphasize continuity with an Indian past.[27] As Ngorchen shows, citation proved an especially potent strategy for establishing authenticity as well as for branding a tradition.

Ngorchen divides his discussion of the mahāsiddhas among the contributions of Nagpopa, Jetari, Indrabhūti, and Vajragarbha, but places particular emphasis on the tradition of Jetari.[28] Jetari's system is unique in its basis in all three Hevajra tantras.[29] Ngorchen also cited mahāsiddha Jetari's *Sādhana of the Four Mudrā* earlier in his argument on body mandala; it appeared in the section devoted to the proper interpretation of Butön's comments on the body mandala of the support.[30] In that context, Ngorchen endorsed Jetari's views as the quintessence of the Sakyapa interpretation of Virūpa's teachings. Here, in the evaluation of Jetari's system among other mahāsiddha traditions, Ngorchen once again cites the *Sādhana of the Four Mudrā* and endorses Jetari's view as being on par with Virūpa's oral instructions. He even devotes a couple folia to a preemptive strike, ruling out any potential contradictions or "doubts" pertaining to Jetari's description of the body mandala practice.[31] Here citation functions as a form of branding of the distinct and authentic Sakyapa inheritance of Hevajra teachings built on a very precise formulation of authenticity or "authenticities."

The Four Authenticities

Throughout his body mandala writings, Ngorchen displays his mastery of the tantric corpus through his citations, enacting the ideal of the exegete as an experienced and skillful interpreter empowered to clarify and transmit authentic meaning. In this section, I interpret a set of four "authenticities" Ngorchen refers to in his conclusion. In so doing, I unearth the rich interplay of ritual practice, epistemology, and exegesis informing his use of citation as his primary tool in defending the Sakya Path and Fruit tradition.

Overall, Ngorchen's style adheres far more closely to the standards of tantric exegesis than of philosophical debate. However, he peppers his text with choice comments that engage his opponent's approach. The tone of these comments is often playful and ironic rather than "axe-grinding." However, toward the end of his treatise, as he completes his map of the Hevajra corpus, Ngorchen's tone shifts away from his more playful mode of critique. He gestures once again to the rhetoric of valid cognition, remarking: "Thus, based on simply not seeing (something), you criticize the profound pith instructions of the mahāsiddha."[32] Ngorchen then transitions from teasing the master of logic who can't see what's in front of him to denouncing that logician's attempts to pass himself off as a tantric exegete. With his final citation in this section, Ngorchen warns of the consequences of faulty exegesis: "There is the prophecy of the Bodhisattva Vajrapāni in the commentary on the praise of Cakrasaṃvara where it says: 'Through erroneous learning manifesting together with arrogance, from apprehending the fault of things which are not seen in the manner of tantra, a root downfall comes about. From the root downfall, one goes to Avīci hell.' So it is said."[33] According to this prophecy, to interpret the tantras irresponsibly without the requisite experience, skill, and intention leads to a karmic sentence more grave than any polemical rebuke. Ngorchen thus expresses the intense soteriological stakes underlying the body mandala debate. Interpreting tantric texts incorrectly not only lands you in hell but also contaminates the understanding and practice of others.

Emerging from his web of citations to wrap up his text, Ngorchen justifies his elaborate defense of the Hevajra body mandala as a necessary effort toward "refuting an inferior doctrine like this which is a mere deterioration of the view."[34] Ngorchen definitively admonishes his opponent with the poetic flourish customary for closing verses, a structure mirroring the form of his introduction in many aspects. These verses confirm a connection between empiricism and authenticity emerging implicitly through his citational strategies throughout the text.

Ngorchen coaxes his reader to be emboldened by his defense of the Hevajra tradition to pursue liberation through tantric practice: "Strive to practice in accord with these oral instructions which are established through the four authenticities (*tshad ma*) through the yoga of the four sessions. Through these methods that accord with the ācāryas of the past, may awakening and likewise, the thirteenth level of Vajradhara manifest."[35] Pointing to the level of Vajradhara, the apex of awakening for those engaged on the Vajrayāna path, Ngorchen encourages practitioners to continue dedicating themselves to practicing sadhāna four times a day. He correlates these four sessions of meditative practice with four "authenticities" (*tshad ma bzhi*). The Tibetan word for "authenticities" (*tshad ma*) is the same term used to describe "valid cognition." This overlap is not coincidental but rather expresses the robust inventory of ways of knowing and ways of accessing the true nature of reality possessed by the Sakyapas. These epistemes encompass ritual, textual, experiential, and relational frameworks.

Although exegetes define the four authenticities in different ways, the Sakyapas embrace this framework as a reflection of the diverse and collaborative quality of the Path and Fruit teachings and of an equally multivalent perspective on authenticity. Many Sakyapa thinkers define these four as "authenticities of the guru (*bla ma*), of experience (*nyams myong*), of the treatise (*bstan bcos*), of basic scriptures (*lung*).[36] These varieties of "authenticity" correlate roughly with four categories of valid cognitions: "the person, of perception, of inference, and of Buddha word."[37] The practitioner, and especially the exegete, relies upon all four of these resources, upon the guru as Buddha on earth as well as upon consciousness, reason, and core texts to establish meanings and to access what is not immediately apparent.

The term *four authenticities* appears in a variety of Sakya sources, including explanatory tantras, teachings of the mahāsiddhas, and the writings of the early Sakya patriarchs, Sachen and his sons.[38] The Tibetan recension of Virūpa's core Path and Fruit treatise, the *Vajra Verses*, contains the term *four authenticities.*[39] Drakpa Gyeltsen used the term as a framework to organize tantric texts like *The Explanation of the Condensed Path*, Sachen's brief exposition of Virūpa's teaching. Another of Sachen's commentaries on Virūpa's texts identifies the authentications of "scripture, i.e., the pure instructions of the Sugata" by which he refers to tantras such as the *Hevajra Tantra*, "of the guru vajra master's pith instructions of experience," "of recollecting the yogis own experience," and "of exposition, i.e., dependent origination of reality" by which he refers to Virūpa's *Vajra Verses.*[40] In a short treatise on valid cognition, Drakpa Gyeltsen used the term *four authenticities* to reference "the awareness of an affliction (experience), the pointing out of the way of its arising (by the guru), a citation from the tantra (scripture), and a citation from the treatise (exposition)."[41] The "four authenticities" thereby connect yogic experience, guru devotion, and textuality as reliable sources for knowing the world and situate citation as central to that endeavor.[42]

Through his citations, Ngorchen unites authenticity in the senses of valid cognition and textual validity (*tshad ma* and *tshad ldan*, respectively). Thus, in his concluding verses, he writes:

> Therefore, the proponent who denies the existence of the explicit explanation from the tantra(s) and the authentic Indian system [does so] in sheer disavowal of direct perception [*mngon sum*]. Because that one creates great obstacles to merit such as bringing about laxity in the practice [of] individuals who wish to cultivate the yoga of the four sessions, one should heed the necessity for refuting an inferior doctrine like this which is a mere deterioration of the view.[43]

With these words, Ngorchen denounces his opponent for acting in defiance of the sources themselves and thereby impeding the efforts of sincere tantric aspirants.

In concluding, Ngorchen hints that he too could fight fire with fire if he chose to do so but that such tactics are just frankly not his style. The manner in which he depicts his choice to reject more aggressive tactics in his defense of the Sakya body mandala practice is key to his unique blending of polemical and commentarial strategies. It also suggests that to denounce overly polemical tactics is itself a polemical maneuver.

Ngorchen's Armor of Citations

In a similar manner to which images reinforce the status of Tibetan gurus as buddhas in lineage portraiture, citation contributes to the exegete's charisma as buddha on earth. Moreover, citation fits within a multifaceted framework for evaluating authenticity. Ngorchen constructs a virtual edifice of citations that attest to his authority as an interpreter. As in his introduction, Ngorchen uses the conclusion to rally sentiment in defense of the Hevajra body mandala practice and to establish its authenticity and superiority. He chastises frauds and sectarians, proclaiming the benefit of the text for "other impartial scholars" (*gzur gnas mkhas gzhan*) like himself.[44] Ngorchen eloquently justifies his own method of argument in opposition to the style of harsh polemics so familiar from Khédrup's text as follows: "Whoever does not take up sharp weapons and does not wear strong armor, by means of the army of flawless scripture and reasoning, how could they not defeat the opponent?[45] Using metaphor, Ngorchen suggests that harsh polemical tactics are unnecessary for an exegete reliant upon knowledge of the Buddhist corpus. Metaphor itself provides a means of issuing a powerful statement in an indirect way, injecting a dash of subtlety and the flourish of the poetic. Even in the rare glimpses of the polemical tone in Ngorchen's text, it is clear that he relies primarily upon the methods of tantric commentary to articulate and defend his position. This commentarial apparatus provides the main framework through which Ngorchen orchestrates his defense by drawing upon a host of texts and placing them in conversation with one another. As with metaphor, commentarial practice allows Ngorchen to make a point by substituting one thing for another. Of course he is familiar with the strategies of philosophical debate relished by Khédrup, as any monk trained in the Sakya scholastic tradition would be. He even pauses at choice moments in the text to playfully exhibit that familiarity with a few loaded comments. But ultimately, Ngorchen claims to defend his tradition "without wielding sharp weapons," using citation to display his mastery of the tantric corpus and to defend his ground.

Having assessed Ngorchen's citational strategies in delineating and defending the Hevajra corpus, I return to earlier sections of his argument where he is citing the Cakrasaṃvara and Guhyasamāja systems. The examples from these sections diversify the portrait of Ngorchen's authorial maneuvers as well as of citation as a device that lends itself to both commentarial and polemical projects. In the process, I also highlight select instances in which Ngorchen's polemical tone becomes a bit more heated, moments in which he relies upon additional tactics beyond his armor of citations to back his opponent into a corner. The manifold uses of contradiction as a polemical device assume prominence in these examples.

CONTRADICTION OR DIVERSITY?: NGORCHEN CITES THE CAKRASAṂVARA CYCLE

Ngorchen's citations of the Cakrasaṃvara system display his particular approach to contradiction in response to Khédrup's charges. In his body mandala chapter in *Ocean of Attainment*, Khédrup suggests a host of discrepancies posed by the ritual mechanics of the Sakya Hevajra body mandala. He uses contradiction, gilded with an overlay of strategies gleaned from Buddhist scholasticism, philosophy, and debate, to destabilize the Path and Fruit tradition. Ngorchen opposes these contradictions by displaying the inherent diversity of the tantric corpus as ripe with variations on body mandala.

In chapter 3, I tackled the problems of the mandala of the support, the body generated as cosmos, protective circle, and celestial palace, within the body mandala debate. I analyzed the way Ngorchen carefully uses citation to critique his opponent's claims as misreadings and misinterpretations of the statements made by the great Tibetan scholar and cataloguer Butön. In the following section of his text (see appendix A, section 2), Ngorchen addresses the contradictions

Khédrup presents regarding the mandala of the supported, the deities inhabiting the celestial palace of the body mandala. Ngorchen rejects

2A. the argument based on the discrepancy between the number of deities in the outer circle and the body mandala;[46]
2B. the argument based on the absence of deities common to inner and outer;[47]
2C. the argument based on not distinguishing body mandala from just arraying deities on the body (*lus la dgod pa*, Skt. *nyāsa*).[48]

Ngorchen cites extensively from texts associated with the *Cakrasaṃvara Tantra* to address these alleged discrepancies regarding the Hevajra body mandala of the Path and Fruit. He includes references to the *Saṃvarodaya* and *Abhidhānottara* explanatory tantras as well as to sādhanas by Indian masters such as Darikapa and Tilopa.[49] I have discussed Khédrup's remarks on distinguishing body mandala from nyāsa (point 2C) in chapters 1 and 3; I examined the ways Khédrup sets body mandala apart as a transformative ritual act of imagination superior to fabricated "mere imaginings." In this section, I address Ngorchen's reply to the charge that the Hevajra body mandala is invalid because the number of deities it contains within the outer mandala contradicts the number in the inner mandala, the body mandala. Ngorchen's citational strategy in the discussion of the relationship of inner and outer mandalas is to show how various accepted authoritative texts would become invalid if such charges were as coherent and absolute as the opponent suggests.

Although there is great variety, basic representations of the Cakrasaṃvara "outer mandala" include five deities, the main father and mother deity in union surrounded by four *dākinīs*, or thirteen deities, adding the eight goddesses guarding the gates and corners of the mandala (figure 4.1). The body mandala, or, as it is sometimes called, the "inner" mandala, typically enumerates a more elaborate form, with sixty-two deities; these deities include the main father and mother, the four dākinīs, and eight goddesses, as well as twenty-four dākinīs with their hero consorts located at various bodily sites. These sites correspond to twenty-four sacred sites of the Indian landscape. Therefore, in the Cakrasaṃvara context, the number of deities in inner and outer mandala does not necessarily match either.

Ngorchen employs density as one tactic in neutralizing this contradiction. A two-folia-long citation from Nāropā's *Wish-Fulfilling Jewel Sādhana* is one example of Ngorchen's use of extensive citations with little to no interruption or interjection.[50] The citation describes what one might call the "outer mandala," although it is to be cultivated in the womb (of the consort presumably). This

4.1 Mandala of the Buddhist Deity Cakrasaṃvara. Nepal, dated 1490. Mineral pigments on cotton cloth, 46 x 34 5/8 in. (116.84 x 87.94 cm). Museum Acquisition Fund (M.73.2.1). Los Angeles County Museum of Art.

mandala is composed of five Heruka father deities with consorts in the cardinal directions and center, with skullcups in the intermediary directions. Then the practitioner transitions to the body mandala of the main deity. First, one imagines the main deity and consort at the center of the lotus at one's heart with the four ḍākinīs at the petals in the cardinal directions, with skullcups of nectar on the intermediary petals. These deities are common to the descriptions of both inner and outer mandala. Ngorchen refers to elements of the twenty-four sites, of the twenty-four heroes (the male consorts of the yoginīs linked with those sites), as well as of the eight guardian goddesses that reside on the bodily gates or orifices in the inner mandala.[51]

The *Wish-Fulfilling Jewel Sādhana* describes the transition from external to internal mandala as effected through a form of "self-blessing" or "self-consecration" (*rang byin brlabs pa*, Skt. *svādhiṣṭhāna*): "When cultivating the body mandala in the body of that main deity, there are the stages of self-consecration [*rang byin brlabs pa'i rim*] and the transformation [*gyur pa*] of the superior body mandala."[52] The range of descriptions of this transition even among the texts selected by Ngorchen suggests that the Indian sādhana literature (and perhaps even the explanatory tantras) vary widely in how they articulate this ritual transition within Cakrasaṃvara body mandala.[53] The diversity of approaches was troubling enough to prompt Ngorchen to deal extensively with the relationships and transitions between inner and outer mandala in another body mandala text.[54] As I have shown in chapter 3, lacunae in the root tantras and in related authoritative texts prompted exegetes to get creative in orchestrating transitions between ritual acts of imagination.

Extensive citations like this one from the *Wish-Fulfilling Jewel Sādhana* have an almost dizzying impact on the reader. Ngorchen confidently concludes the citation with, "So there is the explanation of generating the body mandala in totality."[55] However, he is not content to move on to another argument without providing additional textual examples to neutralize the contradictions in ritual mechanics his opponent has suggested. Ngorchen questions the assumption that body mandala require deities common to the inner and outer mandala in order to be effective. He writes "alternatively the Cakrasaṃvara Buddhakapala sādhana taught in the Cakrasaṃvara *Abhidhānottara Tantra* would become mistaken (*nor bar 'gyur*) on account of the absence of deities common to inner and outer mandala. See how my reasoning is correct."[56] He reinforces his point with two citations from the *Abhidhānottara Tantra*, a source that itself attests to the complexity of citational practices within tantric textuality. The *Abhidhānottara* is one of many Buddhist tantras containing sections derived from Hindu Śaiva tantras.[57] Scholars have theorized a range of explanations for such instances of "repetition" and have also incorporated them as evidence for dating tantric texts. While some scholars claim Hindu and Buddhist tantric texts drew on a common substratum of ritual sources, others argue more decisively for Buddhist appropriation of Hindu sources.[58] Although Ngorchen and Khédrup may not have been directly concerned with the non-Buddhist origins of texts such as the *Abhidhānottara* or with dating it definitively, citation of this text inspires connections to other forms of repetition. Some of these forms refuse the practice of attributing credit to a source. Citation therefore inhabits a broader domain of tantric textuality charged with questions of imitation, influence, and appropriation, questions that plague approaches to representation more broadly.[59]

I have shown how Ngorchen uses citation in this particular section of his argument, on the relationship of inner and outer mandala, to destabilize the opponent's claims and to neutralize contradictions with a host of counterexamples from authoritative texts. In providing a battery of scriptural precedents from the Cakrasaṃvara corpus, Ngorchen creates space for the Sakyapa interpretations of Hevajra body mandala by turning a polemical weapon back on his opponent. He resists the logic of contradiction in the logician's claims by showing that if one were to adhere rigidly to the demand for coherence between different mandala systems like those of inner and outer mandala, all manner of authentic sources would be rendered obsolete as tools for generating body mandala.

FORCING CONSENSUS AND GETTING PERSONAL: NGORCHEN CITES THE GUHYASAMĀJA CYCLE

In selectively citing the Guhyasamāja system, Ngorchen forces consensus and even hones in on the identity of his opponent whose own text is based in that system. He leverages his knowledge of the Ārya Guhyasamāja body mandala to challenge both his opponent's charges on Hevajra as well as that opponent's understanding of the Ārya Guhyasamāja system, the latter being a ritual tradition in which the opponent(/s) is especially invested. Ngorchen uses citations to show that if his opponent's points of argument were indeed sound criteria for invalidating the Hevajra body mandala, the Ārya Guhyasamāja body mandala along with the opponent's own interpretations of it would also be compromised.

In Ngorchen's longer body mandala debate text, *Dispelling Evil Views of the Hevajra Body Mandala* (*Dispelling Evil Views*) [N2], he cites Guhyasamāja sources to implicate, critique, and almost identify his "unnamed" opponent. *Destroyer of the Proponents of Evil* [N1] and *Dispelling Evil Views* [N2] appear side by side in his collected works with nearly identical colophons and identical dates. In *Dispelling Evils Views* [N2], his longer "version," with about forty as opposed to about thirty-five folia sides, Ngorchen ornaments his references to the Guhyasamāja with a polemical flair. Outlining and comparing Ngorchen's citations from the Guhyasamāja system presents possibilities for resolving the relationship of the two versions of his body mandala writings. The heightened polemical tone of N2 suggests Ngorchen's increased confidence in his position, garnered by direct experience of his findings. Ngorchen may have undertaken a deeper investigation of Khédrup's writings between the time of composing N1 and N2.[60] Moreover, the more pointed remarks in the longer text suggest that Ngorchen may have been targeting Khédrup more specifically in this longer text. Although Tsongkhapa may indeed have initiated many of the critiques of the Sakya Hevajra body mandala, for Ngorchen, Khédrup's repetition of them made a difference. Ngorchen's choice to "get personal" by exposing inconsistencies within his opponent's writings and by challenging his knowledge of key texts transmitted by the opponent's lineage serves as a reminder that human as well as textual relationships are at stake in this debate.

Within an especially long divergence from *Destroyer of the Proponents of Evil* [N1] within *Dispelling Evil Views* [N2], Ngorchen invokes the Guhyasamāja cycle to break down his opponent's argument regarding the lack of gods common to inner and outer mandalas.[61] Ngorchen first disputes the claim that the Hevajra body mandala practice is invalidated because it lacks deities shared by both inner and outer mandala. Ngorchen argues that if possessing deities common to both varieties of mandala were to be taken as criteria for assessing the efficacy of a body mandala system, then Ārya Nāgārjuna's commentarial lineage would contradict the Guhyasamāja system. As support, he provides an extensive quotation from Nāgārjuna's disciple Āryadeva's *Caryāmelāpakapradīpa*.[62] Ngorchen summarizes the import of his citation of Āryadeva as follows:

> In short, not arranging the twenty goddesses taught in the outer mandala within the inner mandala and not arranging the thirty-two deities of the inner mandala in the outer mandala and without any deities common to both, this supreme tradition is negated. If you think that one can't establish an absence of deities common to inner and outer [mandala] in this tradition on account of the fact that the deities are arranged on the body of the main deity, you're wrong. The reason is that in the outer mandala the main deity is in union with a consort. For the inner mandala, the main deity is at the heart, and the consort is placed at the vajra door. Monks, in claiming to understand the texts of the

> Ārya cycle, [there is] this insincere speech which neglects the texts of Āryadeva [Aa cu de ba]. What is it but aversion towards phenomena and persons?[63]

Ngorchen shows how this criteria for determining the efficacy of a given body mandala, especially narrowly applied in the way the logician has suggested, would raise problems for the Ārya Guhyasamāja system as well. That outer mandala, as envisioned in figure 3.5, includes a retinue of twenty goddesses. Ngorchen suggests that the absence of these goddesses from the map of the Ārya Guhyasamāja body mandala would invalidate the tradition if his opponent were correct. He even refutes potential defenses his opponent is likely to pose by distinguishing the placement of the main deity and consort in the two varieties of mandala. Whereas in the outer mandala, they appear in union in the central chamber of the palace, in body mandala they are imagined in the heart and genital regions of the tantric practitioner. Ngorchen connects ritual mechanics and interpretive practice to resist the logician's charges. In doing so, he turns the tables to focus on the integrity of the Ārya Guhyasamāja, not as an attack upon the texts of that tradition but rather upon his opponent's command of them.

Ngorchen critiques the unskilled exegete who, while "claiming to understand the texts of the Ārya cycle" is actually poorly versed in its teachings and is therefore a fraud. Ngorchen suggests that without knowing the ins and outs of their own tradition and oblivious to the position of Āryadeva in particular, these fraudulent exegetes make trouble with "insincere speech" driven by impure motivations. Tsongkhapa and Khédrup claimed inheritance of Nāgārjuna's commentarial lineage and used it as a platform for building their emerging Gelukpa tradition. In turning the attention back to the Ārya Guhyasamāja system, the main topic of Khédrup's text as a whole, Ngorchen hones in on the identity of his opponent, and his polemics become increasingly targeted. He employs citation to augment his defense by showing that the opponent is not only wrong about the views of the Path and Fruit but contradicting their own writings on the Ārya Guhyasamāja.

Ngorchen's critique hits even closer to home within a longer divergence from *Destroyer of the Proponents of Evil* [N1] in *Dispelling Evil Views* [N2]. In this instance, he cites the Guhysamāja in conjunction with a heightened polemical tone that spikes with a direct interrogation of the opponent's own writings. In this section of his longer body mandala text, Ngorchen defends against the claim that the Hevajra body mandala is invalid based merely on the fact that the number of deities in the body mandala (157) differs from those in the outer mandala (9).[64] He proves that the same could be said of the Ārya Guhyasamāja tradition. In this passage, Ngorchen connects the opponent so explicitly with their writings on the Guhyasamāja that he seems to barely stop short of naming the logician:

> You babble senselessly without recalling your very own claims. Likewise, your very own Ārya Guhyasamāja commentary becomes invalidated on account of arranging the forty-nine deities in the inner mandala within the mere thirty-two of the outer mandala. The reason is your very own claim: "arranging Amoghasiddhi on the two channels of vital basis, Kṣitigarbha on the two eyes, Vajrapāṇi on the two ears, Rūpavajra on the two eye orifices, Śabdavajra on the two nostrils, Samantabhadra on the twelve joints, Sumbha, on the two feet." You yourself wrote it. Remember?[65]

This paraphrase of Khédrup's text is not immediately recognizable from his body mandala chapter, but corresponds roughly with Khédrup's citation from Nāgārjuna's *Piṇḍikṛta*.[66] Ngorchen uses citation in this passage to insinuate that not only is his opponent deficient in his knowledge of what others say about the body mandala, but that the logician can't even keep track of his own positions or maintain continuity among them. This demand for consistency within an author's writings is endemic to the polemical genre. Despite the fact that scholarly debate is aimed at mutual clarification of ideas, in some ways, there is also a limited tolerance for changing one's mind. Within the polemical context, the failure to live up to demands for consistency with the writings of one's predecessors, as well as with the views expressed across one's own writings, could lead to "internal contradiction" (*nang 'gal*) and consequent defeat.[67]

Earlier in this book, I proposed that the tendency to "get personal" is one indicator of polemical texts. Ngorchen's manner of citing the Guhyasamāja in *Dispelling Evil Views* is intended to hit close to home for his opponent, to compel him to abandon his charges, and to accept defeat. In an earlier polemical text targeted at least in part at Tsongkhapa's teacher Rédaba, Ngorchen adopts a similar strategy of getting personal in conjunction with an orchestrated deployment of the device of contradiction. In that text, *Overcoming Objections to the Three Tantras*, introduced in chapter 2, Ngorchen uses contradiction to accentuate the absurdity of the opponent's claim that the *Hevajra Tantra* espouses a Cittamātrin perspective. In his commentary upon his own root text, Ngorchen's tone shifts to become more polemical and less commentarial in conjunction with an increase in citations from the Guhyasamāja cycle.[68] The "personal" aspect of polemics reflects this heightened awareness of one's opponents' views, their training in particular ritual and textual traditions and methodologies, and their loyalties. In polemics, getting personal often implies the ability to force consensus.

Ngorchen and Khédrup combine citation and contradiction in complex ways in their authorial maneuvers through the body mandala debate. With the examples from Ngorchen's remarks on the Cakrasaṃvara system discussed in the previous section, Ngorchen used contradiction to suggest that all manner of authoritative texts would be invalidated by the opponent's line of reasoning. On numerous occasions, Khédrup generates contradictions by invoking multiple Buddhist discourses simultaneously, bringing the standards of the path of perfections to bear upon the path of secret mantra. Moreover, in the case of correlating goddesses with varieties of *lung* described in chapter 3, Khédrup navigated a series of conflicting accounts among texts accepted as authoritative by his lineage to introduce his own interpretation of the practice. In that same line of argument, he also used a philosophical notion of contradiction based on the mutually exclusive properties of different elements (earth, fire, and so forth) and bodily substances to support his approach to correlating the goddesses with elemental *lung*. Moreover, he used citations from the Vajramālā explanatory tantra to graft sophisticated understandings of the vajra body gleaned from the yoginī tantras onto the Guhyasamāja body mandala. The authors of the body mandala debate therefore combine contradiction and diversity, distinction and synthesis in unique ways deeply tied to their citational practices.

Ngorchen forges an armor of citations fit to defend the Hevajra body mandala. In revealing his process, I have highlighted the unique ways in which he uses citation to balance polemical strategies such as getting personal and forcing consensus with commentarial strategies such as neutralizing contradictions and underlining diversity within canonical sources. Outlining Ngorchen's citations also reveals the impact of these citations to be cumulative. Over the course of his body mandala texts, Ngorchen speaks through the words of his predecessors, displaying his expertise in the diverse cycles and genres of the tantric corpus far beyond the Hevajra context. These are texts in which he has been inculcated through study and reflection, many committed to memory. His facility in repeating them contributes to the impact of his writing by establishing him as an authoritative interpreter of body mandala. Ngorchen is therefore a part of the "difference" in these acts of repetition.

ON CITATION

The Buddhist scholar monk is, in a sense, not what they eat but what they read. Ngorchen and Khédrup perform their expertise through citations that attest to their discipline and experience in studying and even memorizing canonical texts. Like mantra or *dhāraṇī* (inscribed, recited, and mnemonic formulae), citations are simultaneously "vast" and "concise."[69] They can provide a pithy encapsulation of meaning but also threaten to swell like rice in the belly. Outlining the texts of the body mandala debate through their citations has revealed connections to broader Buddhist approaches to intertextuality.

In the body mandala debate, citation is a tool to reinforce or recreate lineage ties and to recast the limits of authority to include Tibetan masters. At times, as in the case of Ngorchen citing Jetari, citations are crucial to a sense of authenticity rooted in connection to an Indian past. However, examples such as Khédrup's reference to Tsongkhapa attest to the value of citations for establishing a Tibetan present and future.

Phrases such as "Thus have I heard," "so it is said," or "some Tibetans say" cue the reader to transition to a different mode of interacting with a text. In analyzing Ngorchen and Khédrup's citations, I have displayed the manner in which these phrases signal the power of repetition to "anticipate acts of renaming" as a form of "repetition with a difference." Tibetan exegetes may claim to "merely" repeat in their endeavors to clarify the words of their predecessors. Yet polemical claims aimed at their opponents suggest that, in their resistance to the charges of fabricating or adding anything new, they "doth protest too much."[70] Learning to see these acts of "renaming" punctures the faulty and frankly unimaginative presumption that when Buddhist authors cite they are "merely" repeating or parroting the words of their predecessors. Understanding what citations do opens up new horizons for appreciating the ingenuity of Buddhist authors as well as an enhanced appreciation of how language and representation work.

When J. L. Austin introduced the category of "speech acts," language that acts in the world in the manner of the conjugal proclamation, "With the power invested in me, I now pronounce you . . . ," he missed a great opportunity.[71] In relegating what he termed "non-serious performances," like the performance of an actor in a play, to the periphery, Austin overlooked the very performances that reveal some of the most compelling insights on what language does, even beyond the spoken word. In some instances, the "non-serious" aspect of a citation makes it all the more ripe for meaning making, like a pun, as in the example of Ngorchen's use of the maxim "Just because you don't see it, doesn't mean it isn't there." Ngorchen uses this citation to reinforce his opponent's inexperience in tantric textuality, to play upon an underlying disparity in the epistemological approaches of the Sakya and the emerging tradition of Tsongkhapa, and to tease as well as chastise the opponent as someone who's supposedly a master of logic who can't see the obvious. In addition, Ngorchen uses the interplay of "valid cognition" and exegesis to define authenticity in terms of a holistic system relating yogic experience, guru devotion, and textuality as reliable sources for knowing the world.

Indeed, not all citations are serious, genuine, or authentic, nor do they by nature demand loyalty to an original. This is the case for fabricated or erroneous citations that prompt corrections like, "Shakespeare never said that" or, for the body mandala debate, "Butön never said that."[72] It is also the case in context-based critiques, like "he did say something like that, but you've got the context all wrong." Today all forms of digital and social media have amplified the sense that texts and images bear the potential for repetition beyond their original contexts. Citation exemplifies this quality of language and representation in extreme ways. As an author, I face the question of how my work might be used in the future in support of philosophies and causes I have somewhat limited control over. Nietzsche presents a classic case of an author whose work was appropriated and redeployed in new contexts to nefarious ends. And yet Derrida, with "unaccustomed bluntness," as one cultural critic observed, remarked on the problematic reiterations of Nietzsche that, "One can't falsify just anything."[73] Similar sentiments come to mind when reading Khédrup's remarks from a later text in which he denies the polemical implications of his claims, writing, "Which Path and Fruit exactly do I refute? How, before whom, and in which text do I refute it?"[74] And yet, Khédrup's longer citations of his "unnamed" opponent make the veil of anonymity even thinner than in the critiques waged before him by Tsongkhapa.

Citation is also a powerful rhetorical strategy for forcing consensus and neutralizing contradiction, making it especially well-suited to tantric polemics, a genre that, as Ngorchen shows us, invites a unique fusion of polemical and commentarial strategies. Ngorchen forces consensus in *Dispelling Evil Views* when he cites Ārya Guhyasamāja texts revered by his opponent's tradition to show how they too would be compromised if the logic of the opponent's critique were applied to them. He even cites his opponent with remarks like "Remember, you yourself wrote," dangling the threat of self-contradiction before him. Khédrup, for his part, often relies upon contradiction as a rhetorical tool for backing his opponent into a corner by creating clashes between different Buddhist discourses or different forms of a practice. Both authors also use citation to resist contradictions. For example, at times Khédrup copes with disparities between authoritative accounts of body mandala by citing sources that allow him to synthesize and reinvent the portrait of the vajra body. On numerous occasions, Ngorchen uses citation to combat Khédrup's logic of contradiction by displaying the inherent diversity of the tantric corpus. These exegetes therefore use citation to both exacerbate and circumvent contradictions.

I have touched upon some of the deeper issues in the development of tantric ritual, issues underlying some of Khédrup and Ngorchen's concerns with ritual mechanics and textual authority in the body mandala debate. In the process, I have provided examples of citational practices as reflecting mandala in the making within the varied domains of art, ritual, and textuality. For example, in invoking tantric texts such as the *Abhidhānottar*a *Tantra*, a text scholars have shown to contain material grafted from Hindu Śaiva sources, Khédrup and Ngorchen interact with broader dynamics of repetition in the world of tantric textuality. Citations gesture toward these forces of imitation, influence, and appropriation at play in representation.

FURTHER OBSERVATIONS ON CITATION AND REPRESENTATION

Citation reveals key dimensions of representation often operating under the radar; citations often conceal the constructed aspect of representations. In concluding these two chapters on citation, I remind the reader of a few additional points on representation I have unearthed in cutting the ground of the body mandala debate together with relevant examples. These reflections pave the way for the exercise I perform in the epilogue of this book, in which I engage contemporary artists and culture critics on questions of citation and representation.

Direct experience of representation matters. Ngorchen responds to the tone of Khédrup's attack by turning the weapon back on his opponent. In presenting Khédrup as a master of valid cognition who can't see what's in front of him, Ngorchen introduces and enacts the ideal of the exegete who always returns to the source to determine its meaning for themselves. He uses the Sakyapa interpretive framework of the four authenticities to posit a link between authenticity and empiricism.

Outlining Khédrup and Ngorchen's citations displays how canon is powered by a generative tension between tradition and innovation. In mapping the Guhyasamāja mandala, Khédrup reinforces a lineage of authoritative sources for the Ārya Guhyasamāja and yet diverges in correlating goddesses with *lung* in new ways. He also confers authority on some sources not universally acknowledged to belong within the canon of the Ārya Guhyasamāja, as in the case of the *Vajrasattva-sādhana* whose authorship by Candrakīrti was somewhat disputed. Examining the varied ways in which Khédrup and Ngorchen use citation reveals how canon manifests in a series of overlapping repetitions through the citation of canonical texts, yet citation is also what makes them canonical. The manner in which citations repeat requires a nuanced approach to the complex dynamics relating original and repetition.

Citations show how representations can force consensus and alienate. In response to Khédrup's tactic to leverage contradiction among sources as grounds for invalidating the Sakya Hevajra body mandala, Ngorchen cites authoritative texts (i.e., Indian sources and *buddha-vacana*) as well as his opponent's own writings (particularly on the Guhyasamāja system) to manipulate the logician into compliance. In addition, Ngorchen performs his command of the vast and diverse genres of tantric textuality to chastise an opponent he regards as possessing insufficient training and experience.

The repetitive dimension of representation lends itself to simulating continuity. Yet this very same dimension of representation often conceals subtle changes. In drawing attention to the mechanism of repetition in citational practices, the sense of origin is destabilized. The evidence that Khédrup was repeating arguments made by his teacher Tsongkhapa troubles the picture of the body mandala debate as an encounter between two solo actors. In tracing the permutations of these arguments backward and forward in time, the origin of the debate in a single text, author, or even encounter between two authors becomes more abstract.

Read as forms of repetition with a difference, citations display the potential of representations to "anticipate renamings." In invoking the authority of masters of the past, Buddhist authors set the stage for new interpretations. Framing these interpretations as clarifications of previous teachings, authors of polemics enact a broader pattern of Buddhist textuality defined as the relation of text and commentary.

Ngorchen and Khédrup also use citations to fill in the blanks where root tantras remain silent. In mapping Ngorchen's citations, I highlighted the centrality of the *Sampuṭa Tantra* to problems of context for the authors of the body mandala debate. The classification of the *Sampuṭa* as an explanatory tantra (*bshad rgyud*) of the "common" (*thun mong*) variety means that it may be brought to bear upon both the Hevajra and Cakrasaṃvara texts. The underdetermined rules of how precisely this works prompt both creativity and conflict. Ngorchen and Khédrup use explanatory tantras to construct and naturalize meaning.

In the final chapter I reveal how explanatory tantras such as the *Sampuṭa* and *Vajramālā* exemplify an important quality of Tibetan textuality relevant for classifying and interpreting both bodies and texts. In exploring a Sakyapa metaphor of the body as explanatory tantra, I expose understandings of the relationship between ritual and exegesis, text and commentary, body and mind utterly central to the task of striving for liberation "in this very body."

As Ngorchen and Khédrup use citations to negotiate the tension between continuity and transformation, they display a form of what Judith Butler termed "citationality."[75] Responding to the essentializing tendencies of contemporary approaches to the categories of sex and gender, Butler posits that citation is not just a way to repeat but also to "rearticulate" meaning. In performing gender, one adopts mannerisms, ornaments the body, and modifies contours, protuberances, hollows, and growths. However, this repetition of gender norms reveals just as much as it conceals. A drag performance destabilizes the very categories it imitates by highlighting the demands gender norms place upon all bodies to emulate an ideal. Khédrup and Ngorchen use citations to map and contour the tantric corpus and to construct a body mandala. Both are creative acts involving manifold varieties of rearticulation. In the final chapter, I explore rearticulation as a unique skill cultivated by the exegete, one who is a guide in executing crucial practices of parsing and supplementing the meanings of bodies and texts.

5

"Aligning the Dependently Arisen Connections"

The Exegete Rearticulates Body and Text

The Buddha rearticulated the meaning of the body by breaking it down into parts, such as form and consciousness, observing each to determine, "This is not mine, this is not I, this is not my self."[1] In this way, Buddhist mnenomic practices of listing and enumerating facilitate a process of breaking free of the confines of the "self" to apprehend impermanence. To repeatedly break down the meaning of the body is to "anticipate an act of renaming."[2] Embodiment, once transformed from an object of desire, becomes the precious opportunity to realize the true nature of reality.

In imagining oneself as a buddha, the tantric practitioner rearticulates the body in enlightened terms. They break down each aspect of their form and establish a divine correlate with a precise number of arms and heads displaying particular gestures and expressions. Like the brain surgery of tantric sādhana, body mandala presents an even more elaborate schema for the basic act of imagining oneself as a buddha. In the case of the Hevajra body mandala, one imagines oneself not only as Hevajra but as a celestial palace filled with buddhas, goddesses, bodhisattvas, and other deities. The goddesses, for example, may take the form of the petals of a lotus or of channels composing the cakras of the vajra body. The practitioner of body mandala repeats such correlative acts of imagination to attune themselves to the hidden potentialities of the body and to rearticulate its meaning in striving to attain liberation. In both the mental representations or imaginings of tantric sādhana as well as in textual representations, repetition and rearticulation are crucial for empowering individuals to clarify meaning.

In this chapter, I make explicit the connections between body and text to which I have gestured throughout the book to reveal a deeper connection between ritual and commentarial practice. I move beyond the ambiguity of the pun of the *corpus* to examine an explicit connection between body and text as well as between ritual and exegesis. I build upon the premise, introduced from the very start of this book, of the support (*rten*) as a shared conceptualization of bodies and representations to consider how exegetes guide us in using these supports to their utmost potential.

The body mandala debate shows how exegesis and tantric ritual practice put different categories of bodies and texts into contact, bringing one to bear upon the meaning of the other in ways that at times are deemed inadmissible and at others illuminating. As a result of this contact, both interpretive and ritual practices entail a degree of soteriological risk. For example, as referenced in the previous chapter, Ngorchen reminds his readers that bad exegesis inhibits the practice of sincere tantric aspirants, those "individuals who wish to cultivate the yoga of the four sessions," and can even land you in Avīci hell.[3] As I discussed in chapter 1, Khédrup is especially concerned with the particular risks of disregarding the boundaries between different kinds of bodies. For him, confusing "defilement" with "wisdom" and "sentient beings" with "buddhas" defeats the whole purpose of Buddhist practice.[4] Yet with these risks come possibilities for refashioning the self in enlightened terms and for creating new forms of body mandala. In chapters 3 and 4, I mapped Ngorchen and Khédrup's texts through their citations. Applying the method of "cutting the ground," I revealed how these authors are rearticulating meaning by breaking down the edifice of the tantric corpus and deploying fragments for contemplation. To repeat can be to reinforce, to maintain, or even to create the force of canon. Repetition can also catalyze a direct experience of what might be taken for granted about sources regarded as standard or canonical. Moreover, as Butler has also suggested in the context of gender norms, rearticulation is a form of repetition that sometimes destabilizes an origin.[5] In the ritual practices of body mandala, the practitioner correlates the parts of the body with the parts of the celestial palace, with the elements of the cosmos, and with the protective circle of the mandala. Through these connections, the tantric adept destabilizes the ordinary sense of self and ultimately unlocks the hidden potential of the vajra body, making it malleable for the task of accessing the profound meaning of enlightenment. In a similar manner, the exegete aligns connections between texts to create meaning.

In this chapter I focus upon the unique skills of the exegete as a guide in rearticulating the meaning of bodies and texts. Exegetes show us how to work with existing representations and make connections between them. They guide us in parsing bodies and texts, distinguishing between subtle and coarse varieties and explicit and implicit meanings. They also demonstrate how to supplement meaning by bringing one representation to bear upon another. In their use of the "explanatory tantra" (*bshad rgyud*, Skt. *vyākhyātantra*), in particular, Ngorchen and Khédrup enact new understandings of the scope of application of one text and its potential to illuminate another. They also effect subtle movements of the boundary between root and commentary. I argue that polemical encounters such as the body mandala debate are the very ground upon which the rules of exegesis are constructed and realigned.

Over the course of this final chapter, I illustrate how Ngorchen and Khédrup use the genre of the explanatory tantra to supplement meaning and to manipulate the interpretive process. I identify two particular qualities of the explanatory tantra that raise crucial questions of context for tantric exegetes: the ambiguity of how widely to apply the "common" explanatory tantra and the way in which the genre as a whole combines different classes of tantric texts. In analyzing Khédrup and Ngorchen's use of two explanatory tantras, the *Sampuṭa* and the *Vajramālā*, I highlight how these exegetes use the challenges posed by the explanatory tantras as opportunities for making the tantric corpus malleable in their hands.

In tracking the ways in which these Tibetan exegetes use the genre of explanatory tantra, I illuminate tools for coping with the perpetual tension between limitation and potential presented by both bodies and texts. I conclude by revealing the ways in which exegetes and tantric practitioners parse, supplement, and rearticulate meaning and align connections as methods for pursuing enlightenment. Crafting and naturalizing meanings proves key to the soteriological process.Through creating, reinforcing, and even moving the boundaries of the meaning-making process, they are "aligning the dependently arisen connections in the body," advancing toward the tantric goal of liberation in this very lifetime and this very body. I begin by introducing a metaphor from the Sakya tradition as a vehicle for navigating this relationship between body and text.

THE SAKYAPA TANTRIC PERSPECTIVE: THE THREE CONTINUA

Continuity has been a guiding theme in approaching the body mandala debate. In exploring the power of imagination in tantric ritual in chapter 1, I described body mandala as one technique for crafting continuity between a practitioner and their enlightened identity as a buddha. Through persistent sādhana practice, the tantric adept cultivates identity with the glimpse of Buddhahood gleaned from consecration and instruction by the guru. In chapter 2, I observed the emphasis upon the continuity of lineage in Tibetan sources, especially in Ngorchen and Khédrup's biographies; in that context, the uninterrupted stream of tantric teachings from guru to disciple across generations was the standard for authenticating particular approaches to body mandala ritual as well as the communities of practice associated with them. Biographers emphasized Ngorchen and Khédrup's continuity with their spiritual predecessors to sanction their interpretations. Ngorchen and Khédrup reinforce those connections in their tantric polemics through their citational practices. Continuity is therefore central to both tantric ritual and exegesis.

Recall that the word *tantra* itself means "thread" or continuity. According to the Path and Fruit tradition of the Sakyapa, the very tradition whose body mandala Ngorchen is charged to defend, continuity assumes a particular form in making sense of the quest for liberation. The Sakyapas parse reality in terms of "three continua" (*rgyud gsum*): the causal continuum of the foundation (*kun gzhi*), the method continuum of the body (*lus*) and the resultant continuum, the *mahāmudrā* (literally, the "great seal"). These three are understood as the cause, in other words, the "universal ground" or underlying potential for buddhahood, the path or method for striving for buddhahood, and the fruit of realizing that potential. The Sakyapas relate cause, path, and fruit through an approach of "taking the result as the path" (*'bras bu lam du byad pa*).[6] From this perspective, the enlightened nature of beings makes their practice possible and potentially efficacious. The body plays an important role in this process. In identifying the body with the path or method continuum, the Sakyapas suggest that the body is a context or process for mediating the relationship between the seed and fruit of enlightened potential.

This Sakya framework of three continua explains the relation of body and mind in tantric practice and their respective roles in the liberation process. The Indian mahāsiddha Virūpa, father of the Path and Fruit teachings, identifies the body with the method continuum in his famous text, the *Vajra Lines*: "For the method continuum of the body and so forth, there is the causal initiation with four triads, the seats and so forth."[7] This verse expresses the significance of tantric initiation rituals for embodied practice. The Tibetan Sakyapa patriach Sachen composed multiple commentaries elucidating the meaning of Virūpa's pithy text. In one of these, Sachen comments upon this verse as follows: "First, this is called the 'method continuum of the body' because the alignment of the dependently arisen connections in the body is the method that brings about the realization of the mind, the universal ground, which exists in the manner of a seed or cause."[8] The mind is the "seed" or "cause," the "universal ground." The process of aligning the karmic amalgamation that is the body with a special attunement to its subtle capacities and meanings allows the practitioner to access the ephemeral nature of the mind. Sachen further clarifies Virūpa's verse with additional detail on the nature and relationship of body and mind: "The 'and so forth' includes the meaning 'the body is the explanatory continuum' because that mind that is the root of samsara and nirvana can be realized by means of aligning the dependently arisen connections in the body."[9] In this analogy, the mind is the root of all perspectives on reality, both ordinary and enlightened, while the body provides the necessary context for realizing the mind. Sachen identifies the role of the body, commonly referred to as the "method continuum" (*thabs rgyud*), here as the "explanatory continuum" (*bshad rgyud*), the same term used for "explanatory tantra."

THE BODY AS EXPLANATORY TANTRA

In beginning to explore Ngorchen's defense of the Hevajra body mandala in the previous chapter, his use of the genre of the explanatory tantra, specifically the *Sampuṭa Tantra*, provoked questions regarding the boundaries of tantric exegesis. These questions consider the position of the explanatory tantra at the boundary between "Buddha word" and commentary. They, in turn, consider its somewhat ambiguous relationship to the different degrees of authority that mark these textual categories. Moreover, there is a lack of consensus on how precisely the explanatory tantra can be used to clarify the meaning of tantric root texts. The body presents similar challenges for the tantric practitioner striving to attain meaning. As a Sakyapa metaphor will illustrate, while body and explanatory tantra share a sense of ambiguity, they also bear a unique potential to clarify.

In this chapter, I consider the relation of body and mind from the Sakyapa tantric perspective in conversation with the metaphor of explanatory and root tantras. I argue that the ambiguity of the explanatory tantra provides unique potential to reinvent the connections between texts. In particular, the explanatory tantra creates opportunities to determine which texts can be brought to bear upon the meaning of others and is therefore deeply linked with questions of authority and the limits of interpretation. Exegetes such as Khédrup and Ngorchen exploit these opportunities to establish, reinforce, and adjust the boundaries of the meaning-making process. I begin by thinking more deeply about what it means to "align the dependently arisen connections in the body." In working through this analogy between corporeality and textuality, I illuminate a connection between embodied ritual action and interpretive practice.

THE FRAGRANCE OF BLISS: BODY AS FLOWER

I had the privilege of an audience with the former head of the Sakya order, the Forty-first Sakya Trizin, in which I introduced my research on the body mandala debate. When asked about the role of the body in tantric practice, Sakya Trizin remarked that it is difficult to purify the mind while focusing on the mind itself. In other words, by focusing on the body, one can more effectively purify the mind.[10] To illustrate this relationship, Sakya Trizin cited a famous mind and body metaphor from the *Hevajra Tantra*. In the tantra, the bodhisattva Vajragarbha asks why practitioners should perform the generation stage of tantric sādhana if the completion process is so blissful. The response vividly depicts the vital role of the body in apprehending the true nature of reality: "Just as the perfume of a flower depends upon the flower, and without the flower becomes impossible, likewise without form and so on, bliss would not be perceived."[11] The mind is the scent inherent in the flower of the body. The body is therefore a container or support for accessing and experiencing the nature of the mind.

From the outset, I have foregrounded the concept of the body as a support (*rten*) for tantric practice. The term *support* accentuates the body's identity as a space for invoking divine presence in tantric consecration. In sādhana practice, the support is the foundation for realizing one's own divine identity. The support refers likewise to bodies and representations. In yet another one of his commentaries upon Virūpa's *Vajra Lines,* Sachen teases out the analogy of mind and body as scent and flower. In so doing, he provides an answer to the question: what precisely does the body contain or "support?" As in the previous citation by Sachen, the context is a discussion of the three continua: the causal continuum of the foundation (*kun gzhi*), the method continuum of the body (*lus*), and the resultant continuum, known as the *mahāmudrā*. Sachen reframes the analogy of mind and body in terms of two categories familiar from the body mandala debate, the support and supported, writing: "The two, support (*rten*) and supported (*brten pa*), are undifferentiated like a mixture of water and milk or the mixture of earth and water called mud. What is separate becomes uniform. The container is like a flower, and the contained is like a scent. Likewise, the scent residing in the flower would be imperceptible without the flower."[12] The body functions as the support for the mind. We perceive them as one, but without the form of the body the mind itself would be beyond our reach. In these excerpts, Sachen presents the mind as subtle and elusive, an aroma perfuming the body. Through the method or explanatory continuum of the body, the practitioner realizes the mind and accesses its subtle and implicit meanings.

Ritual and exegetical action, body and text are poetically intermingled in these statements. Just as the explanatory tantras provide access to the elusive meaning of the root tantra, so the body provides access to the true nature of the mind. The body is a crucial pathway for discovering meaning that is difficult to access, for bringing to light the implicit meanings concealed by our ordinary perceptions of reality. Some Tibetan commentaries even deliberately exploit the semantic overlap of these terms, the double entendre of the root and explanatory continua (*rtsa rgyud* and *bshad brgyud*) as root and explanatory tantras.[13] In light of the important role of explanatory tantras in the arguments that make up the body mandala debate, this double meaning enriches our understanding of the relation of root and explanatory tantras and of mind and body. Through powerful analogies like those of mind and body, supported and support, and perfume and flower, the Sakyapa tantric perspective presents a deep appreciation of the unique potential of both the explanatory tantra and the body in the meaning-making process. Like a commentary on the root text that is the mind, the body provides a context for creating connections, for contextualizing, as a "weaving together" of the threads of continuity essential for crafting meaning.

The overall orientation of the Sakyapa tantric path, of taking the fruit or result as the path, suggests that the schema of three continua is somewhat fluid. This fluidity extends to the interpretation of the body as explanatory continuum. As the location for aligning connections, for weaving together accounts of reality from different contexts and different levels of meaning, the explanatory tantra generates questions regarding the distinctions between text and commentary, between explicit and implicit meaning, and even between ordinary and enlightened being.

Reflecting on the powerful analogy of body and explanatory tantra as locales for "aligning the dependently arisen connections," I take a closer look at how Ngorchen and Khédrup exploit the genre of the explanatory tantra, in particular the *Sampuṭa* and the *Vajramālā*, in their body mandala debate writings.

THE CLARIFICATORY POWER OF THE KING OF EXPLANATORY TANTRAS: NGORCHEN'S USE OF THE *SAMPUṬA TANTRA*

Ngorchen uses the explanatory tantra to establish relationships between different kinds of bodies, texts, and perspectives on reality. Recall that Khédrup's charges regarding the Sakyapa body mandala boil down to a challenge to cite a canonical precedent; for Khédrup such a precedent would be an Indian tantric text attributed to the Buddha or to one of the venerable Indian commentators or tantric adepts recognized by tradition. Ngorchen met this challenge by citing evidence from a diverse range of sources to support the Hevajra body mandala based on the Path and Fruit teachings. These sources included the Hevajra root tantra, explanatory tantras, writings of the mahāsiddhas, and the oral instructions of the guru. In chapter 4, I traced Ngorchen's citational strategies to illuminate the ways in which they legitimate the Sakyapa approach to body mandala by delineating the Hevajra corpus, tracing its outlines, and demarcating its boundaries. Ngorchen also aligns these different genres of the tantric corpus to navigate different kinds of meaning-making, explicit and implicit, those transmitted by word of mouth and in written form, to craft an essence of the Sakyapa Hevajra practice. For Ngorchen, the *Sampuṭa Tantra* played an important role in this process.

Systems of classifying the tantras exemplify the concerns with articulating relationships between different varieties of texts (and bodies) expressed by the authors of the body mandala debate. The Sakyapas classify the *Sampuṭa* as one of the "three tantras" (*rgyud gsum*) of Hevajra, and the text provides a wealth of information on the completion stage of sādhana practice.[14] Recall that the three tantras are the Hevajra root tantra; the *Vajrapañjara Tantra*, often labeled an "uncommon" explanatory tantra (meaning it pertains only to the interpretation of the *Hevajra Tantra*); and the *Sampuṭa Tantra*, a "common" explanatory tantra applied to both the Hevajra and Cakrasaṃvara cycles. In endorsing this system, Ngorchen distinguishes his tradition from other transmissions of the Path and Fruit, namely, the Marpa transmission of the Kagyupa, that do not include the explanatory tantras. The classifications of root and explanatory tantra and, further, of "common" (*mthun mong*) and "uncommon" (*mthun mong ma yin*) explanatory tantra are important for understanding the underlying structure of Ngorchen's commentarial method. Ngorchen shows relating different kinds of texts and different degrees of meaning to be parallel processes. He guides his reader both in supplementing what is incomplete and in aligning connections between representations of body mandala.

The *Sampuṭa* presents solutions for Ngorchen in his process of crafting an armor of citations in defense of the Sakya tradition. I have suggested that the *Sampuṭa* may also be at the crux of the debate, as in the example of the viśvavajra described in chapter 3. The *Sampuṭa*'s classification as a "common" explanatory tantra produces a potential clash of contexts. The ambiguity of how precisely the *Sampuṭa* might be brought to bear on the meaning of different tantric cycles, specifically the Hevajra and Cakrasaṃvara, raises questions for exegetes about the limits of interpretation.

Ngorchen applies the *Sampuṭa* in his defense of the Sakya Path and Fruit tradition of generating the Hevajra body mandala in at least three ways. First, he uses the *Sampuṭa* to substantiate the basis of this body mandala in canonical sources. He also uses the tantra's reference to the vital role of the guru's oral instructions in filling in the blanks found in other authoritative sources to validate the oral transmission of the Path and Fruit. In this vein, he writes: "In short, there is a little bit of explicit teaching of the yoga of the body mandala in the root tantra. The *King of Explanatory Tantras* [i.e., *Sampuṭa*] clarifies the meaning attained [*don thob*]. Through the explanation based in the oral instructions of the pure lama, it is possible to clearly realize the yoga. One should apprehend the main point [*gnad gyi don*] [by these means]."[15] While meaning may remain elusive within the root text, the explanatory tantras clarify. Finally, Ngorchen plays upon the ambiguity of the *Sampuṭa*'s scope of application to shake the very foundation of his opponent's charge.

APPLYING AND CLASSIFYING THE *SAMPUṬA TANTRA*

The importance of systems of classifying tantric texts to the interpretive process underlies the body mandala debate. For example, Khédrup began his allegations against the Sakyapa Hevajra system by referring to what "some Tibetans" describe in the context of the body mandala of the "mother tantras." Tantric interpreters classify texts based upon their level of profundity, the initiations required to study them, the varieties of ritual practices they inspire (in particular sexual union, real or imagined, with a consort), the deities they propitiate, and even their philosophical orientation. In some cases, cataloguers determine the degree of "profundity" of a text on the basis of its antinomian content or the degree to which its true meaning is perceived as "hidden" and demanding exegesis. These more "profound" texts often reveal esoteric meanings of the body, displaying increasingly elaborate depictions of the energetic hubs, pathways, and essences of the vajra body. The Sakya patriach Sönam Tsémo posited four main classes of tantras: *kriyā*, *caryā*, *yoga*, and *niruttatura*; he further divided the final category in three parts: mother, father, and nondual.[16] The *Hevajra Tantra*, the root of the system with which Ngorchen is most concerned, qualifies as a mother tantra of the "unsurpassed" (Skt. *niruttara*) class, as does the *Cakrasaṃvara Tantra*. The ritual practices of the *Guhyasamāja Tantra*, to which Khédrup's larger treatise is devoted, is classed among the father tantras of the "unsurpassed."

Competing accounts suggest that the scope for applying an explanatory tantra such as the *Sampuṭa* could be quite vast or very focused and even defied classificatory boundaries. For example, according to one text connected with Ngorchen, the great Tibetan canon creator Butön regarded the *Sampuṭa* as applicable to the interpretation of thirty-two tantras. The same text specifies that the Sakyapa master Sönam Tsémo applied the *Sampuṭa* to sixteen or seventeen tantras, in which case, "[in addition to the two-part *Hevajra Tantra*], it is most importantly an explanatory tantra for the *Guhyasamāja* . . . *Vajra Catuṣpitha* . . . *Cakrasaṃvara* . . . and [four others] ending in Guhya, because it clarifies their uncommon philosophical systems.]"[17] The variety in this list raises the question of whether or not all parts of the *Sampuṭa* are equally applicable to the understanding and practice of these tantras. Peter-Dániel Szántó narrowed the scope, based upon a comment from Butön's *"Extended Categorization of Tantric Classes"* suggesting the *Cakrasaṃvara* as the primary object of interpretation for the *Sampuṭa*.[18] Shiníchi Tsuda briefly assessed the state of the field of study of the *Sampuṭa*, comparing it with other tantras of the Cakrasaṃvara cyle as follows: "The relations between these tantras and the principles of classification which have been adopted by Butön and other scholars should be discussed after studying each of the tantras carefully. Nearly everything is left to be done in this regard."[19] More specifically, for the purposes of the body mandala debate, the question remains: can the *Sampuṭa* be applied to both the *Cakrasaṃvara* and *Hevajra* tantras (mother tantras) in part or in their totalities or even to the *Guhyasamāja* (a father tantra)?

Even the relationship of an explanatory tantra to the "root" with which it is connected is ambiguous. George Robert Elder claims that while the *Hevajra Tantra* is cited multiple times, the *Guhyasamāja* is the only tantra explicitly referred to by name in the *Sampuṭa*.[20] Szanto identifies the *Sampuṭa* as "a compilation from most major tantras, such as the *Hevajra*, the *Herukābhidhāna*, the *Catuṣpītha*, etc."[21] Yong-Hyun Lee likewise suggests that "the principal purpose" of the text is "to synthesize several Yoga tantras and Yoginī tantras in terms of theory and practice."[22] Both the explanatory tantras I analyze in this chapter share this quality of compendium or "anthology," of bringing different texts and even tantric systems into contact.[23] The category of the "common" explanatory tantra, designating a text shared by multiple tantric systems, accentuates the qualities of synthesis, compilation, and contact that characterize the genre more generally. The explanatory tantra therefore poses significant questions about the role of context in dictating exegetical practice.

The classificatory problems of the explanatory tantra relate to core questions of tantric textuality for making sense of the relationships of text and commentary as well as of source and repetition. I first introduced these questions by analyzing Ngorchen and Khédrup's citational practices. Here I build upon that foundation to show how the problems of the "common" explanatory tantra highlight the volatility of context for representation.

CONTEXTUALIZING BODY MANDALA: RECALLING NGORCHEN'S ARGUMENT ON THE MANDALA OF THE SUPPORT

The question of how to decide which portion of the *Sampuṭa* relates to the ritual system of Hevajra and which to that of Cakrasaṃvara looms heavy over the body mandala debate. As I showed in chapter 3, the debate is shaped in part by controversies between its authors surrounding the ritual mechanics of generating the body mandala of the support. These mechanics include correlating the parts of the body with cosmic elements, with components of the mandala's protective circle, and with aspects of the celestial palace. For example, the placement of the viśvavajra within this network of correlations was deemed especially problematic. These problems of ritual mechanics are problems of ritual context and chronology that interrogate the relationships between discrete acts of imagining the body as mandala. They are intertwined with questions about the context for describing this practice within the canonical sources.

As discussed in chapter 4, in critiquing his opponent, Ngorchen portrays the skilled exegete as a master of context who prioritizes direct experience of the vast array of tantric sources. For example, he locates a damning oversight in the logician's citation of Butön's writings. Ngorchen argues that Butön did not say that the body mandala described "by some Tibetans in the context of the mother tantras," and construed as the Hevajra body mandala of the Sakyapa Path and Fruit tradition, didn't exist in the authentic Indian sources. Instead, according to Ngorchen, Butön merely said that he hadn't seen such an explanation aside from a passing reference. Furthermore, Ngorchen suggests that the context for any potential critique by Butön may only be relevant for the Cakrasaṃvara version of the practice, not for the Hevajra version.[24] He therefore endeavors to expose his opponent's oversight and misunderstanding of context as an indication of their lack of direct and extensive experience of tantric sources. Ngorchen insinuates that his opponent's misunderstanding of context and denial of the legitimacy of the Hevajra body mandala is tied to a failure to appreciate the integral place of the *Sampuṭa* in making sense of the *Hevajra Tantra*.

THE FIVE GODDESSES AND REALIZING BUDDHA POTENTIAL: THE MANDALA OF THE SUPPORTED

Just as cakras and mandalas are expanded, classified, and reformulated in relationship to one another, the vajra body and the tantric corpus of ritual texts and commentaries are supplemented and evolve in tandem. In chapter 3, I introduced this parallel of image, text, and body by highlighting the manner in which visual and textual representations of mandala were mutually crafted. The number of deities, cakras, and especially buddha families were especially charged topics in determining the form of these representations. I revealed Khédrup's attempt to correlate goddesses with winds in the Guhyasamāja body mandala as a form of iconography in the making. These interpretive maneuvers are evidence of a process of experimentation and "renaming" endemic to the history of mandala, but also indicative of a broader phenomenon of dynamic tension informing tantric representations.

Ngorchen invokes the *Sampuṭa* on numerous occasions, together with one of its Indian commentaries, to justify the map of the body mandala offered by the Path and Fruit tradition. According to this map, the mandala of the supported, the deities inhabiting the celestial palace of the body, is composed of five cakras. The practitioner generates five respective goddesses in the five cakras of the vajra body, the body as composed of hidden potentialities in the form of winds, channels for the movement of those energies, and drops of blissful potency. The Hevajra root tantra itself describes only four goddesses, while the Path and Fruit describes five. Ngorchen refers to the *Sampuṭa Tantra* to substantiate the "production of the five main Buddha families in the center of the cakras . . . from a drop." In this vein, he cites the *Sampuṭa*'s enumeration of five wisdoms and five buddhas, identifying the pure nature of the drop with the goddesses.[25] He writes:

> As for the production of the five main [buddha] families in the center of the cakras that are like that from the drop, in the fourth part of the sixth section [it says]: "This wish to abide continuously is the pure vow of all Buddhas. Moreover, the manner which is mirror-like, likewise, sameness, like the rite of discriminating wisdom, [and] earnest activity like that. As for that which is expressed as continuously abiding, [it is] possessed of a totally pure nature. As for that, [there are] Vairocana, moreover Akṣobya and Ratnasambhava and Amitābha, abiding continuously from once upon a time, Amoghasiddhi. The amalgamation of the five nectars, the form of the drop, like the mind, totally pure, very

precious wisdom, possessed of the nature of all goddesses is explained as 'Vajrasattva' [and] expressed as ultimate bliss."[26]

The practitioner generates the primary buddha of each of the five buddha families from a drop (or sometimes a seed syllable) in the center of each cakra.[27] In conjunction with each of these buddha families, the practitioner attains a unique variety of wisdom, such as "mirror-like" or "discriminating," corresponding to a phase of the consecration process. The passage from the *Sampuṭa* adds a fifth buddha, Vajrasattva, to the set of four from the root tantra as the "amalgamation of the five nectars" or summation of their collective enlightened qualities. Ngorchen supplements the *Sampuṭa*'s description with another account of the five goddesses derived from Abhayākāragupta's *Āmnāyamañjarī,* referred to as the "cluster" (*snye ma*), an Indian commentary on the *Sampuṭa*. The *Āmnāyamañjarī,* which I introduced in chapter 4, names the five consorts: Locanā, Māmakī, Pāṇḍaravāsinī, Tārā, and Dorjé Nyema.[28] Ngorchen identifies this last goddess with Vajradhātuīśvarī, who often appears as the consort of Vajrasattva. He explains how all five families are "sealed" by Vajrasattva. Including Vajrasattva and his consort is a standard technique in mandala logic for elaborating a structure from four- to five-fold. In this instance, Ngorchen uses the *Sampuṭa* to justify this departure from the mandala structure suggested by the root tantra. In defending the Path and Fruit version, he demonstrates the way in which, for the body mandala debate, ritual mechanics and textual authority are intertwined.

I now turn to a more detailed analysis of the role of another explanatory tantra within the body mandala debate to reveal how both Khédrup and Ngorchen use the *Vajramālā* to introduce unique approaches to knowing body and text.

THE VAJRAMĀLĀ EXPLANATORY TANTRA: ALIGNING AND PARSING BODY AND TEXT

In this section, I illuminate how Khédrup and Ngorchen use the *Vajramālā* to encourage their readers to cultivate skills for parsing the meanings of both bodies and texts, skills these authors see as vital to the liberation process. I argue that exegetes show us how to use representations as tools for making sense of reality by modeling these skills of aligning and parsing as part of a larger process of rearticulating meaning.

Khédrup cites the *Vajramālā* in every section of his body mandala chapter (see appendix 2), and it appears frequently in the writings of his teacher Tsongkhapa as well. Ngorchen concludes his body mandala debate texts by discussing citations from the *Vajramālā*, although it appears somewhat out of place among the Hevajra texts to which the second half of his treatise is devoted. Khédrup and Ngorchen's citations of the *Vajramālā* in the body mandala debate exemplify the explanatory tantra's potential for bringing different ritual idioms into contact. The *Vajramālā* embodies the qualities of synthesis as an act of "placing together" found in many explanatory tantras and thereby "aligning" tantric ritual and textual systems. In addition to the ambiguity of the explanatory tantra's scope of application, this quality of synthesis creates an opportunity for tantric exegetes to align different approaches to interpreting body mandala.

The *Vajramālā* is an explanatory tantra accepted as the word of the Buddha (Skt. *buddha-vacana*) within the Ārya Guhyasamāja tradition, the tradition associated by some Tibetan exegetes with the lineage of the Madhyamaka author Nāgārjuna.[29] No original Sanskrit text of the *Vajramālā* survives except portions cited in other Ārya Guhyasamāja sources; however, Tibetan translations began to emerge in the eleventh century.[30] It is perhaps most well-known for the forty verses that expound upon the first forty syllables of the *Guhyasamāja Tantra*. These verses are cited in both Candrakīrti's *Pradīpoddyotana* and in part within Āryadeva's *Caryāmelpakapradīpa*.[31] Citation is therefore central to the identity of the *Vajramālā*, exhibiting links with larger questions of tantric textuality, in particular of both dating and reconstructing texts from their repetitions in other sources. The *Vajramālā* synthesizes multiple tantric ritual and textual systems; it has been described as a compendium or "anthology" of practices inclusive of both the Mahāyoga and yoginī tantric interpretations of the Guhyasamāja sādhana.[32] Moreover it focuses upon completion stage practices of tantric sādhana. As a result of this quality of synthesis and its sophisticated ritual focus, the *Vajramālā* contains more elaborate descriptions of the vajra body than those found in many of the other sources on the Guhyasamāja system.

The *Vajramālā* exemplifies the explanatory tantra's potential to synthesize ritual systems, and this quality of synthesis is linked to its history. It was composed during the height of Indian tantra from the eighth to the twelfth centuries, a period of complex influence and borrowing between traditions. Many of the Indian texts describing the Guhyasamāja practice, texts classed within the purview of the father tantras of unsurpassed yoga tantra (and sometimes of mahāyoga), were composed in dialogue with texts of the classes of mother or yoginī tantras. Texts categorized within the latter classes contain especially sophisticated descriptions of the vajra body in the context of completion stage practice. Khédrup therefore uses the *Vajramālā* in a manner that resonates with this quality of the explanatory tantra, bringing its descriptions of completion stage practice across tantric systems to bear upon the interpretation of the generation stage of the Guhyasamāja body mandala.

In the section on "Shifting Portraits of the Vajra Body: Citations from the *Vajramālā*" in chapter 3, I touched upon the ways Khédrup uses this explanatory tantra to synthesize different formulations of the vajra body derived from discrete classes of tantric texts. He repeatedly exploits its sophisticated understandings of the subtle potentialities of the body realized by the tantric adept. In the next section, I return to Khédrup's attempts to correlate the goddesses with elemental winds to reexamine the way he uses the *Vajramālā* to amplify the stakes of ritual and interpretive practice. I argue that, through his manner of citing the explanatory tantra, Khédrup introduces the skill of parsing as vital to both practices.

Dissolving the Body Mandala: Khédrup Parses the Vajra Body

The dissolution of the bodily elements in completion stage practices of tantric sādhana prepares the practitioner for the moment of death, when their own body will disaggregate in this way. Khédrup amplifies his argument for correlating the goddesses with elemental winds in the Guhyasamāja body mandala by interpreting the *Vajramālā*'s description of the goddesses in terms of the ritual logic of dissolution.[33] In incorporating the logic of dissolution into his project of correlating goddesses and winds, despite the fact that his treatise is focused upon the generation versus completion stage, Khédrup reminds the reader of the high stakes at play in getting the ritual mechanics for body mandala right.

Khédrup presents this explanatory tantra's correlation of goddesses with elements together with the qualities and manifestations of those elements to build his larger argument for correlating them with elemental winds or *lung* (*rlung*): "In the *Vajramālā Explanatory Tantra* [it says]: 'Moreover, the Bhagavatī Locanā abides in the earth element, in the fat and so forth of this one. The Bhagavatī Māmakī abides in the water element, the blood and so forth. The Bhagavatī Paṇḍaravāsinī abides in the fire element, heat and so forth. The Bhagavatī Tārā abides in the *lung* element, trembling and so forth.' "[34] When I discussed the significance of Khédrup's acts of mapping and correlating the goddesses in chapter 3, I focused more on his use of the logic of contradiction to make sense of arguments like this one: "How could anyone in their right mind claim that the flesh of the body [is endowed with/made up of] the earth *lung* and the blood [with/of] fire *lung*?[35] Contradiction is certainly one natural consequence of the way in which explanatory tantras, and commentarial practice more broadly, bring different systems into contact. However, here I illuminate a further dimension of his interpretation of the explanatory tantra. Khédrup builds upon his citation of the *Vajramālā* to introduce a critical skill for parsing the body and ritual practice, one that mirrors the exegete's ability to parse the different levels of meaning of a text.

Khédrup solidifies the correlation of the goddesses with particular phases of the dissolution process, writing, "In that case, there is the explanation for dissolving earth, water, fire and *lung* and so forth. At the time of the dissolution the twenty-five coarse [constituents], the potential for producing the consciousnesses dissolves. The bodily deities, the [set of] four, Locanā and so forth, are taught to be dissolved in accord with the dissolution [of] those."[36] When Khédrup refers to the dissolution of "the potential for producing the consciousnesses," he reinforces vital connections between the elements and the varieties of sensory consciousness. When the elements are dissolved, the four goddesses are dissolved.[37]

For Khédrup, developing the skills to parse the psychophysical components of the body relies upon a basic understanding of the ritual spectrum of coarse and subtle. The psychophysical composite of the body includes a range of cosmic elements from the most coarse, earth, to the most subtle, *lung*. Based on this logic, the body in conceived and grows in the womb, beginning with the most subtle and progressing to the most coarse aspects.[38] At death, the process is reversed, as the coarsest elements dissolve into their subtler counterparts along with the different varieties of sensory awareness and consciousness they support. Khédrup unpacks the signs that accompany the stages of this process in writing, "That being the case, at the time of the dissolution of the subtle elements (*khams phra pa*), a vision akin to a mirage manifests on account of the dissolution of earth into water and so forth."[39] The practitioner simulates these signs in sādhana to prepare to recognize them during the death process as indications that the moment of liberation is near. In learning to parse the coarse from the subtle components of the body, their explicit and implicit meanings, through repeatedly enacting the body mandala, the practitioner advances the goal of enlightenment.

Khédrup nuances the categories of coarse and subtle to reveal the internal stratification of the elements. Khédrup specifically reveals the category of *lung* to itself contain a further breakdown of coarse to subtle elemental *lung*: "So here is the teaching concerning the dissolution of the coarse among the many subtle and coarse [components] possessed by the four elemental *lung*."[40] Because there are "many distinct degrees of coarse and subtle for the internal subdivision of *lung* itself,"[41] when *lung lung*, the most subtle of these, is dissolved, the ultimate dissolution of the body is complete.[42] Until then, the body still, in a sense functions as a support for practice.

While everyone possesses the elements of the vajra body, only the tantric adept is able to recognize them. Through training, they develop the skills to harness the body's hidden potential as an instrument for transformation. Knowledge of the body and the ability to parse its coarse and subtle components in therefore a key dimension of tantric practice. Khédrup connects the necessity of parsing the body according to the logic of coarse and subtle with the imperative to realize the most fundamental and implicit aspect of tantric practice. He writes: "If you don't know how to make distinctions like this, not knowing how to distinguish the dissolution of the coarse and the dissolution of the subtle, how would it be possible to realize the essential point of the completion stage?"[43] While his own text is focused upon the generation stage, his consistent references to the *Vajramālā* and the logic of dissolution in mapping the goddesses onto bodily constituents, elements, and winds indicate sophisticated corporeal understandings of completion stage practice. Khédrup's articulation of the "essential point" (*gnad zab mo*), literally the "profound pith" of the completion stage, resonates with his description of body mandala as unique in "piercing to the pith of the body" (*lus la gnad du bsnun*): "The completion stage, which arises from meditation by piercing to the pith of the body, is the main cause of establishing the supreme siddhi."[44] In tantric sādhana, the practitioner uses imagination to generate and dissolve forms, emanations of oneself as a buddha. In the completion stage of this process, the adept harnesses the subtle capacities of the vajra body. According to Khédrup, attaining the full liberating benefit of a practice like body mandala is not possible without the ability to parse the coarse from the subtle and peripheral meanings from the essential point.

Ngorchen and the Vajramālā

Ngorchen uses the Vajramālā explanatory tantra to advocate for the exegete's unique capabilities of knowing both body and text, for parsing their explicit and implicit meanings, and for understanding the relationship between those different varieties of meaning. Following his intensive survey of the Hevajra system, Ngorchen investigates "methods for explaining from other tantric commentaries." Somewhat surprisingly, he devotes his energies in this final section of his argument entirely to the *Vajramālā*. In chapter 4, I showed how Ngorchen uses the quality of synthesis within the genre of explanatory tantra to neutralize contradictions, creating space for variety among interpretations of body mandala. Here, I reveal the way in which Ngorchen affirms the complementarity of skills cultivated in ritual practice and exegesis, skills of learning to discern hidden potential for meaning and to align connections among existing representations.

Through his citations of the *Vajramālā*, Ngorchen defines body mandala as the ritual practice that reenacts the underlying reality of human embodiment through cultivating the channels in the form of deities. He begins his discussion of the *Vajramālā* by referring to three different varieties of body mandala described in its chapters and identifying them with three different tantric cycles. He writes:

> As for the second [i.e., the method of explaining based on other tantric commentaries], in the sixty-seventh chapter of the *Vajramālā*, there is the explanation for applying the twenty-four sites to the twenty-four inner abodes in the manner of the Cakrasaṃvara body mandala. But in the sixty-third chapter, there is the clear explanation of the body mandala of the Guhyasamāja. In the seventeenth chapter, it is taught like this body mandala of Hevajra. So it says: "Distinction in terms of the number of cakras likewise, superior among the excellent. In the six cakras, sixteen containers; in the body, the celestial palace of deities. Just as there is union, there is abiding. Thus there is the abbreviated manner of generating the body as the celestial palace."[45]

As I have shown in other excerpts from the debate, in this passage, Ngorchen displays his expertise in multiple ritual systems and underlines the diversity within the sources themselves. He thus uses the explanatory tantra as a tool for making the tantric corpus malleable for his interpretive maneuvers.

Ngorchen also uses the explanatory tantra to demonstrate why the ritual acts of imagination performed in body mandala, acts of correlating aspects of the vajra body with enlightened forms, are essential. In so doing, he proceeds to chapter 17 of the *Vajramālā* to cite verses describing 5 cakras (*lung*, fire, enjoyment, dharma, and bliss) with 6, 3, 16, 8, and 32 channel-petals respectively, as well as an additional version of 131 channels; an interlinear note in the xylograph of Ngorchen's text corrects this number to 129.[46] Ngorchen skips the next 20 verses of the *Vajramālā*, which name all of the channels that make up the cakras. Instead, he briefly summarizes them before resuming his citation with the following:

> Those [i.e., the *ḍākinīs*] [are] the five elements [and] abide as the five wisdoms. For that reason, by all who strive, they are to be understood as the channel cakras. Likewise, wood which is in the center of water instantly increases. From that, endowed with a fruit and so forth, bestowing in this without a doubt. Likewise, the "wood" is the *skandhas.* Having increased by the water of the channels, by increasing, [there is] the perfect fruit bestowing omniscience. One cultivates the nature of the channels in terms of the nature of the aspects of the deities.[47]

Ngorchen sums up the meaning of the passage with, "As for the meaning of the first two verses, there is cultivation of the five ḍākinīs in the center of the five cakras. The last two verses teach arranging the one hundred and thirty-one goddesses in/as the channel-petals."[48] He directs the reader to the commentary of an Indian master Alamkakalaśa for a more detailed explanation of these profound verses.[49] These verses from the *Vajramālā* describe the relationship of the vajra body to the ordinary body: the channels support the aggregates, the skandhas, and catalyze their development.[50] According to this model, the coarse elements of embodiment rely upon their subtle invisible counterparts. Ngorchen thereby uses the *Vajramālā* to highlight the importance of knowing the elements of the vajra body and of understanding their relationship to the ordinary body of psychophysical aggregates.

Through interpreting the ritual mechanics of body mandala, Ngorchen makes an implicit, rather than explicit, argument for bodily knowledge. He infuses this nuanced corporeal perspective into a highly technical orchestration of source materials in defense of the Hevajra body mandala practice. For example, Ngorchen applies these verses from the *Vajramālā*, an extensive and diverse text presenting many options for relating the ordinary body and vajra body, to bare bones ritual mechanics: generating the five ḍākinīs in the center of the five cakras and arranging the 131 goddesses as the channel-petals; this is likely an allusion to the 129 deities of the Hevajra body mandala of the Sakya Path and Fruit.[51] Through careful citation of the *Vajramālā* and its Indian commentaries, Ngorchen elucidates the relationship between forms of embodiment without diverting his focus from the topic of textual authority.

The use of these explanatory tantras within the body mandala debate highlights the delicate network of relations between root and explanatory tantras as well as between different tantric textual cycles. However, the quality of synthesis of the explanatory tantra, of placing together different versions of body mandala, produces tensions as well as opportunities. Ngorchen betrays these tensions especially potently in one passage from *Dispelling Evil Views* in which he addresses how best to "supplement" the incomplete representations of body mandala found in tantric sources.

PROBLEMS OF SUPPLEMENTING AND SYNTHESIS IN *DISPELLING EVIL VIEWS*

In chapters 3 and 4, I touched upon the practice of "supplementing" (*kha bskangs*), of filling in the blanks in one source from another, by observing Ngorchen and

Khédrup's citational practices. Here I highlight the significance of supplementing as a tool used by the exegete to negotiate lacunae, contradiction, and issues of textual relationship in the context of these authors' engagement with the *Vajramālā*. The example featured in this brief section also solidifies the sense that the scope of application of the explanatory tantra is not always set in stone.

In his body mandala debate writings, Ngorchen validates the practice of supplementing meaning from the oral instructions of the Sakya lineage gurus to explain the process of generating the body mandala of the support. He does so by aligning those instructions of the Tibetan masters with the teachings of the great Indian tantric master Jetari. As I mentioned earlier, Ngor chen's two body mandala debate texts, while often regarded as two "versions" of a single text, differ signficantly in length as well as in the structure of their citations. In the longer "version," *Dispelling Evil Views* [N2], Ngorchen diverges for two folia at this point in the argument. This divergence signals an attempt to synthesize the versions of body mandala from different tantric texts and systems as well as to evaluate their relationship.[52] In *Dispelling Evil Views* [N2], Ngorchen postpones the citation of Jetari's *Sādhana of the Four Seals* found at this juncture in *Destroyer of the Proponents of Evil* [N1] to expound upon the precise methodology of supplementing. Here Ngorchen references the *Vajramālā*, *Sampuṭa*, and *Cakrasaṃvara* tantras together with the writings of the mahāsiddhas Darikapa and Ghantapa in working through potential issues of contradiction. In the process, Ngorchen reveals how synthesis, a process of placing things side by side, in the manner of the explanatory tantra raises question of the limits of the exegete's practice of supplementing (*kha bskangs*), of bringing one text to bear upon another. He writes:

> What's the contradiction in supplementing in the context of Cakrasaṃvara? If you think it's inappropriate to supplement what's not explained in the Cakrasaṃvara texts by drawing upon the Hevajra [corpus], then likewise, your own use of the *Vajramālā* to explicate all cases for the Cakrasaṃvara body mandala . . . would be invalid.[53] This is because you're supplementing what's not actually explained in the Cakrasaṃvara text from a Guhyasamāja explanatory tantra. To supplement the Cakrasaṃvara body mandala with the *Vajramālā explanatory tantra* would be wrong.[54]

This mode of argumentation is familiar from the examples of Ngorchen's exegetical techniques presented in the previous chapter, techniques that are both commentarial and polemical in nature. As in those examples, Ngorchen is neutralizing contradictions and forcing consensus through recourse to his opponent's approach to the interpretation of the Guhyasamāja. However, in this section from *Dispelling Evil Views*, Ngorchen is not merely synthesizing traditions and neutralizing contradictions. He is also drawing attention to the questions surrounding the explanatory tantra's range of application.[55] Ngorchen is not necessarily claiming that there is a problem with applying the *Vajramālā* to interpreting the Cakrasaṃvara practice.[56] In this case, the hypothetical is effective not so much because of its absurdity but because of its concurrent feasibility. The manner in which Ngorchen dangles the possibility before his opponent suggests that there is an unresolved dimension to the way the *Vajramālā* can be used to fill in the blanks in other texts.

The process of bringing explanatory tantras to bear upon the meaning of root tantras, of aligning connections between different varieties of tantric textuality, interrogates the rules for using the explanatory tantras to supplement the meaning of the root tantras. Ngorchen's exegetical moves evoke the analogous qualities of meaning-making that frame both bodies and texts within the body mandala debate. Ngorchen thereby reveals how the tension between "limitation" and "ingenuity," described by Jonathan Z. Smith in the context of canon as a "cultural process," is central to interpretive practice.[57]

PIERCING TO THE PITH (*GNAD DU BSNUN*) AND ATTAINING THE MEANING (*DON THOB*)

The body mandala provides a means for aligning connections between ordinary and enlightened forms and for making sense of the body's explicit and implicit potential. It is is uniquely swift and efficacious in facilitating progress toward the ultimate goal of attaining a buddha body. As Ngorchen reminds the reader in his conclusion, "It is necessary for the Buddha to consecrate the channel winds in the generation of the wisdom of bliss of the completion stage. Other than the body mandala, there is no profound shortcut for achieving that."[58] Ngorchen thereby endorses body mandala as the ultimate tool for ritual transformation, for catalyzing an experience of "bliss" that provides a glimpse of enlightened reality. It is a tool for locating and manipulating the subtle potential of the body in the meaning-making process.

In their writings on body mandala, and most vividly in their citation and interpretation of explanatory tantras, Ngorchen and Khédrup argue for the necessity of knowing the explicit and implicit meanings of body and text. Khédrup, for example, punctuates his argument for correlating the goddesses with elemental winds with a call to develop the abilities to parse the coarse (*rags pa*) from the subtle (*phra ma*) elements of the body. Only by learning to parse the psychophysical components of the body in this way is the practitioner able to cultivate the skills required to access the essential point (*gnad zab mo*) of the ultimate stage of sādhana practice. In a similar way, Ngorchen prioritizes the ability to discern the explicit and implicit meanings of a text alongside a deep understanding of the explicit corporeal meanings of the ordinary body and the implicit meanings of the vajra body. Both capacities for discernment are tools for the process of liberation in this lifetime and this very body. Both ritual and commentarial practice therefore suggest that the body as commentary or explanatory tantra provides a unique role in mediating access to a more profound understanding of reality.

In chapter 1, I discussed anxieties around imagination as fabrication (*bcos ma*) expressed in Khédrup's text. For Khédrup, what makes body mandala unique among mandala representations is its unfabricated quality. Body mandala plays a crucial role in "piercing to the pith of the body" in the completion stage of sādhana practice in which the adept learns to access and harness the hidden potential of the vajra body. I return to a salient passage, discussed in chapter 1, in which Khédrup describes the efficacy of body mandala as follows:

> So, if you ask, "why is the body mandala superior to the two fabricated external mandala?" [I would reply that] the distinction of the superior and inferior emerges based on the fabricated and unfabricated basis of establishment. The completion stage, which arises from meditation by piercing to the pith of the body, is the main cause of establishing the supreme siddhi. By repeatedly cultivating the generation and consecration of all the current parts as deities, the channels, winds and drops of the body become workable (*las rung du gyur*). By piercing to the pith of the body in meditation, the ripening of the effortless generation (*bde blag tu skye ba*) of realizing the completion stage becomes supreme.[59]

According to Khédrup, the power of body mandala as an "unfabricated basis of establishment," or at the very least one that is not "newly fabricated," lies in a process of disambiguating the individual components of the vajra body and rearticulating them by correlating them with divine forms. Repetition, the process of "cultivating over and over," is key to this transformation. In this way, the tantric practitioner is able to "pierce to the pith of the body," to get at the heart of what embodiment is all about. Body mandala makes the vajra body workable and brings a form of naturalness, of "effortless generation" to the fore.

Ngorchen too reinforces the naturalness of body mandala. For example, he affirms the efficacy of body mandala for advancing toward liberation by reinforcing the naturalness of the foundation of the vajra body in writing: "The five channel cakras are naturally established (*rang grub du yod pa*) in the vajra body. Having produced the goddesses and drops in the center of the five cakras together with outer husk channels as the five main deities and consorts, since one visualizes them within the individual sites within the [vajra] body, this is not a mental imputation."[60] The play of the terms for "naturally established" (*rang grub du yod pa*) and "imputation" (*blos brtag pa*) recall controversies within Khédrup's text around the mind's power to fabricate our reality; I described these controversies in chapter 1. Recall that Khédrup asked how tantric ritual acts of imagination are different from other forms of mental fabrication, of superimposing false concepts upon reality. In directly opposing the conflation of body mandala with mental imputation, Ngorchen once again playfully engages Khédrup's concerns with "valid cognition." When Khédrup challenged any intrinsic or "natural" link between bodies and mandala, he used a term (specifically *rang chas su yod pa*) to describe such a link, a term closely resembling Ngorchen's "naturally established" (*rang grub du yod pa*). In this passage, Ngorchen suggests that harnessing the potential of the components of the vajra body and accessing their natural or implicit meanings involves a process of rearticulating its form, breaking down each part to establish a divine correlate.

Cultivating naturalness is integral to both the practice and textual interpretation of body mandala. Ngorchen and Khédrup rearticulate the meaning of body and text through repeatedly breaking down and resuturing meanings to simulate naturalness. In the process, they craft the very essences, piths and meanings they also discover and clarify. For Tibetan authors navigating a delicate balance between syncretism and conservatism, tradition and innovation, the practices of parsing, supplementing, and aligning I have described in this chapter are crucial in making meanings natural.

In the fifteenth-century Tibetan context, polemics and exegesis are powered in part by the imperative to clarify the essence of the words of one's predecessors. I have examined Ngorchen and Khédrup's textual maneuvers, their artful repetition of the words of their predecessors, and the manner in which they align authors, texts, and varieties of meaning. In the process, I have revealed the creative ways in which these exegetes attain a meaning that is not explicit and pierce to the pith of what the body or text is about.

Conclusion

In my conversations with Drakpa Gyatso, the expert scholar monk under whose mentorship I produced my translations of Ngorchen's body mandala writings, we often encountered problems with translating the locative (*la don*) particle in the context of these elaborate tantric ritual acts of imagination. Was the practitioner imagining the goddesses "in," "on," or "as" the body? Was imagination a little less about the "as if" and more about the process of knowing the reality of the body to be such that the goddesses, for example, ARE the channels of the vajra body? The perspectival orientation of the Sakyapas underlies this problem of translation.

The overarching tradition of Mahāyāna Buddhism, of which Vajrayāna Buddhists count themselves a part, posits two truths, two basic ways of viewing reality. The conventional truth is the world of names and concepts that inform the ordinary conventions and confines of inhabiting the world. The ultimate truth is the way things really are, empty. To be empty is to be unconfined by concepts, by dualistic ways of perceiving and interacting with the world, and by the ceaseless grasping at forms and ideas. To be empty is to be free. The Sakyapas overlay this basic two-truth structure with an additional framework of three visions.[1] These visions describe the perspectives of ordinary beings, tantric adepts, and enlightened beings. For the tantric adept, the conventional truth is the mandala, while the ultimate truth is the union of emptiness and appearance (*gsal stong dbyer med*).[2] The practitioner understands that everything, even the body, is an appearance to the mind. Body mandala is one of many tools that tantric practitioners use to understand the true nature of reality, but the tradition preserves some level of distinction between the means and the end. The endgame of liberation involves such a radical form of transformation that the even the notion of an interior and exterior to the body is broken down. Everything becomes the mandala. This distinction of means and end is vital for understanding how representations can be useful even when they are not true, accurate, uncrafted, or natural.

In examining the seams and sutures of the body mandala debate, I have exposed a spectrum of creativity expressed in Buddhist approaches to representation. The tantric practitioner generates images from emptiness, using the mind's power of representation to recreate and realize divine identity. Biographers construct personae and brand traditions while artfully hiding their tracks. Exegetes suture citations, carefully curated fragments, in crafting a tantric corpus and a body mandala that appear seamless. Finally, in aligning connections and parsing and supplementing meanings, these interpreters craft the very essences that they clarify.

Anxieties surface continuously within these representations. Khédrup and Ngorchen betray anxieties around imagination and the negative associations of the mind's generative capacity, specifically its links with delusion and fraudulence. They display concerns with ruptures within the monastic body, especially charged in the case of polemics. They explore contradictions among authoritative sources and creatively justify novel interpretations. They set and modify the boundaries of interpretive practice itself in modeling the manner in which it is possible to bring one text to bear upon the meaning of another.

In chapters 3 and 4, I explored how Ngorchen and Khédrup use citations as a form of "repetition with a difference" to both reinforce and reinvent tradition. In particular, I looked at the ways in which they map the body mandala, creating and modifying the boundaries of the imagined body as well as the ritual framework. In parallel, I evaluated the ways in which they shape and contour the tantric corpus through their citations by placing emphasis on particular texts. In investigating the body mandala debate with attention to citational practices, I have shown how questions of ritual mechanics and textual authority are ultimately intertwined.

Ngorchen and Khédrup reveal both tantric practice and exegesis to be risky processes that repeatedly bring different categories of texts and bodies into contact. In tantric sādhana, the adept negotiates the divide between ordinary being and buddhahood through choreographed acts of imagination. In their interpretations of body mandala, Ngorchen and Khédrup both reinforce and recreate boundaries between such categories. Sometimes I think of the exegete as an architect, struggling to create windows in textuality, to create space for new perspectives without sacrificing the integrity of the structure, a challenge that, as a writer, I deeply identify with. This tension between limitation and ingenuity, tradition and innovation, underlies the forms of representation the body mandala debate exemplifies. In the final chapter, I fleshed out the thoughts on representation I have compiled in analyzing the debate by illuminating the exegete's skill in "aligning the dependently arisen connections" in body and text. In preparing for the interdisciplinary conversation on representation in the epilogue, I briefly review the discoveries about representation featured in the chapters of this book.

Representation is a tool, method, or process for making sense of reality. The Sakya analogy of body and mind, explanatory and root tantra, highlights the connection between ritual and exegetical practice in the body mandala debate. Regarded as supports (*rten*) for divine presence and transformation and as explanatory tantras (*bshad rgyud*) or commentaries for realizing the mind's true nature, bodies, like representations, provide a method for accessing profound meanings.

Representations are a context for "aligning dependently arisen connections" and for rearticulating meaning. Exegetes exploit this quality of representation to weave together existing ideas and interpretations. In so doing, they display their expertise and make the tantric corpus malleable. Ngorchen and Khédrup show us that representations are incomplete. In their body mandala writings, they draw attention to the process of supplementing (*kha bskangs*) meaning, bringing one representation to bear upon the interpretation of another. In tracing their authorial maneuvers, a quality akin to Derrida's "supplementarity" emerges, revealing the manner in which texts demand commentary.[3] Ngorchen and Khédrup invoke systems of classifying texts in ways that suggest that not all authentic or authoritative sources are appropriate to draw upon to complete the meaning of a text. In deploying citations from the genre of explanatory tantra, Ngorchen and Khédrup display underlying ambiguities and nuances of the rules of interpretation.

Exegetes cultivate skills to parse different levels of meaning within representations. Ngorchen shows us how to parse explicit and implicit meanings and to use the resources available to access the main point of a text. He cites the *Vajramāla* in calling his reader to apprehend the relationship between seemingly paradoxical aspects of the body. He underlines the connection between the highly constructed nature of the body as an aggregate of psychophysical components and the more subtle and potentially transformative aspects of the vajra body. In correlating the goddesses of the Guhyasamāja body mandala with elemental winds, Khédrup appeals to the Vajramāla explanatory tantra to emphasize parsing the body's coarse and subtle elements. Khédrup reminds the reader of the urgency of properly interpreting and performing body mandala by connecting these correlations with the process of dissolving the elements of the body at death. When the ordinary constructed body dissolves, the moment for liberation, the opportunity to attain the most profound meaning, easily slips away for those lacking the training to recognize it. To know the body is to know the world. Bodies are not accurate representations of reality. They do, however, provide a context, or support, for "aligning the dependently arisen connections," for working with existing models and for simulating better ones.

Why is it so important to examine the seams and sutures of the body mandala debate? Certainly not to unravel Buddhist meanings in order to expose an erroneous claim to truth. That would be deconstruction at its worst, postmodernism's shadow side, and, in part, the cause of its fall from favor. Rearticulation provides an alternative approach to deconstruction.

Rearticulation highlights creativity and the malleability of boundaries while reinforcing the vital ways in which limitations and meanings are bound together. In translating the body mandala sources, navigating the array of renditions of the vajra body they describe, the contours and boundaries of tantric textuality and of body mandala shifted continuously before my eyes. In this regard, I sympathize with Judith Butler's remarks on the search for the body among the rubble of evidence of its constructedness. Butler describes her own search for the body as follows: "I tried to discipline myself to stay on the subject, but I found that I could not fix bodies as simple objects of thought. Not only did bodies tend to indicate a world beyond themselves, but this movement beyond their own boundaries, a movement of boundary itself, appeared to be quite central to what bodies 'are.' . . . Inevitably, I began to consider that perhaps this resistance to fixing the subject was essential to the matter at hand."[4] The movement of boundaries, the gestures to "a world beyond themselves" along with "resistance to fixing the subject" are dynamics shared by bodies and representations. In making the most of them, we face the paradox of their constructed nature as well as the ways in which they both limit and expand the horizon of possibility. Exegetes lead the way in navigating the contradictions presented by representations (bodies, texts, images) and in locating hidden potential for rearticulating meaning.

The savvy exegete possesses skills to rearticulate meaning in a world characterized by a constant flow of representations. For the Sakyapa, all phenomena, including bodies, are mental creations, representations appearing to the mind. However, the way in which we use these representations matters. As my mentor Drakpa Gyatso pointed out, if used properly, the body provides a chance to achieve nirvana; if used improperly, the body leads to further samsaric suffering.[5] In tantric practice, the poison contains a bit of the cure. Bodies and representations are not just illusions and objects of desire; they are opportunities to overcome the greatest challenges to realizing the mind's clarity in order to see things as they truly are. A similar flow of representations defines contemporary experiences of digital worlds; the barrage of representations in competing media is continuous. Without the exegete's skills, we risk drowning in the perpetual flow of representations. Without the ability to parse, we are unable to sift through them, to recognize the ways in which they act upon us and the ways in which we in turn internalize and even redeploy them. Without the ability to supplement, we overlook the incomplete nature of representations, their demand for commentary and the ways in which they absorb that commentary. Caught in the flow, we fail to see how even when representations seem to disappear they endure in future iterations.

Rearticulation demands that we slow down to take a closer look at what representations are made of and how they are bound together. To rearticulate is to deconstruct and to reassemble repeatedly. To rearticulate is therefore to embrace repetition as a powerful mechanism of representation rife with tensions. The best exegetes train us to cultivate the ability to see the contradictory facets of representations for ourselves. They guide us to make connections and interpretive choices of our own. Following in the footsteps of exegetes such as Khédrup and Ngorchen, we become capable to use representations as opportunities to redefine the human as a movement between limitation and potential.

Epilogue

What does it mean to have a body that has been made into a grammar for whole worlds of meaning?

—C. Riley Snorton, *Black on Both Sides: A Racial History of Trans Identity*

UNSUTURED: *NOTES ON THE MARGIN OF THE BLACK BOOK*

I use this epilogue as an opportunity to showcase a contemporary exegete working beyond the Buddhist context and far beyond the fifteenth century. In doing so, I demonstrate the relevance of the interpretive skills modeled by the Buddhist authors of the body mandala debate for addressing contemporary struggles with representation. In highlighting the strategies of a contemporary artist searching for the body in a book of controversial photographs, I transition to a postmodern moment in which the intersections of race, class, sexuality, and gender assume center stage.

In his 1991–1993 installation, *Notes on the Margin of the Black Book*, contemporary artist Glenn Ligon navigates representations with a keen attunement to the tensions between limitation and potential that power them (figure E.1). Ligon unsutures the ninety-one photographs from Robert Mapplethorpe's 1986 work, *Black Book*, composed entirely of black and white photos of Black male nudes.[1] He arrays the double row of photographs in the order in which they appear in the *Black Book*, with odd-numbered pages on top and even-numbered pages on

FIGURE E.1 Glenn Ligon, *Notes on the Margin of the Black Book,* 1991–1993. Ninety-one offset prints, seventy-eight text pages, each framed: prints 11.5 x 11.5 inches (29.2 x 29.2 cm); text pages 5.25 x 7.25 inches (13.3 x 18.4 cm). Collection of Solomon R. Guggenheim Museum, New York; gift of the Bohen Foundation. Photo Ronald Amstutz © Glenn Ligon; courtesy of the artist, Hauser & Wirth, New York, Regen Projects, Los Angeles, Thomas Dane Gallery, London and Chantal Crousel, Paris. All Robert Mapplethorpe photographs © Estate of Robert Mapplethorpe. Used by permission. All rights reserved.

the bottom, and intersperses them with a double row of seventy-eight citations.[2] Placing text and image together, and framing each, he destabilizes the relationship of image and commentary. In this work, Ligon displays the skills of a modern exegete. He activates the capacity for critical interpretation in his audience and guides them in coping with the paradoxes of representation.

Ligon shows that Mapplethorpe's images can't be viewed in a vacuum; they are connected to a larger system of representation demanding commentary and critique. To contextualize literally means to "weave together." Through citation, Ligon breaks the *Black Book* apart and reframes the images, creating space for his viewers to weave together their meanings. In doing so, he pushes back against the objectifying mode of the photographs and the ways in which they fragment and decontextualize the bodies of these Black men. The citations feature the commentary of artists, critics, men who sat for Mapplethorpe, gender theorists, people Ligon talked to in bars around town, and cultural conservatives. They appear in the same order each time they are installed, beginning with Stuart Hall and ending with an entry from Ligon's own diary.[3] There is not an explicit one-to-one correlation between each text and each image. Instead, Ligon facilitates interactions between text, image, and body. He spatializes the demand for remove, prompting the viewer to alternate between looking closely and taking a step back. The exegete thereby creates the conditions for the viewer to make connections and interpretive choices for themselves. In making image and commentary equally integral to the work, Ligon also reveals how Mapplethorpe's images have absorbed some of the debates that have surrounded them over time.

In the wake of Mapplethorpe's death from AIDS in 1989, the photographer's work became central to censorship debates deeply tied to antigay bigotry. Bodies occupied the front line in these polemics around the limits of representation. The climate prompted by the work of Mapplethorpe together with other photographers, most prominently Andres Serrano, and performance artists such as Karen Finley was described in a 1990 *Artforum* article as follows: "the present terrain of battle is the body, the sexual nature of which some would choose to deny."[4] The most virulent controversies occurred in conjunction with a retrospective of Mapplethorpe's work that debuted in 1988 and began touring just months following his passing. *Robert Mapplethorpe: The Perfect Moment* included images that were contested for a variety of reasons, but much attention was focused upon representations of nude bodies engaged in or implying queer sex acts.[5] Curators were sued on obscenity charges, and some museums even canceled their exhibitions.[6] Conservative watchdog organizations like Morality in Media and the American Family Association and conservative politicians such as Senator Jesse Helms demanded the restriction of public funding for the National Endowment for the Arts and other cultural institutions supporting and exhibiting art deemed morally problematic. The defense of creative freedom transformed into a defense of sexual freedom in the volatile climate of the AIDS epidemic. For many, this was the beginning of the "culture wars" and marked a moment that art institutions continue to reckon with.[7]

Ligon is "restaging a debate" around Mapplethorpe's images in which the most prominent controversies around creative freedom and sexuality obscured the critique of their racist implications.[8] In *Notes on the Margin of the Black Book*, Ligon reveals the echo chamber effect of representations as evoking prejudices and violence from the past and also resonating further into the future. Rather than simply reifying or condemning Mapplethorpe's portraits, Ligon uses them as an opportunity to work through the charged and paradoxical nature of representation.

REGARDING CANON

In the context of canon, to be uncitable is to be invisible and illegible, to be denied a presence. Initially, in perusing his personal copy of the *Black Book*, Ligon commented upon the photographs on the margin but was concerned that this act was a form of "double erasure."[9] To deface the representations would be to efface the bodies of the Black men who posed for Mapplethorpe. To cite Mapplethorpe's images is therefore, in part, to grant ontology to his models and to create the possibility for agency. In the process of making the work, Ligon discovered the diverse and complex attitudes these men had toward their representations. He found that "to erase the complication of that story is another kind of erasure."[10] Ligon therefore took on the challenge of retaining nuance. He created strategies to encourage viewers to resist the temptation to reduce Mapplethorpe's images to a simple reification or exploitation of Black bodies.

Mapplethorpe made it into the canon of modern photography in large part because of his technical mastery in manipulating light to craft bodies evocative of classical sculpture. Some critics celebrated his efforts as acts of inclusion bestowing canonical beauty on neglected bodies. Among the citations featured in Ligon's installation are remarks by critics and by Mapplethorpe himself suggesting that the photographer strove to include Black and queer bodies in a canon from which they were largely absent. However, as Ligon illuminates, Mapplethorpe's own self-proclaimed rationale for exploring Black male nude subjects in the *Black Book* as "an area that hadn't been explored intensively" invites critique of the colonialist and Orientalist moorings of these images.[11]

I first encountered Ligon's *Notes on the Margin of the Black Book* in December 2019 at the Guggenheim Museum in New York, in a show entitled *Implicit Tensions: Mapplethorpe Now.* The exhibit showcased photographs by Mapplethorpe alongside those of artists responding in various ways to Mapplethorpe's legacy and illuminating the role of representation in crafting canon.[12] The curators presented the show not as simple testament to Mapplethorpe's influence but as a "two-way effect" of meaning-making; they highlighted photographic "strategies" for using representation in the "construction of identity," "affirmation of community," and to initiate social change.[13] However, resurrecting Mapplethorpe's images presented a new field of controversy. One critic remarked that the exhibition "which means to lionize the photographer, instead suggests that his sexually explicit images, once shocking, now look like illustrations in a textbook on fetishes, while his glorifications of black men feed into old, odious stereotypes."[14] Such critiques raise a question underlying Ligon's work: why unearth charged and exploitative images from Mapplethorpe's archive rather than allow them to gather dust on a shelf?

According to Ligon, Mapplethorpe had the "lock on Black representation" in the art world of the 1980s.[15] Mapplethorpe's monopoly on representing Black bodies drew Ligon to engage with these photographs. In including Mapplethorpe's images in *Notes on the Margin of the Black Book*, Ligon acknowledges the presence of the bodies of the individuals the images themselves represent. He addresses the place of these images within the canon of modern photography. Finally, he demands accountability from Mapplethorpe as well as from the viewers of the photographs. This task involves raising questions about the larger "grammar," to use C. Riley Snorton's term, in which images and bodies participate.[16] Representations reflect cultural attitudes; they are internalized by individuals and projected outward onto encounters with images and bodies in the world. Much of this movement of representations occurs silently, without explicit acknowledgment of the choices involved in regarding self and world through the lens of representation. Ligon's choice to cite Mapplethorpe's images is therefore both despite and because of the problems posed by the modes of representation they employ. In a strikingly exegetical fashion, Ligon cultivates awareness in his viewers of the slippery quality of representations and of the manner in which they reverberate.

"REPETITION WITH A DIFFERENCE": LIGON'S CITATIONAL PRACTICE

The multiple varieties of visual and textual citation in *Notes on the Margin of the Black Book* attest to a broader repertory of citational practice within Ligon's work. In an interview he remarked, "I'm interested in what happens when a text is difficult to read or frustrates legibility—what that says about our ability to think about each other, know each other, process each other."[17] His canvases have borne the words of Zora Neale Hurston, James Baldwin, and Richard Pryor, to name a few key figures.[18] His invocations of their words have been described as "smart and judicious acts of sampling" and as "acute engagements with the weights and forces . . . of language and image" and "not mere reverential citations."[19] He often works with stencils and oil crayon to transfer these words onto his canvases, and the soft, greasy quality of the crayons blurs the rigid boundaries of the stencils. Ligon describes how for a year he struggled with this aspect of his materials before eventually embracing it. Even on forms of visual and textual repetition employing a matrix, variations occur over a series. The blurred boundaries of the letters evoke the feeling that every use of language is a rupture from a context that bleeds.

Ligon's use of citation speaks to his philosophy on the creative process as both collective and reiterative. He regards the limits of pure "self-expression" and is more interested in taking ideas and images that are out there and engaging with them in a new way.[20] In using methods and materials that emphasize this dynamic, he challenges the idea of creativity as an independent birthing. For example, collaborators execute stages of his paintings that he eventually takes over. Ligon describes how at a certain point it became less important for him to assert total control over every stage of the process.

Artists, like curators, often draw connections between existing representations as a means to reframe reality. Ligon's citation of text and image in *Notes on the Margin of the Black Book* draws attention to the responsibility artists hold for the manner in which they set the stage for a viewing experience. For example, a citation by Richard Bolton, whose book on the culture wars documents much of the controversies surrounding Mapplethorpe's work, the NEA, public funding of the arts, and censorship, issues a call for "artists and art institutions" to "reconsider their pedagogical assumptions" and to "reevaluate our practices and reach beyond them."[21] In the context of interpreting the body mandala debate in the chapters of this book I referred to Felstiner's notion of "repetition with a difference" as way thinking about the citational practice of Buddhist authors. Recall that Felstiner writes of Celan's use of repetition as a way of "holding up something—both displaying and delaying it—for our attention"; in the translation process, these acts of repetition "anticipate an act of renaming."[22] Ligon too models the potential of repetition to cultivate attention and to signal transformation. In breaking down the *Black Book* and reassembling it, repeating the images together with their commentary, he creates space for critique and even for new meanings.

CUTTING THE GROUND

In this book, I introduced cutting the ground (*sa bcad*) as a method of mapping and analyzing citations in Buddhist sources. Cutting the ground of Ligon's *Notes on the Margin of the Black Book* likewise exposes his meaning-making strategies and the complex ways in which he engages his viewer in critical practice. See appendix C for a preliminary attempt at cutting the ground of Ligon's installation. The artist has created a somewhat open-ended experience for viewers as exegetes in the making, leaving a trail of breadcrumbs for a thorough inculcation in art, film, and culture critique. The citations do not include the original instance of their appearance. Therefore, the task of more thoroughly cutting the ground would require exegetes in the making to trace these citations back to the source and to see them in context for themselves. Struck by a particular citation, a viewer might immerse themselves in such a quest. Ligon engages his audience in this critical interpretive practice. He also shows how mastering this practice can be an asset in a world of images in which individuals are constantly making unconscious choices that seem beyond their control.

Mapplethorpe's "technically rigorous" photographs were lauded by many for their seamlessness, for molding smooth surfaces from light in a striking interplay of black and white. Ligon uses citation to exposes their seams and sutures and even to "play in the gray." Tamura Lomax coined this phrase in her study of the life of the Jezebel trope in the contemporary Black church.[23] Lomax illustrates how race and gender interact through representations in a grammar of embodiment that is too pervasive and complex to ignore. Inspired largely by the work of bell hooks, Lomax introduces "play in the gray" to describe an attitude through which individuals may choose to identify with forms of Jezebel as she appears, for example, in hip-hop culture, yet also break down and critique those representations to recognize the manner in which they are instrumentalized to oppress. Through citation, Ligon likewise juxtaposes contradictory and competing readings of Mapplethorpe's photographs in a manner that requires a viewer to make interpretive choices. I include several examples of his citations here to provide a sense of his exegetical skill.

Ligon's selection of voices demands attention to questions of who is authorized to interpret the images of the *Black Book*. The voices of the men who sat for the photographs are especially significant and thought-provoking in this regard. Ligon also incorporates the voices of artists, writers, and theorists, many of whom are Black and many of whom are queer. Mapplethorpe's voice also emerges. Ligon even inserts his own voice in creative ways (a diary excerpt, a personal ad, snippets from a conversation), reflecting on his own experience as an artist who is Black and queer. There are vernacular citations, such as a "jingle" and "photo backdrop from 125th Street" as well as somewhat anonymous voices such as "Drag Queen, patron at Sound Factory" and "Michael, patron at Keller's." Collectively, these citations accentuate the ways in which the idea of a photographic canon restricts not only who is represented in an image but also who can give an image meaning. Moreover, select citations of cultural conservatives attest to the highly polemical status of Mapplethorpe's work in the late eighties and early nineties. Through this panoply of citations, Ligon asserts his own expertise as an authoritative interpreter. He also uncovers the incompleteness of Mapplethorpe's photographs, their demand for the exegete to intervene.

From his very first citation, Ligon makes it clear to his viewer that their role is active, not passive. This in itself is a radical reversal of one of the most troubling aspects of the photographs. To allow such images to act upon you, rather than to ask what they are doing and how, is to be complicit in the violence they perpetuate. Ligon begins by drawing attention to the problematic history of the use of representations as tools for dominating Black people. He cites the words of Stuart Hall to expose the manner in which representations impact Black people's views of themselves: "The way in which black people, black experiences, were positioned and subject-ed in the dominant regimes of representation were the effects of a critical exercise of cultural power and normalization. Not only, in Said's 'Orientalist' sense, were we constructed as different and other within the categories of knowledge of the West by those regimes. They had the power to make us see and experience *ourselves* as 'Other.'"[24] Using Hall's words, Ligon engages the viewer in the interpretive work the images demand. This work includes both a critique of colonialism and racism as well as the task of making sense of how representations mediate the relationship of self and world. In contemplating the photographs alongside these citations, a viewer is lead to consider how representation involves allowing a part to speak for the whole as well as seeing yourself in an image.

The agency of Mapplethorpe's models has been highly contested. Ligon incorporates the voices of these men into his critique. They reflect upon their own relationships to the images and the different ways in which they relate to these representations in a mixture of detachment, admiration, and shame. To represent is to allow a part to speak for the whole. To be represented is to be able to see yourself in an image. Jack Walls remarks, "I could never be embarrassed by it because I just divorce myself from the image and after that it's just a picture."[25] Two separate comments by the same model, Ken Moody, suggest that he saw the images as "a good way for me to at least get to see what I look like." When he regarded the images of himself, there were occasions in which he saw himself as "attractive," and others as "a freak"; Moody adds that the image is "not something I would like to own."[26] Artist Lyle Ashton Harris, a friend of Ligon's, directly confronts the problem of agency, saying: "The whole notion that these men are in control of their representations is tired. We know what Mapplethorpe got out of it. What did these men get?"[27] With these citations, Ligon restores voices to these men and defines the issue of "control of their representations" as central.

At the same time, he displays the contradictory ways in which representations both expand and limit the horizons of possibility.

Ligon questions the reading of images from the *Black Book* as simple glorifications of an underrepresented demographic within the photographic canon. A citation from scholar Richard Dyer, for example, addresses Mapplethorpe's choice to focus only on Black bodies in the *Black Book* as a "passion and single-mindedness" in representing "non-dominant groups" that contributes to their designation as "departures from the norm." Dyer's words reinforce the fraught repercussions of such acts of inclusion: "Meanwhile, the norm has carried on as if it is the natural, inevitable, ordinary way of being human."[28] Through his citations, Ligon also introduces doubt about what the canon is and why Mapplethorpe belongs in it. As artist Thomas Allen Harris suggested to him, Ligon is "kind of killing the 'great white father" with this work.[29] Ligon documents his awareness of the risks involved in citing Mapplethorpe's images within a critical context. In the process of obtaining permission to incorporate the photographs into his installation, curator Tom Sokolowski urged Ligon, "Just explain to the Mapplethorpe Foundation that you're doing a project that celebrates the photos in some way."[30] As I discussed in the context of the body mandala debate, not all citations are "genuine." Repetition has the power to destabilize an original.

Ligon illuminates the ways in which the formal qualities of the images, the manner in which they sculpt, fragment, and decontextualize bodies, connects to broader dynamics of power, race, gender, desire, and grammars of representation. Along with their polarizing aspects, traces of the ambiguity of the images resound in some of the remarks Ligon features. These testimonies to "ambivalence" show the complex ways people engage with Mapplethorpe's photographs. Author Edmund White, for example, acknowledges the potential reading of these images as "reprehensible or somehow objectifying," but still insists upon "the power of his art to awaken within us some of our deepest fears, dreams, and nightmares."[31] Art critics and curators such as Janet Kardon remark on ways in which the formal aesthetic qualities of the images as "symmetrical, frontal, canonical photos, and removed from real life by dramatic light of high contrast" naturalize "homosexuality."[32] Kardon, who curated *Robert Mapplethorpe, the Perfect Moment* for its 1988 debut at the Institute of Contemporary Art at the University of Pennsylvania, observes that decontextualization is key to their impact and to the "sense of disbelief" they produce. However, Mapplethorpe often fragments the bodies of his subjects to present them in a classical mode of canonical beauty. Ligon introduces a critique of this "insulting and endangering" mode of fragmentation from poet and activist Essex Hemphill who denounces Mapplethorpe's replacement of holistic images of some of his subjects with close-ups of their genitalia; for Hemphill, the "minds and experiences" of these men become dangerously trivialized by such acts of fragmentation.[33]

In exposing the constructed nature of Mapplethorpe's photographs as well as their role in constructing norms and naturalness, Ligon shows how these images participate in a grammar of bodies and meanings based in abstraction. Tropes play an important role in this grammar. A citation from David Joselit suggests that Mapplethorpe breathed life into "readable" types such as "classical nudes, jungle inhabitants, athletes, allegorical figures, soldiers, and tough guys" with "power" and "presence."[34] Artist Gary Simmons calls out the troubling resemblance of these sexualized and objectifying images to the colonialist images of the "savage black man with a spear," but also reflects on a potent sense of the power of the men inhabiting this trope. Ligon cites artist and filmmaker Isaac Julien and scholar Kobena Mercer's remarks to unveil the complex maneuvers that make the illusions of power and presence in the photographs possible: "Mapplethorpe appropriates the conventions of porn's racialized codes of representation, and by abstracting its stereotypes into 'art,' he makes racism's phantasms of desire respectable."[35] Such tropes perpetuate a pattern of recognition and projection and accrue force through their repetition. Ligon offsets this force by drawing attention to the way in which tropes work to compel and to oppress, to create legibility and visibility and to deny it.

Ligon pushes back against the unexamined deployment of language and images and asks his viewer to regard processes of naturalizing difference. A citation from artist and polymath Henry Louis Gates Jr. describes race as "the ultimate trope of difference because it is so very arbitrary in its application." Gates observes: "Yet we carelessly use language in such a way as to will this sense of natural difference into our formulations."[36] As an exegete, Ligon therefore trains his viewer to recognize how representations do what they do. His citational strategies attest to the capacity of representation to reveal anxieties that take shape as subterranean desires, fears of "miscegenation," and dread of epidemic. Cumulatively, the force of Ligon's reiterative practice shows how, despite or perhaps even because of their abstracted, fragmentary, and repetitive qualities, representations have real implications for bodies in the world.

In shaking the foundations of the representational framework and its accompanying grammar of bodies, Ligon indicates a web of disparities and injustices that thwart the potential of Mapplethorpe's portraits to serve as unilateral testaments to identity and community. Among the most disturbing of Ligon's citations is a remark by Mapplethorpe that attests to dire inequities resulting from racism: "Most of the blacks don't have health insurance and therefore can't afford AZT. They all died quickly, the blacks. If I go through my Black Book, half of them are dead."[37] To be invisible and illegible, to be fragmented and abstracted, is to lack recourse to judicial and economic power and to medical care. The exegete reveals how representations have the power to both grant and to obscure presence; representations can re-present an absence.

"NOTES ON THE MARGIN": LIGON AS ARTIST AND EXEGETE

In a 2021 interview, Ligon emphasized "the peculiar position of being marginal and central," a theme evoked in his work across media, including black neons, stenciled canvases, and multimedia installations.[38] In *Notes on the Margin of the Black Book*, Ligon upends the hierarchy of margin and center and interrogates the ways in which representations construct the category of Blackness. With his title, Ligon asks the viewer what his act of writing on the margin means. He also references his own position as an artist who is both Black and queer in myriad ways, citing a personal ad he placed and snippets of his conversations, including an exchange with "Drag Queen, patron at Sound Factory," who assumes he is Mapplethorpe. The words of other Black artists also speak to Ligon's position as an artist working within the limits of representations embedded in tropes of domination. For example, Ligon cites Toni Morrison reflecting on "blackness" as a "metaphorical shortcut" she finds unreliable: "I am a black writer struggling with and through a language that can powerfully evoke and enforce hidden signs of racial superiority, cultural hegemony, and dismissive 'othering' of people and language which are by no means marginal or already and completely known and knowable in my work."[39] Ligon shows how looking closely at representations can prompt the realization there is no there there. Citing Stuart Hall's reflections on "black" as an "unstable identity, psychically, culturally and politically" and "something constructed, told, spoken, not simply found," the artist as exegete exposes the constructed nature of representations and expresses their limits.[40] Having collected thoughts on the meaning of the photographs from theorists, models, bartenders, artists, and friends, Ligon provides the final citation from his own diary, 1/24/93: "Left Mapplethorpe on the bar at Sound Factory and danced for hours with Lyle."[41]

Reading Mapplethorpe's images in 2021 from within yet another epidemic that has pronounced race and class differentials and in light of #BlackLivesMatter, the dangers of representing bodies as vulnerabilities as well as the perils of lived vulnerability are undeniable. In "Blackness and the Trouble of Transvisibility," Che

Gossett asks, "Who gets to assume a body? Who gets to assume the integrity and security of that body?"[42] Body, text, and image are entangled in these contemporary questions of representation. Ligon summons the presence of the men who sat for Mapplethorpe through their words and images and also signals their absence, in the manner that "blackness ghosts and haunts the normative, the way it exceeds representational fixity."[43] In *Notes on the Margin of the Black Book*, Ligon harnesses the power of representation and turns it back on itself; or, in tantric terms, he uses a bit of poison in the cure. He breaks down and reassembles the *Black Book* in a manner that encourages his readers to do the same. Like the Buddhist authors whose authorial maneuvers and citational strategies have been the main subject of my book, Ligon is a guide in navigating the paradoxes of representation and in making interpretive choices, choices that are part of being human.

"ALIGNING THE DEPENDENTLY ARISEN CONNECTIONS"

I introduced the concept of "aligning the dependently arisen connections" in chapter 5 to describe the unique ways in which, for Tibetan authors of the Sakyapa tradition, the body functions as a context for realizing the mind's true nature and the true nature of reality. Like searching for meaning in a cryptic tantric root text or the condition of embodiment in the present moment, aligning the dependently arisen connections brings attention to the ways in which all representations, a category that for Buddhists includes bodies, texts, and images, demand commentary. This metaphor proved useful for making sense of the attitudes toward body and text that took shape in the body mandala debate. It helped to describe the manner in which Khédrup and Ngorchen placed texts side by side through their citations, weaving together these textual precedents in innovative ways to generate meaning.

The metaphor of "aligning the dependently arisen connections" also expresses the discipline of the tantric practitioner enacting tantric sādhana. As I have shown, repetition is a powerful tool for making the tantric corpus malleable in both ritual and commentarial contexts. In repeatedly performing ritual sequences, the practitioner of body mandala breaks down the body and rearticulates its parts as divine. Through these repetitions, the adept learns to access the channels, winds, and drops of the vajra body and strives to attain a glimpse of buddhahood and ultimately a buddha body. In a similar manner, the tantric exegete repeats the words of predecessors, breaking down the edifice of the tantric corpus and reassembling the boundaries of the meaning-making process. As I have argued in the preceding chapters, representations are crucial for such tantric approaches to expanding the horizon of possibility, even in the face of persistent tensions between ordinary and enlightened forms and between tradition and innovation. Representations partake of the urgency of pursuing enlightenment here and now.

To return to the question posed at the beginning of this book: why use representations if they are not true? I conclude by proposing a few answers gleaned from these conversations with the exegetes of fifteenth-century Tibet and of the postmodern age. Representations are how we think and make sense of the world. They are the language we use and the images we circulate. Training to become better exegetes involves using representations to attune ourselves to the ways in which meanings are created in tension with limitation. Representations are not "who we are" but proxies for who we are and who we aim to become. Wielded properly, they are tools for defining and interpreting our experiences. Representations provide a context for rearticulating meaning.

Exegetes weave together existing ideas and interpretations and recontextualize them. They create and neutralize contradictions and negotiate lacunae. They parse different levels of meaning. In breaking down the intricacies of how to correlate self with representation, exegetes display the mediating capacity of representations to be of use for liberatory and rearticulatory projects and as tools for realization and transformation. As exegetes in the making, we accept the challenge presented again and again by representations as evidence that our work is not yet done.

Appendix A

"Cutting the Ground" (*sa bcad*) of Ngorchen's body mandala text, *Destroyer of the Proponents of Evil Through Eliminating Objections to the Hevajra Body Mandala* (*Kye'i rdo rje'i lus kyi dkyil 'khor la rtsod spong smra ba ngan 'joms*) (N1)

Part I. (548.2) Explaining the objections [to the Hevajra body mandala]

(548.2–549.1) synopsis of the "logician" (*rtog ge ba*)'s position[1]

the "logician" citing "some Tibetans" on body mandala of the mother tantras

(548.3–.4) "some Tibetans" citing Butön[2]

(548.5–549.1) Butön citing Nagpopa's *Saṃvara-vyākhyā* (*Sdom pa bshad pa*)[3]

The logician's assessment

Part II. (549.1) Ascertaining their rejection

1. (549.2) **Rejecting the argument concerning the body mandala of the support (*rten gyi lus dkyil*)**

1A. (549.2) developing flaws in word

(549.2) reference to Butön's interpretation of the *Yoginī-saṃcāra* (*Rnal 'byor ma kun spyod*)[4] and the commentary on Nagpopa's sādhana (*Nag po pa'i sgrub thabs kyi 'grel pa*)[5]

(549.3) re-citing Butön (see 548.4, i.e., "the logician" citing "some Tibetans" citing Butön)

(549.4) re-citing one line from "the logician" citing "some Tibetans" on body mandala of mother tantras (549.4)

(549.4–.5) "further along in the same text" (*zhes pa'i sogs khong nas*)

(549.5) reference to *Sampuṭa Tantra*

1B. (549.6) entering into flaws in meaning

(549.6) re-citing Butön (see 548.4 & 549.3) and providing hidden meaning

(549.6–550.3) Abhayākaragupta[6]

(550.5–6) "the third of the sixth of the *Sampuṭa*" (*Dpal sam pu ta'i brtag pa drug pa'i gsum pa*)[7]

(551.3–552.1) Lopön Dralé Namgyel's (Jetari's) *Sādhana of the Four Seals* (*Phyag rgya bzhi yi sgrub thabs* / Skt. *Caturmudrā-sādhana*)[8]

(552.2) abbreviated reference to citation from 548.2 in clarifying Butön's intent

2. (552.3) Rejecting the argument concerning the body mandala of the supported (*brten pa lus dkyil*)

2A. (552.4) rejecting the argument of the disjunction of the number of gods of the outer circle (*phyi dkyil*) and the body mandala (*lus dkyil*)

(552.5 & .6) reference to Darikapa's five and thirteen-deity Cakrasaṃvara sādhana (*grub chen dha ri ka pa'i bde mchog lha lnga dang bcu gsum pa'i sgrub thabs*) (see below)

(552.6–554.3) *Sri Cakrasaṃvara-sādhana tattvasaṃgraha* (referenced here as *Sgrub thabs de kho na nyid bsdus pa*)[9]

(554.3) reference to the *Cakrasaṃvara Samvarodaya sādhana* (*Bde mchog sdom 'byung gi sgrub thabs*)[10]

(554.4–5) chapter 13 of *Samvarodaya Tantra* (*Sdom pa 'byung pa'i rgyud*)[11]

(554.5–555.2) the commentary on that *Samvarodaya Tantra*[12]

2B. (555.3) rejecting the argument of the absence of deities common to inner and outer

(555.3) re-cites portion of the "logician's" claim from 548.6

(555.3) reference to Tilopa's sādhana of the five-deity Cakrasaṃvara (*Bde mchog lha lnga'i sgrub thabs*)

(554.4–557.4) *The Wish-Fulfilling Jewel Sādhana* (*Sgrub thabs yid bzhin nor bu*)[13]

(557.5) reference to the Buddhakapala sādhana taught in the *Cakrasaṃvara Abhidhānottara* (*Bde mchog mngon brjod bla mar gsungs pa'i sang rgyas thod pa'i sgrub thabs*)

(557.6–?559.2) chapter 26 of that tantra (*rgyud de'i le'u nyi shu rtsa drug pa*)[14]

2C. (559.3) rejecting the argument of not distinguishing the body mandala (*lus dkyil*) and the arraying of deities on the body (*lus la dgod pa*)

(559.3) re-cites portion of the "logician's" claim from 548.6

(559.4–5) "the tantra of the six-faced (one)" (*Gdong drug gi rgyud*)[15]

(559.6–560.1) Dorjé Drilbu (Ghantapa/Ghaṇṭapāda)[16]

(560.1) Ācārya Prajñārakṣita[17]

(560.2–3) Lopön Drönma Chen's school's explanation of the Hevajra body mandala

3. (560.6) Rejecting the argument that it (the body mandala) is not contained in the tantras or Indian sources

(560.6–561.1) citing the "logician"

(561.1) citing Rikpé Wangchuk[18]

3A. method of explaining from Hevajra commentaries

3Ai. (561.2) Explaining from the tantra and oral instructions

(561.3) Hevajra root tantra[19]

(561.4–562.1) third chapter of "the sixth" (*drug pa'i rab byed gsum mar*) of Saṃpuṭa explanatory tantra[20]

(562.2–5) chapter 4 of "the first" (*dang po'i rab byed bzhi par*)[21]

(562.6–563.2) in "the fourth cluster" (*snye ma bzhi par*)[22]

(563.3) refers back to citation on 562.5

(563.4–564.1) the fourth of the sixth section (*brtag pa drug pa'i bzhi par . . .*)[23]

(564.1–2) the cluster of commentary on that (*de'i 'grel pa snye mar*)[24]

(564.3) the fourth of the first section (*brtag pa dang po'i bzhi par*)[25]

(564.4) the cluster of commentary on that (*de'i 'grel pa snye mar*)[26]

(565.1) further along in this text (*lung de'i rjes kho na la*)[27]

(565.3) condensed teaching of the body mandala of the introduction of the Vajrapañjara explanatory tantra . . . in chapter 7 (*bshad pa'i rgyud rdo rje gur gyi gleng gzhi'i skabs su lus dkyil mdor bstan tsam 'byung la . . . le'u bdun par*)[28]

(565.4) in chapter 8 (of the *Vajrapañjara*)

(565.5–6) reference to oral instructions of Virūpa

(565.6) reference to the "condensed path" (*lam bsdus pa*)[29]

3Aii. (565.6) The commentarial method by the other mahāsiddhas

3Aiia. Nagpopa's position

(566.1–566.5) Nagpopa

(567.1–567.3) The commentary of the vajra song (*rdo rje'i glu'i 'grel pa*)

(567.4–5) "in the subsequent tantra" (*rtsa rgyud phyi mar* Skt. *Uttaratantra*)[30]

(567.5) the great commentary of Nāropa (*na ro 'grel chen*)[31]

3Aiib. Dralé Namgyel's (Jetari's) position

3Aiib1. (568.1) the scriptural explanation

Dralé Namgyel (568.1–570.1)[32]

3Aiib2. (570.1) **uncovering doubts in relation to that**

(570.3) Dārikapa[33]

(570.3–.4) Ācārya Tathāgatavajra (*slob dpon de bzhin gshegs pa'i rdo rje*)[34]

(571.3–.4) chapter 8 of the *Vajrapañjara Tantra*

(572.1) reference to the "Ornament of the Tent" (*gur rgyan*) by the venerable precious second Vajradhara (*rje btsun rin po che rdo rje 'chang gnyis pa*)[35]

3Aiic. (572.2) Indrabhūti's position

(572.2–573.3) the commentary on the *Sampuṭa* by King Indrabhūti (*mi'i dbang po in dra bhu ti'i zhabs kyi sam pu ta'i 'grel*)[36]

3Aiid. (573.4) **Dorjé Nyingpo's (Vajragarbha's) position**

(573.4–575.4) the bodhisattva Vajragarbha's commentary (*byang chub sems dpa' rdo rje snying po'i 'grel par*)[37]

(575.6–576.1) The prophecy by Vajrapāṇi in the commentary on the praises of Cakrasaṃvara (*phyag na rdo rjes bde mchog bstod 'grel du lung bstan te*)

3B. (576.1) Method of explaining from other tantric commentaries

(576.2) reference to chapters 63 and 67 of the *Vajramālā*[38]

(576.3–577.6 & 577.1–.3) chapter 17 of the *Vajramālā*[39]

(577.4–5) reference to Alamkakalaśa's commentary on the *Vajramālā*[40]

(577.5–6) "from that same chapter" (*le'u de nyid las*)[41]

Appendix B

"Cutting the Ground" (*sa bcad*) of chapter three of Khédrup's *Ocean of Attainment of the Guhyasamāja Generation Stage* (*Gsang 'dus bskyed rim dngos grub rgya mtsho*)[42]

THE DETAILED EXPLANATION OF THE MANNER OF GENERATING THE BODY MANDALA [233.6]

I. (234.1) Refuting the tradition of others

(234.1) Lopön Dorjé Drilbupa (Ācārya Ghantapa/Ghaṇṭapāda)[43]

(238.6) Pakpa Lujang (Nāgabodhi)[44]

(239.1) Vajramālā explanatory tantra (*Bshad rgyud rdo rje 'phreng ba*)[45]

(239.2) "some Tibetan lamas of the Guhyasamāja say" (*bod kyi 'dus pa ba'i bla ma kha cig na re*)

(239.2–.3) *Piṇḍī-kṛta* (*Mdor byas*)[46]

(239.5–.6) reference to *Piṇḍī-kṛta* and to Vajramālā explanatory tantra

(240.1–.2) reference to *Samāja sādhana vyavasthole* [*sthāli*] (*Rnam gzhag rim pa*)[47]

(240.2–.3)[48] and (240.4–.5) *Piṇḍī-kṛta*[49]

(240.6–241.1) *Samāja sādhana vyavasthole* [*sthāli*] and its "connections" (*mtshams sbyor*)[50]

(242.1) reference to *Piṇḍī-kṛta*

(242.3) both the *Samāja sādhana vyavasthole* [*sthāli*] and the *Pradīpoddyotana* (*Sgron gsal*) quote the *Vajramālā*[51]

(243.1–.2) *Piṇḍī-kṛta*[52]

(243.2–.3) *Samāja sādhana vyavasthole* [*sthāli*][53]

(243.4) chapter 8 of the (Guhyasamāja) root tantra (*Rtsa rgyud kyi le'u brgyad pa*)[54]

(243.4) reference to *Sūtra-melāpaka* (*Mdo bsres*)[55]

(243.4–244.4) the commentary on that from the *Pradīpoddyotana* (*de'i 'grel pa sgron gsal las*)[56]

(244.4–.5) *Piṇḍī-kṛta*[57]

(245.1) reference to previously cited root tantra

(245.3) reference to previously cited *Pradīpoddyotana*

(246.4) Candrakīrti's *Vajrasattva-sādhana* (*Dpal ldan zla ba grags pas rdo rje sems dpa'i sgrub thabs*)[58]

(246.6–247.1) Vajramālā explanatory tantra[59]

(248.1) reference to *Sampuṭa Tantra*[60]

(248.2) reference to *Piṇḍī-kṛta*

(248.3–.4) *Vajrasattva-sādhana*

(248.4) *Piṇḍī-kṛta sādhana* (*sgrub thabs mdor byas*)

(248.5–.6) The analogies in the *Vajrasattva-sādhana* (*Rdo rje sems dpa'i sgrubs thabs kyi dpe' dag pa rnams*)

(248.6–249.1) *Piṇḍī-kṛta*

(249.1–.2) the "garland commentary" (*'Grel pa rin 'phreng*)[61]

(249.2) Vajramālā explanatory tantra[62]

(249.3) "Some unlearned Tibetans say" (*bod kyi ma sbyangs pa kha cig na re*)

(249.4–.5) *Samāja sādhana vyavasthole* [*sthāli*][63]

(249.5–.6) *Guhyasamāja Uttaratantra* (*'Dus pa'i rgyud phyi ma*)

(250.1–.2) Vajramālā explanatory tantra[64]

II. (250.4) Establishing my own tradition

A. (250.5) the general explanation of the manner of establishing the body mandala of the support and the supported (*lus rten dang brten pa'i dkyil 'khor*)

(251.3) re-citing Lopön Dorjé Drilbupa (Ācārya Ghantapa/Ghaṇṭapāda) from 234.1

(251.5-.6) Lopön Dorjé Drilbupa (Ācārya Ghantapa/Ghaṇṭapāda)

(253.6–254.1) *Sūtra-melāpaka*

(254.2) Reference to *Vajramālā Tantra* (*Rgyud rdor 'phreng*) and *Samāja sādhana vyavasthole* [*sthāli*]

(254.6–255.1) "Some Tibetans say, 'in the many body mandalas of mother tantras . . ." (*bod dag gis ma rgyud kyi lus dkyil mang por*)

(255.2–.3) Butön Rinpoche on the *Saṃvara-vyākhyā* (*bu ston rin po ches sdom pa bshad par*)[65]

B. the detailed explanation of generating any deity from any seed syllable on any place on the body [255.5]

(255.6–256.4) *Vajramālā Tantra* (*Rgyud rdor 'phreng*)[66]

(256.5) "A few lamas of the past" (*bla ma nga ma mkha' cig*)

(256.6[67] and 257.1[68]) *Vajramālā Tantra* (*Rgyud rdor 'phreng*)

(257.4–258.6) *Piṇḍī-kṛta*[69]

(259.1) repeats one line from *Piṇḍī-kṛta* quote [259.1]

(259.3) *Vajramālā Tantra* (*Rgyud rdor 'phrengs*)[70]

(259.3) *Vajrasattva-sādhana*[71]

(259.4) *Vajrasattva-sādhana*[72]

(259.5–.6) reference to *Pradīpoddyotana* and "the garland of perfect yoga" (*Rnal 'byor dzogs 'phreng*) (refers to *Niṣpannayogāvalī*)[73] and *Vajrasattva pūja vidhi* (*Nag po pa'i rdo rje sems dpa'i mchod cho ga rnams*)[74] and the explanation from the *Vajra hṛdaya alaṃkāra Tantra* which accords with the *Guhyasamāja* (*'dus pa'i phyogs mthun kyi rgyud rdo rje snying po rgyan gyi rgyud las kyang bshad pas*)[75]

(259.6) reference to the Jñānapāda tradition (*Ye shes zhabs lugs*) & "Tibetan lamas of the past" (*bod kyi bla ma snga ma dag*)

(260.1) the Ārya tradition (*'Phags pa yab sras kyi gzhung*) and
Pradīpoddyotana (*Rab tu sgron gsal*) and
Niṣpannayogāvalī (*Rnal 'byor rdzogs 'phreng*)[76] and
the "garland commentary" (*'Grel pa rin 'phreng*)[77]

(260.2) reference to *Vajra-hṛdaya-alaṃkāra Tantra* (*Rdo rje snying po rgyan gyi rgyud*) and the texts of the Jñānapāda tradition (*Ye shes zhabs lugs kyi gzhung rnams*)

(260.2) Nakpo Damtsik Dorjé (Kṛṣṇasamayavajra)[78] and "Tibetans" (*bod dag*)

(260.3) *Vajrasattva-sādhana*

(260.3–.4) the commentary on this by Līlāvajra (*de'i 'grel pa li la ba dzras mdzad par*)[79]

(260.5–.6) Vajramālā explanatory tantra

(261.2) *Vajramālā Tantra* (*Rgyud rdor 'phreng*)[80]

(261.4) reference to chapter 9 of the *Cakrasaṃvara Abhidhānottara Tantra* (*bde mchog gi lus dkyil mngon brjod kyi le'u dgu pa*)

(261.5) the case of Luipa and Ghantapa (*La'u Dril sogs skabs*)

(261.6) the explanation from the *Abhidhānottara* (*Mngon brjod nas bshad pa*)[81]

Appendix C

PRELIMINARY MAP OF GLENN LIGON'S *NOTES ON THE MARGIN OF THE BLACK BOOK*

Images

Robert Mapplethorpe[82]

Citations

Stuart Hall[83]
Henry Louis Gates Jr.
Richard Dyer
James Baldwin
Isaac Julien and Kobena Mercer
Alan Hollinghurst
Ingrid Sischy
Thomas Yingling
David Joselit
Edmund White
Toni Morrison
Richard Dyer
Walter Annenberg
Rita Burke
Hilton Kramer

Janet Kardon
Joshua P. Smith
Carol Vance
James Baldwin
Unidentified voice in *Paris is Burning*
Trinh T. Minh-ha
Juan Sanchez
Robert Mapplethorpe
Essex Hemphill
Kobena Mercer
bell hooks
Gary Simmons
Photo backdrop, 125th St.
Judith Butler
Thomas Allen Harris
Tom Sokolowski
Roland Barthes
Ntozake Shange
Jane Gaines
Marlon Riggs
Jingle
Jack Walls
Robert Mapplethorpe
Ingrid Sischy
Janet Kardon
Stuart Morgan
Milton Thorne
David Joselit
Essex Hemphill
Kobena Mercer
Frantz Fanon
David Joselit
Michael, patron at Keller's
Judith Butler
Harry Mapplethorpe
Jane Gaines
bell hooks
Bill T. Jones
Cliff Chase

Personal Ad
Hilton Als
Essex Hemphill
James Baldwin
Robert Mapplethorpe
Janet Kardon
Alan Hollinghurst
Christian Walker
Lyle Ashton Harris
Isaac Julien and Kobena Mercer
Robert Mapplethorpe
Ken Moody
Jack Walls
Bill Joseph
Drag Queen, patron at Sound Factory
Fabian Thomas
Greg, bartender at Keller's
Jack Walls
Ken Moody
Ken Moody
Essex Hemphill
Audrey Lorde
Greg Tate
Diary, 1/24/93

Notes

INTRODUCTION

1. The term *subtle body* is often used to describe these more elusive aspects of human potentiality. As the term is linked with movements that have decontextualized Asian religious traditions, I choose not to employ it in this book. Later in this introduction, I provide further detail on my use of the term *vajra body*.
2. To explore this style of "autotheory" within larger stylistic trends in art, philosophy, and criticism, see Lauren Fournier, *Autotheory as Feminist Practice in Art, Writing, and Criticism* (Cambridge, MA: MIT Press, 2021).
3. To "comment" (*'grel ba*) is to "clarify" (*gsal ba byed*), to make easier to understand (*go sla ba*), and to unravel (*bkrol*). See entries for *'grel ba* and the related *bkrel ba* in *Bod rgya tshig mdzod chen mo* (Pe cing: Mi rigs dpe skrun khang, 2003), 1:85, 515. I am indebted to an anonymous reviewer for reminding me of this etymology. See also thlib.org.
4. Yael Bentor has been influential in highlighting the dual role of "supports" (*rten*) as body and image in tantric ritual practice and in analyzing paradoxes around the consecration of these vessels in the writings of tantric authors. See her introduction for an overview on these topics. Yael Bentor, *Consecration of Images and Stūpas in Indo-Tibetan Tantric Buddhism* (Leiden: Brill, 1996). See also Janet Gyatso, "Image as Presence: The Place of the Work of Art in Tibetan Religious Thinking," in *The Newark Museum Tibetan Collection III: Sculpture and Painting*, ed. Valrae Reynolds, Amy Heller, and Janet Gyatso (Newark, NJ: Newark Museum, 1986), 30–35.

   For a study of the analogy of body and image in the tantric consecration rites of Newar Buddhism, see Alexander von Rospatt, "Remarks on the Consecration Ceremony in Kuladatta's *Kriyāsaṃgrahapañjikā* and Its Development in Newar Buddhism," in *Hindu and Buddhist Initiations in Nepal and India*, ed. Astrid Zotter and Christof Zotter (Wiesbaden: Harrassowitz, 2010), 199–262.
5. On the complex dynamics and polemics around the use of images in the history of Christianity, see Hans Belting, *Likeness and Presence: A History of the Image Before the Era of Art*, trans. Edmund Jephcott (Chicago: University of Chicago Press, 1994).
6. On the Sanskrit terminology for images, see Robert DeCaroli, *Image Problems: The Origin and Development of the Buddha's Image in Early South Asia* (Seattle: University of Washington Press, 2015), 59–66. DeCaroli's study highlights complex attitudes toward images within South Asian

Buddhism and makes connections with other Indic traditions. He explores themes of image "aversion" and "appeal" that resonate with my own interests in the paradoxical nature of representations and their role in Buddhist meaning-making.

7. For examples of such debates around the status of "supports" *(rten)* in the ritual context, see Bentor, *Consecration of Images and Stūpas.*
8. Ngor chen kun dga' bzang po, *Kye'i rdo rje'i lus kyi dkyil 'khor la rtsod spong smra ba ngan 'joms* [*Destroyer of the Proponents of Evil Through Eliminating Objections to the Hevajra Body Mandala*] in *gsung 'bum,* Kun dga' bzang po. *Ngor chen kun dga' bzang po'i bka' 'bum,* comp. Bsod nams rgya mtsho and reproduced from the Sde dge block prints (Dehra dun: photomechanical print from a set of prints from the Sde dge dgon chen blocks [W11577]) 1:545–580.

   ______, *Kye rdo rje'i lus kyi dkyil 'khor la rtsod spong lta ba ngan sel* [*Dispelling Evil Views of the Hevajra Body Mandala*] in *gsung 'bum,* Kun dga' bzang po, 1:580–625.
9. Mkhas grub rje dge legs dpal bzang po (1385–1438), *Gsang 'dus bskyed rim dngos grub rgya mtsho* [*Ocean of Attainment of the Guhyasamāja Generation Stage*] in New Zhol par khang edition of *gsung 'bum,* Mkhas grub rje *(zhol),* TOH 5481 (New Delhi: Mongolian Lama Guru Deva, 1980–82), TBRC W384 (*ja*), 7:5–384. See 233–262.
10. Ngor chen, *Destroyer of the Proponents of Evil,* 578.6.
11. See Mkhas grub, *Ocean of Attainment,* 250.6–251.3. I discuss this passage in further depth in chapter 1.
12. See Jackson's analysis of this painting. David P. Jackson, *The Nepalese Legacy in Tibetan Painting* (New York: Rubin Museum of Art, 2010), 179–181 and figure 8.2. This painting will be discussed further in chapter 1.
13. Ary highlights the significance of such representations of Khédrup and Tsongkhapa's encounter in visual and textual sources, linking them to an event from Khédrup's hagiography. Elijah S. Ary, *Authorized Lives: Biography and the Early Formation of Geluk Identity* (Somerville, MA: Wisdom, 2015).
14. The painting from the collection of Shelly and Donald Rubin is one of many depicting Khédrup offering a mandala to his teacher. Tsongkhapa assumes various forms in these images. For example, see Himalayan Art Resources (HAR) #56, as well as HAR #23391 from a private collection, #71928 from Tibet House, Delhi, an example from the Freer and Sackler Galleries (Acc. #F1905.74), and one from the Asian Art Museum of San Francisco (B62D37). I am grateful to Wen-shing Chou for bringing the latter two examples to my attention.
15. The inscription reads: "The Venerable Dharmarājā Tsongkhapa offers the empowerment and vows of Vajrabhairava to Khédrupjé Gélek Pel who clarifies interpolations from the scripture, 'Offering and service of the Six-armed protector.'" *rje btsun chos kyi rgyal po tsong kha pas/rdo rje 'jigs byed dbang dang gdams pa gnang/phyag drug dgon po'i bsnyan bsgrubs be bum la/lha zhugs bsal mdzad Mkhas grub dge legs dpal.* An inscription on the back of the painting also refers to Khédrup's status as a previous incarnation in the line of Panchen Lamas. See Jeff Watt's description of this painting and his translation of the inscription on https://www.himalayanart.org/items/56.
16. Ary, *Authorized Lives.*
17. Ferdinand Lessing and Alex Wayman, trans. mKhas Grub rJe's *Fundamentals of Buddhist Tantra,* Indo-Iranian Monographs v. 8 (The Hague: Mouton, 1968).
18. On Ngorchen's 1404 text and Rédaba's role as opponent, see Rae Dachille, "Running the Numbers for the Path of Mantra: Distinguishing the Thirteenth Bhūmi in Fifteenth-Century Tibet," *Religions* 12, no. 3 (20210309): 175.
19. Ngor chen kun dga' bzang po (1382–1456), *Zung 'jug rdo rje 'chang chen po'i sa mtshams rnam par bshad pa log rtog ngan sel* [*Dispelling Evil Misunderstandings of the Explanation of the Ground of Union Vajradhara*] in *Gsung 'bum,* Kun dga' bzang po. *Ngor chen kun dga' bzang po'i bka' 'bum.* Compiled by Bsod nams rgya mtsho and reproduced from the Sde dge block prints. Dehra dun:

photomechanical print from a set of prints from the Sde dge dgon chen blocks, BDRC W1157, 1:659–91.

20. Ngor chen kun dga' bzang po (1382–1456), *Rgyud gsum gnod 'joms* [*Overcoming Objections to the Three Tantras*] in Ngor chen kun dga' bzang po'i bka' 'bum, *The Collected Works of Ngor chen Kun dga' bzang po*, compiled by Bsod nams rgya mtsho. Tokyo: Sa skya pa'i bka' 'bum, *The Complete Works of the Great Masters of the Sa skya Sect of the Tibetan Buddhism* (Toyo Bunko, 1968–9) 9:155d–157a.

 ______. "Commentary on Overcoming Objections to the Three Tantras," *Rgyud gsum gnod 'joms kyi 'grel pa*, 9:157a–164b. For a literary reading of Ngorchen's treatment of polysemy in this text, see Rae Dachille, "'Empty Like the Sky': Polysemy and the Problem of 'Mere Clear Awareness' at the Intersection of Sūtra and Tantra in Fifteenth-Century Tibet," *Revue d'Etudes Tibétaines*, no. 58 (April 2021): 208–236.

21. Bentor most recently proposed that Khédrup is replying directly to Rédaba's writings on the Guhyasamāja cycle in *Ocean of Attainment*, an extensive text in which the body mandala chapter plays but one part. In this article, Bentor describes Rédaba's stance on aspects of the sādhana practice and on the related texts. She also illuminates ways in which Tsongkhapa and Khédrup distinguish their interpretations from those of Rédaba. Yael Bentor, "Tsongkhapa's Guhyasamāja Sādhana and the Ārya Tradition," in *Vimalakīrti's House: A Festschrift in Honor of Robert A.F. Thurman on the Occasion of His Seventieth Birthday*, ed. Christian K. Wedemeyer, John D. Dunne, and Thomas F. Yarnall (New York: American Institute of Buddhist Studies, 2015), 165–192. Bentor is building upon initial observations she made in her earlier work regarding Butön Rinchen Drup (1290–1364) and Rédaba's roles as Khédrup's "unnamed opponents." See Bentor, "Identifying the Unnamed Opponents of Tsong kha pa and Mkhas grub rje Concerning the Transformation of Ordinary Birth, Death, and the Intermediary State into the Three Bodies," in *Tibetan Buddhist Literature and Praxis: Studies in Its Formative Period, 900–1400*, ed. Ronald M. Davidson and Christian Wedemeyer (Leiden: Brill, 2006), 185–200.

 For additional and more abbreviated references to Rédaba's part in the complex dynamics of lineage and exegesis, see Bentor, "Did mKhas grub rje Challenge the Authenticity of the Sa skya Lam 'bras Tradition?" in *Towards a History of Fifteenth Century Tibet: Cultural Blossoming, Religious Fervour and Political Unrest*, ed. Volker Caumanns and Marta Sernisi (Lumbini, Nepal: Lumbini International Research Institute, 2017), 237; see also Bentor, "Divergent Perspectives on the Guhyasamāja Sādhana in Tibet: Dge lugs vs. Sa skya," 密教文化 = *Journal of Esoteric Buddhism* / 密教研究会 編. 237 (2016): 70–44, 118.

22. Judith Butler, *Bodies That Matter: On the Discursive Limits of "Sex"* (New York: Routledge, 1993), xxi–xxii.

23. Amy Hollywood, "Performativity, Citationality, Ritualization," in *Bodily Citations: Religion and Judith Butler*, ed. Ellen T. Armour and Susan M. St. Ville (New York: Columbia University Press, 2006), 252–75. See 261.

24. Ngor chen, *Destroyer of the Proponents of Evil*, 560.3–.4.

25. For an exploration of the tensions inherent in Tibetan discourses of the vajra body in the fourteenth century, see Willa Blythe Miller, "Secrets of the Vajra Body: Dngos po'i gnas lugs and the Apotheosis of the Body in the Work of Rgyal ba Yang dgon pa" (PhD diss., Harvard University, 2013). Miller explores the positive valences of embodiment articulated in the work of a fourteenth-century Tibetan Kagyupa master. Through tracing the use of the term *dngos po'i gnas lugs*, translated as "the nature of things" or "the nature of material substance," she shows how Yangönpa Gyeltsen Pel shifted the conversation on the ordinary versus enlightened body in significant ways.

26. The notion of a vajra body in Buddhist texts also predates the tantric tradition and is linked to conversations around the paradoxes of the Buddha's embodiment. For example, Radich inventories instances from early Buddhist texts in which the Buddha's body is compared to "adamant" and highlights a connection in Chinese translations after 400 C.E. of the Buddha's adamantine

body with immortality. Michael David Radich, "The Somatics of Liberation: Ideas About Embodiment in Buddhism from Its Origins to the Fifth Century C.E." (PhD diss., Harvard University, 2007), 1072–1093, 1485–1486.

27. In the introduction to their edited volume on the "subtle body," Samuel and Johnston trace the Western usage of the term back to a translation of the Vedantic term *sukṣma-śarīra* employed by members of the Theosophical Society. They account for the challenges posed by the history of the term while preserving it as a workable category for a complex network of concepts and practices suggested by early Upaniṣadic, late Vedic, and classical Vedantic literature in addition to their more explicit and familiar development in yogic as well as Buddhist and Hindu tantric literature. Geoffrey Samuel and Jay Johnston, eds., *Religion and the Subtle Body in Asia and the West: Between Mind and Body* (Abingdon, Oxon: Routledge, 2013), 2.
28. I am grateful to Max Strassfeld for recommending this particularly salient example of Stryker's work to me and to Susan Stryker for taking the time to discuss my interests in religion, embodiment, and transformation. Susan Stryker, "My Words to Victor Frankenstein Above the Village of Chamounix," *GLQ* 1, no. 3 (1994): 237–254. This essay is based on a performance piece delivered by Stryker at the "Rage Across the Disciplines Conference" held at California State University in 1993.
29. Stryker, 239.
30. Stryker, 240–241.
31. Tourmaline, Eric A. Stanley, and Johanna Burton, eds., *Trap Door: Trans Cultural Production and the Politics of Visibility* (Cambridge, MA: MIT Press, 2017).
32. *rig pa'i dbang phyug gis/ma mthong phyir na med pa min.* Ngorchen, *Destroyer of the Proponents of Evil,* 561.1.
33. Ronald Davidson positioned the debate within a broader framework of tantric polemical writings and especially "Sakyapa apologetics." R. M. Davidson, "Reflections on the Maheśvara Subjugation Myth: Indic Materials, Sa-skya-pa Apologetics, and the Birth of Heruka," *Journal of the International Association of Buddhist Studies* 14, no. 2 (1991): 197–235. Additional works by Davidson relevant to the debate are "The Ngor-pa Tradition," *Wind Horse* 1 (1981): 79–98; and "Preliminary Studies on Hevajra's Abhisamaya and the Lam-'bras Tshogs-bshad," in *Tibetan Buddhism, Reason, and Revelation*, ed. Steven D. Goodman and Ronald M. Davidson (Albany: State University of New York Press, 1992), 107–132.

    Van der Kuijp also laid the groundwork for the study of the debate through the lens of tantric polemics in his seminal article: Leonard W. J. van der Kuijp, "A Text-Historical Note on *Hevajratantra* II: V:1–2." *Journal of the International Association for Buddhist Studies* 8, no. 1 (1985): 83–89.
34. Donald Lopez, "Polemical Literature (dGag lan)," in *Tibetan Literature: Studies in Genre*, ed. J. I. Cabezón and R. R. Jackson, 217–228 (Ithaca, NY: Snow Lion, 1996).
35. Bentor has produced focused articles exploring the relationship between ritual and lineage raised by the debate. See Yael Bentor, "Identifying the Unnamed Opponents"; "Tsongkhapa's Guhyasamāja Sādhana"; "Interpreting the Body *Maṇḍala*: Tsongkhapa Versus Later Gelug Scholars," *Revue d'Etudes Tibétaines* 31 (February 2015): 63–74; "Tibetan Interpretations of the Opening Verses of Vajraghanta on the Body Mandala," in *Chinese and Tibetan Esoteric Buddhism*, ed. Yael Bentor and Meir Shahar (Boston: Brill, 2017), 230–259; and "Did mKhas grub rje Challenge."
36. For examples of this critique, see José Ignacio Cabezón and Geshe Lobsang Dargyay, *Freedom from Extremes: Gorampa's "Distinguishing the Views" and the Polemics of Emptiness* (Boston: Wisdom, 2007), 2–10. Donald S. Lopez, "Burnouf and the Birth of Buddhist Studies," *Eastern Buddhist* 43, no. 1/2 (2012): 25–34; Jonathan Z. Smith, "Religion, Religions, Religious," in *Critical Terms for Religious Studies*, ed. Mark C. Taylor (Chicago: University of Chicago Press, 1998), 179–195.

37. Cabezón and Dargyay, 7. In his work on philosophical exchanges involving Ngorchen's student Gorampa, Cabezón introduces an important distinction between "sectarian differentiation" and "sectarianism" in terms of "belonging" and "pathology" respectively.
38. Bentor, "Did mKhas grub rje Challenge," 238.
39. Jörg Heimbel, *Vajradhara in Human Form: The Life and Times of Ngor chen Kun dga' bzang po* (Lumbini, Nepal: Lumbini International Research Institute, 2017), 239–240. He references the body mandala debate to flesh out the socioreligious and scholastic context for the engagement of the Sakya and Geluk traditions; see 229–224. For a recent article on the complexities of engaging the historical sources of the debate, see Jörg Heimbel, "The Dispute Between mKhas grub rJe and Ngor chen: Its Representation and Role in Tibetan Life Writing," in *Towards a History of Fifteenth Century Tibet*, 249–90. For an earlier preliminary study of Ngorchen, see Jörg Heimbel, "Biographical Sources for Researching the Life of Ngor chen Kun dga' bzang po (1382–1456)," *Revue d'Etudes Tibétaines*, No. 22 (2011): 47–91.
40. Ary, *Authorized Lives.*
41. Jonathan Z. Smith , oral communication (1989) cited by Laurie Patton, *Myth as Argument: The Brhaddevata as Canonical Commentary* (Berlin: De Gruyter, 1996), fn6.
42. Felstiner coined the phrase "repetition with a difference" to describe the ways in which Paul Celan used repetition to expand and transform the potential of words to suggest meaning. John Felstiner, *Paul Celan: Poet, Survivor, Jew* (Urbana: University of Illinois Press, 2001), 211.
43. For examples of influential approaches to de-essentializing Buddhism, see Charles Hallisey, "Roads Taken and Not Taken in the Study of Theravāda Buddhism," in *Curators of the Buddha: The Study of Buddhism Under Colonialism*, ed. Donald Lopez (Chicago: University of Chicago Press, 1995); Donald S. Lopez, *Prisoners of Shangri-La: Tibetan Buddhism and the West* (Chicago: University of Chicago Press, 1998); Robert H. Sharf, "Buddhist Modernism and the Rhetoric of Meditative Experience," *Numen* 42, no. 3 (1995): 228–283, reprinted in *Buddhism: Critical Concepts in Buddhist Studies*, ed. Paul Williams (London: Routledge, 2005), 2:255–298; William Schweiker and José Ignacio Cabezón, "The Discipline(s) and Its (Their) Other(s): A Response to José Ignacio Cabezón," *Journal of the American Academy of Religion* 74, no. 1 (2006): 39–46.
44. Scholarship in Tibetan Buddhism produced in the 1990s also engaged and theorized the themes of gender, embodiment, and identity in generative ways. See especially David Germano, "Remembering the Dismembered Body of Tibet: Contemporary Visionary Movements in the People's Republic of China," in *Buddhism in Contemporary Tibet: Religious Revival and Cultural Identity*, ed. Melvyn C. Goldstein and Matthew T. Kapstein, 53–94 (Berkeley: University of California Press, 1998); Janet Gyatso, "Down with the Demoness: Reflections on a Feminine Ground in Tibet," in *Feminine Ground: Essays on Women and Tibet*, ed. Janet D. Willis, 33–51 (Ithaca: Snow Lion, 1987). Anne C. Klein, *Meeting the Great Bliss Queen: Buddhists, Feminists, and the Art of the Self* (Boston: Beacon, 1994).
45. On the construction of the body through discipline and the role of representations, see Michel Foucault and Alan Sheridan, *Discipline and Punish: The Birth of the Prison* (New York: Vintage, 1979). On the construction of meaning through reconnaissance, see Michel Foucault, "Nietzsche, Genealogy, History," in *Nietzsche: Critical Assessments*, ed. Daniel W. Conway and Peter S. Groff (London; New York: Routledge, 1998).
46. Jacques Derrida, "Signature, Event, Context," in *A Derrida Reader: Between the Blinds*, ed. Peggy Kamuf (New York: Columbia University Press, 1991), 80–111. See 97.
47. Butler, "Afterword," in *Bodily Citations*, 276–292.
48. Butler, *Bodies That Matter*, xii.
49. Nearly twenty years ago, Said asserted the urgency of developing sharper skills for approaching representations in the contemporary world. Edward W. Said, *Humanism and Democratic Criticism* (New York: Columbia University Press, 2004).

I. IMAGINING THE BODY MANDALA

1. Thub-bstan-ye-shes, Jonathan Landaw, and Philip Glass, *Introduction to Tantra: The Transformation of Desire* (Boston: Wisdom, 2014), 29.
2. Tomabechi and Hong make the important point that there is no Sanskrit evidence for the term *Ārya tradition* (Tib. *'Phags lugs*), and therefore, we must be cautious about projecting such terms upon the Indian context. See Candrakīrti, Hong Luo and Toru Tomabechi, "Introduction," in *Candrakīrti's Vajrasattvaniṣpadanasūtra = Vajrasattvasādhana: Sanskrit and Tibetan Texts* (Beijing: China Tibetology, 2009), note 2. They refer likewise to Toru Tomabechi's "Vitapāda, Śākyamitra, and Āryadeva: On a Transitional Stage in the History of Guhyasamāja Exegesis," in *Esoteric Buddhist Studies: Identity in Diversity* (Koyasan University: Proceedings of the International Conference on Esoteric Buddhist Studies, 2008), 171–177, for further detail.
3. *rdzogs rim bde ba'i ye shes bskyed pa la/rtsa rlung rgyal bas byin gyis brlabs pa dgos/de nyid sgrub la lus kyi dkyil 'khor las/gzhan ba'i myur lam zab mo yod ma yin.*

   Ngor chen kun dga' bzang po, *Kye'i rdo rje'i lus kyi dkyil 'khor la rtsod spong smra ba ngan 'joms* [*Destroyer of the Proponents of Evil Through Eliminating Objections to the Hevajra Body Mandala*], in *gsung 'bum*, Kun dga' bzang po. *Ngor chen kun dga' bzang po'i bka' 'bum*, comp. Bsod nams rgya mtsho and reproduced from the Sde dge block prints (Dehra dun: photomechanical print from a set of prints from the Sde dge dgon chen blocks [W11577]) 1:545–580. See 578.6.
4. While I generally adopt the conventional translation of term *byin gyis brlabs* as "consecrate" in this book, it is noteworthy that my Tibetan mentors opted for alternatives such as "bless" and "transform." The Sanskrit equivalent of the term, *adhiṣṭhāna*, denotes the act of installing a presence within an abode and is commonly used to describe the infusion of sacred presence into an image during image consecration rituals. *Abhiṣekha*, on the other hand, is consecration proper; the root *abhi-ṣic* conveys the act of anointing in a royal consecration and has been extended to the consecration of practitioners in tantric initiation rites. In Tibetan, the inconsistent use of *dbang* to refer to both Sanskrit terms has generated confusion.
5. Mkhas grub rje dge legs dpal bzang (1385–1438), *Gsang 'dus bskyed rim dngos grub rgya mtsho* [*Ocean of Attainment of the Guhyasamāja Generation Stage* (*Ocean of Attainment*)] . BDRC W384.Vol. 7 (*ja*), 5–384: See 233–262. New Zhol par khang edition of *gsung 'bum, Mkhas grub rje (zhol)*. Reproduced from a set of prints from the 1897 Lhasa Old Zhol (Ganden Puntso Ling) blocks, TOH 5481 (New Delhi: Mongolian Lama Guru Deva, 1980–2), BDRC W384, 252.1–.2.
6. Gavin Flood, *The Tantric Body: The Secret Tradition of Hindu Religion* (London: I. B. Tauris, 2006): 110. Sanderson provides some textual sources for this concept of becoming a god to worship a god: JS 12.1; MTV II (*Mṛgendratantravṛtti*) 29, 9–10; SvT (*Svacchandratantra*) 2.55 ab. Alexis Sanderson, "Mandala and Āgamic Identity in the Trika of Kashmir," in *Mantras et Diagrammes Rituelles dans l'Hindouisme*, ed. Andre Padoux, équipe no. 249, "L'hindouisme: textes, doctrines, pratiques" (Paris: CNRS, 1986) 169–214, note 30.
7. Dan Martin (DM) defines *dra ba dra phyed* as: "Fabric temple-hanging forming a kind of latticework of jewels and auspicious symbols which seem to be spit out of the mouth of a kīrtimukha"; https://www.thlib.org/.
8. Mkhas grub, *Ocean of Attainment*, 254.6–255.1. In Ngorchen's text, *Destroyer of the Proponents of Evil*, the final line reads: *lce dang mchu 'dod yon gyi snam bu*, "the corridors(/terraces) of the desire goddesses."
9. The remainder of Khédrup's claim and Ngorchen's objection to it is more explicitly tied to issues of textual authority rather than to ritual mechanics.
10. Drakpa Gyatso, International Buddhist Academy, personal communication, Spring 2012.
11. The Path and Fruit texts in current use were created by Ngorchen Könchok Lhündrup (1495–1557), the tenth abbot of Ngor monastery. They supplanted those of Ngorchen's disciple Müchen

Könchok Gyeltsen (1388–1469), although they were largely modeled on them. In considering Ngorchen's own influences in formulating his approach to the Hevajra sādhana, including the body mandala, Davidson emphasizes the role of Lama Dampa Sönam Gyeltsen; he also reflects upon the significance of the absence of explicit references to that teacher in Ngorchen's extensive Hevajra abhisamaya text, the *Gnad kyi zla zer*. Ronald M. Davidson, "Preliminary Studies on Hevajra's Abhisamaya and the Lam-'bras Tshogs-bshad," in *Tibetan Buddhism, Reason and Revelation*, ed. Steven D. Goodman and Ronald M. Davidson (Albany: State University of New York Press, 1992), 112–114.

12. See the digital Sakya *Lam 'bras* collection, 10:140–143. I am grateful to Rory Lindsay for his help in locating this text. This appears to be the same text referred to in Davidson within the collection of the *Pod gser ma*, or the *Yellow Book* compilation of esoteric instructions [(?) *Lus kyi dkyil 'khor*, in *Pod-ser-ma* (Bhir:'Jam dbyangs lung-rtogs dpal-bzang, 1970), 169.3–173.4], and in Jan-Ulrich Sobisch's *Hevajra and Lam 'bras Literature* (cited at the end of this note), title list #290 [(*Lam la sags pa'i chos nyi shu la*) *lus kyi dyil 'khor, Sa skya Lam 'bras* series 11: 68r–69v]. While Davidson attributes this particular text to Drakpa Gyeltsen, Sobisch does not specify its authorship. Davidson, "Preliminary Studies," note 26.

    The *Yellow Book* was intended to transmit the esoteric teachings passed down orally until the time of Sachen. This text is one of twenty-three in that collection clarifying Virūpa's teachings and Sachen's explanations of them. Many of the twenty-three texts are indeed by Drakpa Gyeltsen. The inclusion of this text as one of the twenty-three within his own title list of the work might support this attribution. Jan-Ulrich Sobisch, *Hevajra and Lam 'bras Literature* (Wiesbaden: Reichert, 2008), 101.

13. ('Phags pa) Blo gros rgyal mtshan (1235–1280), *Kyai rdo rje lus dkyil gyi sgrub thabs* [*Hevajra Body Mandala Sādhanam*], in *Sa skya bka' 'bum, Collected Writings of the First Five Great Patriarchs of the Sakya Order*. Includes the three supplementary volumes recently published by Khenpo Tsultrim Gyaltsen, listed separately [W20751], reprinted from a set of Dege Parkhang prints (Dehra dun: Sakya Center, 1992–1993), BDRC W22271, 13: 538–542.

14. Bentor identifies a similar correlation schema in the Hevajra sādhana composed by Ngorchen in 1410, the *Dpal kye rdo rje'i lus kyi dkyil 'khor gyi sgrub pa'i thabs rnal 'byor snying po*. This text, not included in Ngorchen's collected works, opens up new pathways for future explorations of the body mandala debate. Yael Bentor, "Did mKhas grub rje Challenge the Authenticity of the Sa skya Lam 'bras Tradition?" in *Towards a History of Fifteenth-Century Tibet: Cultural Blossoming, Religious Fervour, and Political Unrest*, ed. Volker Caumanns and Marta Sernisi (Lumbini, Nepal: Lumbini International Research Institute, 2017), 239.

15. *Visuddhimagga* 8.39–8.60; Buddhaghosa and Nāṇamoli, *The Path of Purification-Visuddhimagga* (Kandy, Sri Lanka: Buddhist Publication Society, 2010), 238–240.

16. *Visuddhimagga,* 8.139; Buddhaghosa and Nāṇamoli, *The Path of Purification,* 257.

17. Flood, *The Tantric Body,* 121.

18. On this ritual purification of the hands, see Richard O. Meisezahl, *Hastapūjāvidhi-Texte: Der Handritus im anuttarayogischen Kult Götterpaares Cakrasambhara und Vajravārahī* (Sankt Augustin, Germany: VGH Wissenschaftsverlag, 1985).

19. Flood, *The Tantric Body,* 114.

20. Flood, 116.

21. English has astutely noted the resemblances between body mandala practice and tantric technologies of purifying and protecting the body of the practitioner by associating the components of the body with deities, armoring the body through nyāsa, and preparing the hands for ritual performance through *hastapūjā-vidhi*. Elizabeth English, *Vajrayoginī: Her Visualizations, Rituals, and Forms* (Boston: Wisdom, 2002). On body mandala, see English, *Vajrayoginī,* 197–203. For observations on the similarity of these ritual technologies existing side by side in the Vajravārāhi sādhana

that is the focus of her study, see for examples: English, *Vajrayoginī,* 116, 166, 197. On associating body parts with deities, see English, *Vajrayoginī,* 114–119. On armoring, see English, *Vajrayoginī,* 163–166. On *hastapūjā-vidhi*, see English, *Vajrayoginī,* 218–220.

22. James Mallinson and Jason Birch are among the scholars who continue to uncover intriguing connections between modes of mapping the body found in Indian *Vajrayāna* texts like the *Amṛtasiddhi* and sources associated with the Hatha Yoga tradition. For examples, see James Mallinson and Mark Singleton, *Roots of Yoga* (London: Penguin, 2017), 199–200. James Mallinson, "The *Amṛtasiddhi*: Haṭhayoga's Tantric Buddhist Source Text," in *Śaivism and the Tantric Traditions: Essays in Honour of Alexis G. J. S. Sanderson*, ed. Dominick Goodall, Shaman Hatley, Harunaga Isaacson, and Srilata Raman (Leiden: Brill, 2020), 409–425. Jason Birch, "The Amaraughaprabodha: New Evidence on the Manuscript Transmission of Any Early Work on Haṭha- and Rājayoga," *Journal of Indian Philosophy* 47 (2019): 947–977.

23. Mkhas grub, *Ocean of Attainment*, 251.6–251.1.

24. *'gro ba 'di dag rang bzhin gyis/sgrub pa'i dkyil 'khor gnyis med pa'o*. The verse also appears in Mkhas grub, *Ocean of Attainment*, 234.1 with a slight variation of *grub* versus *sgrub*. For the source of the citation in Ghantapa's text, see Ghantapa, *Dpal 'khor lo sdom pa'i dbang gi bya ba mdor bsdus pa,* Toh. 1431, *D* 21: 438–444 (ie.219v–222v). See folio 219 b (p438.5–.6). See also Bentor's discussion of this verse in Yael Bentor, "Tibetan Interpretations of the Opening Verses of Vajraghanta on the Body Mandala," in *Chinese and Tibetan Esoteric Buddhism*, ed. Yael Bentor and Meir Shahar (Boston: Brill, 2017), 230–259. For details on the editions, see notes 15 and 16 in that article.

25. Mkhas grub, *Ocean of Attainment*, 234.1–.2. The passage appears in the context of Khédrup's critique of others' interpretations as presented in 234.1–238.2 of *Ocean of Attainment.*

26. Mkhas grub, *Ocean of Attainment*, 234.2–.3.

27. Mkhas grub, 234.3–.4.

28. Mkhas grub, 234.5–.6.

29. Mkhas grub, 234.6–235.1.

30. Mkhas grub, 235.2–235.3.

31. One of the very first texts Ngorchen wrote, dated to 1404, addresses the distinction of the tantric path, culminating in the thirteenth ground of the Union Vajradhara, from the eleventh ground that is the apex of the perfections vehicle. (Ngor chen) Kun dga' bzang po (1382–1456), "Dispelling Evil Misunderstandings of the Explanation of the Ground of Union Vajradhara" [*Zung 'jug rdo rje 'chang chen po'i sa mtshams rnam par bshad pa log rtog ngan sel*], in *Gsung 'bum,* Kun dga' bzang po. Ngor chen kun dga' bzang po'i bka' 'bum. Compiled by Bsod nams rgya mtsho and reproduced from the Sde dge block prints. Dehra dun. [W11577], 1: 659–691. On Ngorchen's approach to classifying texts and soteriological goals in tandem in this work, see Rae Dachille, "Running the Numbers for the Path of Mantra: Distinguishing the Thirteenth Bhūmi in Fifteenth-century Tibet," *Religions* 12, no. 3 (2021): 175.

For a comparable Sakayapa perspective on the fruits of sutra and tantra, see chapter 5 in Verrill's translation of the Sakyapa patriarch Sonam Tsemo's (1142–1182) *The Yogini's Eye.* Bsod nams rtse mo, Wayne Verril, and Sonam Gyatso, Ngor Thartse Khenpo, *The Yogini's Eye: Comprehensive Introduction to Buddhist Tantra,* vol. 1: *Systematization and Interpretation* (Xlibris, 2012), 119–180.

32. Tsong-kha-pa Blo-bzang-grags-pa, and Gavin Kilty, *A Lamp to Illuminate the Five Stages Teachings on Guhyasamāja Tantra* (Boston: Wisdom, in association with the Institute of Tibetan Classics, 2013):117.

33. Medical literature also provides rich accounts of causality, as Frances Garrett shows in her study of how Tibetan Buddhist texts use embryological accounts as both a deterrent to craving rebirth in a human body and as positive model for spiritual transformation. Garrett presents the complex theories of causes and conditions that pervade embryological accounts from Tibetan medical works

and their Indian sources. Frances Garrett, *Religion, Medicine, and the Human Embryo in Tibet* (New York: Routledge, 2008).

34. Hirakawa Akira and Paul Groner, *A History of Indian Buddhism: From Śākyamuni to Early Mahāyana* (Delhi: Motilal Banarsidass, 1998), 180; Buddhaguhya, *The Mahā-Vairocana-Abhisambodhi Tantra*, trans. Stephen Hodge (New York: RoutledgeCurzon, 2003), note 10.5.

35. See *Abhidharma-kośa* II.56–58, as referenced in Buddhaguhya, *The Mahā-Vairocana-Abhisambodhi Tantra*, note 10.5. For an example of a Madhyamaka understanding of Abhidharmic causality, see Nāgārjuna and David J. Kalupahana, *Mūlamadhyamakakārikā of Nāgārjuna: The Philosophy of the Middle Way: Introduction, Sanskrit Text, English Translation and Annotation* (Delhi: Motilal Banarsidass, 1996), 110–111, 284.

36. I have encountered numerous references in secondary scholarship suggesting that the ability to produce a form body by means of the "similar type cause" was regarded as a distinguishing feature of the tantric path. For example, see Tsong-kha-pa Blo-bzang-grags-pa, *Tantra in Tibet: The Great Exposition of Secret Mantra*, vol. 1 (Delhi: Motilal Banarsidass, 1987), 68, 137.

37. Mkhas grub, *Ocean of Attainment*, 236.3.

38. José Ignacio Cabezón and Geshe Lobsang Dargyay, *Freedom from Extremes: Gorampa's "Distinguishing the Views" and the Polemics of Emptiness* (Boston: Wisdom, 2007), 26–27.

39. Georges Dreyfus, *Recognizing Reality: Dharmakīrti's Philosophy and Its Tibetan Interpretations* (Albany: SUNY Press, 1997), 25.

40. Dreyfus, 176.

41. Dreyfus, 26.

42. Dreyfus, 371, 376–77.

43. In particular, the question of the relationship of universals and particulars was at the heart of the controversy.

44. In discussing Khédrup's interpretation of Dharmakīrti's chapter on *pramāṇasiddhi*, van der Kuijp demonstrates the link created between this chapter and the Kadampa stages of the path (*lam rim*) teachings to "form the hermeneutic grid along which the soteriology of Buddhist *pramāṇavāda* came to be established." Leonard van der Kuijp, "Studies in the Life and Thought of Mkhas grub rje I: Mkhas grub rje's Epistemological Oeuvre and His Philological Remarks on Dignāga's *Pramāṇasamuccaya*," *Berliner Indologische Studien* 1 (1985), 75–105, 75–77. He is responding to Ernst Steinkellner's "Tshad ma'i skyes bu: Meaning and Historical Significance of the Term," in *Contributions on Tibetan Language, History, and Culture: Proceedings of the Csoma de Körös Memorial Symposium*, ed. Ernst Steinkellner and Helmut Tauscher (Vienna: Arbeitskreis für Tibetische und Buddhistische Studien, Universität Wien, 1983), 275–283 (especially 282–283). See also Jackson's 1993 edition and translation of the *pramāṇasiddhi* chapter. Roger R. Jackson and Rgyaltshab Dar-ma-rin-chen, *Is Enlightenment Possible?: Dharmakīrti and rGyal tshab rje on Knowledge, Rebirth, No-self, and Liberation* (Ithaca, NY: Snow Lion, 1993).

45. Dreyfus, *Recognizing Reality*, 252. For more on the role of representations in Dharmakīrti's thought, see Dreyfus, 220.

46. Dreyfus, 252.

47. Dreyfus, 252.

48. Mkhas grub, *Ocean of Attainment*, 236.6–237.2.

49. Khenpo Choying Dorjee, reading session with author, UC Berkeley, Spring 2011.

50. Mkhas grub, *Ocean of Attainment*, 237.3–.6.

51. Khédrup may have been following the lead of his Indian predecessors in appropriating pramāṇa discourse to confer prestige upon certain aspects and interpretations of tantric practice over others. Davidson addresses the use of *pramāṇa* terminology in the writings of medieval Indian authors on meditative, and in particular, esoteric practice in connection with "institutionalization of

esoteric Buddhism, a purpose well served by this language." R. M. Davidson, "Masquerading as Pramāṇa: Esoteric Buddhism and Epistemological Nomenclature," in *Dharmakīrti's Thought and Its Impact on Indian and Tibetan Philosophy: Proceedings of the Third International Dhamakīrti Conference, Hiroshima, November 4–6, 1997*, ed. Shoryu Katsura (Vienna: Verlag der Österreichischen Akademie der Wissenschaften, 1999), 25–35.

52. Klaus-Dieter Mathes, *A Direct Path to the Buddha Within: Gö Lotsāwa's Mahāmūdrā Interpretation of the Ratnagotravibhāga* (Boston: Wisdom, 2008), 45.

53. Translation from Mathes, *A Direct Path*, 45. See also 25–129. *chos sku de ni gdod nas spros dang bral/ spros dang bral ngo shes pas bden par grub.*

    Dol po pa Shes rab rgyal msthan. (1292–1361) *The Ocean of Definitive Meaning of Mountain Dharma.* (Jo nang) *Ri chos nges don rgya mtsho* (Beijing: Mi rigs dpe skrun khang, 1998), 446.26–447.

54. Dolpopa writes, "As to how the three kāyas are attained, it is [here] maintained that the fruit, [namely] the three kāyas of a perfect Buddha, are attained owing to a cause, [namely] these two naturally present and fortified potentials. First, the naturally present potential is perfected through many accumulations of wisdom, and becomes free from all adventitious stains, and . . . the svābhāvikakāya, the dharmatā endowed with both purities, is thereby attained. Second, the accumulation of merit is perfected by increasing the fortified potential, and the latter kāyas, namely the sambhogakāya and the nirmāṇakya, which appear to disciples near and far, are thereby attained." Translation from Mathes, *A Direct Path*, 83–84 and note 436; Dolpopa, *Nyi ma'i 'od zer* 987.3–.6. *Theg pa chen po rgyud bla ma'i bstan bcos legs bshad nyi ma'i 'od zer. The 'Dzam-thang Edition of the Collected Works of Kun mkhyen Dol-po-pa Shes-rab rgyal-mtshan*, 4 (ma): 883–1161 (Delhi: Shedrup, 1992).

55. Mkhas grub, *Ocean of Attainment*, 237.5–.5.

56. Mkhas grub, 238.1–.2.

57. Ferdinand Lessing and Alex Wayman, trans., mKhas Grub rJe's *Fundamentals of Buddhist Tantra*, Indo-Iranian Monographs v.8 (The Hague, Mouton, 1968), 49–51.

58. Bentor notes that although the issue of *tathāgatagarbha* isn't "central" for Khédrup, it is one of the sectarian claims emerging in the present text. Through reference to Ruegg, and to Lessing and Wayman, Bentor clarifies Khédrup's position on the *svābhāvikakāya*, namely that it is not found in the continua of all sentient beings and cannot be equated with Buddha nature, counter the Jonangpa position. She compares Khédrup's position with that of Butön, who equates the *svābhāvikakāya* with Buddha nature but denies its inclusion in the mindstream of all sentient beings. In his *Fundamentals of Buddhist Tantra* [*Rgyud sde spyi rnam*], Khédrup differs both from the Jonangpa as well as from certain aspects of Butön's writings with regard to sutra teachings on *tathāgatagarbha* theory. Bentor highlights the fact that in that text Khédrup is explicit in identifying the objects of his critiques. Bentor, "Identifying the Unnamed Opponents of Tsong kha pa and Mkhas grub rje Concerning the Transformation of Ordinary Birth, Death and the Intermediary State Into the Three Bodies," in *Tibetan Buddhist Literature and Praxis: Studies in Its Formative Period, 900–1400*, ed. Ronald M. Davidson and Christian Wedemeyer, 185–200, note 39. Lessing and Wayman, mKhas Grub rJe's *Fundamentals of Buddhist Tantra*, 48–49. David Seyfort Ruegg, *La Théorie du Tathāgatagarbha et du Gotra: Études sur la Sotériologie et la Gnoséologie du Bouddhisme* (Paris: École Française d'Extrême-Orient, 1968), note 501.

59. Khenpo Choying Dorjee, personal communication, reading session, UC Berkeley, Spring 2011.

60. Cabezón, likewise, highlights that these exchanges were multidirectional, including Jonangpa critiques of Tsongkhapa and so forth. Cabezón and Dargyay, *Freedom from Extremes*, 43, note 207. Tsongkhapa's Sakyapa teacher Rédaba refuted the Jonangpas on many issues beyond Buddha nature, including aspects of interpreting the Kālacakra system. Khenpo Choying Dorjee, personal communication, reading session, UC Berkeley, Spring 2011.

61. Bentor, "Tibetan Interpretations," 233–237.
62. Yael Bentor, "Did mKhas grub rje Challenge," 236.
63. For a thorough exploration of the early Buddhist evolution of attitudes toward embodiment in the Indian context, see Michael David Radich, "The Somatics of Liberation: Ideas About Embodiment in Buddhism from its Origins to the Fifth Century C.E." (PhD diss., Harvard University, 2007).
64. Mkhas grub, *Ocean of Attainment*, 250.5–253.4.
65. Mkhas grub, 251.5–.6. As for the reference in this passage to the lower tantric classes, biographical sources as well as secondary scholarship suggest that Khédrup and Ngorchen clashed on topics surrounding cultivating deities in practices associated with the lower tantric classes; this controversy will be addressed briefly in chapter 2. The implication in this particular passage seems to be that the higher tantric classes contain more profound and elaborate forms of corporeal transformation. Different degrees of ritual initiation prepare practitioners to engage in these higher tantric practices. These controversies suggest further dimensions of the volatile status of imagination in fifteenth-century Tibet. Contentious issues include who is qualified to imagine themselves as what kind of deity and what kinds of ritual preparation are required for imaginative activity.
66. Mkhas grub, *Ocean of Attainment*, 250.6–251.3.
67. Mkhas grub, 251.3–.4. I have emended *rang bzhi* to *rang bzhin* as it appears in 234.1 where the same quote by Ghantapa appears with the variation of *sgrub* versus *grub*. Thanks to Khenpo Yeshe for noting this discrepancy.
68. Khenpo Choying Dorjee, reading session, UC Berkeley, Spring 2011
69. Dreyfus, *Recognizing Reality*, 222.
70. Dreyfus, 222.
71. In his *Fundamentals of Buddhist Tantra*, Khédrup explains the "drop of springtime" in the context of Cakrasaṃvara body mandala practice as a drop in the heart of the "ground Heruka" from which the main deities in union are generated. Lessing and Wayman, mKhas Grub rJe's *Fundamentals of Buddhist Tantra*, 305.
72. Mkhas grub, *Ocean of Attainment*, 251.4–5. I have emended *bsgrub bzhi* to *bsgrub gzhi* on the basis of the numerous appearances of that term in similar contexts within this text.
73. Bentor, "Identifying the Unnamed Opponents," 186, note 4.
74. The context for the quotation is a discussion of the bliss resulting from the union of compassion and emptiness. Kilty, *A Lamp*, 107.
75. Tsongkhapa displays concern with where the body mandala practice, included in body isolation (*lus dben*), fits in relation to these classificatory schema. This concern may signal the problematic status of the body itself at the intersection of fabricated and natural realities and ordinary and extraordinary bodies.
76. Kilty, *A Lamp*, 85–6, note 147.
77. *lus la gnad du bsnun pa'i dkyil 'khor ni bcos ma gnyis la mi bya'i lus dkyil la bya dgos te.* Tsong kha pa, *The Jewel Treasury: The Rite of Empowerment of the Body Mandala of Ghantatapa, the Lord of Yoga. Rnal 'byor dbang phyug dril bu lugs bde mchog lus dkyil gyi dbang chog rin po che'i bang mdzod.* Tsong kha pa, 10:57–106; Toh 5327, 61.3–4. For Tsongkhapa's citation of Ghantapa, see 58.6–59.3. I tracked this source down based upon a reference in Bentor, "Identifying the Unnamed Opponents," 196.
78. Khenpo Choying Dorjee, personal communication, Spring 2011.

    I explored the concept of "piercing to the pith of the body" in an article in which I remark upon the challenge of locating the Sanskrit equivalent of *gnad du bsnun* and of securing the Indian origins of this practice. Rae Erin Dachille, "Piercing to the Pith of the Body: The Evolution of Body Mandala and Tantric Corporeality in Tibet," special issue of the Society for Tantric Studies Proceedings (2016), *Religions* 8, no. 9 (2017): 189.

As I have noted there, the meaning of "piercing to the pith" may shift across different tantric cycles and transmissions. The etymology of "mandala" reflects the notion of "taking the pith." See Yong-Hyun Lee, *Synthesizing a "Liturgical" Heritage: Abhayākaragupta's "Vajrāvalī" and the Kālacakramaṇḍala* (PhD diss., University of Wisconsin, Madison, 2003, UMI dissertation Information Service), 130, note 4. The notion of the pith seems to evolve in the representations of the vajra body found in ritual practices like body mandala. For example, it is possible that the practice of "piercing to the pith" may have been elaborated in conjunction with acts of reading the yoginī tantras back into the Guhysamāja system. In their chapter on the yogic body, Mallinson and Singleton include references to piercing the cakras and knots (*granthi*) from the *Netratantra* and *Yogabīja* respectively. Mallinson and Singleton, *Roots of Yoga*, 203, 215–216. The term *granthi-bhedana* is one possible equivalent for "piercing to the pith" in the yogic context. James Mallinson, email communication, June 2017.

79. Mkhas grub, *Ocean of Attainment*, 251.6–252.2.
80. Mkhas grub, 252.2–.3.
81. While the term *lhag mos* (Skt. *adhimokṣa*) has a range of associations with conviction, belief, and zeal, in this context it is best translated as imaginative activity. In our discussions of Khédrup's text, Khenpo Choying Dorjee clarified the term *lhag mos* as meaning something like "imagine inside your mind" and as indicating a process similar to the process of assuming the "the pride of the deity" (*lha'i nga rgyal*). He also noted the subtle connotation of *mos* as implying that something is not the case. Khenpo Choying Dorjee, reading session, UC Berkeley, Spring 2011. Bentor translates *lhag mos* [Skt. *adhimokṣa*] as "special visualization." Bentor, "Identifying the Unnamed Opponents."
82. Mkhas grub, *Ocean of Attainment*, 252.5–253.2. The phrase *lus la bsdus pa* here is one of many instances of the term *bsdus* within the body mandala texts. Although I have opted for "dissolution" as a translation here, "gathering" is also appropriate.
83. Yael Bentor, "Interpreting the Body *Maṇḍala*: Tsongkhapa Versus Later Gelug Scholars," *Revue d'Etudes Tibétaines,* no. 31 (February 2015): 72.
84. Bentor, 70–72. Bentor also demonstrates how Tsongkhapa differed from later Geluk thinkers on the mechanics of generating the body as the celestial palace. See Bentor, 66–67.
85. Yael Bentor, "Women on the Way to Enlightenment," in *From Bhakti to Bon: Festschrift for Per Kvaerne*, ed. Hanna Havnevik and Charles Ramble (Oslo: Institute for Comparative Research in Human Culture, Novus Press, 2015); Holly Gayley, "Revisiting the 'Secret Consort' (*gsang yum*) in Tibetan Buddhism," *Religions* 9, no. 6 (2018): 179; Sarah Jacoby, *Love and Liberation: Autobiographical Writings of the Tibetan Buddhist Visionary Sera Khandro* (New York: Columbia University Press, 2014); Christian Wedemeyer, *Making Sense of Tantric Buddhism: History, Semiology, and Transgression in the Indian Traditions* (New York: Columbia University Press, 2012).
86. Mkhas grub, *Ocean of Attainment*, 253.2–.4.
87. Mkhas grub, 260.4–.261.3
88. The passage reads: *bod la grags pa'i lus dkyil mang po zhig la de 'dra ba'i rnam gzhag gang yang sbyar rgyu med pa'i blos btags 'ba' zhig la man ngag dang zab chos su byed par snang bas.* Mkhas grub, 263.5.

2. CONSTRUCTING THE BODY MANDALA DEBATE

1. Ngor chen kun dga' bzang po, *Kye'i rdo rje'i lus kyi dkyil 'khor la rtsod spong smra ba ngan 'joms* [*Destroyer of the Proponents of Evil Through Eliminating Objections to the Hevajra Body Mandala*] in *gsung 'bum*, Kun dga' bzang po. *Ngor chen kun dga' bzang po'i bka' 'bum*, comp. Bsod nams rgya mtsho and reproduced from the Sde dge block prints (Dehra dun: photomechanical print from a set of prints from the Sde dge dgon chen blocks [W11577]), 1:545–580. See 546.1–.2.

Ngorchen refers here to his tantric lama, Yongdzin Yéshé Gyeltsen. For an account of the teachings Ngor chen received from this master, see (Ngor chen,) Kun dga' bzang po (1382–1456), *Thob yig rgya mtsho* [*Record of Received Teachings*], in *gsung 'bum,* Kun dga' bzang po, *Ngor chen kun dga' bzang po'i bka' 'bum* [W11577], 1:179–434, especially 179–263.

2. Christian Luczanits, "Siddhas, Hierarchs, and Lineages: Three Examples for Dating Tibetan Art," in David P. Jackson and Christian Luczanits, eds., *Mirror of the Buddha: Early Portraits from Tibet* (New York: Rubin Museum of Art, 2011), 170–197.
3. For an illuminating study of Tibetan lineage portraiture, see Jackson and Luczanits.
4. See Jackson's analysis of this painting. David P. Jackson, *The Nepalese Legacy in Tibetan Painting* (New York: Rubin Museum of Art, 2010), 179–181 and figure 8.2.
5. Jackson, 179.
6. Jackson, 179.
7. Ngor chen, *Destroyer of the Proponents of Evil,* 546.3–.4.
8. *kho bos lam bras gang du bkag/ gang gi tshe bkag/ tshul ji ltar du bkag/ su zhig gi mdun du bkag.* Mkhas grub, *Dge ba'i bshes gnyen kon ting gug shri ba'i dris lan* [*Reply to the Questions of the Kalyānamītra Kon ting gug śrī ba*]. *Thor-bu Collected Works,* TBRC W384, vol. 9, pp. 775–808; see 775.4.
9. Michel Foucault, "Nietzsche, Genealogy, History," in *Nietzsche: Critical Assessments,* ed. Daniel W. Conway with Peter S. Groff (London: Routledge, 1998), 142.
10. Kapstein and Davidson are among the most useful historical references for this period in Tibetan history. Ronald M. Davidson, *Tibetan Renaissance: Tantric Buddhism in the Rebirth of Tibetan Culture* (New York: Columbia University Press, 2005); Matthew Kapstein, *The Tibetans* (Oxford: Blackwell, 2006). See also Michael Aris, *Hidden Treasures and Secret Lives: A Study of Pemalingpa (1450–1521) and the Sixth Dalai Lama (1683–1706)* (London: Kegan Paul International, 1989); Elijah Sacvan Ary, *Authorized Lives: Biography and the Early Formation of Geluk Identity* (Boston: Wisdom, 2015). David P. Jackson, *The Early Abbots of 'Phan-po Ne-len-dra: The Vicissitudes of a Great Tibetan Monastery in the Fifteenth Century* (Vienna: Arbeitskreis für Tibetische und Buddhistische Studien, Universität Wien, 1989); Turrell V. Wylie, "Monastic Patronage in Fifteenth-Century Tibet," in *The History of Tibet,* ed. Alex McKay (London: Routledge Curzon, 2003).
11. The fourteenth century was also a time marked by attempts at organizing and standardizing Buddhist iconography to reflect the connection of deities with particular texts in that canon.
12. Peter Schwieger, "Significance of Ming Titles Conferred Upon the Phag mo gru Rulers: A Reevaluation of Chinese-Tibetan Relations During the Ming Dynasty," *Tibet Journal* 34, nos. 2/3 (2009): 315. For more on the Pakmo Dru, see Luciano Petech, *Central Tibet and the Mongols: The Yüan Sa-Skya Period of Tibetan History* (Rome: Instituto italiano per il Medio ed Estremo Oriente, 1990), 85–138.
13. Franz-Karl Ehrhard, "Spiritual Relationships Between Rulers and Preceptors: The Three Journeys of Vanaratna (1384–1468) to Tibet," in *The Relationship Between Religion and State (chos srid zung 'brel) in Traditional Tibet: Proceedings of a Seminar Held in Lumbini, Nepal, in March 2000* (= LIRI Seminar Proceedings, 1) (Lumbini, 2004), 249.
14. Ehrhard documents the travels of one such master, Vanaratna (1384–1468). He suggests that Ngorchen, the other protagonist of this book, was actually the first master Vanaratna encountered on his first trip to Tibet in 1426. This is the same year that Ngorchen composed his body mandala texts. Vanaratna proceeded on to Gyantsé where he established a relationship with Rongtön, Khédrup's "opponent" in the elusive debate referenced later in this chapter. Ehrhard, "Spiritual Relationships," 246. For another excellent resource on the visitation of Indian masters to Tibet (and China) in the fifteenth century, see Arthur McKeown, *Guardian of a Dying Flame: Śāriputra (c. 1335 1426) and the End of Late Indian Buddhism* (Cambridge, MA: Harvard University Press, 2018).
15. Sperling describes the distinct dynamics of relationship expressed by this visit: "Thus, although the Ming circles harked back to the T'ang for their theoretical lessons in Sino-Tibetan affairs, and

although Ch'eng-tsu attempted to imitate the Yuan dynasty's ties with the Sa-skya-pa, early Ming Tibetan relations existed upon a footing of their own amidst new circumstances for Tibet and China." Eliot Sperling, "The Fifth Karmapa and Some Aspects of the Relationship Between Tibet and the Early Ming," in *The History of Tibet*, ed. Alex McKay (London: Routledge Curzon, 2003), 478. For a study of the miraculous events surrounding the Karmapa's visit and its representation in visual sources, see Patricia Ann Berger, "Miracles in Nanjing: An Imperial Record of the Fifth Karmapa's Visit to the Chinese Capital," in *Cultural Intersections in Later Chinese Buddhism*, ed. Marsha Weidner (Honolulu: University of Hawai'i Press, 2001), 145–169.

16. As I was reminded by Kyabgön Phakchok Rinpoche, current head of the Taklung Kagyu order of Tibetan Buddhism, the term *debate* implies that there is a residual absence of understanding on the part of the participants. "If there were clarity, there would be no need for debate." Audience with Kyabgön Phakchok Rinpoche, Kathmandu, August 31, 2011.

17. See Dreyfus for a thorough exploration of the pedagogical dimensions of debate. Georges Dreyfus, *The Sound of Two Hands Clapping: The Education of a Tibetan Monk* (Berkeley: University of California Press, 2003).

18. Lopez provides this translation of the term in his study of the genre of polemical literature through the Gelukpa scholar Séra Jétsünpa's replies to his Sakyapa and Kagyupa contemporaries. Donald Lopez, "Polemical Literature (dGag lan)," in *Tibetan Literature: Studies in Genre*, ed. José Ignacio Cabezón and Roger R. Jackson (Ithaca, NY: Snow Lion, 1996).

19. The imagined debate between Manjuśri and Vimalakīrti based on the *Vimalakīrti-nirdeśa-sūtra* assumes a similar iconic status as attested by its popularity in Chinese art. See Berger's introduction and Dunhuang cave 103 for some examples. Patricia Ann Berger, *Empire of Emptiness: Buddhist Art and Political Authority in Qing China* (Honolulu: University of Hawaii Press, 2003), 1–13.

20. Based upon his comparison of Ngorchen and Khédrup's biographical materials, Heimbel concludes that Ngorchen and Khédrup did not meet during their lifetimes. Jörg Heimbel, "The Dispute Between mKhas grub rJe and Ngor chen: Its Representation and Role in Tibetan Life Writing," in *Towards a History of Fifteenth Century Tibet: Cultural Blossoming, Religious Fervour, and Political Unrest*, ed. Volker Caumanns and Marta Sernisi (Lumbini, Nepal: Lumbini International Research Institute, 2017), 249–290. See 250 and also note 3, including Heimbel's reference to the *Dus kyi me lce* 51.1–.4.

21. Mkhas grub rje dge legs dpal bzang po (1385–1438), *Gsang 'dus bskyed rim dngos grub rgya mtsho* [*Ocean of Attainment of the Guhyasamāja Generation Stage*(Ocean of Attainment)] in New Zhol par khang edition of *gsung 'bum*, Mkhas grub rje *(zhol)*, TOH 5481 (New Delhi: Mongolian Lama Guru Deva, 1980–82), TBRC W384 (*ja*), 7:5–384; see 233–262.

22. Ngor chen, *Destroyer of the Proponents of Evil*. Ngor chen, *Kye rdo rje'i lus kyi dkyil 'khor la rtsod spong lta ba ngan sel* in *gsung 'bum* [*Dispelling Evil Views* of the *Hevajra Body Mandala* (*Dispelling Evil Views*)] [W11577], 1:580–625.

23. Yael Bentor, "Did mKhas grub rje Challenge the Authenticity of the Sa skya Lam 'bras Tradition?," in *Towards a History of Fifteenth-Century Tibet*, 227–248.

24. Bentor, 237.

25. Gorampa's text, *Illuminating the Pith: Dispelling Objections to the Moonrays of the Pith* [*Gnad gyi zla zer la rtsod pa spong ba gnad kyi gsal byed*], is a response to critiques of Ngorchen's positions in the *Moonrays of the Pith of the Generation Stage of the Precious Explanation of the Hevajra Sādhana* [*Dpal kye rdo rje'i sgrub thabs kyi rgya cher bshad pa bskyed rim gnad kyi zla zer*]. See Ronald M. Davidson, "The Ngor-pa Tradition," *Wind Horse* 1 (1981): 88, note 25.

26. Ronald M. Davidson, "Reflections on the Maheśvara Subjugation Myth: Indic Materials, Sa-skya-pa Apologetics, and the Birth of Heruka," *Journal of the International Association of Buddhist Studies* 14, no. 2 (1991): 197–235. See 221–222.

27. Davidson, 221–222.

28. I am grateful to an anonymous reviewer for reinforcing the human tendency to construct relatable narratives.
29. Bentor also introduced the term "unnamed opponents" in that article. Yael Bentor, "Identifying the Unnamed Opponents of Tsong kha pa and Mkhas grub rje Concerning the Transformation of Ordinary Birth, Death, and the Intermediary State Into the Three Bodies," in *Tibetan Buddhist Literature and Praxis: Studies in Its Formative Period, 900–1400*, ed. Ronald M. Davidson and Christian Wedemeyer, 185–200.
30. Yael Bentor, "Tsongkhapa's Guhyasamāja Sādhana and the Ārya Tradition," in *Vimalakīrti's House: A Festschrift in Honor of Robert A. F. Thurman on the Occasion of His Seventieth Birthday* (New York: Columbia University Press, 2015), 165–192. Two other recent works by Bentor are relevant: Yael Bentor, "Interpreting the Body *Maṇḍala*: Tsongkhapa Versus Later Gelug Scholars," *Revue d'Etudes Tibétaines* No. 31 (February 2015): 63–74; Yael Bentor, "Tibetan Interpretations of the Opening Verses of Vajraghanta on the Body Mandala," in *Chinese and Tibetan Esoteric Buddhism*, ed. Yael Bentor and Meir Shahar (Boston: Brill, 2017), 230–259. On Rédaba as an opponent in Ngorchen's early polemical texts, see Rae Dachille, "Running the Numbers for the Path of Mantra: Distinguishing the Thirteenth Bhūmi in Fifteenth-century Tibet," *Religions* 12, no. 3 (March 2021): 175.
31. On Kanha, see Cyrus Stearns, trans., *Taking the Result as the Path: Core Teachings of the Sakya Lamdré Tradition* (Boston: Wisdom, 2006), 9–13, part 1, note 12.
32. ["Notes for the Correct Explication of How to Enter Into the Writings of the Venerable Sa skya pas: Opening Wide in a Hundred Directions the Dharma Gates to Which All Beings of Tibet are Guided"] *Rje btsun sa skya pa'i gsung rab la 'jug tshul legs par bshad pa'i yi ge bod yul 'gro kun bsgrod pa'i chos sgo phyogs brgyar ring du phye ba*, ed. A-med-zhabs and originally composed by Chos dpal bzang po; collected works, vol. kha, fols. 384r–393v, as cited in Jan-Ulrich Sobisch, *Hevajra and Lam 'bras Literature of India and Tibet as Seen Through the Eyes of A-mes-zhabs* (Wiesbaden: Reicher, 2008), 5–6.
33. Scholars of religion such as Jonathan Z. Smith have provided compelling reasons to question the tendency to reduce debates to conflicts in philosophical perspectives defined by sectarianism. For one influential example, see Jonathan Z. Smith, "Religion, Religions, Religious," in *Critical Terms for Religious Studies*, ed. Mark C. Taylor (Chicago: University of Chicago Press, 1998), 179–195. Within Tibetan studies, two comparable critiques can be found in José Ignacio Cabezón and Geshe Lobsang Dargyay, *Freedom from Extremes: Gorampa's "Distinguishing the Views" and the Polemics of Emptiness* (Boston: Wisdom, 2007), 2–10; Donald S. Lopez, "Burnouf and the Birth of Buddhist Studies," *Eastern Buddhist* 43, nos. 1/2 (2012): 25–34.
34. Cabezón and Dargyay, *Freedom from Extremes*, 7.
35. Davidson, for example, has also noted a disjuncture between the perceived terms of the "debate" between the two figures and the details of their biographies. Davidson, "Reflections on the Maheśvara Subjugation Myth," 221–221. Bentor and Heimbel also pursue these problems; while Heimbel is more interested in the biographical sources, Bentor addresses the concerns as they arise in ritual writings of the two traditions, with attention to the relation of ritual and lineage. Heimbel, "The Dispute"; Bentor, "Did mKhas grub rje Challenge?"
36. Elijah Sacvan Ary, "Logic and Lineage: Jetsun Chokyi Gyaltsen's Ascension and the Secret Biography of Khedrup Geleg Pelzang" (PhD Diss., Harvard University, 2007), 13.
37. In part 4 of his recent monograph on Ngorchen, Heimbel emphasizes the pivotal and sectarian nature of the body mandala debate and calls for a rigorous study of the details. He summarizes its import as follows: "In general, the dispute over the interpretation of the body mandala was not merely a polemical exchange written in a cutting tone, but was also conducted from a sectarian standpoint that shaped the historical and religious realities of fifteenth-century Tibet." Jörg Heimbel, *Vajradhara in Human Form: The Life and Times of Ngor chen Kun dga' bzang po* (Lumbini, Nepal: Lumbini International Research Institute, 2017), 239, 229–248.

38. Ary observes: "while Tsongkhapa's followers may have not have initially seen themselves as members of a new and distinct Tibetan religious order, over time they came to distinguish themselves more and more from the Sakyas. Eventually, Tsongkhapa was perceived as having diverged from the interpretations accepted by the Sakyas, for which he was greatly criticized by some of the latter tradition's foremost scholars. Consequently the Gelukpas' nascent self-identity began to solidify as a distinct religious order centered upon the acceptance of the authority of Tsongkhapa's particular interpretations." Ary, *Authorized Lives*, 83-84.
39. Mkhas-grub Dge-legs-dpal-bzang-po and José Ignacio Cabezón, *A Dose of Emptiness: An Annotated Translation of the sTong thun chen mo of mKhas-grub dGe-legs-dpal-bzang* (Albany: State University of New York Press, 1992), 15.
40. Bentor, for example, describes the "passionate" and "hyperbolic" dimensions of Khédrup's style. Bentor, "Did mKhas grub rje Challenge?," 240.
41. Mkhas grub rje, *Ocean of Attainment*, 380.6
42. Khédrup's epithet "Changra Master of Ten Treatises" (*lcang ra bka' bcu pa*) reflects his integral connection with this monastery. Mkhas-grub and Cabezón, *A Dose of Emptiness*, 15 and note 36.
43. Wylie, however, dates the founding of Pelkhor Déchen to 1418. Turrell V. Wylie, "Lama Tribute in the Ming Dynasty," in *Tibetan Studies in Honour of Hugh Richardson* (Warminster: Aris and Phillips, 1980), note 10.
44. Mkhas-grub and Cabezón, *A Dose of Emptiness*, 16.
45. Jackson posits 1425 as the year in which Khédrup composed his "anti-Sakya tantric polemics;" this seems to be a reference to the body mandala debate. Jackson, *The Nepalese Legacy*, 178.
46. For a study and translation of this text, see Mkhas-grub and Cabezón, *A Dose of Emptiness*.
47. Cabezón suggests that Rongtön is among the scholars whose approaches to Madhyamaka thought Khédrup "may have very well found anathema." Mkhas-grub and Cabezón, *A Dose of Emptiness*, 6, note 29. In this book, Cabezón conducted the initial comparison of biographical accounts of the debate with Rongtön. Both of the main biographies Cabezón consults as resources on this event appear in Khédrup's *Collected Works*. See Rje brtsun chos kyi rgyal mtshan, *Gsang ba'i rnam thar* (SNT) *Collected Works*, vol. a: 421–493. Gnas rnying 'Jam dbyangs kun dga' dge legs rin chen rgyal mtshan, *Rnam thar mkhas pa'i yid 'phrog* (KYP), Collected Works, vol. ka: 1–22.
48. For more on Rapten, see Ary, "Logic and Lineage," note 267. Ary, *Authorized Lives*, 40–41, note 119. Nag-dbang-blo-bzang-rgya-mtsho and Zahiruddin Ahmad, *The History of Tibet* (Bloomington: Indiana University, Research Institute for Inner Asian Studies, 1995), 149. Wylie, "Lama Tribute in the Ming Dynasty," 484.
49. Wylie identifies this trend by "local rulers appointed by the Fifth Lha-tsun of Phag-mo-gru, Gong-ma Grags-pa rgyal-mtshan, who was known for his patronage of Tsong kha pa and his disciples." Wylie, "Lama Tribute in the Ming Dynasty," 485. Alternatively, Ehrhard highlights the gradual autonomy the princes of Gyantsé gained against the Pakmo Dru hegemony. Ehrhard also points out that Rapten Künzang possessed titles from both Gongma Drakpa Gyeltsen and the Yongle emperor. Ehrhard, "Spiritual Relationships," 249. Wylie's argument suggests the need to reconsider the degree of "independence" that a Chinese title might indicate during the Ming versus during the Yuan.
50. Jackson, *The Nepalese Legacy*, 178–179.
51. Mkhas-grub and Cabezón, *A Dose of Emptiness*, 17.
52. As translated by Cabezón in appendix 1 from this letter cited in KYP 6a–7a. Mkhas-grub and Cabezón, *A Dose of Emptiness*, 390.
53. Mkhas-grub and Cabezón, *A Dose of Emptiness*, 390.
54. See also Ary, *Authorized Lives*, 40–41, fn119. For his translation of the encounter within Jétsünpa's secret biography of Khédrup, see Ary, *Authorized Lives*, 128, note 334, 131–133, 140.

55. Leonard W. J. van der Kuijp, "Studies in the Life and Thought of Mkhas grub rje I: Mkhas grub rje's Epistemological Oeuvre and His Philological Remarks on Dignaga's *Pramāṇasamuccaya*," *Berliner Indologische Studien* 1 (1985): 98, note 18.
56. Translation of Jétsün Chökyi Gyaltsen (Jétsünpa's)'s *Secret Biography* (SNT) by Elijah Sacvan Ary, *Authorized Lives*, 128.
57. Ary, 128.
58. Jétsünpa describes Tsongkhapa as possessing similar skills. Ary reveals how Jétsünpa promoted Khédrup's image as one of Tsongkhapa's "main disciples" and also promoted Khédrup's philosophical interpretations by replacing the current philosophical textbook in use at Sera monastery with one authored by Khédrup. Ary, *Authorized Lives*, x, 60, 65–66, 93–94, note 277, 96, note 287, 97–98, 101, 105.
59. Cabezón remarks: "The fifteenth century Sa skya scholars Go and Śāk, as they were known to the dGe lugs pas, were also fond of polemics, many of their criticisms being directed against Tsong kha pa's interpretation of the Madhyamaka." Mkhas-grub and Cabezón, *A Dose of Emptiness*, 6, note 26. Heimbel elaborates upon Jétsünpa's involvement in debates, showing how biographical sources on Jétsünpa himself, such as that by Délek Nyima, emphasize the contentious nature of his polemics with these Sakyapa masters in contrast with more "cordial exchange(s) between like-minded scholars." Heimbel, "The Dispute," 261–263.
60. Translation of Jétsünpa's *Secret Biography* of Mkhas grub 11b by Ary, *Authorized Lives*, 132.
61. Cabezón identifies "the status of the dGe lugs pa colleges at Dpal 'khor sde chen" as the real source of Khédrup's concern." Mkhas-grub and Cabezón, *A Dose of Emptiness*, 17, note 44.
62. Jackson, *The Nepalese Legacy*, 179.
63. As is the case with many of Khédrup's texts, the colophon offers no date of composition, only the location, Ganden. See Mkhas grub rje dge legs dpal bzang (1385–1438), *Phyin ci log gi gtam gyi sbyor ba la 'jug pa'i smra ba ngan pa rnam par 'thag pa bstan bcos gnam lcags 'khor lo* [The Thunderbolt Wheel Treatise Which Utterly Decimates the Evil Proponents Engaged in Erroneous Speech (*Thunderbolt Wheel of Reply to Ngor*)] in Collected Works [*zhol*] Vol. 2, 7–100. See also the modern publication: *Dgag lan phyogs bsgrigs*. Ch'eng tu: Si khron Mi rigs Dpe skrun khang, 1997. Chinese colophon title: Pien lun wen hsuan pien, 1–68. Ary described this modern collection as "a compilation of works by five authors refuting non-Geluk criticisms of Tsongkhapa's Madhyamaka views." Ary, *Authorized Lives*, 84 fn247.
64. Translation of or Jétsünpa's *Secret Biography* (SNT) 17b–18a by Ary, *Authorized Lives*, 140.
65. Further research is needed to determine the identity of Chöjé Sönam Lodrö. Ary suggests that this may be a "Khewang Sönam Lodrö." Ary, *Authorized Lives*, 140 fn352. Heimbel suggests that this figure is the teacher of Ngor's third abbot, Jamyang Shérap Gyatso (1396–1474). Heimbel, "The Dispute," 255.
66. Sangs rgyas phun tshogs (b. 1649, d. 1705), *Rgyal ba rdo rje 'chang kun dga' bzang po'i rnam par thar pa legs bshad chu bo 'dus pa'i rgya mtsho yon tan yid bzhin nor bu'i 'byung gnas* [The Source of the Wish Fulfilling Jewel, the Oceanic Qualities Which Gather the Rivers: The Biography ("Liberation Story") of the Victorious Vajradhara Kun dga' bzang po]. Scanned from the Sde dge blocks carved at the time of Sa skyong tshe dbang rdo rje rig 'dzin, dkar mdzes khul: Sde dge. [written 1688], 531.4–.5.

    For more on Rongtön in Ngorchen's biography, see 531.4–532.1.
67. Translation of Jétsünpa'as *Secret Biography* (SNT) 17b–18a by Ary, *Authorized Lives*, 140.
68. Heimbel presents a compelling theory that Jétsünpa confuses the arguments from *The Thunderbolt Wheel* with those made in a different reply by Khédrup, the *Reply to the Questions of the Kalyānamītra Kon ting gug śrī ba*, to be discussed later in this chapter. Both texts open up possibilities for exploring further "rounds" of the body mandala debate. If Jétsünpa is in error, while

his confusion of the two texts may be in earnest, it is also possible that his choices reflect a concern to construct a coherent narrative of the debate.

69. Translation of *Secret Biography* (SNT) by Jétsün Chökyi Gyeltsen (or Jétsünpa) 7b–8a by Ary, *Authorized Lives,* 128.
70. Heimbel, "The Dispute," 253.
71. *The Thunderbolt Wheel* also provides important clues for resolving the relationship between Ngorchen's two texts, *Destroyer of the Proponents of Evil* [N1] and the other "version," *Dispelling Evil Views* [N2]. In *The Thunderbolt Wheel,* Khédrup cites selected points from Ngorchen's argument, and upon preliminary investigation, these selections appear to be from the longer "version," *Dispelling Evil Views* [N2].
72. Mkhas grub, *Reply to the Questions.*
73. Heimbel dates the text to the period between 1427 and 1431. Heimbel, "The Dispute," note 24.
74. Rockhill translated this title as "Holy Anointed Adviser (Preceptor) of the Realm." William Woodville Rockhill, *The Land of the Lamas: Notes of a Journey through China, Mongolia and Tibet with Maps and Illustrations* (New York: Century, 1891), 199, note 1. The first Tibetan teacher to receive the title was the Sakyapa abbot Khétsün Namkha Lekpé Gyeltsen (1305–43) from the Yuan emperor Yesün Temür (r. 1323–1328). The Ming emperors conferred the title upon laymen as well, for example, upon the Pakmo Dru administrators. Schwieger, "Significance of Ming Titles," 315. Roerich indicates that the title was conferred upon the abbots of Tsurpu in the form of a seal by the Yongle/Ming emperor. Gos Lo-tsā-ba Gzhon-nu-dpal and George Roerich, *The Blue Annals* (Delhi: Motilal Banarsidass, 1988).
75. Schwieger, "Significance of Ming Titles," 314. Schwieger refers to the work of Shen Weirong in considering how the conferral of these titles during the Ming may have been less politically significant than during the Yuan. Shen Weirong, "On the History of Gling tshang Principality mDo khams During the Yuan and Ming Dynasties: Study on Sources Concerning Tibet in the Ming Shilu (I)," in *Tibetstudien: Festschrift für Dieter Schuh zum 65. Geburtstag* ed. Dieter Schuh, Petra H. Maurer, and Peter Schwieger (Bonn: Bier'sche Verlagsanstalt, 2007).
76. Translation, also cited earlier, of *Secret Biography* (SNT) by Jétsün Chökyi Gyeltsen (or Jétsünpa), 7b–8a, by Ary, who has identified this figure as "Kunting Gushri Namkha Sangpo," but no additional information is provided. Ary, *Authorized Lives,* 128 note 336. Cabezón also make note of a reference to a Sakyapa "Kan ting gu śrī" as one of Khédrup's "opponents" cited in the *Secret Biography.* Mkhas-grub and Cabezón, *A Dose of Emptiness,* 6, note 29.
77. Heimbel bases his theory on a comment in the *Mdo smad chos 'byung* of Könchok Tenpa Rapgyé (1801–1866). Heimbel, *Vajradhara in Human Form,* 232, note 95. He ties this figure to Sakya Nyidé Labrang. Heimbel, "The Dispute," 252.
78. Leonard van der Kuijp, "Miscellanea Apropos of the Philosophy of Mind in Tibet: Mind in Tibetan Buddhism," *Tibet Journal* 10, no. 1 (Spring 1985): 34. Also cited in Heimbel, *Vajradhara in Human Form,* 232, note 95. See TBRC P3565, which lists this figure's lifespan as 1349–1425. There appears to be some confusion with the notes for this entry, potentially conflating this Tekchen Chöjé with a figure invited to the Ming court in 1438 and conferred titles. If we consider the somewhat less likely possibility that Könting Gushrī may have been a contemporary of Tsongkhapa but not of Khédrup himself, some additional possibilities present themselves. For example, Künga Rinchen (1339–1399) [TBRC P1862], the sixteenth throne holder of Zhitok Labrang at Sakya, was also granted the title Könting Gushrība by the Ming emperor.
79. Davidson, "Preliminary Studies," 21, note 64.
80. Mkhas grub, *Reply to the Questions,* 776.3.
81. Mkhas grub, 775.2–.3. Heimbel has proposed that the first part of this text is a response to Ngorchen's 1419 *Moonrays of the Pith* [*Gnad kyi zla zer*], a comprehensive exposition of the Hevajra sādhana, while the second part responds to a recently discovered short sādhana text. The latter,

the *Dpal kye rdo rje'i lus kyi dkyil 'khor gyi sgrub pa'i thabs rnal 'byor snying po*, is dated to 1410 but does not appear in Ngorchen's collected works. Heimbel's theory provides a compelling avenue for future body mandala debate studies If he is correct, it would provide another example of the layered nature of the body mandala debate and the challenges of evaluating an author's stated purpose for composing a polemical text versus the issues they actually explore in the text.. However, it should be noted that Khédrup claims to be responding to a critique of his commentary on the Guhyasamāja sādhana within which his body mandala remarks appear. Heimbel, *Vajradhara in Human Form*, 233, note 99. For Ngorchen's 1419 Hevajra sādhana text, see *Dpal kye rdo rje'i lus kyi dkyil 'khor gyi sgrub pa'i thabs rnal 'byor snying po*. In *Sa skya'i chos mdzod chen mo, Si khron bod yig dpe rnying 'tshol bsdu rtsom sgrig khang* (2013), 28:296–312.

82. Mkhas grub, *Reply to the Questions*, 775.4–776.1.
83. Mkhas grub, 776.5–777.1.
84. The calculations may concern the date of the Buddha's passing, which, according to Sapen, predates Jétsün Drakpa Gyeltsen's death in 1216 by 3,350 years. Jowita Kramer, *A Noble Abbot from Mustang: Life and Works of Glo-bo mKhan-chen (1456–1532)*, Wiener Studien zur Tibetologie und Buddhismuskunde 68 (Vienna: Arbeitskreis für Tibetische und Buddhistische Studien, 2008), 148, note 29.
85. Heimbel posits a shift in audience here, with the first part of the text targeting Kon ting's "misconception of Buddhism, in general," and the second focused on Ngorchen "as a religious master who, though having received Vajrayāna teachings from Tsong kha pa, discarded his tantric pledges like grass out of hope for riches and honours in this life and disparaged Tsong kha pa holding much hate and jealousy." Heimbel, "The Dispute," 253.
86. Mkhas grub, *Reply to the Questions*, 782.5–783.1.
87. Heimbel remarks, "That mKhas grub rJe was slightly mischaracterised has recently been shown by Yael Bentor." Heimbel, *Vajradhara in Human Form*, 235. See Bentor, "Did mKhas grub rje Challenge?"
88. Bentor identifies Tsongkhapa's *Lam rim chen mo*, his comprehensive work on the stages of the path of practice, as well as his *'Dod 'jo*, a commentary on Cakrasaṃvara practice, as sources for some of Khédrup's arguments in *Ocean of Attainment*. Bentor, "Did mKhas grub rje Challenge?," 238.
89. In his review of Thurman's dissertation on Tsongkhapa's *Legs bshad snying po*, van der Kuijp questions Thurman's claim that Rédaba disapproved of Tsongkhapa's tantric inclinations. Van der Kuijp traces this claim to Khédrup's biographical writings on Tsongkhapa and critiques its accuracy. See Leonard van der Kuijp, "Apropos of a Recent Contribution to the History of Central Way Philosophy in Tibet: Tsong kha pa's Speech of Gold," *Berliner Indologische Studien* 1 (1985): 47–74, see 47. For Thurman's remark, see Robert A. F. Thurman, *The Central Philosophy of Tibet: A Study and Translation of Jey Tsong Khapa's Essence of True Eloquence* (Princeton: Princeton University Press, 1984), 69.
90. Van der Kuijp, "Apropos of a Recent Contribution," 50.
91. Van der Kuijp points to the importance of confirming a more specific date for Khédrup's biography of Tsongkhapa than the colophon provides. Based upon the colophon's statement that the text was written in Nyangtö in Tsang, van der Kuijp deduces that it was composed after Tsongkhapa's death in 1419 and before Khédrup's tenure as throneholder at Ganden beginning in 1431. Van der Kuijp, "Apropos of a Recent Contribution," note 8.
92. On the history of Virūpa's quintessential Path and Fruit text, the *Rdo rje tshig rkang*, including Ngorchen's assessment of that history, see Cyrus Stearns, *Luminous Lives: The Story of the Masters of the Lam 'Bras Tradition in Tibet* (Boston: Wisdom, 2001), 8–12.
93. Cabezón and Dargyay, *Freedom from Extremes*, 25; van der Kuijp, "Apropos of a Recent Contribution," 47–74; Davidson, "Reflections on the Maheśvara."
94. Davidson introduced this term. Davidson, "Reflections on the Maheśvara."

95. Sangyé Püntsok's biography is one of the two available biographies out of six that were written. The first was written in 1455, mostly during Ngorchen's lifetime, by his disciple Müchen Könchok Gyeltsen. Heimbel describes Sangyé Püntsok's biography of Ngorchen, composed in 1688, as "a much later compilation of Ngorchen's biographies written by Ngorchen's direct disciples, including Mus chen." Sangyé Püntsok's role in disseminating this work through supervising the carving of the woodblocks for the xylograph at Dégé is of particular interest. Heimbel, "The Dispute," 273.

96. Sangs rgyas phun tshogs, *The Source*, 546.2–.3. I cite this same passage in my introduction to Ngorchen's root text and his commentary for *Overcoming Objections to the Three Tantras* in Rae Dachille, "'Empty Like the Sky': Polysemy and the Problem of 'Mere Clear Awareness' at the Intersection of Sūtra and Tantra in Fifteenth-century Tibet," *Revue d'Etudes Tibétaines*, no. 58 (April 2021): 208–236; see 210.

97. Within his text and autocommentary, Ngorchen mostly uses the terms *Vijñapti-vada* (*rnam rig smra ba*) and *Vijñapti-mātra* (*rnam rig tsam*) rather than *Cittamātra* (*sems tsam pa*) to describe this "Consciousness Only" orientation. See Dachille, "'Empty Like the Sky,'" 211, note 9.

98. Khenpo Tashi Dorje described a more recent conversation that occurred at a 2004 conference in Vārāṅasī between two luminaries of the contemporary Sakya and Geluk traditions on this very problem. Khenpo Gyatso of Sakya College and His Holiness the Fourteenth Dalai Lama revisited the problem of Virūpa's philosophical perspective. Khenpo Gyatso claimed that the faulty identification of Virūpa as a Cittamātrin was the result of confusing two different historical masters; apparently His Holiness accepted the claim. This exchange reinforces the enduring significance of the tantric polemics that are the focus of this book. Reading session with author, International Buddhist Academy (IBA), Kathmandu, Fall 2011.

99. Khenpo Tashi Dorje suggested that Rédaba was the one to demand a reply to this challenge and that Tsongkhapa supported him in this demand. Reading session, IBA, Fall 2011. Van der Kuijp identifies both Rédaba and Bodong Penchen as Ngorchen's opponents in these texts. Leonard W. J. van der Kuijp, "A Text-Historical Note on *Hevajratantra* II: V:1–2." *Journal of the International Association for Buddhist Studies* 8, no. 1 (1985): 87.

    In an upcoming article, I explore this text together with its autocommentary in detail, with particular attention to the role of Rédaba as one of Ngorchen's unnamed opponents. I argue that, as a site of interpenetration and potential cross-contamination of the Sakya and Geluk lineages, Rédaba posed a challenge for both traditions. Ngorchen's efforts to disambiguate his own interpretation of the Sakya perspective from that of Rédaba are symptomatic of this discomfort.

100. Sangs rgyas phun tshogs, *The Source*, 546.3–.5.

101. Khenpo Tashi Dorje, reading session, IBA, Fall 2011.

102. *dpal ldan kun dga'i lung rigs lha dbang gis/ rdo rje log rtog lha min kun bcil nas/ thub bstan skabs gsum rgyas par mdzad* [547.1] *pa yis/ mdzad pa bzang po e ma ngo mtshar phul*. Sangs rgyas phun tshogs, *The Source*, 546–547.1. Khenpo Tashi Dorje suggested that *skabs gsum* may here refer to the three vows. The three vows are the *prātimokṣa* vows of monastic conduct, the bodhisattva vows of altruistic intention, and the *samaya* vows guarding tantric practice. Khenpo Tashi Dorje, reading session, IBA, Fall 2011.

103. *snga ma sa skya pa'i rgyud gsum man ngag dang bcas pa'i lta ba sems tsam yin zer ba dang / sa skya pa'i lus dkyil gyud gzhung nas ma bshad zer ba'i rtsod pa byung nas*. Sangs rgyas phun tshogs, *The Source*, 537.4.

104. *sa skya pa'i dge bshes rnams 'thor sa med pa'i bca' khrims byas nas 'byon stabs ma byung*. Sangs rgyas phun tshogs, 537.4.

105. Sangs rgyas phun tshogs, 537.5. Sangyé Püntsok refers to Lobo here as "*rje mkhan chen po*."

106. Kramer notes that the details of Ngorchen's visits to Lomöntang assume a prominent role in Lobo's autobiography (approximately 40 percent of the text), despite the fact that the two masters never

met. She describes this prominence as testament to Lobo's "strong obligation . . . to this great master of the Ngor pa tradition." Kramer, *A Noble Abbot*, 56.

107. Kramer, *A Noble* Abbot, 146–147. Glo bo mkhan chen bsod nams lhun grub (1456–1532), *Rje btsun bsod nams lhun grub legs pa'i 'byung gnas rgyal mtshan dpal bzang po'i rnam par thar pa zhus lan,* manuscript 6a–b.
108. *bka' bcu* is a synonym of *bka' chen,* indicating one who "observes the ten precepts" and "equivalent to the Geshe degree." https://www.thlib.org (RY).
109. Heimbel, *Vajradhara in Human Form*, 282–283. Heimbel's sixth chapter is a study of Ngorchen's three journeys to Lomöntang. Heimbel, 274–299.
110. There are certainly instances of threats to the physical safety of monks resulting from their involvement in polemics. I am grateful to José Cabezón for suggesting this possibility for interpreting the travel ban. Conversation with the author, International Association of Tibetan Studies, Paris, July 2019.
111. Heimbel, "The Dispute," 250.
112. José Cabezón, email communication, November 2019.
113. Jackson, *The Nepalese Legacy,* 178. See also Jörg Heimbel, "Biographical Sources for Researching the Life of Ngor chen Kun dga' bzang po (1382–1456)," *Revue d'Etudes Tibétaines* 22 (2011): 54, note 23. Heimbel consults several biographies of Ngorchen's student and eventual abbatial successor, Müchen Könchok Gyeltsen (1388–1469) to flesh out Ngorchen's activities in the time leading up to the founding of Ngor.
114. Heimbel, "Biographical Sources," 48.
115. Heimbel, 48.
116. Heimbel, *Vajradhara in Human Form*, 226. Heimbel adjusts the dating of this threat from 1426–1427, as found in the biographies, to 1425–1426.
117. Heimbel likewise considers sorcery as a significant narrative convention in Khédrup and Ngorchen's biographical sources. Heimbel, "The Dispute."
118. *Ngor chen gyi rnam thar* 2: 522.2–.4, Translated in Heimbel, *Vajradhara in Human Form*, 227, note 71.
119. Heimbel, "Biographical Sources," 48.
120. Sangs rgyas phun tshogs, *The Source*, 524.3. I considered emending the reading to "bar" or "drinking place" (*chang sa*). However, as Heimbel points out, all versions of the text indeed read *chang ma*. Heimbel, "Biographical Sources," 49, note 5.
121. Mahākāla even confesses: "The Sakyapas definitely don't like you. They gave me ritual cakes and told me to harm Tsongkhapa and his spiritual heirs, particularly you!" in Chöden Ranjor's *Short Biography of Mkhas grub*, 30a, translated in Ary, *Authorized Lives*, 112.
122. Sangs rgyas phun tshogs, *The Source*, 536.5–539.2.
123. Sangs rgyas phun tshogs, 540.6 for a description of Ngorchen's activities at Lomöntang, see the biography, 536.5–539.2, and Heimbel, *Vajradhara in Human Form*, 274–299. For important background on the region through the lens of oratory, see David P. Jackson, *The Mollas of Mustang: Historical, Religious, and Oratorical Traditions of the Nepalese-Tibetan Borderland* (Dharamsala: Library of Tibetan Works and Archives, 1984).
124. See, for example, Kramer, *A Noble Abbot*, 151, 153. See also Sangs rgyas phun tshogs, *The Source*, 539.1.
125. On Ngorchen's ordination of Amapel, see Kramer, *A Noble Abbot*, 145–146. See also Sangs rgyas phun tshogs, *The Source*, 538.4–.5. On his ordination of the king of Gugé, see Kramer, *A Noble Abbot*, 148, note 27.
126. Kramer's translation of Amapel; see Kramer, *A Noble Abbot*, 147.
127. Kramer's translation of Amapel; see Kramer, 153.
128. Heimbel, "Biographical Sources," 55, note 27.

129. Bodong was one of Khédrup's teachers in Buddhist logic and philosophy. See Adams, treasuryoflives .org (2007). Jétsünpa's *Secret Biography* of Khédrup (6a–6b) describes a debate between Khédrup and Bodong held at Ngamring when the latter was only sixteen. According to the account, Khédrup emerged victorious. See Ary, *Authorized Lives*, 39, 126–127, note 331. For more on the tradition of Bodong, see Gene E. Smith and Kurtis R. Schaeffer, "Buddhist Literary and Practical Arts According to Bo dong Pan chen Phyogs las rnam rgyal," in *Among Tibetan Texts: History and Literature of the Himalayan Plateau* (Boston: Wisdom, 2001), 179–208.
130. Khenpo Tashi Dorje, personal communication, IBA, Fall 2011.
131. For more on Ngorchen and Rongtön's relationship, see Heimbel, *Vajradhara in Human Form*, 360, note 635.
132. See Sangs rgyas phun tshogs, *The Source*, 537.3. Recall that Bodong has been posited as one of Ngorchen's opponents in his early polemical text and commentary for *Overcoming Objections to the Three Tantras*.
133. Cabezón and Dargyay, *Freedom from Extremes*, 42
134. Heimbel, "Biographical Sources," 47–48.
135. Jackson, *The Nepalese Legacy*, 178. See also Sangs rgyas phun tshogs, *The Source*, 527.6: "Although Dakchen Chumikpa had offered the land, when he [Ngor chen] arrived at Chumik he requested a letter of permission and offered a crystal bowl and so forth as payment." Sangyé Püntsok [530.6] lists Ngorchen's half-brother, Dakchen Chumikpa Drakpa Lodrö, first in his enumeration of Ngorchen's disciples and patrons.
136. See reference to Sönam Drakpa's *Deb ther mar po gsar ma* in Cabezón and Dargyay, *Freedom from Extremes*, 44.
137. Bsod-nams-grags-pa and Giuseppe Tucci, *Deb ther dmar po gsar ma Tibetan chronicles* (Roma: Istituto Italiano per il Medio ed Estremo Oriente), 99aa, 239–40, as cited in Cabezón and Dargyay, *Freedom from Extremes*, 44.
138. Cabezón and Dargyay, *Freedom from Extremes*, 44.
139. Cabezón and Dargyay, *Freedom from Extremes*, 44 fn215. For more on the patron Norzang and on Sönam Drakpa's depiction of Ngorchen—including the Fifth Dalai Lama's critique of it—see Heimbel, "The Dispute," 265–269, and Heimbel, *Vajradhara in Human Form*, 242–244.
140. Cabezón and Dargyay, *Freedom from Extremes*, 44.
141. Cabezón cites Guru Trashi's *Ngag dbang blo gros Stag sgang mkhas mchog* in *Gu bkra'i chos 'byung*, 992. Cabezón speculates that, in that instance, "what was at stake was not so much the authenticity of texts as their interpretations and ritual enactment." Cabezón and Dargyay, *Freedom from Extremes*, 25, note 16. Heimbel, *Vajradhara in Human Form*, 237, note 130. I would argue that in the case of the body mandala debate questions of authenticity and ritual and interpretive practice cannot be so easily separated.
142. Ronald M. Davidson, "The Ngor-pa Tradition," *Wind Horse* 1 (1981): 86, note 17.
143. Davidson, 86.
144. Sangs rgyas phun tshogs, *The Source*, 547.1–2
145. Jeffrey Hopkins and Kevin Vose, *Tantric Techniques* (Ithaca, NY: Snow Lion, 2009), 303–318. Lessing and Wayman, mKhas Grub rJe's *Fundamentals of Buddhist Tantra*, 163–171.
146. Davidson, "The Ngor-pa Tradition," 86.
147. Sangs rgyas phun tshogs, *The Source*, 547.1–.2.
148. Davidson, "The Ngor-pa Tradition," 86. See Ngorchen's collected works for these texts: Ngor chen kun dga' bzang po, *Spyod rgyud spyi'i rnam gzhag legs bshad sgron me* [*Lamp of Eloquent Explanation for Classifying the Kriyā Tantras*] in *gsung 'bum*, Kun dga' bzang po. TBRC W11577. 4:135–204. Ngor chen kun dga' bzang po, *Bya rgyud spyi'i rnam bshad legs bshad rgya mtsho* [*Ocean of Eloquent Explanation of the Caryā Tantras*] in *gsung 'bum*, Kun dga' bzang po. TBRC W11577. 4:204–418.

149. Khenpo Tashi Dorje, reading session, IBA, Fall 2011. See also Davidson, "The Ngor-pa Tradition," 84. There still remains some ambiguity around the circumstances of this failed encounter.
150. Heimbel, *Vajradhara in Human Form*, 225. This particular exchange between Ngorchen and Tsongkhapa deserves further attention, particularly in light of disparities between accounts and their Buddhological interpretations. It is possible that Ngorchen's interest in "reviving" the lower classes of tantras had genuine pedagogical grounding in his vision for monastic education, but the value of the higher tantric classes as central to the ritual programs of both Sakya and Gelukpa traditions is undeniable.
151. Heimbel, "The Dispute," 252, note 17, 275, note 82.
152. Bentor locates Ngorchen's critique of Tsongkhapa on the Guhyasamāja in his *Shin tu rnal 'byor gyi khyad par sgrub thabs kyi yan lag tu bris pa*, an appendix to his 1423 text, *Dpal gsang ba 'dus pa'i dkyil 'khor gyi sgrub thabs dngos grub rgya mtsho*. The critique appears in a somewhat cryptic statement on distinguishing forms of atiyoga: "Therefore, it seems that the later lamas (*phyis kyi bla ma rnams*) who wrote many inadequate explanations by only taking into account one method of the *atiyoga*, did not investigate this matter in detail." Bentor locates Ngorchen's critique of Tsongkhapa's interpretation of Cakrasaṃvara in his *Dril bu pa'i lus dkyil gyi bshad pa*. Bentor writes: "One of these rounds is highly critical of Tsong kha pa. Though this work is undated, it cites verbatim Tsong kha pa's *sNgags rim chen mo* written in 1405, and his commentary on the practice of Cakrasamvara, which may have been written in 1415." Bentor, "Did mKhas grub rje Challenge?," 230–231.

3. "CUTTING THE GROUND"

1. Scholars have begun to explore the potential of intertextuality as a category for analyzing Buddhist texts. Cabezón was at the forefront in inviting a rigorous inquiry into Tibetan "intertextual promiscuity" to engage with cross-cultural and interdisciplinary conversations on authorship. José Cabezón, "Authorship and Literary Production in Classical Buddhist Tibet," in *Changing Minds*, ed. Guy Newland (Ithaca, NY: Snow Lion, 2001), 233–264. Wedemeyer uses citations by Tibetan exegetes as evidence of the array of different Tibetan translations of Indian texts available to them. Our studies share an interest in "discursive strategies of legitimation of authority in fourteenth–fifteenth century Tibetan scholastic discourse." Christian Wedemeyer, "Tantalising Traces of the Labours of the Lotsawas: Alternative Translations of Sanskrit Sources in the Writings of Rje Tsong Kha Pa," in *Tibetan Buddhist Literature and Praxis: Studies in Its Formative Period, 900–1400*, ed. Ronald Davidson and Christian Wedemeyer (Leiden: Brill, 2006), 149–182. More recent fruitful examples of the diversity of approaches to intertextuality appear in "Reuse and Intertextuality in the Context of Buddhist Texts," ed. Elisa Freschi, Cathy Cantwell, and Jowita Kramer, special issue, *Buddhist Studies Review* 33, nos. 1–2 (2016). Among these, Paul Hackett addresses issues especially germane to this chapter. He highlights intertextuality within Guhyasmāja sources as well as the framing of the commentarial apparatus as "recovery" versus "discovery" of meaning. Paul G. Hackett, "Re-making, Re-marking, or Re-using? Hermeneutical Strategies and Challenges in the Guhyasamāja Commentarial Literature," in Freschi, Cantwell, and Kramer, 163–169.
2. *rdo rje theg pa'i sde snod la sbyang pa yun ring du ma byas pa'i rtog ge pa dag 'di skad 'dzer te.* Ngor chen kun dga' bzang po, *Kye'i rdo rje'i lus kyi dkyil 'khor la rtsod spong smra ba ngan 'joms* [*Destroyer of the Proponents of Evil Through Eliminating Objections to the Hevajra Body Mandala*] in *gsung 'bum*, Kun dga' bzang po. *Ngor chen kun dga' bzang po'i bka' 'bum*, comp. Bsod nams rgya mtsho and reproduced from the Sde dge block prints (Dehra dun: photomechanical print from a set of

prints from the Sde dge dgon chen blocks [W11577]), 1:545–580. See 548.1–2. I have emended *sbyad pa* to *sbyang pa* in accord with Ngorchen's longer text.

3. Susan Stryker, "My Words to Victor Frankenstein Above the Village of Chamounix," *GLQ: A Journal of Lesbian and Gay Studies* 1, no. 3 (June 1994): 237–254; see 240. I discuss the larger context for Stryker's remarks in the introduction.
4. John Felstiner, *Paul Celan: Poet, Survivor, Jew* (Urbana: University of Illinois Press, 2001), 211.
5. Jacques Derrida, "Signature, Event, Context," in *A Derrida Reader: Between the Blinds,* ed. Jacques Derrida and Peggy Kamuf (New York: Columbia University Press, 1991), 80–111.
6. Jonathan Z. Smith, "Sacred Persistence: Toward a Redescription of Canon," in *Imagining Religion: From Babylon to Jonestown* (Chicago: University of Chicago Press, 1982), 52.
7. For example, for studies of the Pāli, Chinese, and Tibetan canons, respectively, see Steven Collins, "On the Very Idea of the Pali Canon," *Journal of the Pali Text Society* 15 (1990): 89–126; and Charles Hallisey, "Roads Taken and Not Taken in the Study of Theravāda Buddhism," in *Curators of the Buddha: The Study of Buddhism Under Colonialism*, ed. Donald Lopez (Chicago: University of Chicago Press, 1995); Jiang Wu and Lucille Chia, *Spreading Buddha's Word in East Asia: The Formation and Transformation of the Chinese Buddhist Canon* (New York: Columbia University Press, 2016); Kurtis R. Schaeffer, *The Culture of the Book in Tibet* (New York: Columbia University Press, 2014).
8. Phillip Stanley, "The Tibetan Buddhist Canon," in *The Wiley Blackwell Companion to East and Inner Asian Buddhism*, ed. Mario Poceski (Oxford: Wiley, 2014), 383–407.
9. The Buddhist Digital Resource Center and the Tibetan and Himalayan Library are two key resources for accessing digital versions of the Tibetan canon. See https://library.bdrc.io/ and https://www.thlib.org/encyclopedias/literary/canons/kt/catalog.php#cat=d.
10. Smith, "Sacred Persistence."
11. Ngor chen, *Destroyer of the Proponents of Evil, 548.1–.2.* See note 2, this chapter.
12. Mkhas grub rje dge legs dpal bzang po (1385–1438), *Gsang 'dus bskyed rim dngos grub rgya mtsho* [*Ocean of Attainment of the Guhyasamāja Generation Stage*] in New Zhol par khang edition of *gsung 'bum/*, Mkhas grub rje *(zhol)*, TOH 5481 (New Delhi: Mongolian Lama Guru Deva, 1980–82), TBRC W384 (*ja*), 7:5–384. See 233–262, especially 250.4–263.3.
13. Mkhas grub, *Ocean of Attainment*, 250.6–252.5.
14. Mkhas grub, 252.5–254.5.
15. For his interpretation, see Mkhas grub, 253.4–254.6. This is a complicated and very technical section of Khédrup's argument. For more detail on Tsongkhapa's version of these ritual mechanics, see Yael Bentor, "Interpreting the Body *Maṇḍala*: Tsongkhapa Versus Later Gelug Scholars," *Revue d'Etudes Tibétaines*, no. 31 (February 2015): 65–67, note 23. Bentor refers to Ngorchen's disputation of Tsongkhapa's position in his *Commentary on the Ghantapa Body Mandala Practice.* I include here references to two different versions of this text by Ngorchen: (Ngor chen) Kun dga' bzang po (1382–1456), *Dril bu pa'i lus dkyil gyi bshad pa* [*Commentary on the Ghantapa Body Mandala Practice*] in *gsung 'bum*, Kun dga' bzang po. *Ngor chen kun dga' bzang po'i bka' 'bum*, compiled by Bsod nams rgya mtsho and reproduced from the Sde dge block prints (Dehra dun: photomechanical print from a set of prints from the Sde dge dgon chen blocks. BDRC W11577), 4:735–766; Ngor chen. *Commentary on the Ghantapa Body Mandala Practice. Dril bu pa'i lus dkyil gyi bshad pa.* In *Sa skya pa'i bka' 'bum* (Tokyo: Toyo Bunko, 1969), vol. 10, folios 117b–140a, 398.1.1–405.4.1.
16. Mkhas grub, *Ocean of Attainment*, 254.5–.6. This is the only moment in his body mandala chapter in which Khédrup cites Tsongkhapa as an authority "by name," albeit in a somewhat open way with the title *Jé Rinpoché*, literally the "venerable precious one." The only other instance in which he mentions a specific Tibetan master, as opposed to the more evasive and often critical "some Tibetans say" or "some earlier lamas said," is his citation (or mis-citation) of Butön on the mandala of the support.
17. Mkhas grub, *Ocean of Attainment*, 254.5–.6. Khédrup's reference to the extraordinary or uncommon (*thun mong ma yin pa*) context of Cakrasaṃvara merits further research in light of several

questions. These regard the commonality of practices to multiple ritual systems and the relevance of some texts, specifically the explanatory tantras, to the interpretation of multiple texts. I address such questions more fully in my analysis of the genre of explanatory tantra in the final chapter. See also chapter 4 for my discussion of a passage from Ngorchen's writings on the "commonality" of the mandala of support to the Cakrasaṃvara and Hevajra systems. Ngorchen, *Destroyer of the Proponents of Evil,* 561.4–562.1.

18. *bod dag gis ma rgyud kyi lus dkyil mang por/spyi bo sna tshogs rdo rje/rkang mthil rdo rje'i sa gzhi/ rtsib ma rdo rje'i ra ba/pags pa rdo rje'i gur dang bla re /ba spu mda'i dra ba/ sen mo me ri rab tu 'bar ba/zhes pa dang snying ga'i rtsa bzhi po sgo bzhi/mig pa 'tsa re kha'i rtsig pa/sna rin po che'i pha gu/ so dra ba dra phyed/ lce dang mchu 'dod yon gyi snam bu/ zhe sogs bris pa la/.* Ngor chen, *Destroyer of the Proponents of Evil,* 548.2–.3.

19. Mkhas grub, *Reply to the Questions of the Kalyānamītra Kon ting gug śrī ba. Dge ba'i bshes gnyen kon ting gug shri ba'i dris lan. Thor-bu Collected Works,* TBRC W384, vol. 9, pp. 775–808. See 775.4. I discuss this passage in chapter 2.

20. For a detailed account of the history of classifying the tantras in Tibet, see Jacob P. Dalton, "A Crisis of Doxography: How Tibetans Organized Tantra During the Eighth–Twelfth Centuries," *Journal of the International Association of Buddhist Studies* 28, no. 1 (2005): 115–181.

21. [?]Grags pa rgyal mtshan (1147–1216), *Lus kyi dkyil 'khor* [*Body mandala*] in Digital Sakya *lam 'bras* collection, 10:140–143.

('Phags pa) Blo gros rgyal mtshan (1235–1280), *Kyai rdo rje lus dkyil gyi sgrub thabs* [*Hevajra Body Mandala Sādhanam*], in *Sa skya bka' 'bum, Collected Writings of the First Five Great Patriarchs of the Sakya Order* (Dehra dun: Sakya Center, 1992–1993), BDRC W22271, 13:538–542.

For additional detail on these two texts, see my introduction to the tantric practice of correlating the aspects of the body with enlightened forms, found in chapter 1. See also the footnote there indicating that Bentor identifies a similar correlation schema in the Hevajra *sādhana* composed by Ngorchen in 1410, the *Dpal kye rdo rje'i lus kyi dkyil 'khor gyi sgrub pa'i thabs rnal 'byor snying po.* Yael Bentor, "Did mKhas grub rje Challenge the Authenticity of the Sa skya Lam 'bras Tradition?" in *Towards a History of Fifteenth-century Tibet: Cultural Blossoming, Religious Fervour, and Political Unrest,* ed. Volker Caumanns and Marta Sernisi (Lumbini, Nepal: Lumbini International Research Institute, 2017), 239.

22. Butön is citing Nagpopa's text, *Saṃvara-vyākhyā.* Full title in Tibetan: *Sdom pa bshad pa.* Toh. 1460. Bstan 'gyur, rgyud 'bum, 22, ff. 6a–10b: 12–20. The source of this citation is found on page (13)7a.4 of the Sde dge edition with a minor variations: *lus skye ni* vs. *lus skye nas.*

23. *zhe sogs bris pa la/ thams cad mkhyen pa bu ston rin po ches/ sdom pa bshad par/go rims bzhin du lus skye nas/rdo rje phur pu lhan cig skyes/ bcings pa thig skud rab tu ldan/shin tu mtshams med brtan par bcings. gur ni rus pa'i phreng ba nyid/ces pa tsam ma gtogs rgya gzhung gang na'ang de 'dra ba bshad pa mi 'dug go.* Ngor chen, *Destroyer of the Proponents of Evil,* 548.3–.4. For Bentor's discussion of this section of Ngorchen's text, see Yael Bentor, "Did mKhas grub rje Challenge?," 242 and note 74.

24. The nine deities likely refer to the Hevajra *yab yum* —Hevajra in union with his consort Nairātmyā—and eight goddesses of their retinue.

25. *zhes gsungs pa ni shin tu med de/lus gzhal yas khang du bskyed tshul de 'dra ba dang/phyi'i dkyil 'khor la lha dgu las med pa la/lus dkyil gyi lha brgya lnga bcu rtsa bdun la sogs pa bkod cing/lus dkyil gyi lha'i nang na phyi dkyil la dgod pa dang thun mong gi lha gcig kyang med pa sogs rgyud dang rgya gzhung tshad ldan gang nas kyang ma bshad cing/don thob la'ang med kyang/lus dkyil dang/lus la lha dgod pa tsam gyis khyad par ma phyed pa'i blos brtag la/man ngag mchog tu ming btags pa'i mun sprul du ma zhig/bod kyi lus dkyil sgrub tshul rnams la snang ste/' dir dgag sgrub rgyas par ma spros so. zhes bya ba bris so.* Ngor chen, *Destroyer of the Proponents of Evil,* 548.4–549.1.

26. On this parallel between the conventional and ultimate paradigm and the wisdom beings and pledge beings of tantric ritual, see the introduction to Yael Bentor, *Consecration of Images and Stūpas in Indo-Tibetan Tantric Buddhism* (Leiden: Brill, 1996).
27. Yael Bentor, "Did mKhas grub rje Challenge the Authenticity," 231;238; fn 27; fn54. (Tsong kha pa) Blo bzang grags pa (1357–81), *The Wish-Granting Extensive Explanation of the Cakrasaṃvara Abhisamaya. Bcom ldan' das dpal' khor lo mde mchog gi mngon par rtogs pa'i rgya cher bshad pa 'dod pa 'jo ba*, Collected Works, New Delhi: Ngawang Gelek Demo, 1975–1979. 27 vols. Old bkra shis lhun po redaction, 14, ff. 195: 72–460. See 124a, p445.2–4. Bentor suggests that Tsongkhapa may have composed this text as late as 1415.
28. *bu ston thams cad mkhyen pas/rnal 'byor ma kun spyod dang/ nag po pa'i sgrub thabs kyi 'grel par/ tshigs phal cher de ltar bshad kyang/gur ni rus pa'i 'phreng pa nyid/ces pa tsam ma gtogs/ gzhan bde mchog gi chos skor gang na'ang 'dug pa ma mthong ngo zhes* bya ba yod kyi/rgya gzhung gang na'ang de 'dra ma bshad. ces pa med bzhin du mngon sum la rdzun du smra bas dgos pa ci zhig bsgrub.* Ngor chen, *Destroyer of the Proponents of Evil* [N1], 549.2–.4. Beginning after *zhes**, Ngorchen's longer text, *Dispelling Evil Views* [N2] reads: *mde mchog gi skor nas ma bshad ces bris kyi/ rgya gzhung gang na'ang de 'dra ba ma bshad ces gang du yang ma bris pas/ 'di lta bu'i mngon sum la rdzun du smra ba mi mdzad du gsol.* The tone here is slightly more direct. Rather than questioning the opponent's rationale for lying, Ngorchen simply entreats them to refrain from doing so. Ngor chen, [*Dispelling Evil Views*]. *Kye rdo rje'i lus kyi dkyil 'khor la rtsod spong lta ba ngan sel*, in *gsung 'bum* [W11577], 1: 580–625. See 584.1.
29. Bentor, "Did mKhas grub rje Challenge the Authenticity," 240 and note 64. Bentor, who located Butön's remark within that author's commentary on the *Yoginī-sañcaryā Tantra* (Toh. 375), further nuances the comparison of Khédrup and Tsongkhapa's iterations of Butön in terms of the language of vision and perception introduced in this section. Namely, Bentor suggests that Butön only claimed not to "see" such an account in the Cakrasaṃvara corpus. However, while Tsongkhapa faithfully conveyed that message, Khédrup manipulated it to say that such teachings didn't exist in the Indian sources. Such issues of "not seeing" something versus it "not being there" are central to my interpretation of the body mandala debate as it continues to unfold in the next chapter. For Butön's text: Bu ston Rin chen grub (1290–1364), *The Commentary on the Yoginī-saṃcāra-tantra, the Utterly Clear Meaning of Cakrasaṃvara. Rnal 'byor ma kun tu spyod pa'i rgyud gyi bshad pa bde mchog gi don rab tu gsal ba. Collected Works,* 76 folios (New Delhi: International Academy of Culture, 1967), vol. 6 [*cha*], pp. 719–869, folio 39a. See 795.1–.4.
30. Ulrike Roesler, "'As it is said in a Sutra': Freedom and Variation in Quotations from the Buddhist Scriptures in Early Bka'-gdams-pa Literature," *Journal of Indian Philosophy* 43, nos. 4/5 (November 2015): 493–510. I am grateful to Jan-Ulrich Sobisch for recommending this article.
31. *lus gzhal yas khang du bskyed tshul kye rdor du bshad pa rnams/ bu ston thams cad mkhyen pas bkag go zhes 'dad pa yang/ rnam par ma brtags ste.* Ngor chen, *Dispelling Evil Views* [N2], 583.3-.4.
32. *yang/lce dang mchu 'dod yon gyi snam bu zhes sogs bris pa la/zhes pa'i sogs khong nas/rkang mthil rlung/sum mdo me/lto ba chu/snying ga sa/sgal tshigs ri rab/mgo bo'i rab kyi stod kyi cha/lus 'dom gang gru bzhi gzhal yas khang/rkang brgyad ka ba rnams 'don pa yin na ni/de rnams sam pu tar bshad pas rgyud 'gog par 'gyur la/ de las gzhan pa ni phyogs ngas khas ma blangs pas dgag sgrub med pa kho na'o.* Ngor chen, *Destroyer of the Proponents of Evil* [N1], 549.4–6.
33. For an intriguing approach to tantric lacunae, see David Gray, "Disclosing the Empty Secret: Textuality and Embodiment in the *Cakrasamvara Tantra*," *Numen* 52, no. 4 (2005): 417–444.
34. Dongsung Shabdrung Rinpoche, personal communication, Fall 2013.
35. No mention is made of the cremation grounds here. However, as a key feature of both the Cakrasaṃvara and Hevajra body mandala and outer mandala, as well as of yoginī tantra more largely, their place within this version of body mandala is of interest. The incorporation of

cremation grounds into painted representations of mandala has also raised questions about the evolution of mandala iconography.

36. Ngor chen, *Destroyer of the Proponents of Evil,* 550.1. In returning to Nagpopa's text to find the section Butön was citing, I discovered that it appeared within a larger section describing elemental mandalas located in the soles of the feet, stomach, chest, throat, and crown (as well as perhaps an elusive description of the "secret place"). Nag po pa, *Saṃvara-vyākhyā,* (13)7a.5–(14)7b.1.

37. Ngor chen, *Destroyer of the Proponents of Evil,* 550.3–.4. The reference to "this transmission" (*lung 'dis*) presents ambiguity for understanding this passage. The Tibetan experts I consulted differed in their interpretations of the phrase, specifically in whether it refers to Nagpopa's words or those of "some Tibetans."

38. The relation of the elements of protective circle and cremation ground in mandala representations evolves over time. In figure 3.1, the progression to the mandala's outer limit proceeds from protective circles of lotuses, vajras, and flames to the cremation grounds. For an excellent visual resource on the iconography of the Hevajra mandala, see https://www.himalayanart.org/pages/hevajramandala/index.html.

39. Dongsung Shabdrung Rinpoche, personal communication, Fall 2013.

40. Yael Bentor, "Interpreting the Body *Maṇḍala*: Tsongkhapa Versus Later Gelug Scholars," *Revue d'Etudes Tibétaines*, no. 31 (February 2015): 63–74. Bentor also suggests a distinction between Tsongkhapa's interpretation of the relationship between the different versions of the visualization of the body as the celestial palace and the interpretations of later Geluk thinkers.

41. (Tsong kha pa) Blo bzang grags pa, "*The Wish-Granting Extensive Explanation,*" folio 122b, 442.5–.6, as translated in Bentor, "Interpreting the Body *Maṇḍala*," 66. Bentor also refers to Ngorchen's commentary on the Ghantapa transmission of the Cakrasaṃvara body mandala practice to demonstrate that Ngorchen disagreed with Tsongkhapa's interpretation. Bentor cites folio 375b, 402.2.1–.2 in the following version: Ngor chen, *Commentary on the Ghantapa Body Mandala Practice, Sa skya pa'i bka' 'bum* (Tokyo: Toyo Bunko, 1969), vol. 10, folios 117b–140a, 398.1.1–405.4.1. Bentor, "Interpreting the Body *Maṇḍala*," 67, note 23.

42. For example, in his writings on the Path and Fruit teachings of the "Outer Creation Stage" of Hevajra, sixteenth-century Sakyapa master Jamyang Khyentse Wangchuk (1524–1568) distinguished the viśvavajra at the base of the celestial palace from that at the base of the protective circle. His comments suggest that there was some controversy over the viśvavajra at the base of the celestial palace: "Some claim that this is the crossed vajra of the protection cakra, but we maintain that that is invisible, obscured by the tiny vajras spread out like barley. This is the seat of the celestial mansion." In this case, the exegete compensates for the absence of clear relationships between these elements by distinguishing two viśvavajra. Jamyang Khyentse Wangchuk, "Summarizing Notes of the Outer Creation Stage from the Expansion of the Great Secret Doctrine: Summarizing Notes of Guidance for the Precious Teaching of the 'Path with the Result,'" as translated in *Taking the Result as the Path: Core Teachings of the Sakya Lamdré Tradition*, ed. Thupten Jinpa and Cyrus Stearns (Boston: Wisdom, 2006),: 503.

43. *mdor na rje btsun gong ma la / bu ston thams cad mkhyen pas/ bde mchog gi rten lus dkyil la dgag pa mdzad pa ma yin no. rtsib ma rdo rje'i ra ba sogs/ zhal gyis mi bzhes pa'i phyir ro. kye rdor gyi skabs su zhal gyis bzhes kyang skyon med de/man ngag nas 'byung ba bzhin lung du bshad pa'i phyir ro. des na lus gzhal yas khang du bskyed tshul de 'dra ba mi 'thad ces pa'ang don ma go bar zad do.* Ngor chen, Destroyer of the Proponents of Evil, 552.1–.3.

44. As previously noted, this point merits further research, in light of a different passage, discussed in the next chapter, in which Ngorchen suggests a commonality between the Hevajra and Cakrasaṃvara approaches to the mandala of the support. See Ngor chen, *Destroyer of the Proponents of Evil,* 561.4–562.1.

45. For an example of how extracanonical materials influenced the form of the tantras, see Jacob P. Dalton, "How Dhāraṇīs WERE Proto-Tantric: Liturgies, Ritual Manuals, and the Origins of the Tantras," in *Tantric Traditions on the Move*, ed. David B. Gray and Ryan Overbey (Oxford: Oxford University Press, 2016), 199–229. Dalton describes ritual manuals as "the DNA of early tantric Buddhism" and as "the principal creative source of early tantric innovation," revealing the processes by which "the tantras were written, and rewritten, to encapsulate and canonize these ritual changes." (202)
46. Christian Luczanits, "On the Earliest Mandalas in a Buddhist Context," in *Mahāyāna Buddhism: History and Culture,* Sambhota Series XV, ed. Darrol Bryant and Susan Bryant (New Delhi: Tibet House, 2008), 111–136. See 113–115. See also Christian Luczanits, "Ritual, Instruction and Experiment: Esoteric Drawings from Dunhuang," in *The Art of Central Asia and the Indian Subcontinent in Cross Culture Perspective*, ed. Anupa Pande and Mandira Sharma (New Delhi: National Museum Institute–Aryan Books International, 2009), 140–49 and eleven figures.
47. David Snellgrove, *Indo-Tibetan Buddhism: Indian Buddhists and Their Tibetan Successors* (Boston: Shambhala, 1992), 189–213.
48. Michelle Wang uses similar language of "mandalas in the making" in her study of the evolution of mandala in the visual culture of the Dunhuang caves. Wang discusses the Guimet example I reference here in her third chapter. Michelle C. Wang, *Maṇḍalas in the Making: The Visual Culture of Esoteric Buddhism at Dunhuang* (Leiden: Brill, 2018), 180–184.
49. The comparison of the relationship between the role of *rlung* (*rlung*) in cosmic creation and destruction (derived from the Abhidharma tradition) and its role in tantric conceptions of bodily creation and dissolution is compelling. See Kong-sprul Blo-gros-mtha'-yas, Elio Guarisco, and Ingrid McLeod, *The Treasury of Knowledge: Book Six, Part Four: Systems of Buddhist Tantra* (Ithaca, NY: Snow Lion, 2005), 176–180 and note 47.

    Kittay observes that the five winds presented in the *Vajramālā* accord with those found in the *Visuddhimagga* 11:37. David Kittay, "Interpreting the Vajra Rosary: Truth and Method Meets Wisdom and Method" (PhD diss, Columbia University, 2011), 133.
50. Even the bodhisattva still has *lung* when reborn with karma. Within the thirteen-stage model of the Buddhist path, *lung* is at play until you reach the stage of Vajradhara. Khenpo Choying Dorjee, personal communication, Spring 2011.
51. On the medical conception of *lung*, see Frances Garrett, *Religion, Medicine, and the Human Embryo in Tibet* (New York: Routledge, 2008), 62–63. The three humors are *lung*, bile, and phlegm; each is construed in terms of five types. Further research is needed into both tantric and medical systems to determine subtleties in their understandings of *rlung*. For important developments in this line of research, see Garrett, chapters 4 and 6; and Janet Gyatso, *Being Human in a Buddhist World: An Intellectual History of Medicine in Early Modern Tibet* (New York: Columbia University Press, 2015), chapter 4.
52. For Khenpo Choying Dorjee, it was important to specify that the medical definition is just one aspect of what the Vajrayāna describes as *rlung*. Khenpo Choying Dorjee, personal communication, Spring 2011.
53. Garrett links the intensified interest in *lung* among tantric authors to the increased production in fourteenth- and fifteenth-century Tibet of ritual formulations of the intermediate state based in the six doctrines of Nāropā. Manipulation of and control over the channels, winds, and drops of the of the vajra body was essential to these practices. Garrett notes that, by the fifteenth century, the winds also became more important to Tibetan medical accounts of fetal gestation, suggesting that religious texts actually influenced medical ones. Garrett, *Religion, Medicine, and the Human Embryo*, 110, 153. Garrett further refers to Bryan J. Cuevas, *The Hidden History of The Tibetan Book of the Dead* (New York: Oxford University Press, 2003).
54. Sayer assesses the relationship of Locanā and Māmakī in detail in the context of Nāgārjuna's *Piṇḍikṛta-sādhana* on the *Guhyasamāja* in Rhonwen Sayer, "The Guhyasamāja *Piṇḍikṛta-sādhana*

and Its Context" (masters thesis, School of Oriental and African Studies, London, 2010), 37–43, 46–47, and appendixes A and B. In this sādhana, the position of the two goddesses is reversed. Sayer discounts Tsuda's theory that the authors of the sādhana misunderstood the tantra and questions the asserted relevance of links between the *Sarva-tathāgata-tattva-saṃgraha* (STTS) and the *Guhyasamāja*. Instead, Sayer points to the inclusion of the goddesses Locanā, Māmakī, Pāṇḍaravāsinī, and Tārā in an eighth-century translation of the *Sarva-durgati-pariṣodhana-tantra* (SDPT) in place of Vajralāsyā and the other inner offering goddesses (shared by STTS and SDPT). The inner offering goddesses are then relegated to the next level of the mandala where they reside alongside the outer offering goddesses. Sayer concludes that the source for this set of four goddesses (Locanā, Māmakī, Pāṇḍaravāsinī, and Tārā) is therefore the SDPT rather than the STTS. As for the reversal of the positions of Locanā and Māmakī, Sayer suggests that the reason is the "promotion of Akṣobhya" of the vajra family to the center of the mandala—thereby reversing the positions of Akṣobhya and Vairocana—occurring in the Ārya Guhyasamāja mandala. There are even places within the STTS and related practices where the vajra family emerges primary. Mallmann states that Māmakī can be associated with either Akṣobhya or Ratnasambhava. Marie-Thérèse de Mallmann, *Introduction à l'iconographie du tantrisme bouddhique* (Paris: En vente, Librairie Adrien-Maisonneuve, 1975).

55. Mkhas grub, *Ocean of Attainment*, 240.1–.2.

56. Toh 1809 Sde dge *bstan 'gyur* 35 ff. 121a–131a by Nāgabodhi. For partial editions, see Kimiaki Tanaka, "Nāgabodhi's *Śrī-guhyasamāja-maṇḍalopāyikā-viṃśati -vidhi*, 8 akasasutrapatanavidhi," *Journal of Indian and Buddhist Studies* 50, no. 1 (2001): 315–320; and his "Nāgabodhi's Śrī-guhyasamāja-maṇḍalopāyikā-vimśatī-vidhi: The Tibetan Translation and Sanskrit Text of Chapters 5 and 6," in *Three Mountains and Seven Rivers: Prof. Musashi Tachikawa's Felicitation Volume* (Delhi: Motilal Banarsidass, 2004), 857–869; and also his "Nāgabodhi's *Śrī-guhyasamāja-maṇḍalopāyikā-vimśatī-vidhi*: The Sanskrit Text Restored from the *Vajrācārānayottam*," in *Genesis and Development of Tantrism, Institute of Oriental Culture Special Series*, ed. Shingo Einoo (Tokyo: Institute of Oriental Culture, 2009), 23:425–434. For Tsongkhapa's position on the attribution of such texts to Nāgabodhi, see Tsong-kha-pa Blo-bzang-grags-pa and Gavin Kilty, *A Lamp to Illuminate the Five Stages: Teachings on Guhyasamāja Tantra* (Boston: Wisdom and Institute of Tibetan Classics, 2013), 65–66.

57. The *Samāja-sādhana-vyavasthole* addresses the four goddesses as follows: "The arrangement of the goddesses is taught. Moharatī Locanā is the earth element. Dveśaratī Māmakī is water. Rāgaratī Pāṇḍaravāsinī is fire. Vajraratī Tārā is *rlung*. We look to the root tantra to clarify the meaning: 'As for the element of earth, it is explained as Locanā. As for the element of water, it is explained as Māmakī. As for the element of fire, it is explained as Pāṇḍaravāsinī. As for the element of *lung*, it is known as Tārā.' So it is said." The *Samāja-sādhana* itself refers to this set of four as "goddesses" (*lha mo*), not "mothers" (*yum*), and makes no mention of a fifth goddess or of the body of a consort. I located and translated this passage using Kimiaki Tanaka's partial critical edition, 323–330, which has been emerging over the course of a series of articles. See Tanaka, "Nāgabodhi's . . . 8," "Nāgabodhi's . . . The Tibetan Translation," and Nāgabodhi's . . . The Sanskrit Text." Tanaka identified this citation from the Guhyasamāja root tantra, chapter 17, verse 51.

58. Sayer dated the *Piṇḍīkṛta* to between 800 and 950 CE. Sayer, "The Guhyasamāja *Piṇḍikṛta-sādhana*," 7.

59. Sayer notes that Tsongkhapa's text elaborates upon the basis of the *Piṇḍīkṛta* but "maintains the same sequence of visualizations and mantras." Sayer, "The Guhyasamāja *Piṇḍikṛta-sādhana*," 54. See also appendix A, in which Sayer compares the structure of the two texts. See Tsongkhapa T5303: *Dpal gsang ba 'dus pa'i sgrub thabs rnal 'byor dag pa'i rim pa*.

60. Sayer, "The Guhyasamāja *Piṇḍikṛta-sādhana*," 8.

61. Mkhas grub, *Ocean of Attainment*, 240.2–.4.
62. Nāgārjuna (*Klu sgrub*), *Piṇḍī-kṛta sādhana*. Full title in Tibetan: *Sgrub pa'i thabs mdor byas pa* (*Mdor byas*). Toh. 1796. Bstan 'gyur, rgyud 'bum, vol. 35, ff. 1b–11a, pp. 4–23. See Sde dge, 10.4. See also Sayer, "The Guhyasamāja *Piṇḍikṛta-sādhana*," v. 96–97. In the context of laying out the body mandala of the father deity in the *atiyoga* section of the text, the *Piṇḍīkṛta* instructs: "With Moharatī, the mantrin should place them on the earth (element), and so forth: that with solidity, that with fluidity, that with warmth and that with airiness respectively," Sayer v. 61 in section v. 52–69.
63. Sayer, "The Guhyasamāja *Piṇḍikṛta-sādhana*," appendix B.2. and B.4.
64. The closing phrase *zhes zer ro* suggests that it is a quotation, although it is possible that Khédrup is simply paraphrasing, perhaps even from a Tibetan source. For example, Bentor has demonstrated Butön to be the target of some of Khédrup's critiques within the *Ocean of Attainment*. Yael Bentor, "Identifying the Unnamed Opponents of Tsong kha pa and Mkhas grub rje Concerning the Transformation of Ordinary Birth, Death and the Intermediary State Into the Three Bodies," in *Tibetan Buddhist Literature and Praxis: Studies in Its Formative Period, 900–1400*, ed. Ronald M. Davidson and Christian Wedemeyer (Leiden: Brill, 2006), 185–200. Among the texts she cites is Butön's commentary on the *Piṇḍīkṛta*. See Bu ston Rin chen grub (1290–1364), *Dpal gsang ba 'dus pa'i sgrub thabs mdor byas kyi rgya cher bshad pa bskyed rim gsal byed*, in *The Collected Works of Bu-ston* (New Delhi: International Academy of Indian Culture, 1967), 9:683–877. In her more recent work, Bentor has given additional attention to Rédaba's role as another unnamed opponent. See Yael Bentor, "Divergent Perspectives on the Guhyasamāja Sādhana in Tibet: Dge lugs vs. Sa skya," 密教文化 = *Journal of Esoteric Buddhism* / 密教研究会 編 237 (2016): 70–44.
65. Mkhas grub, *Ocean of Attainment*, 245.4–.5.
66. Mkhas grub, 245.5–.6.
67. See entries by OT, IW, and RY on thlib.org on the five root winds: *srog 'dzin, gyen rgyu, khyab byed, me mnyam, thur sel*. Garrett describes how these five root winds (together with five subsidiary winds) are common in tantric physiological accounts, citing the twelfth-century Sakyapa patriarch Drakpa Gyeltsen as one example. She locates the winds at areas of the body: *thur sel* in the anus, *mnyam gnas* (or *me mnyam)* in the navel, *srog 'dzin* in the heart, *gyen rgyu* in the throat, and *khyab byed* throughout the body. Thise winds bear associations with the elements and with colors as well as bodily functions. Garrett, *Religion, Medicine and the Human Embryo*, 65–66.
68. Mkhas grub, *Ocean of Attainment*, 245.6–246.2.
69. Mkhas grub, 246.2–.3.
70. For more on the principle of contradiction in Buddhist philosophical debate, see Georges B. J. Dreyfus, *The Sound of Two Hands Clapping: The Education of a Tibetan Buddhist Monk* (Berkeley: University of California Press, 2003), especially 212–213.
71. I am grateful to Khenpo Yeshe for clarifying the logic of this statement: personal communication, Spring 2011.
72. See *Vajrasattva-sādhana*. *Gser bris bstan 'gyur* 35:436–61.
73. Candrakīrti, Hong Luo, and Toru Tomabechi, *Candrakīrti's Vajrasattvaniṣpadanasūtra*, x.
74. On the distinction of "practical" and "formal" canons, see Stanley, "The Tibetan Buddhist Canon," 385.
75. Mkhas grub, *Ocean of Attainment*, 246.3–.5.
76. The sādhana espouses a three-buddha body system. According to this system, in producing the *dharmakāya*, the practitioner generates deities, absorbs them, places them on the body, and dissolves them into emptiness. In producing the *sambhoghakāya*, the practitioner manifests as white Vajradhara. Finally, in producing the *nirmāṇakāya*, the practitioner locates the deities on the body. The mapping of these three bodies onto the sādhana structure becomes significant in the Tibetan interpretation of the Guhyasamāja as a technology for manipulating the process of death and

rebirth. Later on in the sādhana, there is also a section devoted to consort yoga; this text appears to identify Sparśavajra as Akṣobhya's consort.

77. Bentor, "Divergent Perspectives," 105–107.
78. Mkhas grub, *Ocean of Attainment,* 246.5–247.1. This passage can be found in the sde dge edition of the *Vajramālā* 270a.3–.4 [539.3–.4] where the only real difference in *mi bskyod* vs. *bskyod pa.*
79. Mkhas grub, 247.1.
80. On the classification of the yoginī tantras, see Elizabeth English, *Vajrayoginī: Her Visualizations, Rituals, and Forms* (Boston: Wisdom, 2002), 3–5.
81. Dalton suggests that there may even have been "two lines of development" within the *niruttara* class in which the tantras fitting within the mahāyoga category developed "from the *Guhyasamāja,* to *Guhyagarbha* and *Māyājāla*" evolving alongside those associated with the "*anuttara" category from "the *Sarvabuddhasamayoga,* to *Cakrasaṃvara* and *Hevajra.*" Dalton, "A Crisis of Doxography," note 90.

4. NGORCHEN'S ARMOR OF CITATIONS

1. Ngor chen kun dga' bzang po, *Kye'i rdo rje'i lus kyi dkyil 'khor la rtsod spong smra ba ngan 'joms* [*Destroyer of the Proponents of Evil Through Eliminating Objections to the Hevajra Body Mandala*] in *gsung 'bum,* Kun dga' bzang po. *Ngor chen kun dga' bzang po'i bka' 'bum,* comp. Bsod nams rgya mtsho and reproduced from the Sde dge block prints (Dehra dun: photomechanical print from a set of prints from the Sde dge dgon chen blocks [W11577]), 1:545–580; see 578.2–.3.
2. Ngor chen, 546.6–547.1, 579.4.
3. See Jackson's analysis of this painting: David P. Jackson, *The Nepalese Legacy in Tibetan Painting* (New York: Rubin Museum of Art, 2010), 179–181, figure 8.2. I discuss this painting in the introduction and chapter 2.
4. For this transmission history, see Cyrus Stearns, *Luminous Lives: The Story of the Early Masters of the Lam 'bras Tradition in Tibet* (Boston: Wisdom, 2001), 9–26.
5. José Ignacio Cabezón and Geshe Lobsang Dargyay, *Freedom from Extremes: Gorampa's "Distinguishing the Views" and the Polemics of Emptiness* (Boston: Wisdom, 2007), 25.
6. Ngorchen, for example, credited Darpaṇa Ācārya as citing Virūpa's *Vajra Verses* in his tantric liturgical compendium, the *Kriyāsamuccaya.* For examples, Stearns refers both to Ngorchen's *Lam 'bras bu dang bcas pa'i man ngag gi byung tshul gsung ngag rin po che bstan pa rgyas pa'i nyi 'od,* 110.3 and Müchen's Dkon mchog rgyal mtshan's *Lam 'bras bu dang bcas pa'i gnad kyi gsung sgros zin bris,* 448. Stearns, *Luminous Lives,* 10, note 15.
7. Ronald M. Davidson, "Reflections on the Maheśvara Subjugation Myth: Indic Materials, Sa-skya-pa Apologetics, and the Birth of Heruka," *Journal of the International Association of Buddhist Studies* 14, no. 2 (1991): 12.
8. In this regard, I agree with Bentor's assessment of both Ngorchen and Khédrup's roles as "systematizers" of their respective traditions. Yael Bentor, "Did mKhas grub rje Challenge the Authenticity of the Sa skya Lam 'bras Tradition?" in *Towards a History of Fifteenth-century Tibet: Cultural Blossoming, Religious Fervour, and Political Unrest,* ed. Volker Caumanns and Marta Sernisi (Lumbini, Nepal: Lumbini International Research Institute, 2017), 243.
9. Sa-skya Paṇḍi-ta Kun-dga-rgyal-mtshan, Jared Rhoton, and Victoria R. M. Scott, *A Clear Differentiation of the Three Codes: Essential Distinctions Among the Individual Liberation, Great Vehicle, and Tantric Systems . . . ; Six Letters* (New York: State University of New York Press, 2002).
10. *spyi don gsum rgyud rgya gzhung las ma bshad pa'i rtsod pa spang ba brjod par bya ste/de la khyed kyis rgyud dang rgya gzhung tshad ldan gang nas kyang ma bshad cing/ don thob la yang*

med do zhes smra ba yang rang gis gzhung lugs rgya chen po ni lta zhog gi/ phyogs re tsam yang ma mthong ngo zhes pa'i tshig yin la/ rig pa'i dbang phyug gis/ ma mthong phyir na med pa min/ zhes bshad pa ltar /kho bos legs par bshad kyis/ mang du thos pa dang bral ba dag rna ba blags te nyon cig. Ngor chen, *Destroyer of the Proponents of Evil,* 560.6–561.2. N2 reads *khyod* vs. *dag* and *lhag* versus *blags.*

Throughout this book, I adopt a more colloquial translation of the proverbial statement *ma mthong phyir na med pa min* as "Just because you don't see it doesn't mean it isn't there." A more literal translation would be: "If on account of not seeing, not absent." Ngorchen attributes this statement to the "lord of reasoning" (*rig pa'i dbang phyug*). It appears in Dharmakīrti's *Pramāṇavarttika-kārikā.* Full title in Tibetan: *Tshad ma rnam 'grel gyi tshig le'ur byas pa,* toh. 4210, Bstan 'gyur (Sde dge), vol. 174, ff. 94v–151r, 189–304.

11. See the *Hevajra Tantra,* Sde dge 2b.7. Cited in Ngor chen, *Destroyer of the Proponents of Evil,* 561.3.
12. One would expect this to be a reference to Māmakī.
13. Ngor chen, *Destroyer of the Proponents of Evil,* 561.3–.4.
14. Ngor chen, 561.4–562.1. For the citation from the *Samputa Tantra,* full title in Tibetan: *Yang dag par sbyor ba'i rgyud chen po,* toh. 381, bka' 'gyur, rgyud 'bum, vol. 79, ff. 73b–157b, 148–318; see 113b.3 and .5–.6.
15. Alternatively, in a different passage, discussed in chapter 3, Ngorchen suggests that the Sakya masters may not necessarily accept the parity of the modes of generating the mandala of the support according to the Cakrasaṃvara and Hevajra systems. See Ngor chen, *Destroyer of the Proponents of Evil,* 552.1–.3.
16. *Sampuṭa Tantra,* Sde dge 81a.5–81b.1. See Ngor chen, *Destroyer of the Proponents of Evil,* 562.2–.6.
17. This passage from the *Sampuṭa* was discussed in chapter 3 in the context of Khédrup's argument surrounding the location of the goddesses in the Guhyasamāja body mandala practice. Khédrup referred to the *Sampuṭa*'s arrangement of the goddess Locanā in the navel, the abode of earth, and of the goddess Tārā in the crown, the abode of *lung.* His reference occurs in the process of his attempt to establish the goddesses' association with elemental *lung* rather than merely with the elements. See Mkhas grub rje dge legs dpal bzang po (1385–1438), *Gsang 'dus bskyed rim dngos grub rgya mtsho* [*Ocean of Attainment of the Guhyasamāja Generation Stage*] in New Zhol par khang edition of *gsung 'bum,* Mkhas grub rje *(zhol),* TOH 5481 (New Delhi: Mongolian Lama Guru Deva, 1980–82), TBRC W384 (*ja*), 7:5–384. See 248.1–.2.
18. Within the *Āmnāyamañjarī,* "cluster" (*snye ma)* refers to the set of commentary upon the equivalent chapter (*rab byed*) in the *Sampuṭa Tantra.* Abhayākāragupta. *Dpal yang dag par sbor ba'i rgyud kyi rgyal po'i rgya cher 'grel pa man ngag gi snye ma. Āmnāyamañjarī.* Toh 1198 cha 1v–316r, in *Bstan 'gyur* (Snar thang). BDRC W22704. 21: 5–708. [Narthang]. The fourth "cluster" (*snye ma*) appears to be roughly equivalent to the fourth chapter, 44b–59a of the Sde dge edition; this citation is found at 56a. I am grateful to the ACIP and Kurt Keutzer for their efforts in making a digital version of this extensive text accessible.

Szanto remarks on the *Āmnāyamañjarī*: "The influence of this text on Tibetan authors, most significantly Tsong kha pa, is a well-known fact to Tibetanists and should not be insisted on further." See Péter-Dániel Szántó, "Before a Critical Edition of the Samputa," *Zentralasiatische Studien* 45 (2016): 397–422. See 2013 version page 6. Tsongkhapa, for example, cites the *Āmnāyamañjarī* frequently in his *Lamp to Illuminate the Five Stages,* a commentary associated with the Guhyasamāja,. See Tsong-kha-pa Blo-bzang-grags-pa and Gavin Kilty, *A Lamp to Illuminate the Five Stages: Teachings on Guhyasamāja Tantra* (Boston: Wisdom and Institute of Tibetan Classics, 2013). See also Tsong-kha-pa Blo-bzang-grags-pa, Robert A. F. Thurman, and Thomas F. Yarnall, *Brilliant Illumination of the Lamp of the Five Stages (Rim lnga rab tu gsal ba'i sgron me): Practical Instruction in the King of Tantras, the Glorious Esoteric Community* (New York: American Institute of Buddhist Studies, 2010).

19. Ngorchen's citations from the *Āmnāyamañjarī* may provide clues to the evolving and at times ambiguous attitudes of Sakyapa authors toward Abhayākāragupta's texts in the particular case of Hevajra-affiliated teachings. In reviewing the Hevajra literature outlined by the later Sakyapa scholar Amézhap (1597–1659), Jan-Ulrich Sobisch discusses the ambiguous status of Abhayākāragupta for the Sakyapa commentators, an ambiguity observed by Amézhap himself. In response to Amézhap's remarks that contemporary (seventeenth century) scholars are more inclusive of Abhayākāragupta's contributions, Sobisch observes the ecumenical nature of Amézhap's assessment. The problematic aspect of the Indian commentator's approach is traced to a critique by Sapen in which he questions Abhayākāragupta's inclusion of the four initiations in the lower tantras and both generation and completion stages in the Amoghapāśa practice. Sobisch has identified this critique within Gorampa's commentary on Sapen's text, the *Sdom gsum rab dbye'i rnam bshad* (94r). See Jan-Ulrich Sobisch, *Hevajra and Lam 'bras Literature of India and Tibet as Seen Through the Eyes of A-mes-zhabs* (Wiesbaden: Reicher, 2008), 76, note 217; and reference to Sa-skya Paṇḍi-ta Kun-dga-rgyal-mtshan, Rhoton, and Scott, *A Clear Differentiation of the Three Codes,* 105, 186, note 20. Most important, the earliest Sakyapa patriarchs, Sachen, Sonam Tsemo and Drakpa Gyeltsen, disregarded Abhayākāragupta's perspective in their interpretation of the *Lam 'bras* teachings. However, apparently Lama Dampa, upon whom Ngorchen is regarded to have relied heavily for his writings on the *Lam 'bras,* referred to Abhayākāragupta often.

    Ngorchen also refers to Abhayākāragupta by name in a more general context in his citation describing the protective circle. Ngor chen, *Destroyer of the Proponents of Evil,* 550.1–550.3. That citation directly precedes Ngorchen's explicit introduction of the Hevajra body mandala context with a quote from the *Sampuṭa* itself.
20. Ngor chen, *Destroyer of the Proponents of Evil,* 562.6–563.2
21. Ngor chen, 563.2–.4.
22. Following the passage on the great bliss cakra, Ngorchen's longer body mandala debate text, *Dispelling Evil Views of the Hevajra Body Mandala* [N2], diverges. N2 adds another citation from the *Āmnāyamañjarī,* one that enumerates seven cakras, once again gesturing toward the inherent diversity of the Indian sources. Ngor chen, [*Dispelling Evil Views of the Hevajra Body Mandala*]. *Kye rdo rje'i lus kyi dkyil 'khor la rtsod spong lta ba ngan sel.* In *gsung 'bum* [W11577], 1: 580–625. See 610.2–.4. Ngorchen quotes an excerpt from the first "cluster" (*snye ma*) enumerating seven cakras in the *uṣṇiṣa,* crown, throat, heart, navel, secret place, and jewel (which likely refers to the drop of bodhicitta at the tip of the penis). He also provides the number of petals for each one and describes them as taking the form of a knot (*mdud pa*) within the womb and cakra.
23. See references to chapters 7 and 8 of the Vajrapañjara explanatory tantra and the reference to its introduction. Ngor chen, *Destroyer of the Proponents of Evil,* 565.3–.5.
24. Drakpa Gyatso suggested that in this instance "Condensed Path" (*lam bsdus*) refers to the condensed Hevajra sādhana based in Virūpa's teachings (as opposed to the middle or extended length versions). Personal communication, IBA, Summer 2018. I also considered that this might be a reference to Sachen's *Lam bsdus pa'i bshad pa* but did not locate the citation there.
25. Ngor chen, *Destroyer of the Proponents of Evil,* 565.5–.6.
26. Ronald M. Davidson, *Tibetan Renaissance: Tantric Buddhism in the Rebirth of Tibetan Culture* (New York: Columbia University Press, 2005), 315–321.
27. For an excellent discussion of how these relationships were articulated and promoted through lineage portraiture, a topic I touched upon in the introduction and in chapter 2, see Christian Luczanits, "Siddhas, Hierarchs, and Lineages: Three Examples for Dating Tibetan Art," in *Mirror of the Buddha: Early Portraits from Tibet,* ed. David Paul Jackson and Christian Luczanits (New York: Rubin Museum of Art, 2011).
28. Sobisch published a study of Amézhap's (1597–1659) *Notes on How to Enter Into the Writings of the Sakapas,* a text primarily composed by Chos dpal bzang po (fifteenth century) based on

Ngorchen's own teachings. The *Notes* is a valuable resource for making sense of the role of these four Indian adepts within the Sakya transmission of Hevajra practice. It outlines eight categories of transmission of the Hevajra instruction; these include the two systems of pith instructions of Marpa(-Nāropā) and of Virūpa(-Kanha) discussed earlier as well as "six great chariot systems" (*shing rta'i srol chen po drug*) of teachings connected with: Ḍombī[heruka]; Mtsho skyes rdo rje (Saroruhavajra/Padmavajra); Nag po Dam tshig rdo rje (Kṛṣṇa Samayavajra); Shāntipa (Ratnākaraśānti); Snyan grags bzang po (Yaśobhadra?); Gnyis med rdo rje (Advayavajra/Avadhūtipa/Maitrīpa). The *Notes* further specifies that of these six chariots, the first three are perfectly transmitted by the Sakyapas at that time. The centrality of the first two "chariots" to the Sakyapa Hevajra practice is attested by the fact that they serve as the basis for the middle and extended Hevajra sādhana practice respectively. The significance of the others is more nuanced. Sobisch, *Hevajra and Lam 'bras,* 30, 39.

29. Sobisch, 48.
30. In that citation, the four mudrā schema described four aspects of the mandala of the support, correlating the parts of the body with the protective circle, cremation grounds/sacred sites, cosmic elements, and the celestial palace, respectively. See Ngor chen, *Destroyer of the Proponents of Evil,* 551.3–552.1. See also Jetari (Slob dpon dgra las rnam rgyal), *Caturmudrā-sādhana*. Full title in Tibetan: *Phyag rgya bzhi yi sgrub thabs.* Gser bris *bstan 'gyur* 2695, 75: 387–393; Snar thang *bstan 'gyur,* vol. 76, ff.142v–144v, 284–288.
31. Ngor chen, *Destroyer of the Proponents of Evil,* 570.1–572.2.
32. *des na rang gis ma mthong ba kho na rgyu mtshan du byas nas/ grub chen gyi gdams ngag zab mo la skur pa 'debs pa ni/* Ngor chen, *Destroyer of the Proponents of Evil,* 575.6.
33. Ngor chen, 575.6–576.1.
34. Ngor chen, 578.1–.2.
35. Ngor chen, 578.3–.4.
36. Jan-Ulrich Sobisch, "Tibetan Interpretations of Authenticity," in *The Illuminating Mirror: Tibetan Studies in Honour of Per K. Sørensen on the Occasion of his Sixty-fifth Birthday*, ed. Per K. Sørensen, Olaf Czaja, and Guntram Hazod (Wiesbaden: Dr. Ludwig Reichert Verlag, 2015), 461. In this article, Sobisch explores the "four authenticities," (*tshad ma bzhi*) in both the Sakya and Drigumang traditions. For additional remarks on the "four authenticities," see Sobisch, *Hevajra and Lam 'bras,* 99–100.
37. Sobisch, "Tibetan Interpretations of Authenticity," 461.
38. Interestingly, the term *four authenticities* also occurs in connection with the exegesis of the *Sampuṭa Tantra,* a text at the center of this book's final chapter. Sobisch, "Tibetan Interpretations of Authenticity," 463. On the importance of both the *Sampuṭa* and *Āmnāyamañjarī* for articulating the "four authenticities" (*tshad ma bzhi*), see Leonard van der Kuijp, "Studies in Btsun pa Ston gzhon's *Pramāṇavārttika* Commentary of ?1297: Part One: Preliminary Observations and the Import of its Title," *Revue d'Etudes Tibétaines* no. 30 (October 2014): 111–198; see especially 150–159.
39. Sobisch, "Tibetan Interpretations of Authenticity," 463.
40. Sobsich refers here to Sachen's *Sras don ma*. Sobisch, "Tibetan Interpretations of Authenticity," 464. The latter variety of *tshad ma* as "exposition" is alternately described by a term frequently understood as "history" (*lo rgyus*). See Sobisch, "Tibetan Interpretations of Authenticity," 465–466.
41. This is one rendition of a variety of levels for interpreting the four authenticities within Drakpa Gyeltsen's brief text, the *Tshad ma bzhi'i yi ge*. Note that the text references the *Sampuṭa Tantra* on multiple occasions. Among the compelling aspects of this text's view of the four authenticities, Sobisch highlights the interconnection of the four and their role in generating qualities such as

"devotion" and "conviction," the emphasis upon a particular kind of relationship between guru and disciple, and a unique logic of cause and effect in which they participate. Sobisch, "Tibetan Interpretations of Authenticity," 468–470.

42. Sobisch concludes his analysis of the Sakya approach to the four authenticities in observing the manner in which it contributes to the authority of the guru and exegete: "By perceiving both the personal *guru* and the *guru* who is the author of the treatise as being the Buddha, Sakyapa spirituality has thus allocated a quasi *buddhavacana* status to some of the tantric treatises of India." Sobisch, "Tibetan Interpretations of Authenticity," 476.
43. Ngor chen, *Destroyer of the Proponents of Evil,* 577.6–578.2.
44. Ngor chen, 579.2–.3.
45. *gang gis rno ba'i mtshon cha ma bzung zhing/ sra ba'i go cha lus la btags min kyang/ skyon med lung dang rigs pa'i dpung tshogs kyis/ phyir rgol pham par byas pa min nam ci.* Ngor chen, 579.4. I have emended *kyas* to *kyis.*
46. For the beginning of this counterargument, see Ngor chen, 552.4.
47. For the beginning of this counterargument, see Ngor chen, 555.3.
48. For the beginning of this counterargument, see Ngor chen, 559.3.
49. In nuancing understanding of the various types of tantric literature of the Cakrasaṃvara cycle, Tsuda problematizes the unqualified application of the label "explanatory tantra" to such texts. On the vast amount of "internal evidence" still to be collected from these tantras, Tsuda remarks: "we must be content with the bare fact that some mutual relation exists between the *Laghusaṃvara,* the *Saṃvarodaya* and the *Abhidhānottara* which, apart from the *Yōginīsamcāra,* can also be taken as a mūla-tantra." *The Saṃvarodaya Tantra: Selected Chapters,* ed. and trans. Shiníchi Tsuda (Tokyo: Hokuseido, 1974), 45. For his discussion of these issues in dialogue with the tantric classifications of both Butön and Tsongkhapa, see 40–45.
50. Ngor chen, *Destroyer of the Proponents of Evil,* 555.4–557.5. For Nāropā's text, see *Dpal 'khor lo sdom pa'i sgrub thabs yid bzhin nor bu.* Nāropa. Trans. Marpa chos kyi blo gros, in *Mkha' 'gro snyan brgyud kyi yig rnying,* 307–328. Darjeeling, w.b.: Kargyud sungrab nyamso khang.
51. These citations are elliptical, in that they use a limited number of members of a set to refer to the set as a whole. Both names and locations are provided for some of these members.
52. Ngor chen, *Destroyer of the Proponents of Evil,* 556.4. Ngorchen also provides another citation from Darikapa's *Sri Cakrasṃvara-sādhana tattvasaṃgraha,* which describes this transition after generating the "outer circle" of thirteen deities, as proceeding from the cultivation of the *nirmāṇakāya* to that of the *sambhogakāya*; see 552.6–554.3.
53. Tsunehiko Sugiki's work illuminates the diversity among Cakrasaṃvara body mandala brilliantly. See his "Five Types of Internal Mandala Described in the Cakrasaṃvara Buddhist Literature: Somatic Representations of One's Innate Sacredness," *Tōyō Bunka Kenkūjo Kiyō* 144 (2003): 157–231. See also Tsunehiko Sugiki, "The Structure and Traditions of the Systems of Holy Sites in the Buddhist Saṃvara Cycle and Its Related Scriptural Cycles in Early Medieval South Asia: The Geography of Esoteric Buddhism in the Eyes of the Compilers of the Scriptures," in *Genesis and Development of Tantrism,* Institute of Oriental Culture Special Series, ed. Shingo Einoo (Tokyo: Institute of Oriental Culture, 2009), 23: 515–562.
54. Yael Bentor, "Interpreting the Body *Maṇḍala*: Tsongkhapa Versus Later Gelug Scholars," *Revue d'Etudes Tibétaines,* no. 31 (February 2015):67, note 23. Ngor chen, *Dril bu pa'i lus dkyil gyi bshad pa* [*Commentary on the Ghantapa Body Mandala Practice*] in *gsung 'bum,* Kun dga' bzang po. *Ngor chen kun dga' bzang po'i bka' 'bum,* comp. Bsod nams rgya mtsho and reproduced from the Sde dge block prints (Dehra dun: photomechanical print from a set of prints from the Sde dge dgon chen blocks [W11577]) 4: 735–766. See alternate edition in *Sa skya pa'i bka' 'bum* (Tokyo: Toyo Bunko, 1969), vol. 10, folios 117b–140a, 398.1.1–405.4.1.

55. Ngor chen, *Destroyer of the Proponents of Evil*, 557.4–.5.
56. Ngor chen, 557.5.
57. Alexis Sanderson, "The Śaiva Age: The Rise and Dominance of Śaivism During the Early Medieval Period," in *Genesis and Development of Tantrism*, Institute of Oriental Culture Special Series, ed. Shingo Einoo (Tokyo: Institute of Oriental Culture, 2009), 23:41–349. Alexis Sanderson, "Vajrayāna: Origin and Function," in *Buddhism Into the Year 2000: International Conference Proceedings* (Bangkok: Dhammakaya Foundation, 1994), 94–95.
58. Sanderson explicitly challenges the substratum theory. Sanderson, "Vajrayāna," 92–93.
59. For example, Sanderson coins the term, "iconography of subjection" to describe the violent tantric imagery of Buddhist and Hindu tantric deities trampling upon deities of the rival tradition. Sanderson, "Vajrayāna," 96. Davidson analyzes the Buddhist appropriation of Śaiva myth as a tool for reinforcing the superiority of Buddhist tantric methods. He displays the direct relevance of such tropes for the Indo-Tibetan context of the body mandala debate. Ronald M. Davidson, "Reflections on the Maheśvara Subjugation Myth: Indic Materials, Sa-skya-pa Apologetics, and the Birth of Heruka," *Journal of the International Association of Buddhist Studies* 14, no. 2 (1991): 197–235.
60. I am grateful to Jacob Dalton for proposing this possibility.
61. Ngor chen, *Dispelling Evil Views*, 599.4–602.3.
62. See Ngor chen, 599.6–601.4. Note that Khédrup does not quote Āryadeva's text in his chapter on body mandala; he relies more heavily upon Candrakīrti's recension of Nāgārjuna's Ārya transmission. For an annotated translation of Āryadeva's text, see Christian K. Wedemeyer, *Āryadeva's Lamp That Integrates the Practices (Caryāmelāpakapradīpa): The Gradual Path of Vajrayāna Buddhism According to the Esoteric Community Noble Tradition* (New York: Columbia University Press, 2007).
63. Ngor chen, *Dispelling Evil Views*, 602.1–.3.
64. Ngor chen, *Dispelling Evil Views* [N2], 591.6–594.4.
65. Ngor chen, *Dispelling Evil Views*, 594.4–.6.
66. See Mkhas grub, *Ocean of Attainment*, 257.4–259.1. It is also possible that the paraphrase refers to another portion of Khédrup's text outside of the body mandala chapter or to Tshongkhapa's writings. Ngorchen's own compositions on the Guhyasamāja system between 1423 and 1425 just preceding his 1426 body mandala texts involved investigation and critique of Tsongkhapa's writings on the Guhyasamāja system. Another source for research is Rédaba's extensive Guhyasamāja treatise. (Red mda' ba) Gzhon nu blo gros, *Dpal gsang ba 'dus pa'i 'grel pa sgron ma gsal ba dang bcas pa'i bshad sbyar yid kyi mun sel zhes bya ba'i legs bshad rgya mtsho'i tshogs*, in *Gsung 'bum: Gzhon nu blo gros*, TBRC W23629. 3:7–760. (Kathmandu: Sa skya rgyal yongs gsung rab slob gnyer khang, 1999). In chapter 2, I briefly reference Rédaba's delicate position as a site of cross-contamination between the Sakyapa and emerging Gelukpa tradition.
67. Jackson explores the link of lineage and self-contradiction in Sapen's *Sdom gsum rabs dbye*. David Jackson, *Enlightenment by a Single Means: Tibetan Controversies on the "Self-sufficient white remedy" (dkar po chig thub)* (Vienna: Verlag der Österreichischen Akademie der Wissenschaften, 1994), 106.
68. Ngor chen Kun dga' bzang po (1382–1456), "Overcoming Objections to the Three Tantras." *Rgyud gsum gnod 'joms*. In Ngor chen kun dga' bzang po'i bka' 'bum = The Collected Works of Ngor chen Kun dga' bzang po / compiled by Bsod nams rgya mtsho. Tokyo: Sa skya pa'i bka' 'bum = The Complete works of the great masters of the Sa skya sect of the Tibetan Buddhism; vv. 9–10. Toyo Bunko, 1968–9. 9: 155d–157a.

    "Commentary on Overcoming Objections to the Three Tantras." *Rgyud gsum gnod 'joms kyi 'grel pa*. 9: 157a–164b. For this shift in tone, see the second half of the commentary, in which Ngorchen outlines seven undesirable consequences that would follow from the opponent's conclusions. There he uses argument by consequence in conjunction with the logic of contradiction to inform his style of argumentation.

69. Janet Gyatso, "Letter Magic: A Peircean Perspective on the Semiotics of Rdo Grub-chen's Dhāraṇī Memory," in *In the Mirror of Memory: Reflections on Mindfulness and Remembrance in Indian and Tibetan Buddhism,* ed. Janet Gyatso (Albany: State University of New York Press, 1992), 175.
70. William Shakespeare, *Hamlet,* second quarto edition, act 3, scene 2.
71. J. L. Austin, *The Works of J. L. Austin,* electronic ed.: *How to Do Things with Words* (Charlottesville, VA: InteLex, 2000), http://pm.nlx.com/xtf/view?docId=austin/austin.01.xml.

    I assume Derrida's stance here in regarding Austin's position as a missed opportunity. See Jacques Derrida, "Signature, Event, Context," in *A Derrida Reader: Between the Blinds,* ed. Jacques Derrida and Peggy Kamuf (New York: Columbia University Press, 1991), 80–111; see especially 102–107.
72. I am grateful to Jan-Ulrich Sobisch for suggesting the connection to Shakespeare. Conversation with author, International Association of Tibetan Studies, Paris, July 2019.
73. Alex Ross, "Nietzsche's Eternal Return," *New Yorker,* October 14, 2019.
74. Mkhas grub rje dge legs dpal bzang (1385–1438), *Reply to the Questions of the Kalyānamītra Kon ting gug śrī ba. Dge ba'i bshes gnyen kon ting gug shri ba'i dris lan. Thor-bu Collected Works,* TBRC W384, 9: 775–808. See 775–6. I discuss this quotation in chapter 2.
75. Judith Butler, *Bodies That Matter: On the Discursive Limits of "Sex"* (New York: Routledge, 1993), xxi–xxii.

5. "ALIGNING THE DEPENDENTLY ARISEN CONNECTIONS"

1. "Anatta-lakkhana Sutta: The Discourse on the Not-self Characteristic" (SN 22.59), trans. Ñanamoli Thera, *Access to Insight (BCBS Edition),* June 13, 2010, https://www.accesstoinsight.org/tipitaka/sn/sn22/sn22.059.nymo.html.
2. John Felstiner, *Paul Celan: Poet, Survivor, Jew* (Urbana: University of Illinois Press, 2001), 211.
3. See Ngor chen kun dga' bzang po, *Kye'i rdo rje'i lus kyi dkyil 'khor la rtsod spong smra ba ngan 'joms* [*Destroyer of the Proponents of Evil Through Eliminating Objections to the Hevajra Body Mandala*] in *gsung 'bum,* Kun dga' bzang po. *Ngor chen kun dga' bzang po'i bka' 'bum,* comp. Bsod nams rgya mtsho and reproduced from the Sde dge block prints (Dehra dun: photomechanical print from a set of prints from the Sde dge dgon chen blocks [W11577]), 587.6–588.2 and 575.6, both discussed in chapter 4.
4. See Mkhas grub rje dge legs dpal bzang po (1385–1438), *Gsang 'dus bskyed rim dngos grub rgya mtsho* [*Ocean of Attainment of the Guhyasamāja Generation Stage*] in New Zhol par khang edition of *gsung 'bum,* Mkhas grub rje *(zhol),* TOH 5481 (New Delhi: Mongolian Lama Guru Deva, 1980–82), TBRC W384 (*ja*), 234.5–.6, discussed in chapter 1.
5. Judith Butler, *Bodies That Matter: On the Discursive Limits of "Sex"* (New York: Routledge, 1993), xii.
6. Stearns traces "taking the result as the path" to Drakpa Gyeltsen's commentary on Sachen's *Explication of the Treatise for Nyak* (11b), translated by Stearns in this same volume. Cyrus Stearns, trans., *Taking the Result as the Path: Core Teachings of the Sakya Lamdré Tradition* (Boston: Wisdom, 2006), note 1.
7. Citation of Virūpa in Sachen's *Explication of the Treatise for Nyak,* as translated by Stearns, *Taking the Result,* 28.
8. Sachen's *Explication of the Treatise for Nyak,* as translated by Stearns, 28.
9. Stearns, 28. In this text, Sachen further identifies the body mandala as the inner dependently arisen connection necessary for enlightenment, while the outer connections are receiving the initiations from a *nirmāṇakāya* emanation. See Stearns, 96.

    Davidson translates *bshad brgyud* as "articulate continuity." See his reference to variations among the commentaries on this point. Ronald M. Davidson, *Tibetan Renaissance: Tantric*

Buddhism in the Rebirth of Tibetan Culture (New York: Columbia University Press, 2005), appendix 2, 477, note 3.

10. The Forty-first Sakya Trizin Ngawang Kunga, private audience, Lumbini, November 2011.
11. *ji ltar me tog la gnas dri/ me tog dngos med shes mi 'gyur/ de bzhin gzugs sogs dngos med pas/ bde ba nyid kyang dmigs med 'gyur. Hevajra Tantra*, II.2.36. See Sde dge bka' 'gyur 18: 15b.3–.4. I am grateful to Kurt Keutzer for identifying the source of this passage.
12. *rten dang brten pa gnyis chu dang 'o ma 'dres pa'am/ sa dang chu 'dres pa la 'jim pa zer ba bzhin tha mi dad par gnas/ grub sde gcig par gnas te/ rten ni me tog lta bu la/ brten pa ni dri lta bu ste/ ji ltar me tog la gnas dri; me tog dngos med shes mi 'gyur.*

    Sa chen kun dga' snying po, *Sras don ma* in Kun dga' snying po, Sa skya pa chen po. *Lam 'bras. Stod cha. Pod nyi shu. Dpal ldan sa skya pa'i gsung rab* (Beijing: Mi rigs dpe skrun khang, 2004), 33.
13. Stearns, *Taking the Result*, note 19.
14. Jan-Ulrich Sobisch, *Hevajra and Lam 'bras Literature of India and Tibet as Seen Through the Eyes of A-mes-zhabs* (Wiesbaden: Reicher, 2008), 6.
15. Ngor chen, *Destroyer of the Proponents of Evil*, 565.2–.3.
16. Jacob P. Dalton, "A Crisis of Doxography: How Tibetans Organized Tantra During the Eighth–Twelfth Centuries," *Journal of the International Association of Buddhist Studies* 28, no. 1 (2005):115–181; see 159.
17. Sonam Tsemo, trans. by Ngor Thartse Khenpo Sonam Gyatso (Hiroshi Sonami) and Wayne Verrill, *The Yogini's Eye: Comprehensive Introduction to Buddhist Tantra*, vol. 1: *Systematization and Interpretation* (Xlibris, 2012), 328. This excerpt is a translation of "Notes on Ngor chen kun dga' bzang po by Dpal gyi brgyal mtshan in A mes zhabs." A-med-zhabs's collected works, 21:76.2. This text is the same text Sobisch is working with as *Notes*, in *Hevajra and Lam 'bras Literature*, but a different edition. On this text, see also note 28, chapter 3, this volume.
18. I translate the relevant statement by Butön as follows: "Being the explanatory tantra of many tantras generally, the Saṃvara is primary. This is on account of distinguishing Vajrasattva Saṃvara as the main deity of the mandala of this one. [Another reason is] to be explained in the introduction of the Saṃvara. [And also since] the commentaries count it as an explanatory tantra of Saṃvara." Bu-ston Rin-chen-grub, *The Jewel Ornament of Tantric Classes: The Classification of the General Tantric Classes. Rgud sde spyi'i rnam par gzhag pa rgyud sde rin po che'i mdzes rgyan*, in *The Collected Works of Bu ston* (Vol. Ba), ed. Lokesh Chandra (New Delhi: International Academy of Indian Culture, 1966), 429. The passage is cited in Peter-Dániel Szántó, "Before a Critical Edition of the *Samputa*" in *Zentralasiatische Studien* 45 (2016), 397–522, note 24.
19. Shiníchi Tsuda, *Saṃvarodaya Tantra: Selected Chapters* (Tokyo: Hokuseido, 1974), 40, note 1.
20. George Robert Elder, "The Saṃputa Tantra: Edition and Translation, Chapters I-IV" (PhD diss., Columbia University, 1978), 15.
21. Szántó, "Before a Critical Edition," 402. Szántó also provides clues for dating the text such as the "conspicuous absence" of the Kālacakra (ca. 1030) from its contents as well as the likelihood it was quoted by Durjayacandra (ca. 1000).
22. Yong-Hyun Lee, *The Niṣpannayogāvalī by Abhayākāragupta: A New Critical Edition of the Sanskrit Text*, rev. ed. (Seoul: Baegun, 2004), 35.
23. The root tantras also exhibit qualities of assimilating and fusing tantric systems. Dalton's discoveries on the formative role of ritual manuals in constructing the tantras facilitate an appreciation of the syncretic nature of the tantras and of their historical development. Jacob P. Dalton, "How Dhāraṇīs WERE Proto-Tantric: Liturgies, Ritual Manuals, and the Origins of the Tantras," in *Tantric Traditions on the Move*, ed. David B. Gray and Ryan Overbey (Oxford: Oxford University Press, 2016), 199–229.
24. As mentioned earlier, Ngorchen suggests the Sakayapa masters may not necessarily accept the allegedly problematic version of generating the body as the cosmic elements and celestial palace for

Cakrasaṃvara practice in the first place. Ngor chen, *Destroyer of the Proponents of Evil,* 552.1–.2. As I have noted, more research is required to resolve this particular line of argument as Ngorchen also states at another point that the account of the body mandala of the support at issue in the debate is common to both the Hevajra and Cakrasaṃvara systems. Ngor chen, *Destroyer of the Proponents of Evil,* 562.1.

25. In his own mapping of the Guhyasamāja body mandala, Khédrup also briefly refers to the *Sampuṭa*'s articulation of the goddesses in the context of correlating the goddesses with elemental winds. Mkhas grub, *Ocean of Attainment,* 233–262, especially 248.1–.2.
26. Ngor chen, *Destroyer of the Proponents of Evil,* 563.6–564.1. The phrase *sangs rgyas kun gyi sdom pa* likely refers to *chos dbyings ye shes*. Consulted thlib.org entry on *ye shes lnga*.
27. Drakpa Gyatso, International Buddhist Academy (IBA), Kathmandu. Reading session with author, spring 2012.
28. *Āmnāyamañjarī*, Sde dge 227a. See Ngor chen, *Destroyer of the Proponents of Evil,* 564.1–.2. On his blog, *Tibeto-logic*, Dan Martin speaks to the problem of determining the Sanskrit equivalent for Dorjé Nyema. Citing chapter 28 in the *Vajrāvalī*, edited by Mori, and Abhayākaragupta's *Abhayapaddhati*, he suggests Vajragarvā. Masahide Mori, ed., *Vajrāvalī of Abhayākaragupta: A Edition of Sanskrit and Tibetan Versions* (Tring: Institute of Buddhist Studies, 2009), 2:428–429. Abhayākaragupta and Chog Dorje, *Abhayapaddhati of Abhayākaragupta: Commentary on the Buddhakapālamahātantra* (Sarnath, Varanasi: Central Institute of Higher Tibetan Studies, 2009), Skt. 3, Tib. 93.
29. Yukei Matsunaga, editor of a critical edition of the *Guhyasamāja Tantra*, suggests that the Ārya Guhyasamāja figures composed explanatory tantras like this one themselves. Yukei Matsunaga, *The Guhyasamāja Tantra: A New Critical Edition* (Osaka: Toho Shuppan, 1978).

    Yael Bentor, "Divergent Perspectives on the Guhyasamāja Sādhana in Tibet: Dge lugs versus Sa skya," 密教文化 *Journal of Esoteric Buddhism* / 密教研究会 編 237 (2016): 103.
30. David Kittay, *The Vajra Rosary Tantra (Vajramalatantra)* (New York: American Institute of Buddhist Studies, 2013), 5–6. This explanatory tantra assumes particular significance in Tibet. As noted by Kittay, the Fourteenth Dalai Lama identifies the *Vajramālā* as the source of guru yoga practice: "The origins of the instructions on this *Lama Chöpa* practice are traced back to the explanatory tantra called *Vajramala*, in which the visualization of the body mandala deities on the guru's body is explained according to Guhyasamaja. Since the integral practice of the three deities Yamantaka, Guhyasamaja, and Heruka has great merit and advantages, *Lama Chöpa* explains how to do it on the basis of this guru yoga practice." See Bstan-'dzin-rgya-mtsho and Thupten Jinpa, *The Union of Bliss and Emptiness: Teachings on the Practice of Guru Yoga* (Ithaca, NY: Snow Lion, 1988), 11.
31. Kittay, *The Vajra Rosary Tantra,* 5–6.
32. Kittay, 21–22. Kittay considers the possibility that the text is an "anthology" and also notes that chapters of the text explicitly clarify this Mahāyoga or yoginī-tantric basis for interpretation.
33. I established the groundwork for my argument on Khédrup's link between correlation and dissolution in Rae Erin Dachille, "Piercing to the Pith of the Body: The Evolution of Body Mandala and Tantric Corporeality in Tibet," special Issue in the Society for Tantric Studies Proceedings (2016), *Religions* 8, no. 9 (2017): 189.
34. Mkhas grub, *Ocean of Attainment,* 245.5–247.1, citing *The Vajramālā (Explanatory Tantra),* Sde dge bka' 'gyur, 270a.3–.4 [539.3–.4], where the only real difference in *mi bskyod* versus *bskyod pa*. This excerpt is from chapter 64 of the tantra on "The Explanation of Mandala of Body, Speech and Mind." Kittay summarizes this chapter as a detailed description of arraying the body mandala on the body of the guru according to the Ārya tradition. Kittay, *The Vajra Rosary Tantra,* 80. I have also cited this passage in chapter 3.
35. Mkhas grub, 247.1.
36. Mkhas grub, 247.1–.3.
37. Khenpo Choying Dorjee, personal communication, spring 2011.

38. On the logic of coarse and subtle in tantric embryological accounts and links to exerting control of the death process through ritual means, see Frances Garrett, *Religion, Medicine, and the Human Embryo in Tibet* (New York: Routledge, 2008), 96–102 and 112–117. See also Willa Blythe Miller, "Secrets of the Vajra Body: *Dngos po'i gnas lugs* and the Apotheosis of the Body in the Work of Rgyal ba Yang dgon pa" (PhD diss., Harvard University, 2013), especially chapters 4 and 5.
39. Mkhas grub, *Ocean of Attainment*, 247.3
40. Mkhas grub, 247.3.
41. *rlung rang gi nang gses kyi dbye ba la phra rags kyi khyad par rim pa du ma zhig yod do.* Mkhas grub, *Ocean of Attainment*, 247.4–.5. Khenpo Choying Dorjee suggested that Khédrup may be citing a root text here. Reading session, spring 2011.
42. Khédrup then elaborates upon the breakdown of *lung* (*rlung*) to describe what we have termed the elemental *lung.* See Mkhas grub, *Ocean of Attainment*, 247.5–248.1. He clarifies how each of the five root winds shares a common color and location with the one of the elements (earth, water, fire, *lung*). Khédrup then distinguishes these varieties of *lung* from the larger category of the element *lung* by producing an example based in Abhidharmic theory and the pan-Indian conception of the cosmos as composed of three realms.
43. Mkhas grub, 247.3–.4.
44. This passage was discussed in detail in chapter 1. Mkhas grub, 252.1.
45. Ngor chen, *Destroyer of the Proponents of Evil,* 576.2–.4. The citation in 576.3–576.6 accords with *Vajramālā*, Sde dge bka' 'gyur, 228b.3–228b.6 (456.3–456.6). Note that Ngorchen's chapter references are slightly different from Kittay's version of the *Vajramālā* where chapters 64 and 68 refer to the Guhyasamāja and Cakrasaṃvara respectively. Kittay bases his translation primarily upon the Lhasa recension of the text and references the Degé and Pédurma as well.
46. Ngor chen, 576.4–577.1. The note inserted at the top of the xylograph page 577 appears to be a correction of this enumeration to 129 versus 131 goddesses. Kittay confirms that the Degé, Peking, and Nartang editions of Alaṃkakalaśa all enumerate 131. Kittay, *The Vajra Rosary Tantra*, note 1460.
47. Ngor chen, 577.2–.4.
48. Ngor chen, 577.4–.5.
49. See Alaṃkakalaśa (Tshul khrims rin chen), *Rnal 'byor chen po'i rgyud dpal rdo rje phreng ba'i rgya cher 'grel pa zab mo'i don gyi 'grel pa*, in bstan 'gyur (sde dge), BDRC W23703, 34:4–442 (Delhi: Delhi karmapae choedhey, gyalwae sungrab partun khang, 1982–1985).
50. Jamgön Kongtrül Lodrö Thayé (1813–1899) explains the relation of gross and subtle bodies as follows: "that which is supported, the body of habitual tendencies; and the support, the innate body." Blo-gros-mtha'-yas, Elio Guarisco, and Ingrid McLeod, *The Treasury of Knowledge: Book Six, Part Four: Systems of Buddhist Tantra* (Ithaca, NY: Snow Lion, 2005), 169.
51. See note 46, this chapter, on the problem of enumerating 131 versus 129 goddesses.
52. Ngor chen, *Kye rdo rje'i lus kyi dkyil 'khor la rtsod spong lta ba ngan sel* [*Dispelling Evil Views of the Hevajra Body Mandala*] [N2] in *gsung 'bum,* Kun dga' bzang po. *Ngor chen kun dga' bzang po'i bka' 'bum*, comp. Bsod nams rgya mtsho and reproduced from the Sde dge block prints (Dehra dun: photomechanical print from a set of prints from the Sde dge dgon chen blocks [W11577]), 1:580–625; see 585.4–587.3.
53. I have elided the long quotation Ngorchen includes here from the *Vajramālā*. Ngor chen, *Dispelling Evil Views*, 585.5–586.3. It describes the body mandala of the support by equating the parts of the body with parts of the celestial palace. Khédrup cited the same *Vajramālā* passage to describe how to generate the body mandala of the support. See Mkhas grub, *Ocean of Attainment,* 255.6–256.4.
54. Ngor chen, *Dispelling Evil Views*, 585.4–.5, 586.3–.4.
55. Ngorchen's argument in this section of *Dispelling Evil Views* [N2] is complex and suggests he may even be drawing an explicit boundary for the *Vajramālā*'s scope of application. My provisional translation of the following passage in which he sums up his two-page divergence suggests such boundary drawing: "For those reasons [based on those citations], it's wrong to supplement by

using the *Vajramālā* in the context of Cakrasaṃvara because it agrees with the mother tantra, [but] it's utterly correct to supplement from the Hevajra cycle. The manner of teaching in accord with the scriptures will be extensively explained below." Ngor chen, 587.2–.3.

56. In addition to the citation of Jetari, the corresponding section of *Destroyer of the Proponents of Evil* [N1] includes the comments—referenced multiple times in this book—regarding the position of Butön and the Sakyapa ancestors on the body mandala of the support in the contexts of Hevajra and Cakrasaṃvara systems. This divergence between Ngorchen's two body mandala debate texts therefore merits further exploration in resolving the ambiguities of his argument here.
57. Jonathan Z. Smith, "Sacred Persistence: Toward a Redescription of Canon," in *Imagining Religion: From Babylon to Jonestown* (Chicago: University of Chicago Press, 1982), 52. See my discussion of canon in dialogue with Smith's definition in chapter 3.
58. Ngor chen, *Destroyer of the Proponents of Evil* [N1], 578.6. I cited Ngorchen's statement in the introduction and chapter 1 of this book as well.
59. Mkhas grub, *Ocean of Attainment*, 252.1–.3.
60. *rtsa 'khor lo lnga rdo rje'i lus la rang grub du yod pa de/lha mo rnams dang 'khor lo lnga'i dbus kyi thig le phyi shun gyi rtsa dang bcas pa gtso bo yab yum lngar bskyed nas/ lus kyi nang so so'i gnas su bsgom pas blos brtag pa ma yin no.* Ngor chen, *Destroyer of the Proponents of Evil*, 560.3–.4. I referenced this passage in the introduction as well.

CONCLUSION

1. For a sixteenth-century formulation of this triad, see Dkon-mchog-lhun-grub, Lobsang Dagpa, and Jay Goldberg, *The Three Visions: Fundamental Teachings of the Sakya Lineage of Tibetan Buddhism* (Ithaca, NY: Snow Lion, 2002).
2. Many thanks to Drakpa Gyatso for his explanations of the notion of "the union of emptiness and appearance." Drakpa Gyatso, reading session, IBA, summer 2018. For my discussion of another text in which Ngorchen explores this unique form of "union" in depth, see Rae Erin Dachille, " 'Empty Like the Sky': Polysemy and the Problem of 'Mere Clear Awareness' at the Intersection of Sūtra and Tantra in Fifteenth-century Tibet," *Revue d'Etudes Tibétaines* 58 (April 2021): 208–236.
3. Jacques Derrida, Gayatri Chakravorty Spivak, and Judith P. Butler, *Of Grammatology* (Baltimore: Johns Hopkins University Press, 2016).
4. Judith Butler, *Bodies That Matter: On the Discursive Limits of "Sex"* (New York: Routledge, 1993), viii.

   Saba Mahmood presents a critical response to Butler's approach to performativity, one that speaks for the entanglement of limitation and meaning. In her study of piety among contemporary Egyptian women, Mahmood emphasizes that "resistance" to or transcendance of limitations or boundaries is not a universal quality of performative agency. Saba Mahmood, "Agency, Performativity, and the Feminist Subject," in *Bodily Citations: Religion and Judith Butler*, ed. Ellen T. Armour and Susan M. St. Ville (New York: Columbia University Press, 2006).
5. Drakpa Gyatso, reading session.

EPILOGUE

1. Robert Mapplethorpe, *Black Book* (New York: St. Martin's, 1986). The earliest published editions of Mapplethorpe's book were titled *Black Book* while most later editions appeared with the title *The Black Book*. Throughout the epilogue, I refer to "the *Black Book*," in sync with Ligon's title.

2. Jonah Groeneboer, archivist, Glenn Ligon Studio, e-mail communication with author, May 12, 2020. I am grateful to Jonah Groeneboer for generously providing me with research images and installation details for Ligon's work.
3. Jonah Groeneboer, e-mail communication with author, May 8 and 12, 2020.
4. Thomas W. Sokolowski, "Iconophobics Anonymous," Summer 1990, https://www.artforum.com/print/199006/iconophobics-anonymous-34059.
5. Among the most controversial images were Mapplethorpe's representations of children and his representations of individuals engaged in BDSM. See Ingrid Sischy, "White and Black," *New Yorker*, November 5, 1989 (November 13 issue), https://www.newyorker.com/magazine/1989/11/13/white-and-black.
6. In 1989, the Corcoran (then the Corcoran Gallery of Art, now the Corcoran School of Arts and Design) canceled their exhibition of *Robert Mapplethorpe: The Perfect Moment* in response to these pressures. When the exhibition opened in April 1990 at the Contemporary Art Center in Cincinnati, Hamilton County prosecutors brought obscenity charges against the museum's director and the institution itself. The verdict in the high-profile trial was ultimately "not guilty." Alex Palmer, "When Art Fought the Law and the Art Won," *Smithsonian Magazine,* October 2, 2015, https://www.smithsonianmag.com/history/when-art-fought-law-and-art-won-180956810/.
7. In 2019, the Corcoran reexamined the place of *The Perfect Moment* in their history by mounting *6.13.89: The Canceling of the Mapplethorpe Exhibition*, an archival unearthing of documents and photographs related to the controversy and protest surrounding the decision; Kriston Capps, "A Museum Canceled Its Robert Mapplethorpe Show—and Decades Later, It's Finally Trying to Make Amends," *Washington Post,* June 12, 2019, https://www.washingtonpost.com/entertainment/museums/a-museum-canceled-its-robert-mapplethorpe-show—and-decades-later-its-finally-trying-to-make-amends/2019/06/12/692f2744-83ce-11e9-bce7-40b4105f7ca0_story.html.

   In 2015, the Contemporary Art Center in Cincinnati commemorated the twenty-fifth anniversary of the trial with a symposium as well as with an exhibition entitled *After the Moment: Reflections on Robert Mapplethorpe.* Palmer, "When Art Fought the Law"; Grace Dubosh, "25 Years Later: Cincinnati and the Obscenity Trial Over Mapplethorpe Art," *Washington Post,* October 24, 2015, https://www.washingtonpost.com/entertainment/museums/25-years-later-cincinnati-and-the-obscenity-trial-over-mapplethorpe-art/2015/10/22/07c6aba2-6dcb-11e5-9bfe-e59f5e244f92_story.html.
8. "Glenn Ligon, Condition Report," Hammer Museum, https://hammer.ucla.edu/take-it-or-leave-it/artists/glenn-ligon.
9. "A Conversation with Glenn Ligon: Parts 1 & 2," Solomon R. Guggenheim Museum, https://www.guggenheim.org/audio/track/a-conversation-with-glenn-ligon-part-1, https://www.guggenheim.org/audio/track/a-conversation-with-glenn-ligon-part-2.
10. Ben Luke, "'America Is Both a Shining Beacon and the Death Star': Glenn Ligon on Andy Warhol, Ambivalence, and His Stevie Wonder Obsession," *Art Newspaper*, August 19, 2021, https://www.theartnewspaper.com/interview/glenn-ligon-interview-black-artist-hauser-wirth-conceptual-art-podcast.
11. Robert Mapplethorpe, as cited in Ligon's *Notes on the Margin of the Black Book*.
12. Along with Ligon, the exhibition featured the work of Rotimi Fani-Kayode, Lyle Ashton Harris, Zanele Muholi, Catherine Opie, and Paul Mpagi Sepuya.
13. *Implicit Tensions: Mapplethorpe Now*, Solomon R. Guggenheim Museum, July 24, 2019–January 5, 2020, https://www.guggenheim.org/exhibition/mapplethorpe. The exhibition was curated by Lauren Hinkson and Susan Thompson with Levi Prombaum.
14. Arthur Lubow, "Has Robert Mapplethorpe's Moment Passed," *New York Times,* July 25, 2019, https://www.nytimes.com/2019/07/25/arts/design/robert-mapplethorpe-guggenheim.html.
15. Luke, "America Is Both."
16. C. Riley Snorton, *Black on Both Sides: A Racial History of Trans Identity* (Minneapolis: University of Minnesota Press, 2017), 11.

17. Hilarie M. Sheets, "The Writing on the Wall: Glenn Ligon on Borrowing Text to Expose American Racism, in 2011," *Art News*, January 15, 2016, https://www.artnews.com/art-news/retrospective/the-writing-on-the-wall-glenn-ligon-on-borrowing-text-to-expose-american-racism-in-2011-5658/.
18. "Glenn Ligon," *Art 21*, https://art21.org/artist/glenn-ligon/?gclid=CjwKCAiAhc7yBRAdEiwAplGxXwKZpdBULQ6l4CbxHy_rTe41RaektGizBZPFS866KMuluddYvLHC_BoC4hgQAvD_BwE.
19. A reviewer of the catalog accompanying Ligon's retrospective, *Glenn Ligon: AMERICA*, describes the complexities of Ligon's citational practice in this way. The reviewer suggests Ligon's 1990 painting *Untitled (I Remember the Very Day That I Became Colored)*, which derives its title from an essay by Zora Neale Hurston, as an especially apt example of Ligon's approach to citation. Pete L'Official, "Words, Words, Words: On Glenn Ligon," *Los Angeles Review of Books*, November 1, 2011, https://lareviewofbooks.org/article/words-words-words-on-glenn-ligon/.
20. "Glenn Ligon," *Art 21*.
21. Richard Bolton, as cited in Ligon's *Notes on the Margin of the Black Book*. See Richard Bolton, *Culture Wars: Documents from the Recent Controversies in the Arts* (New York: New Press, 1992).
22. John Felstiner, *Paul Celan: Poet, Survivor, Jew* (Urbana: University of Illinois Press, 2001), 211. See chapter 3 for my discussion of "repetition with a difference" in the context of Ngorchen and Khédrup's body mandala debate.
23. Tamura A. Lomax, *Jezebel Unhinged: Loosing the Black Female Body in Religion and Culture* (Durham: Duke University Press, 2018).
24. Stuart Hall, as cited in Ligon's *Notes on the Margin of the Black Book*. This passage appears in Hall's essay, "Cultural Identity and Diaspora," first published in *Framework*, no. 36 (1989): 222–237.
25. Jack Walls, as cited in Ligon's *Notes on the Margin of the Black Book*.
26. Ken Moody, as cited in Ligon's *Notes on the Margin of the Black Book*.
27. Lyle Ashton Harris, as cited in Ligon's *Notes on the Margin of the Black Book*.
28. Richard Dyer, as cited in Ligon's *Notes on the Margin of the Black Book*.
29. Thomas Allen Harris, as cited in Ligon's *Notes on the Margin of the Black Book*.
30. Tom Sokolowski, as cited in Ligon's *Notes on the Margin of the Black Book*.
31. Edmund White, as cited in Ligon's *Notes on the Margin of the Black Book*.
32. Janet Kardon, as cited in Ligon's *Notes on the Margin of the Black Book*. See also Janet Kardon, David Joselit, and Kay Larson, *Robert Mapplethorpe: The Perfect Moment* (Philadelphia: University of Pennsylvania, Institute of Contemporary Art, 1988).
33. Essex Hemphill, as cited in Ligon's *Notes on the Margin of the Black Book*. See Hemphill's introduction to Essex Hemphill and Joseph Beam, *Brother to Brother: Collected Writings by Black Gay Men* (Boston: Alyson, 1991), xl.
34. David Joselit, as cited in Ligon's *Notes on the Margin of the Black Book*. Joselit contributed an essay to the exhibition catalog for *Robert Mapplethorpe, the Perfect Moment*.
35. Isaac Julien and scholar Kobena Mercer, as cited *in Ligon's Notes on the Margin of the Black Book*.
36. Henry Louis Gates Jr. as cited in Ligon's *Notes on the Margin of the Black Book*. See Henry Louis Gates Jr., "Editor's Introduction: Writing 'Race' and the Difference It Makes," *Critical Inquiry* 12, no. 1, "Race," Writing, and Difference (Autumn 1985): 1–20.
37. Robert Mapplethorpe, as cited in Ligon's *Notes on the Margin of the Black Book*.
38. In a recent interview, Ligon elaborated upon these tensions between marginality and centrality in Black American identity addressed in his work. He reflected on his citation of James Baldwin's writings, observing that, in some ways, "being at the margins of a culture you see it better." Speaking of his use of coal dust in those pieces, Ligon described the "elevation" of material refuse as a way of referencing Baldwin's "transformation of his positionality." Luke, "America Is Both."

39. Toni Morrison, as cited in Ligon's *Notes on the Margin of the Black Book*. See also Toni Morrison, *Playing in the Dark: Whiteness and the Literary Imagination* (Cambridge, MA: Harvard University Press, 1992).
40. Stuart Hall, as cited in Ligon's *Notes on the Margin of the Black Book*.
41. Glenn Ligon, as cited in Ligon's *Notes on the Margin of the Black Book*.
42. Che Gossett, "Blackness and the Trouble of Transvisibility," in *Trap Door: Trans Cultural Production and the Politics of Visibility*, ed. Tourmaline, Eric A. Stanley, and Johanna Burton (Cambridge, MA: MIT Press, 2017), 184. Many thanks to Max Strassfeld for encouraging me to return to the work in this volume.
43. The full quotation reads, "Visibility politics, or the kind of queer and transpolitics we might call neoliberal, cannot account for the ways that blackness ghosts and haunts the normative, the way it exceeds representational fixity." Gossett, "Blackness and the Trouble of Transvisibility," 187.

APPENDIXES

1. This entire section (548.2–549.1) is a direct citation of Khédrup's argument from his body mandala chapter. Mkhas grub rje dge legs dpal bzang po (1385–1438), *Gsang 'dus bskyed rim dngos grub rgya mtsho* [*Ocean of Attainment of the Guhyasamāja Generation Stage*] in New Zhol par khang edition of *gsung 'bum*, Mkhas grub rje *(zhol)*, TOH 5481 (New Delhi: Mongolian Lama Guru Deva, 1980–82), TBRC W384 (*ja*), 7:5–384; see 233–262, especially 254.6–255.5.

   See my discussion in chapter 3. As I mention there, Bentor has shown that Khédrup is reiterating Tsongkhapa's argument from *The Wish-Granting Extensive Explanation of the Cakrasaṃvara Abhisamaya* (*Bde mchog mngon rtogs rgya cher bshad pa 'dod pa 'jo ba*). Yael Bentor, "Did mKhas grub rje Challenge the Authenticity of the Sa skya Lam 'bras Tradition?," in *Towards a History of Fifteenth-Century Tibet: Cultural Blossoming, Religious Fervour and Political Unrest*, ed. Volker Caumanns and Marta Sernisi (Lumbini, Nepal: Lumbini International Research Institute, 2017), 231, note 27, 238, note 54. Bentor locates the citation in (Tsong kha pa) Blo bzang grags pa (1357–81), *Bcom ldan 'das dpal 'khor lo mde mchog gi mngon par rtogs pa'i rgya cher bshad pa 'dod pa 'jo ba*, in *Collected Works* (New Delhi: Ngawang Gelek Demo, 1975–1979), 27 vols., Old bkra shis lhun po redaction, vol. 14, 195 folios, 72–460; see 124a, pp. 445.2–4.
2. Bu ston Rin chen grub (1290–1364), *The Commentary on the Yoginī-saṃcāra-tantra, the Utterly Clear Meaning of Cakrasaṃvara. Rnal 'byor ma kun tu spyod pa'i rgyud gyi bshad pa bde mchog gi don rab tu gsal ba*. Bu ston's *Collected Works*, Zhol par khang, vol. 6, pp. 725–876. See 795.1–.4.
3. Nag po pa, *Saṃvara-vyākhyā*. Full title in Tibetan: *Sdom pa bshad pa*. Toh. 1460. Bstan 'gyur, rgyud 'bum, vol. 22, ff. 6a–10b, pp. 12–20. The source of this citation is found on page (13)7a.4 of the Dégé edition.
4. Bu ston Rin chen grub (1290–1364), *The Commentary on the Yoginī-saṃcāra-tantra*.
5. Bu ston, *Nagpopa's Cakrasaṃvara Sādhana*, Bu ston Rin chen grub (1290–1364). *Nagpopa's Cakrasaṃvara Sādhana, Free from Errors or Impurities. Bde mchog nag po pa'i sgrub thabs 'khrul ba'i dri bral*. Toh. 5049. In *Gsung 'bum*, Rin chen grub, Zhol par khang, TBRC W1934, 7:151–186. Lha sa: Zhol par khang, 2000. See 254.6–255.5.
6. Abhayākaragupta, *Niṣpannayogāvalī*. Full title in Tibetan: *Rdzogs pa'i rnal 'byor gyi phreng ba*. Toh. 3121. Bstan 'gyur, rgyud 'bum, vol. 75, ff. 94b–151a, pp. 188–301; see 189.4–.6.
7. *Sampuṭa Tantra*. Full title in Tibetan: *Yang dag par sbyor ba'i rgyud chen po*. Toh. 381. Bka' 'gyur, rgyud 'bum, vol. 79, ff. 73b–157b, pp. 148–318. The citation can be found at 113b.3–.5.
8. Jetari (Slob dpon dgra las rnam rgyal), *Caturmudrā-sādhana*. Full title in Tibetan: *Phyag rgya bzhi yi sgrub thabs*. Gser bris bstan 'gyur 2695, vol. 75, pp. 387–393; see 388.4–389.2; Snar thang bstan 'gyur, vol. 76, ff. 142v–144v, pp. 284–288; see 286.5–287.2.

9. Darikapa, *Sri Cakrasaṃvara-sādhana tattvasaṃgraha*. Full title in Tibetan: *Dpal 'khor lo sdom pa'i sgrub thabs de kho na nyid bsdud pa*. Toh. 1429. Bstan 'gyur, rgyud 'bum, vol. 21, ff.197b–203b, pp. 396–408. Gser bris bstan 'gyur 147, vol. 13, pp. 531–428. In the latter edition, the citations can be found at 538.1–2, 538.5–539.2, 539.4–5, 540.2, 541.6–542.1.
10. Consider Bu ston Rin chen grub (1290–1364), *Cakrasaṃvara Samvarodaya sādhana. Dpal bde mchog 'khor lo sdom pa 'byung ba'i sgrub thabs*. Rin chen grub, Rin chen rnam rgyal, Lokesh Chandra, In *Gsung 'bum*, Zhol par ma (Ldi lir bskyar par brgyab pa), TBRC W22106. In his study of the *Samvarodaya Tantra*, Tsuda also refers to an Indian commentary. See Kṣāntiśrī. *Śrī-samvarodaya sādhana*. Full title in Tibetan: *Dpal sdom pa 'byung ba'i sgrub thabs*. Toh. 1515. Bstan 'gyur, rgyud 'bum, vol. 22, ff. 374b–379a, pp. 750–760. Shiníchi Tsuda, *The Saṃvarodaya Tantra: Selected Chapters* (Tokyo: Hokuseido, 1974), 6.
11. *Samvarodaya Tantra*. Full title in Tibetan: *Dpal bde mchog 'byung ba zhes bya ba'i rgyud kyi rgyal po chen po*. Toh. 373. Bka' 'gyur, rgyud 'bum, vol. 78, ff.137a–264b, pp. 531–624.
12. One possibility is Ratnarakṣita, *Śrī-samvarodaya-mahātantrarāja-padmini-nāma-pañjikā*. Full title in Tibetan: *Dpal sdom pa 'byung ba'i rgyud kyi rgyal po chen po'i dka' 'grel padma can*. Toh. 1420. Bstan 'gyur, rgyud 'bum, vol. 21, ff. 1b–101b, pp. 4–204.
13. Nāropa, trans. Marpa chos kyi blo gros. *Dpal 'khor lo sdom pa'i sgrub thabs yid bzhin nor bu*, in *Mkha' 'gro snyan brgyud kyi yig rnying*. Darjeeling, w.b.: kargyud sungrab nyamso khang, pp. 307–328. Another possibility was Ghantapa, Tshul khrims rin chen, *Bcom ldan 'das 'khor lo bde mchog sgrub pa'i thabs rin po che yid bzhin gyi nor bu*. In Sde dge bstan 'gyur. TBRC W23703. 21:468–476 (233v–237v).
14. *Abhidhānottara Tantra*. Full title in Tibetan: *Mngon par brjod pa'i rgyud bla ma*. Toh. 369. Bka' 'gyur, rgyud 'bum, vol. 77, ff. 247a–370a, pp. 495–741. The citation is located in Sde dge 310b.5–311b.1; 311a.3–.4; 311b.1–.2.
15. Consider both: *Kṛṣṇayamāri Tantra*. Full title in Tibetan: *De bzhin gshegs pa thams cad kyi sku gsung thugs gshin rje gshed nag po zhes bya ba'i rgyud*. Toh. 442. Bka' 'gyur, rgyud 'bum, vol. 83, ff. 134b–151b, pp. 270–304.

    Yamāri kṛṣṇakarmasarvacakrasiddhikara Tantra. Full title in Tibetan: *Gshin rje'i gshed dgra nag po'i 'khor lo las thams cad grub par byed pa zhes bya ba'i rgyud kyi rgyal po*. Toh. 474. Bka' 'gyur, rgyud 'bum, vol. 83, ff. 175b–185b, pp. 351–372.
16. Ghantapa (*Rdo rje dril bu pa*). *Śrī-cakrasaṃvarasekaprakriyopadeśa*. Full title in Tibetan: *Dpal 'khor lo sdom pa'i dbang gi bya ba mdor bsdus pa*. Toh. 1431. Bstan 'gyur, rgyud 'bum, vol. 21, 219b–222b, pp. 440–446.
17. Prajñārakṣita (Śāśvatavajra) is an eleventh-century tantric scholar versed in the Luipa (Lūyīpāda) transmission of the Cakrasaṃvara cycle. Butön catalogued four of his works. Munenobu Sakurai, "Another Version Prajñārakṣita's Balividhi," in *Three Mountains and Seven Rivers: Musashi Tachikawa's Felicitation Volume*, ed. Musashi Tachikawa, Shoun Ino, and Toshihiro Wada (Delhi: Motilal Banarsidass, 2004), 815–828. See 815. Rngog blo ldan shes rab (1059–1109) co-translated four to five of Prajñārakṣita's texts with Sumatikīrti. These include *Abhisamaya-nāma-pañjika* (P2182), *Cakrasaṃvarameghamañjari* (P2183), *Cakrasaṃvarabalimañjari* (P2184), *Cakrasaṃvara hastapūjavidhi* (P2185), and *Cakrasaṃvaramaṇḍalavidhisaṃgraha* (P2186). See Ralf Kramer, *The Great Tibetan Translator: Life and Works of Rngog blo ldan shes rab (1059–1109)* (Munich: Indus, 2007); see 55, 68, and 121–122.
18. As the citation appears in his *Pramāṇavarttika-kārikā*, the "lord of reasoning" here is Dharmakīrti. *Pramāṇavarttika-kārikā*. Full title in Tibetan: *Tshad ma rnam 'grel gyi tshig le'ur byas pa*. Toh. 4210. Sde dge bstan 'gyur, vol. 174, ff. 94v–151r, pp. 189–304.
19. *Hevajra Tantra*. Full title in Tibetan: *Kye'i rdo rje zhes bya ba rgyud kyi rgyal po*. Toh. 417, Bka' 'gyur, rgyud 'bum, vol. 80, ff. 1a–13b, pp. 3–28; see citation at 2b.7.
20. *Sampuṭa Tantra*, Sde dge bka' 'gyur, 113b.3 and .5–.6.
21. *Sampuṭa Tantra*, Sde dge bka' 'gyur, 81a.5–81b.1.

22. Abhayākaragupta. *Āmnāyamañjarī.* Full title in Tibetan: *Dpal yang dag par sbyor ba'i rgyud kyi rgyal po'i rgya cher 'grel pa man ngag gi snye ma.* Toh. 1198, cha 1b–316a; see 56a (ACIP input).
23. *Sampuṭa Tantra*, Sde dge bka' gyur, 117b.5–.7.
24. Abhayākaragupta, *Āmnāyamañjarī*, Sde dge bstan gyur, 227.
25. *Sampuṭa Tantra*, Sde dge bka' 'gyur, 80b.3–4.
26. Abhayākaragupta, *Āmnāyamañjarī*, Sde dge bstan gyur, 52b.
27. Abhayākaragupta, 52b.
28. For more detail, see *Vajrapañjara Tantra.* Full title in Tibetan: *'Phags pa mkha' 'gro ma rdo rje gur zhes bya ba'i rgyud kyi rgyal po chen po'i brtag pa.* Toh. 419. Bka' 'gyur, rgyud 'bum, vol. 80, ff. 30r–65v, pp. 59–130.
29. "Condensed Path" (*Lam bsdus pa*) likely refers to the condensed Hevajra sādhana based in Virūpa's teachings. Drakpa Gyatso, personal communication, IBA.
30. In my preliminary search for this citation, I was not able to locate it either in the *Guhyasamāja Uttaratantra* or in the *Hevajra Tantra.*
31. (Nāropāda or *Snyan grags bzang po*), *Vajrapada-sāra-saṁgraha-pañjikā.* Full title in Tibetan: *Rdo rje'i tshig gi snying po bsdus pa'i dka' 'grel*, Toh. 1186. Bstan 'gyur, rgyud 'bum, vol. 4 ff. 58b–146b, pp. 118–294; Dpe sdur ma, vol. 2, pp. 87–1110. See citation at p. 926. I am grateful to Kurt Keutzer for his assistance in identifying this text. Sobisch describes this text as a commentary on the *Hevajra Tantra*, the *Kyai rdor don bsdus*, with an incomplete subcommentary, the *Kyai rdor don bsdus kyi 'grel pa.* See Sobisch's Title List # 12 and 134, respectively. According to Sobisch, Ngorchen disputed this text's attribution to Nāropā; however, he maintained its value and compatibility with the generation stage of mahāsiddha Saroruha and with the completion stage of Kālacakra. Jan-Ulrich Sobisch, *Hevajra and Lam 'bras Literature of India and Tibet as Seen Through the Eyes of A-mes-zhabs* (Wiesbaden: Reicher, 2008), 43, 136, and 146.
32. Jetari (Slob dpon dgra las rnam rgyal). *Caturmudrā-sādhana.* Full title in Tibetan: *Phyag rgya bzhi yi sgrub thabs.* Gser bris bstan 'gyur 2695, vol. 75, pp. 387–393; Snar thang bstan 'gyur, vol. 76, ff. 142v–144v, pp. 284–288. This same text is cited by Ngorchen on 551.3–552.1 in the section on "entering into flaws in meaning."
33. Darikapa, *Sri Cakrasaṃvara-sādhana tattvasaṃgraha.* Full title in Tibetan: *Dpal 'khor lo sdom pa'i sgrub thabs de kho na nyid bsdud pa*, Toh. 1429. Bstan 'gyur, rgyud 'bum, vol. 21, ff. 197b–203b, pp. 396–408. Gser bris bstan 'gyur 147, vol. 13, pp. 531–428.
34. Tathāgatavajra (*Slob dpon de bzhin gshegs pa'i rdo rje*), *Luyipābhisamaya-vṛttiṭikā-viśeṣadyota.* Full title in Tibetan: *Lū yi pa'i mngon par rtogs pa'i 'grel pa'i ṭī kā khyad par gsal byed.* Toh. 1510. Bstan 'gyur, rgyud 'bum, vol. 22, ff. 285a–308b, pp. 571–618.
35. See Drakpa Gyeltsen's commentary on the *Vajrapañjara Tantra.* Kun dga' snying po, Bsod nams rtse mo, Grags pa rgyal mtshan, Kun dga' rgyal mtshan, Blo gros rgyal mtshan. *Commentary on the Vajrapañjara. 'Phags pa rdo rje gur gyi rgyan zhes bya ba'i rnam 'grel.* In Sa skya bka' 'bum, TBRC W00EGS1017151. 7:9–166 (Kathmandu: Sachen International, 2006).
36. See the commentary on the *Sampuṭa* attributed to Indrabhūti. *Smṛti-saṃdarśanāloka.* Full title in Tibetan: *Dpal kha sbyor thig le zhes bya ba rnal 'byor ma'i rgyud kyi rgyal po'i rgya cher 'grel pa yang dag par lta ba'i dran pa'i snang ba.* Bstan 'gyur, rgyud 'bum, vol. 6, ff. 94b–313b, pp. 190–627.
37. See Vajragarbha. *Hevajrapiṇḍārthaṭikā.* Full title in Tibetan: *Kye'i rdo rje bsdu pa'i don gyi rgya cher 'grel pa.* Toh. 1180. Bstan 'gyur, rgyud 'bum, vol. 2, ff. 1b–126a, pp. 2–253.
38. *The Vajramālā (Explanatory) Tantra.* Full title in Tibetan: *Rnal 'byor chen po'i rgyud dpal rdo rje 'phreng ba mngon par brjod pa rgyud thams cad kyi snying po gsang ba rnam par phye ba zhes bya ba.* Toh. 445. Bka' 'gyur, rgyud 'bum, vol. 81, ff. 208a–277b, pp. 415–554.
39. 576.3–576.6 accords with the *Vajramālā*, Sde dge bka' 'gyur, 228b.3–228b.6 (456.3–456.6). After Ngorchen paraphrases, he returns to cite a passage further along in the *Vajramālā*; 577.1–.3 of Ngorchen's text corresponds with 229b.3–229b.4 (458.3–458.4) of the *Vajramālā.*

40. Alaṃkakalaśa. *Śri Vajramālā-mahāyoga- ṭantra-tīkā-gambhīrārtha-dīpikā*. Full title in Tibetan: *Rnal 'byor chen po'i rgyud dpal rdo rje phreng ba'i rgya cher 'grel pa zab mo'i don gyi 'grel pa*. Toh. 1795. Bstan 'gyur, rgyud 'bum, vol. 33, ff. 1b–220a.
41. *Vajramālā*, Sde dge bka' 'gyur, 230b.7 (460.6–.7).
42. Mkhas grub rje dge legs dpal bzang po (1385–1438), *Gsang 'dus bskyed rim dngos grub rgya mtsho. Ocean of Attainment of the Guhyasamāja Generation Stage*. In New Zhol par khang edition of *Gsung 'bum (zhol)*, TOH 5481 (New Delhi: Mongolian Lama Guru Deva, 1980–82), TBRC W384 (*ja*), 7:5–384; see 233–262.
43. Ghantapa (*Rdo rje dril bu pa*), *Śrī-cakrasaṃvarasekaprakriyopadeśa*. Full title in Tibetan: *Dpal 'khor lo sdom pa'i dbang gi bya ba mdor bsdus pa*. Toh. 1431. Bstan 'gyur, rgyud 'bum, vol. 21, 219b–222b, pp. 440–446; see 438.5–6. For Tsongkhapa's analysis of Ghantapa's verse, see his citation of Ghantapa in (Tsong kha pa) Blo bzang grags pa (1357–81). *The Jewel Treasury: The Rite of Empowerment of the Body Mandala of Ghantapa, the Lord of Yoga. Rnal 'byor dbang phyug dril bu lugs bde mchog lus dkyil gyi dbang chog rin po che'i bang mdzod*, vol. 10, Toh. 5327, pp. 57–106; see 58.6 to 59.3. For Bentor's discussion of disagreements around Ghantapa's work, see Yael Bentor, "Tibetan Interpretations of the Opening Verses of Vajraghanta on the Body Mandala," in *Chinese and Tibetan Esoteric Buddhism*, ed. Yael Bentor and Meir Shahar (Leiden: Brill, 2017), 165–192. See also Yael Bentor, "Identifying the Unnamed Opponents of Tsong kha pa and Mkhas grub rje Concerning the Transformation of Ordinary Birth, Death, and the Intermediary State Into the Three Bodies," in *Tibetan Buddhist Literature and Praxis: Studies in Its Formative Period, 900–1400*, ed. Ronald M. Davidson and Christian Wedemeyer (Leiden: Brill, 2006), 196.
44. See 249.5-.6 for the citation of this passage. As noted there, it is derived from chapter 2 of the *Samāja sādhana vyavasthole* [*sthāli*] citing the *Uttaratantra*, the eighteenth chapter of the *Guhyasamāja Tantra*, See Nāgabodhi (*Klu'i blo*), *Samāja sādhana vyavasthole* [sthāli]. Full title in Tibetan: *'Dus pa'i sgrub pa'i thabs rnam par gzhag pa'i rim pa*. Toh. 1809. Bstan 'gyur, rgyud 'bum, vol. 35, ff. 121a–131a, pp. 243–263. *Uttaratantra. Rgyud phyi ma*. Toh. 443. Bka' 'gyur, rgyud 'bum, vol. 81, ff. 148a–157b, pp. 297–316. See Tanaka's edition and chart of citation derivations. Kimiaki Tanaka, "Nāgabodhi's Śrī-guhyasamāja-maṇḍalopāyikā-viṃśati-vidhi, 8 akasasutrapatanavidhi." *Journal of Indian and Buddhist Studies* 50, no. 1 (2001): 315–20.9.

    Kimiaki Tanaka, "Nāgabodhi's Śrī-guhyasamāja-maṇḍalopāyikā-viṃśati-vidhi: The Tibetan Translation and Sanskrit Text of Chapters 5 and 6," in *Three Mountains and Seven Rivers: Prof. Musashi Tachikawa's Felicitation Volume* (Delhi: Motilal Banarsidass, 2004), 857–869.

    Kimiaki Tanaka,"Nāgabodhi's Śrī-guhyasamāja-maṇḍalopāyikā-viṃśati-vidhi: The Sanskrit Text Restored from the Vajrācārānayottam," in *Genesis and Development of Tantrism, Institute of Oriental Culture Special Series*, ed. Shingo Einoo (Tokyo: Institute of Oriental Culture, 2009), 425–434.
45. *Vajramālā*, see Sde dge 275a.2 [549.2] and 275a.6 (chapter 68).
46. Nāgārjuna (*Klu sgrub*), *Piṇḍī-kṛta sādhana*. Full title in Tibetan: *Sgrub pa'i thabs mdor byas pa* (*Mdor byas*). Toh. 1796. Bstan 'gyur, rgyud 'bum, vol. 35, ff. 1b–11a, pp. 4–23. See Sde dge p.7.3 for the relevant passage. For a valuable translation and study of the *Piṇḍī-kṛta* , see Rhonwen Sayer, "The Guhyasamāja Piṇḍikṛta-sādhana and Its Context" (Masters thesis, School of Oriental and African Studies, 2010). For this verse, see Sayer translation verse 55.
47. ? Nāgabodhi (*Klu'i blo*), *Samāja sādhana vyavasthole* [*sthāli*]. Full title in Tibetan: *'Dus pa'i sgrub pa'i thabs rnam par gzhag pa'i rim pa*. (*Rnam gzhag*), Toh. 1809, Sde dge bstan 'gyur, vol. 35, ff. 121a–131a. See partial editions by Tanaka listed in note 44 of this appendix.
48. *Piṇḍī-kṛta*. See Sde dge, p10.4. See also Sayer, "The Guhyasamāja Piṇḍikṛta-sādhana," v 96 and 97.
49. *Piṇḍī-kṛta*. See Sde dge, p10.4.-.5. See Sayer, "The Guhyasamāja Piṇḍikṛta-sādhana," v 97 and 98.

50. *Samāja sādhana vyavasthole* [*sthāli*] (chapter 2). See Tanaka, Nāgabodhi's Śrī-guhyasamāja-maṇḍalopāyikā-viṃśati-vidhi."
51. *Vajramālā* (chapter 64), "The Explanation of the Mandalas of Body, Speech, and Mind," Sde dge 270a.2 (539.2). It is also cited in both the *Piṇḍī-kṛta* and *Samāja sādhana vyavasthole* [*sthāli*].
52. *Piṇḍī-kṛta*. See Sayer, "The Guhyasamāja Piṇḍikṛta-sādhana, v62.
53. *Samāja sādhana vyavasthole* [*sthāli*] (chapter 2). See Tanaka, Nāgabodhi's Śrī-guhyasamāja-maṇḍalopāyikā-viṃśati-vidhi."
54. *Guhyasamāja Tantra*. Full title in Tibetan: *De bshin gzhegs pa thams cad kyi sku gsung thugs kyi gsang chen gsang ba 'dus pa zhes bya ba brtag pa'i rgyal po chen po*. Toh. 442. Bka' 'gyur, rgyud 'bum, vol. 81, ff. 40a–148a, pp. 181–297. The citation appears at 203.4.
55. ? Nāgārjuna (*Klu sgrub*). *Śrī guhyasamāja-mahayogatantra-utpattikrama-sādhana-sūtra- melāpaka-nāma*. Full title in Tibetan: *Rnal 'byor chen po'i rgyud dpal gsang ba 'dus pa'i bskyed pa'i rim pa bsgom pa'i thabs mdo dang bsres pa*. Toh. 1797. Bstan 'gyur, rgyud 'bum, vol. 35, ff. 11a–15b, pp. 23–32. The citation appears on 24.5–.6.
56. Candrakīrti (*Zla ba grags pa*), *Pradīpoddyotana-nāma-tīkā*. Full title in Tibetan: *Sgron ma gsal bar byed pa zhes bya ba'i rgya cher bshad pa*. Toh. 1785. Bstan 'gyur, rgyud 'bum, vol. 29, ff.1b–201b. This citation is found on 118.4–119.3.
57. See 239.2–.3 and, later, 257.5–.6 where this verse in cited in its totality. See also Sayer, "The Guhyasamāja Piṇḍikṛta-sādhana," v55.
58. ? Candrakīrti (*Zla ba grags pa*), *Vajrasattva-sādhana*. Full title in Tibetan: *Dpal ldan zla ba grags pas rdo rje sems dpa'i sgrub thabs*. Toh. 1814. Bstan 'gyur, rgyud 'bum, ff. 195b–204b, pp. 390–408. See also 49.15–19 [III.2] in Candrakīrti, Hong Luo, and Toru Tomabechi. *Candrakīrti's Vajrasattvaniṣpadanasūtra: Vajrasattvasādhana: Sanskrit and Tibetan Texts*. Beijing: China Tibetology, 2009.
59. *Vajramālā,* Sde dge bka' 'gyur, 270a.3–.4 [539.3–.4]. This excerpt is from chapter 64, "The Explanation of Mandala of Body, Speech, and Mind."
60. *Sampuṭa Tantra*. Khédrup is likely referring to a passage appearing in 81a.5–81b.1 of the Dégé edition where the four goddesses are named, associated with a mudrā (karma, dharma, *mahā-*, *samaya*), given alternate names connecting them with particular virtues, located within a cakra, envisioned as a lotus at a particular site on the body, and, finally, correlated with a seed syllable and an element. Ngorchen cites this passage in his text. Ngor chen kun dga' bzang po, *Kye'i rdo rje'i lus kyi dkyil 'khor la rtsod spong smra ba ngan 'joms* [*Destroyer of the Proponents of Evil Through Eliminating Objections to the Hevajra Body Mandala*], in *Gsung 'bum, Ngor chen kun dga' bzang po'i bka' 'bum*, comp. Bsod nams rgya mtsho and reproduced from the Sde dge block prints. Dehra dun: photomechanical print from a set of prints from the Sde dge dgon chen blocks, W11577, 1:545–580; see 552.1–562.5.
61. Ratnākaraśānti, *Piṇḍikṛta-sādhanopāyikā-vṛtti-ratnāvalī*. Full title in Tibetan: *Mdor bsdus thabs gyi 'grel pa rin chen 'phreng ba*. Toh. 1825. Bstan 'gyur, rgyud 'bum, vol. 36, ff. 1b–95a, pp. 4–191.
62. *Vajramālā*, Sde dge bka' 'gyur, 270a.4–.5 (539.5–.6).
63. This quotation from chapter 2 of the *Samāja sādhana vyavasthole* [*sthāli*] quoting the *Uttaratantra,* chapter 18 of the Guhyasamāja, was cited by Khédrup earlier in the text at 238.6–7. See also Tanaka's edition and chart of citation derivations.
64. *Vajramālā,* Sde dge bka' 'gyur, 275a.2 (549.2) & 275a.5–.6 (549.5–.6) respectively.
65. Ngor chen cites this entire section of Khédrup's text (254.6–255.5) as his object of refutation. See Appendix A, Part I. For the details of how Khédrup is citing Butön who is citing Nagpopa and of how Khédrup's argument is reiterating Tsongkhapa's own, see chapter 3 and notes 1–3 of these appendixes.
66. *Vajramālā,* Sde dge bka' 'gyur, 275a.2–.6 [549.2–.6]. This citation is derived from the detailed description of the body mandala of the support in chapter 68 of the *Vajramālā*, titled, "The Collection of All *Siddhis*."

67. *Vajramālā,* Sde dge bka' 'gyur, 237a.4 [473.4]. This citation is derived from chapter 24 of the *Vajramālā*, titled "Ascertaining the Three Tips of the Nose."
68. *Vajramālā,* Sde dge bka' 'gyur, 237a.7 [473.7]. This citation is also taken from chapter 24.
69. This excerpt corresponds with verses 53–68 in Sayer, the *atiyoga* section of the *Piṇḍikṛta sādhana*; Sayer, "The Guhyasamāja Piṇḍikṛta-sādhana," verses 53–68.
70. *Vajramālā,* Sde dge bka' 'gyur, 270a.7 [539.7]. The citation is from chapter 64, "The Explanation of the Mandala of Body, Speech, and Mind."
71. See Candrakīrti, Hong Luo and Tomabechi, *Candrakīrti's Vajrasattvaniṣpadanasūtra*, p. 50, line 8.
72. See Candrakīrti, Hong Luo, and Tomabechi, p. 50, lines 11–12.
73. Consider Abhayākaragupta, *Niṣpannayogāvalī*. Full title in Tibetan: *Rdzogs pa'i rnal 'byor gyi phreng ba*. Toh. 3121. Bstan 'gyur, rgyud 'bum, vol.75, ff. 94b–151a, pp. 188–301.
74. Nag po pa, *Vajrasattva-pūja-vidhi*. Full title in Tibetan: *Rdo rje sems dpa' mchod pa'i cho ga*. Toh. 1820. Bstan 'gyur, rgyud 'bum, vol. 35, ff. 258b–261a, pp. 518–523.
75. *Vajra-hṛdaya-alaṃkāra Tantra*. Full title in Tibetan: *Dpal rdo rje snying po rgyan gyi rgyud*. Toh. 451 (Sde dge 449). Bka' 'gyur, rgyud 'bum, vol. 82, ff. 36a–58b, pp. 73–118.
76. Abhayākaragupta, *Niṣpannayogāvalī,* Sde dge Bstan 'gyur, 189.4–.6.
77. Ratnākaraśānti. *Piṇḍikṛta-sādhanopāyikā-vṛtti-ratnāvalī.*
78. There were two possible matches with associated works for this Indian pandit in TBRC. P4CZ15180 is a figure from the eleventh century who wrote a commentary on the *Māyājāla*. P4CZ15250 is a figure from the ninth century with three associated works in the Tengyur, including a commentary on the *Pañcakrama*. Consider Kṛṣṇasamayavajra (*Nag po dam tshig rdo rje*). *Pancakramapañjika*. Full title in Tibetan: *Rim pa lnga'i dka' 'grel*. Toh. 1841. Bstan 'gyur, rgyud 'bum, vol. 37, ff. 157b–187a, pp. 316–376.
79. Līlavajra. *Vajrasattva-sādhana-nibandha*. Full title in Tibetan: *Rdo rje sems dpa'i sgrub thabs kyi 'grel pa*. Toh. 1815. Bstan 'gyur, rgyud 'bum, vol. 35, ff. 204b–209a, pp. 410–419.
80. This citation appears to be derived from chapter sixty-eight of the *Vajramālā*. However, the Dégé edition 275b.4 reads slightly differently: *kun bzang tshigs kyi msthams dbus bzhugs*.
81. *Abhidhānottara Tantra*. Full title in Tibetan: *Mngon par brjod pa'i rgyud bla ma*. Toh. 369. Bka' 'gyur, rgyud 'bum, vol. 77, ff. 247a–370a, pp. 495–741.
82. Robert Mapplethorpe, *Black Book* (New York: St. Martin's, 1986).
83. I have included each citation here. As several individuals are cited more than once, many of their names appear multiple times in the list. As I discuss in the epilogue, this is only a preliminary map of these citations, laying the groundwork for future exploration of their precedents.

Bibliography

TIBETAN REFERENCES

Tibetan Kangyur

Abhidhānottara Tantra. Full title in Tibetan: *Mngon par brjod pa'i rgyud bla ma*. Toh. 369. Bka' 'gyur, rgyud 'bum, vol. 77, ff. 247a–370a, pp. 495–741.

Guhyasamāja Tantra. Full title in Tibetan: *De bshin gzhegs pa thams cad kyi sku gsung thugs kyi gsang chen gsang ba 'dus pa zhes bya ba brtag pa'i rgyal po chen po*. Toh. 442. Bka' 'gyur, rgyud 'bum, vol. 81, ff. 40a–148a, pp. 181–297.

Hevajra Tantra. Full title in Tibetan: *Kye'i rdo rje zhes bya ba rgyud kyi rgyal po*. Toh. 417, Bka' 'gyur, rgyud 'bum, vol. 80, ff. 1a–13b, pp. 3–28.

Kṛṣṇayamāri Tantra. Full title in Tibetan: *De bzhin gshegs pa thams cad kyi sku gsung thugs gshin rje gshed nag po zhes bya ba'i rgyud*. Toh. 442. Bka' 'gyur, rgyud 'bum, vol. 83, ff. 134b–151b, pp. 270–304.

Sampuṭa Tantra. Full title in Tibetan: *Yang dag par sbyor ba'i rgyud chen po*. Toh. 381. Bka' 'gyur, rgyud 'bum, vol. 79, ff. 73b–157b, pp. 148–318.

Samvarodaya Tantra. Full title in Tibetan: *Dpal bde mchog 'byung ba zhes bya ba'i rgyud kyi rgyal po chen po*. Toh. 373. Bka' 'gyur, rgyud 'bum, vol. 78, ff. 137a–264b, pp. 531–624.

Uttaratantra. *Rgyud phyi ma*. Toh. 443. Bka' 'gyur, rgyud 'bum, vol. 81, ff. 148a–157b, pp. 297–316.

Vajra hṛdaya alaṃkāra Tantra. Full title in Tibetan: *Dpal rdo rje snying po rgyan gyi rgyud*. Toh. 451 (Sde dge 449). Bka' 'gyur, rgyud 'bum, vol. 82, ff. 36a–58b, pp. 73–118.

Vajramālā (Explanatory) Tantra. Full title in Tibetan: *Rnal 'byor chen po'i rgyud dpal rdo rje 'phreng ba mngon par brjod pa rgyud thams cad kyi snying po gsang ba rnam par phye ba zhes bya ba*. Toh 445. Bka' 'gyur, rgyud 'bum, vol. 81, ff. 208a–277b, pp. 415–554.

Vajrapañjara Tantra. Full title in Tibetan: *'Phags pa mkha' 'gro ma rdo rje gur zhes bya ba'i rgyud kyi rgyal po chen po'i brtag pa*. Toh. 419. Bka' 'gyur, rgyud 'bum, vol. 80, ff. 30r–65v, pp. 59–130.

Yamāri kṛṣṇakarmasarvacakrasiddhikara Tantra. Full title in Tibetan: *Gshin rje'i gshed dgra nag po'i 'khor lo las thams cad grub par byed pa zhes bya ba'i rgyud kyi rgyal po*. Toh. 474. Bka' 'gyur, rgyud 'bum, vol. 83, ff. 175b–185b, pp. 351–372.

Tibetan Tengyur

Abhayākaragupta. *Āmnāyamañjarī*. Full title in Tibetan: *Dpal yang dag par sbyor ba'i rgyud kyi rgyal po'i rgya cher 'grel pa man ngag gi snye ma*. Toh. 1198. Bstan 'gyur, rgyud 'bum, vol. 7, ff. 1b–316a, pp. 4–633.

Abhayākaragupta. *Niṣpannayogāvalī*. Full title in Tibetan: *Rdzogs pa'i rnal 'byor gyi phreng ba*. Toh 3121. Bstan 'gyur, rgyud 'bum, vol.75, ff. 94b–151a, pp. 188–301.

Alaṃkakalaśa. *Śri Vajramālā mahāyoga ṭantratīkā-gambhīrārthadīpikā*. Full title in Tibetan: *Rnal 'byor chen po'i rgyud dpal rdo rje phreng ba'i rgya cher 'grel pa zab mo'i don gyi 'grel pa*. Toh. 1795. Bstan 'gyur, rgyud 'bum, vol. 33, ff. 1b–220a.

Candrakīrti (Zla ba grags pa). *Pradīpoddyotana-nāma-tīkā*. Full title in Tibetan: *Sgron ma gsal bar byed pa zhes bya ba'i rgya cher bshad pa*. Toh. 1785. Bstan 'gyur, rgyud 'bum, vol. 29, ff. 1b–201b.

? Candrakīrti (Zla ba grags pa). *Vajrasattva-sādhana*. Full title in Tibetan: *Rdo rje sems dpa'i sgrub thabs*. Toh. 1814. Bstan 'gyur, rgyud 'bum, ff. 195b–204b, pp. 392–410.

Darikapa. *Sri Cakrasaṃvara-sādhana tattvasaṃgraha*. Full title in Tibetan: *Dpal 'khor lo sdom pa'i sgrub thabs de kho na nyid bsdud pa*. Toh. 1429. Bstan 'gyur, rgyud 'bum, vol. 21, ff. 197b–203b, pp. 396–408. *Gser bris bstan 'gyur* 147, vol. 13, pp. 531–428.

Dharmakīrti. *Pramāṇavarttika-kārikā*. Full title in Tibetan: *Tshad ma rnam 'grel gyi tshig le'ur byas pa*. Toh. 4210. Bstan 'gyur, Sde dge, vol. 174, ff. 94v–151r (pp.189–304). Delhi: Delhi Karmapa Choeday, Gyalwae sungrab partun khang, 1982–1985.

Ghantapa (Rdo rje dril bu pa). *Śrī-cakrasaṃvarasekaprakriyopadeśa*. Full title in Tibetan: *Dpal 'khor lo sdom pa'i dbang gi bya ba mdor bsdus pa*. Toh. 1431. Bstan 'gyur, rgyud 'bum, vol. 21, ff. 219b–222b, pp. 440–446.

Ghantapa, Tshul khrims rin chen. *Bcom ldan 'das 'khor lo bde mchog sgrub pa'i thabs rin po che yid bzhin gyi nor bu*. In bstan 'gyur, Sde dge, TBRC W23703, 21:468–476, 233v–237v.

Indrabhūti. *Smṛti-saṃdarśanāloka*. Full title in Tibetan: *Dpal kha sbyor thig le zhes bya ba rnal 'byor ma'i rgyud kyi rgyal po'i rgya cher 'grel pa yang dag par lta ba'i dran pa'i snang ba*. Bstan 'gyur, rgyud 'bum, vol. 6, ff. 94b–313b, pp. 190–627.

Jetari (Slob dpon dgra las rnam rgyal). *Caturmudrā-sādhana*. Full title in Tibetan: *Phyag rgya bzhi yi sgrub thabs*. Gser bris bstan 'gyur 2695. vol. 75, pp. 387–393; Snar thang bstan 'gyur vol. 76, ff. 142v–144v, pp. 284–288.

Kṛṣṇasamayavajra (Nag po dam tshig rdo rje). *Pañcakramapañjika*. Full title in Tibetan: *Rim pa lnga'i dka' 'grel*. Toh. 1841. Bstan 'gyur, rgyud 'bum, vol. 37, ff. 157b–187a, pp. 316–376.

Kṣāntiśrī. *Śrī-samvarodaya sādhana*. Full title in Tibetan: *Dpal sdom pa 'byung ba'i sgrub thabs*. Toh. 1515. Bstan 'gyur, rgyud 'bum, vol. 22, ff. 374b–379a, pp. 750–760.

Līlavajra. *Vajrasattva sādhana nibandha*. Full title in Tibetan: *Rdo rje sems dpa'i sgrub thabs kyi 'grel pa*. Toh. 1815. Bstan 'gyur, rgyud 'bum, vol. 35, ff. 204b–209a, pp. 410–419.

? Nāgabodhi (Klu'i blo). *Samāja sādhana vyavasthole* (*sthāli*). Full title in Tibetan: *'Dus pa'i sgrub pa'i thabs rnam par gzhag pa'i rim pa*. Toh. 1809. Bstan 'gyur, rgyud 'bum, vol. 35, ff. 121a–131a, pp. 243–263.

Nāgārjuna (Klu sgrub). *Piṇḍī-kṛta sādhana*. Full title in Tibetan: *Sgrub pa'i thabs mdor byas pa*. Toh. 1796. Bstan 'gyur, rgyud 'bum, vol. 35, ff. 1b–11a, pp. 4–23.

? Nāgārjuna (Klu sgrub). *Śrī guhyasamāja-mahāyogatantra-utpattikrama-sādhana-sūtra- melāpaka-nāma*. Full title in Tibetan: *Rnal 'byor chen po'i rgyud dpal gsang ba 'dus pa'i bskyed pa'i rim pa bsgom pa'i thabs mdo dang bsres pa*. Toh. 1797. Bstan 'gyur, rgyud 'bum, vol. 35, ff. 11a–15b, pp. 23–32.

Nag po pa. *Saṃvara-vyākhyā*. Full title in Tibetan: *Sdom pa bshad pa*. Toh. 1460. Bstan 'gyur, rgyud 'bum, vol. 22, ff. 6a–10b, pp. 12–20.

Nag po pa. *Vajrasattva pūja vidhi*. Full title in Tibetan: *Rdo rje sems dpa' mchod pa'i cho ga*. Toh. 1820. Bstan 'gyur, rgyud 'bum, vol. 35, ff. 258b–261a, pp. 518–523.

Nāropa. *Dpal 'khor lo sdom pa'i sgrub thabs yid bzhin nor bu*. Translated by Marpa chos kyi blo gros. In *Mkha' 'gro snyan brgyud kyi yig rnying*, 307–328. Darjeeling: Kargyud sungrab nyamso khang.

(Nāropāda or Snyan grags bzang po). *Vajrapada-sāra-saṁgraha-pañjikā.* Full title in Tibetan: *Rdo rje'i tshig gi snying po bsdus pa'i dka' 'grel.* Toh. 1186. Bstan 'gyur, rgyud 'bum, vol. 4, ff. 58b–146b, pp. 118–294; Dpe sdur ma, vol. 2, pp. 87–1110.

Ratnākaraśānti. *Piṇḍikṛta-sādhanopāyikā-vṛtti-ratnāvalī.* Full title in Tibetan: *Mdor bsdus thabs gyi 'grel pa rin chen 'phreng ba.* Toh.1825. Bstan 'gyur, rgyud 'bum, vol. 36, ff. 1b–95a, pp. 4–191.

Ratnarakṣita. *Śrī-samvarodaya-mahātantrarāja-padmini-nāma-pañjikā.* Full title in Tibetan: *Dpal sdom pa 'byung ba'i rgyud kyi rgyal po chen po'i dka' 'grel padma can.* Toh. 1420. Bstan 'gyur, rgyud 'bum, vol. 21, ff. 1b–101b, pp. 4–204.

Tathāgatavajra (Slob dpon de bzhin gshegs pa'i rdo rje). *Luyipābhisamaya-vṛttiṭīkā-viśeṣadyota.* Full title in Tibetan: *Lū yi pa'i mngon par rtogs pa'i 'grel pa'i ṭī kā khyad par gsal byed.* Toh. 1510. Bstan 'gyur, rgyud 'bum, vol. 22, ff. 285a–308b, pp. 571–618.

Vajragarbha. *Hevajrapiṇḍārthaṭikā.* Full title in Tibetan: *Kye'i rdo rje bsdu pa'i don gyi rgya cher 'grel pa.* Toh. 1180. Bstan 'gyur, rgyud 'bum, vol. 2, ff. 1b–126a, pp. 2–253.

Sources Attributed to Tibetan Authors

(Tsong kha pa) Blo bzang grags pa (1357–81). *The Jewel Treasury: The Rite of Empowerment of the Body Mandala of Ghantapa, the Lord of Yoga. Rnal 'byor dbang phyug dril bu lugs bde mchog lus dkyil gyi dbang chog rin po che'i bang mdzod,* Toh. 5327, 10:57–106.

Blo bzang grags pa. *The Stage of Pure Yoga: The Guhyasamāja Sādhana. Dpal gsang ba 'dus pa'i sgrub thabs rnal 'byor dag pa'i rim pa.* Toh. T5303. In *Gsung 'bum,* Tsong kha pa, Bla brang par ma. TBRC W22273, 7:623–678. Bla brang: Bla brang bkra shis 'khyil.

Blo bzang grags pa. *The Wish-Granting Extensive Explanation of the Cakrasaṃvara Abhisamaya. Bde mchog mngon rtogs rgya cher bshad pa 'dod pa 'jo ba.* In *Gsung 'bum,* Tsong kha pa, Bla brang par ma. TBRC W22273, 9:195–592. Bla brang: Bla brang bkra shis 'khyil, 199?.

Blo bzang grags pa. *The Wish-Granting Extensive Explanation of the Buddha Cakrasaṃvara Abhisamaya. Bcom ldan 'das dpal 'khor lo mde mchog gi mngon par rtogs pa'i rgya cher bshad pa 'dod pa 'jo ba.* In Collected Works, 27 vols. Old Bkra shis lhun po redaction, 14:195, ff. 72–460. New Delhi: Ngawang Gelek Demo, 1975–1979.

('Phags pa) Blo gros rgyal mtshan (1235–1280). *Hevajra Body Mandala Sādhana. Kyai rdo rje lus dkyil gyi sgrub thabs.* In *Sa skya bka' 'bum, Collected Writings of the First Five Great Patriarchs of the Sakya Order.* Includes the three supplementary volumes recently published by Khenpo Tsultrim Gyaltsen, listed separately [W20751]. Reprinted from a set of Dege Parkhang prints. TBRC W22271, 13:538–542. Dehra dun: Sakya center, 1992–1993.

Bod rgya tshig mdzod chen mo, vol. 1. Pe cing: Mi rigs dpe skrun khang, 2003.

(Go rams pa) Bsod nams seng ge (1429–1489). *Illuminating the Pith: Dispelling Objections to the Moonrays of the Pith. Gnad gyi zla zer la rtsod pa spong ba gnad kyi gsal byed.* In *Gsung 'bum,* Bsod nams seng ge, TBRC W1PD1725, 12:557–694.

Bu ston Rin chen grub (1290–1364). *Nagpopa's Cakrasaṃvara Sādhana, Free from Errors or Impurities. Bde mchog nag po pa'i sgrub thabs 'khrul ba'i dri bral.* Toh. 5049. In *Gsung 'bum,* Rin chen grub, Zhol par khang, TBRC W1934, 7:151–186. Lha sa: Zhol par khang, 2000.

Bu ston. *The Commentary on the Yoginī-saṃcāra-tantra, the Utterly Clear Meaning of Cakrasaṃvara. Rnal 'byor ma kun tu spyod pa'i rgyud gyi bshad pa bde mchog gi don rab tu gsal ba.* Bu ston's *Collected Works,* Rin chen grub, Zhol par khang, 6:725–876. See also *Collected Works.* New Delhi: International Academy of Culture, 1967. vol. 6 (cha), 76 folios, pp. 719–869.

Bu ston. *Cakrasaṃvara Samvarodaya sādhana.* Rin chen grub, Rin chen rnam rgyal, Lokesh Chandra. *Dpal bde mchog 'khor lo sdom pa 'byung ba'i sgrub thabs.* In *Gsung 'bum,* Rin chen grub, Zhol par ma (ldi lir bskyar par brgyab pa). TBRC W22106, 7:479–504. New Delhi: International Academy of Indian Culture, 1965–1971.

Bu ston. *Clarifying the Generation Stage: The Extensive Explanation of the Guhyasamāja Piṇḍī-kṛta sādhana. Dpal gsang ba 'dus pa'i sgrub thabs mdor byas kyi rgya cher bshad pa bskyed rim gsal byed.* In *The Collected Works of Bu-ston,* 683–877. New Delhi: International Academy of Indian Culture, 1967.

Chos ldan rab 'byor. *Short Biography of the Omniscient Mkhas grub. Mkhas grub thams cad mkhyen pa'i rnam thar bsdus pa.* Collected writings of Mkhas grub dge legs dpal gzang. vol. ka, pp. 109–34.

Dol po pa Shes rab rgyal msthan (1292–1361). *The Ocean of Definitive Meaning of Mountain Dharma.* (Jo nang) *Ri chos nges don rgya mtsho.* Beijing: Mi rigs dpe skrun khang, 1998.

Glo bo mkhan chen bsod nams lhun grub (1456–1532). *Reply to Questions: The Biography ("Liberation Story") of the Venerable Bsod nams lhun grub, the Execellent Victory Banner, Source of All Goodness. Rje btsun bsod nams lhun grub legs pa'i 'byung gnas rgyal mtshan dpal bzang po'i rnam par thar pa zhus lan.* Tōyō Bunko, 41–683.

Gnas rnying 'Jam dbyangs kun dga' dge legs rin chen rgyal mtshan. *The Captivating Scholar's Liberation Story. Rnam thar mkhas pa'i yid 'phrog* (KYP), Collected works of *Mkhas grub rje,* vol. ka, pp. 1–22.

Grags pa rgyal mtshan (1147–1216). *Body mandala. Lus kyi dkyil 'khor.* Digital Sakya *lam 'bras* collection, 10:140–143.

Grags pa rgyal mtshan. Kun dga' snying po, Bsod nams rtse mo, Grags pa rgyal mtshan, Kun dga' rgyal mtshan, Blo gros rgyal mtshan. *Commentary on the Vajrapañjara. 'Phags pa rdo rje gur gyi rgyan zhes bya ba'i rnam 'grel.* In *Sa skya bka' 'bum,* TBRC W00EGS1017151, 7:9–166. Kathmandu: Sachen International, 2006.

Mkhas grub rje dge legs dpal bzang (1385–1438). *Collected Works.* New Zhol par khang edition of *Gsung 'bum,* Mkhas grub rje (*zhol*), TOH 5481, TBRC W384. New Delhi: Mongolian Lama Guru Deva. 1980–82.

Mkhas grub. *The Thunderbolt Wheel Treatise Which Utterly Decimates the Evil Proponents Engaged in Erroneous Speech* (*Thunderbolt Wheel of Reply to Ngor*). *Phyin ci log gi gtam gyi sbyor ba la 'jug pa'i smra ba ngan pa rnam par 'thag pa bstan bcos gnam lcags 'khor lo.* TBRC W384, 2:7–100.

Mkhas grub. *Some Difficult Points in the Generation Stage of the Ghantapa Body Mandala. Dril bu lus dkyil gyi byang du byas pa'i bskyed rim gyi bka' gnas 'ga' zhig.* TBRC W384, 6:765–787.

Mkhas grub. *Ocean of Attainment of the Guhyasamāja Generation Stage. Gsang 'dus bskyed rim dngos grub rgya mtsho.* TBRC W384, 7:5–384.

Mkhas grub. *Dispelling Delusions regarding the Hevajra Sādhana. Kyai rdo rje'i sgrub thabs 'khrul spong.* TBRC W384, 8:89–135.

Mkhas grub. *The Extensive Explanation for Classifying the Divisions of Tantra. Rgyud sde spyi'i rnam par bzhag pa rgyas par bshad pa. Collected Works* (Zhol), 8:443–630.

Mkhas grub. *Reply to the Questions of the Kalyānamītra Kon ting gug śrī ba. Dge ba'i bshes gnyen kon ting gug shri ba'i dris lan.* In *Thor-bu Collected Works,* TBRC W384, 9:775–808.

Mkhas grub. *Thunderbolt Wheel of Reply to Ngor. Ngor lan gnam lcags 'khor lo. Dgag lan phyogs bsgrigs.* Chinese colophon title: Pien lun wen hsuan pien, 1–68. Ch'eng tu: Si khron Mi rigs Dpe skrun khang, 1997.

(A myes zhabs) Ngag dbang kun dga' bsod nams (b. 1597–d. 1659/60). "Notes for the Correct Explication of How to Enter Into the Writings of the Venerable Sa skya pas: Opening Wide in a Hundred Directions the Dharma Gates to Which All Beings of Tibet Are Guided." (Notes). *Rje btsun sa skya pa'i gsung rab la 'jug tshul legs par bshad pa'i yi ge bod yul 'gro kun bsgrod pa'i chos sgo phyogs brgyar ring du phye ba.* Edited by A-med-zhabs and originally composed by Chos dpal bzang po; *Collected Works,* vol. kha, fol. 384r–393v.

(Ngor chen) Kun dga' bzang po (1382–1456). *Collected Works. Gsung 'bum,* Kun dga' bzang po. *Ngor chen kun dga' bzang po'i bka' 'bum.* Compiled by Bsod nams rgya mtsho and reproduced from the Sde dge block prints. Dehra dun: photomechanical print from a set of prints from the Sde dge dgon chen blocks. TBRC W11577.

Ngor chen. *Catalogue of Hevajra Commentaries. Kye rdo rje'i 'grel pa'i dkar chag.* TBRC W11577, 2:452–453.

Ngor chen. Commentary on *Overcoming Objections to the Three Tantras. Rgyud gsum gnod 'joms kyi 'grel pa.* TBRC W11577, 1:630–659.

Ngor chen. *Commentary on the Ghantapa Body Mandala Practice. Dril bu pa'i lus dkyil gyi bshad pa.* TBRC W11577, 4:735–766.

Ngor chen. *Commentary on the Ghantapa Body Mandala Practice. Dril bu pa'i lus dkyil gyi bshad pa.* In *Sa skya pa'i bka' 'bum*, vol. 10, folios 117b–140a, 398.1.1–405.4.1. Tokyo: Tōyō Bunko, 1969.

Ngor chen. *Destroyer of the Proponents of Evil through Eliminating Objections to the Hevajra Body Mandala* [N1]. *Kye'i rdo rje'i lus kyi dkyil 'khor la rtsod spong smra ba ngan 'joms.* TBRC W11577, 1:545–580.

Ngor chen. *Dispelling Evil Misunderstandings of the Explanation of the Ground of Union Vajradhara. Zung 'jug rdo rje 'chang chen po'i sa mtshams rnam par bshad pa log rtog ngan sel.* TBRC W11577, 1:659–691.

Ngor chen. *Dispelling Evil Views of the Hevajra Body Mandala. Kye rdo rje'i lus kyi dkyil 'khor la rtsod spong lta ba ngan sel* [N2]. TBRC W11577, 1:580–625.

Ngor chen. *The Essential Yoga: The Sādhana of the Hevajra Body Mandala. Dpal kye rdo rje'i lus kyi dkyil 'khor gyi sgrub pa'i thabs rnal 'byor snying po.* In *Sa skya'i chos mdzod chen mo,* 28:296–312. Si khron bod yig dpe rnying 'tshol bsdu rtsom sgrig khang, 2013.

Ngor chen. *Extraordinary Ocean of Biographies of Lineage Lamas and the Manner of Arising of the Hevajra Tantra. Kye rdo rje'i byung tshul dang brgyad pa'i bla ma'i rnam thar ngo mtshar rgya mtsho.* TBRC W11577, 2:425–451.

Ngor chen. *Lamp of Eloquent Explanation for Classifying the Kriyā Tantras. Spyod rgyud spyi'i rnam gzhag legs bshad sgron me.* TBRC W11577, 4:135–204.

Ngor chen. *Moonrays of the Pith of the Generation Stage of the Precious Explanation of the Hevajra sādhana. Kye rdo rje'i sgrub thabs kyi rgya cher bshad pa bskyed rim gnad kyi zla zer.* TBRC W11577, 2:5–418.

Ngor chen. *The Ocean of Attainment of the Sādhana of the Guhyasamāja Mandala. Gsang 'dus dkyil 'khor gyi sgrub thabs dngos grub rgya mtsho.* TBRC W11577, 3:369–4.

Ngor chen. *Ocean of Eloquent Explanation of the Caryā Tantras. Bya rgyud spyi'i rnam bshad legs bshad rgya mtsho.* TBRC W11577, 4:204–418.

Ngor chen. *Overcoming Objections to the Three Tantras. Rgyud gsum gnod 'joms.* TBRC W11577, 1:625–630.

Ngor chen. *Record of Received Teachings. Thob yig rgya mtsho.* TBRC W11577, 1:179–434.

(Red mda' ba) Gzhon nu blo gros. *The Gathering of the Ocean of Excellent Explanation: Clearing Mental Darkness, a Commentary on the Guhyasamāja, together with the Pradīpoddyotana. Dpal gsang ba 'dus pa'i 'grel pa sgron ma gsal ba dang bcas pa'i bshad sbyar yid kyi mun sel zhes bya ba'i legs bshad rgya mtsho'i tshogs.* In *Gsung 'bum: Gzhon nu blo gros.* TBRC W23629. 3:7–760. Kathmandu: Sa skya rgyal yongs gsung rab slob gnyer khang, 1999.

Rje brtsun chos kyi rgyal mtshan. *Secret Biography* (of Mkhas grub rje). *Gsang ba'i rnam thar* (SNT) *Collected Works,* a:421–493.

Sangs rgyas phun tshogs (1649–1705). *The Source of the Wish Fulfilling Jewel, the Oceanic Qualities Which Gather the Rivers: the Biography ("Liberation Story") of the Victorious Vajradhara Kun dga' bzang po. Rgyal ba rdo rje 'chang kun dga' bzang po'i rnam par thar pa legs bshad chu bo 'dus pa'i rgya mtsho yon tan yid bzhin nor bu'i 'byung gnas.* Scanned from the Sde dge blocks carved at the time of Sa skyong tshe dbang rdo rje rig 'dzin, Dkar mdzes khul: Sde dge, written 1688.

Other References

Abhayākaragupta, Dorje. *Abhayapaddhati of Abhayākaragupta: Commentary on the Buddhakapālamahātantra.* Sarnath, Varanasi: Central Institute of Higher Tibetan Studies, 2009.

Akira, Hirakawa. *A History of Indian Buddhism: From Śākyamuni to Early Mahāyana,* ed. Paul Groner. Honolulu: University of Hawai'i Press, 1990.

"Anatta-lakkhana Sutta: The Discourse on the Not-self Characteristic" (SN 22.59). Trans. Ñanamoli Thera. *Access to Insight (BCBS Edition)*, June 13, 2010. https://www.accesstoinsight.org/tipitaka/sn/sn22/sn22.059.nymo.html.

Aris, Michael. *Hidden Treasures and Secret Lives: A Study of Pemalingpa (1450–1521) and the Sixth Dalai Lama (1683–1706)*. London: Kegan Paul International, 1989.

Art 21. "Glenn Ligon." https://art21.org/artist/glenn-ligon/?gclid=CjwKCAiAhc7yBRAdEiwAplGxXwKZpdBULQ6l4CbxHy_rTe41RaektGizBZPFS866KMuluddYvLHC_BoC4hgQAvD_BwE.

Ary, Elijah Sacvan. *Authorized Lives: Biography and the Early Formation of Geluk Identity*. Boston: Wisdom, 2015.

——. "Logic and Lineage: Jetsun Chokyi Gyaltsen's Ascension and the Secret Biography of Khedrup Geleg Pelzang." PhD diss., Harvard University, 2007.

Austin, J. L. "The Works of J.L. Austin. Electronic edition: How to Do Things with Words." http://pm.nlx.com/xtf/view?docId=austin/austin.01.xml.

Bell, Catherine. *Ritual Theory, Ritual Practice*. New York: Oxford University Press, 1992.

Belting, Hans. *Likeness and Presence: A History of the Image Before the Era of Art*. Translated by Edmund Jephcott. Chicago: University of Chicago Press, 1994.

Bentor, Yael. *Consecration of Images and Stūpas in Indo-Tibetan Tantric Buddhism*. Leiden: Brill, 1996.

——. "Divergent Perspectives on the Guhyasamāja Sādhana in Tibet: Dge lugs vs. Sa skya." 密教文化 = *Journal of Esoteric Buddhism* / 密教研究会 編 237 (2016): 70–44.

——. "Did mKhas grub rje Challenge the Authenticity of the Sa skya Lam 'bras Tradition?" In *Towards a History of Fifteenth-century Tibet: Cultural Blossoming, Religious Fervour and Political Unrest*, ed. Volker Caumanns and Marta Sernisi, 227–248. Lumbini, Nepal: Lumbini International Research Institute, 2017.

——. "Identifying the Unnamed Opponents of Tsong kha pa and Mkhas grub rje Concerning the Transformation of Ordinary Birth, Death and the Intermediary State Into the Three Bodies." In *Tibetan Buddhist Literature and Praxis: Studies in Its Formative Period, 900–1400*, ed. Ronald M. Davidson and Christian Wedemeyer, 185–200. Leiden: Brill, 2006.

——. "Interpreting the Body *Maṇḍala*: Tsongkhapa Versus Later Gelug Scholars." *Revue d'Etudes Tibétaines*, no. 31 (2015): 63–74.

——. "Tibetan Interpretations of the Opening Verses of Vajraghanta on the Body Mandala." In *Chinese and Tibetan Esoteric Buddhism*, ed. Yael Bentor and Meir Shahar, 230–259. Leiden; Boston: Brill, 2017.

——. "Tsongkhapa's Guhyasamāja Sādhana and the Ārya Tradition." In *Vimalakīrti's House: A Festschrift in Honor of Robert A.F. Thurman on the Occasion of His Seventieth Birthday*, ed. Christian K. Wedemeyer, John D. Dunne, and Thomas F. Yarnall, 165–92. New York: Columbia University Press, 2015.

——. "Women on the Way to Enlightenment." In *From Bhakti to Bon: Festschrift for Per Kvaerne*, ed. Hanna Havnevik and Charles Ramble, 89–96. Oslo: Institute for Comparative Research in Human Culture: Novus, 2015.

Berger, Patricia Ann. *Empire of Emptiness: Buddhist Art and Political Authority in Qing China*. Honolulu: University of Hawai'i Press, 2003.

——. "Miracles in Nanjing: An Imperial Record of the Fifth Karmapa's Visit to the Chinese Capital." In *Cultural Intersections in Later Chinese Buddhism*, ed. Marsha Weidner, 145–169. Honolulu: University of Hawai'i Press, 2001.

Birch, Jason. "The Amaraughaprabodha: New Evidence on the Manuscript Transmission of any Early Work on Haṭha- and Rājayoga." *Journal of Indian Philosophy* 47 (2019): 947–977.

Blo-gros-mtha'-yas, Elio Guarisco, and Ingrid McLeod. *The Treasury of Knowledge: Book Six, Part Four: Systems of Buddhist Tantra*. Ithaca, NY: Snow Lion, 2005.

Bolton, Richard. *Culture Wars: Documents from the Recent Controversies in the Arts*. New York: New Press, 1992.

Bourdieu, Pierre. *The Logic of Practice*. Stanford: Stanford University Press, 1990.

——. *Practical Reason: On the Theory of Action*. Stanford: Stanford University Press, 1998.

Bstan-'dzin-rgya-mtsho, and Thupten Jinpa. *The Union of Bliss and Emptiness: Teachings on the Practice of Guru Yoga*. Ithaca, NY: Snow Lion, 1988.

Buddhaghosa, and Ñāṇamoli. *The Path of Purification-Visuddhimagga*. Kandy: Buddhist Publication Society, 2010.

Buddhaguhya. *The Maha-Vairocana-Abhisambodhi Tantra: With Buddhaguhya's Commentary*. Trans. Stephen Hodge. New York: Routledge, 2005.

Buddhist Digital Archives. https://library.bdrc.io/.

Butler, Judith. "Afterword." In *Bodily Citations: Religion and Judith Butler*, edited by Ellen T. Armour and Susan M. St. Ville, 261. New York: Columbia University Press, 2006.

——. *Bodies That Matter: On the Discursive Limits of "Sex."* New York: Routledge, 1993.

Cabezón, José Ignacio. "Authorship and Literary Production in Classical Buddhist Tibet." In *Changing Minds: Contributions to the Study of Buddhism and Tibet in Honor of Jeffrey Hopkins*, ed. Guy Newland, 233–64. Ithaca, NY: Snow Lion, 2001.

——. *Sexuality in Classical South Asian Buddhism*. Somerville, MA: Wisdom, 2017.

Cabezón, José Ignacio, and Geshe Lobsang Dargyay. *Freedom from Extremes: Gorampa's "Distinguishing the Views" and the Polemics of Emptiness*. Boston: Wisdom, 2007.

Candrakīrti, Hong Luo, and Toru Tomabechi. *Candrakīrti's Vajrasattvaniṣpadanasūtra = Vajrasattvasādhana: Sanskrit and Tibetan Texts*. Beijing: China Tibetology, 2009.

Capps, Kriston. "A Museum Canceled Its Robert Mapplethorpe Show—and Decades Later, It's Finally Trying to Make Amends." *Washington Post*, June 12, 2019. https://www.washingtonpost.com/entertainment/museums/a-museum-canceled-its-robert-mapplethorpe-show—and-decades-later-its-finally-trying-to-make-amends/2019/06/12/692f2744-83ce-11e9-bce7-40b4105f7ca0_story.html.

Chandra, Lokesh, ed. *The Collected Works of Bu ston*. New Delhi: International Academy of Indian Culture, 1966.

Cixous, Hélène, Keith Cohen, and Paula Cohen. "The Laugh of the Medusa." *Signs* 1, no. 4 (1976): 875–893.

Collins, Steven. "On the Very Idea of the Pali Canon." *Journal of the Pali Text Society* 15 (1990): 89–126.

Cuevas, Bryan J. *The Hidden History of The Tibetan Book of the Dead*. New York: Oxford University Press, 2003.

Dachille, Rae. "'Empty Like the Sky': Polysemy and the Problem of 'Mere Clear Awareness' at the Intersection of Sūtra and Tantra in Fifteenth-century Tibet." *Revue d'Etudes Tibétaines*, no. 58 (April 2021): 208–236.

——. "Piercing to the Pith of the Body: The Evolution of Body Mandala and Tantric Corporeality in Tibet" Special issue in the Society for Tantric Studies Proceedings (2016), *Religions* 8, no. 9 (2017): 189.

——. "Running the Numbers for the Path of Mantra: Distinguishing the Thirteenth Bhūmi in Fifteenth-century Tibet." *Religions* 12, no. 3 (2021): 175.

Dalton, Jacob P. "A Crisis of Doxography: How Tibetans Organized Tantra During the Eighth–Twelfth Centuries," *Journal of the International Association of Buddhist Studies* 28, no. 1 (2005): 115–181.

——. "How Dhāraṇīs WERE Proto-Tantric: Liturgies, Ritual Manuals, and the Origins of the Tantras." In *Tantric Traditions on the Move*, ed. David B. Gray and Ryan Overbey, 199–229. Oxford: Oxford University Press, 2016.

Davidson, Ronald M. "Masquerading as Pramāṇa: Esoteric Buddhism and Epistemological Nomenclature." In *Dharmakīrti's Thought and Its Impact on Indian and Tibetan Philosophy: Proceedings of the Third International Dhamakīrti conference, Hiroshima, November 4–6, 1997*, ed. Shoryu Katsura, 25–35. Vienna: Verlag der Österreichischen Akademie der Wissenschaften, 1999.

——. "The Ngor-pa Tradition." *Wind Horse*, no.1 (1981): 88.

——. "Preliminary Studies on Hevajra's Abhisamaya and the Lam-'bras Tshogs-bshad." In *Tibetan Buddhism, Reason and Revelation*, ed. Steven D. Goodman and Ronald M. Davidson, 26. Albany: State University of New York Press, 1992.

——. "Reflections on the Maheśvara Subjugation Myth: Indic Materials, Sa-skya-pa Apologetics, and the Birth of Heruka." *Journal of the International Association of Buddhist Studies* 14, no. 2 (1991): 197–235.

——. *Tibetan Renaissance: Tantric Buddhism in the Rebirth of Tibetan Culture*. New York: Columbia University Press, 2005.

DeCaroli, Robert. *Image Problems: The Origin and Development of the Buddha's Image in Early South Asia*. Seattle: University of Washington Press, 2015.

de Mallmann, Marie-Thérèse de. *Introduction à L'iconographie du Tantrisme Bouddhique*. Paris: Librairie Adrien-Maisonneuve, 1975.

Derrida, Jacques. "Signature, Event, Context." In *A Derrida Reader: Between the Blinds*, ed. Peggy Kamuf, 80–111. New York: Columbia University Press, 1991.

Derrida, Jacques, Gayatri Chakravorty Spivak, and Judith P. Butler. *Of Grammatology*. Baltimore: Johns Hopkins University Press, 2016.

Dge-legs-dpal-bzang-po, Mkhas-grub, and José Ignacio Cabezón. *A Dose of Emptiness: An Annotated Translation of the sTong thun chen mo of mKhas-grub dGe-legs-dpal-bzang*. Albany: State University of New York Press, 1992.

Dkon-mchog-lhun-grub, Lobsang Dagpa, and Jay Goldberg. *The Three Visions: Fundamental Teachings of the Sakya Lineage of Tibetan Buddhism*. Ithaca, NY: Snow Lion, 2002.

Dreyfus, Georges. *Recognizing Reality: Dharmakīrti's Philosophy and Its Tibetan Interpretations*. Albany: State University of New York Press, 1997.

——. *The Sound of Two Hands Clapping: the Education of a Tibetan Monk*. Berkeley: University of California Press, 2003.

Dubosh, Grace. "25 Years Later: Cincinnati and the Obscenity Trial Over Mapplethorpe Art." https://www.washingtonpost.com/entertainment/museums/25-years-later-cincinnati-and-the-obscenity-trial-over-mapplethorpe-art/2015/10/22/07c6aba2-6dcb-11e5-9bfe-e59f5e244f92_story.html.

Ehrhard, Franz-Karl. "Spiritual Relationships Between Rulers and Preceptors: The Three Journeys of Vanaratna (1384–1468) to Tibet." In *The Relationship Between Religion and State (chos srid zung 'brel) in Traditional Tibet*. Lumbini: Lumbini International Research Institute, 2004.

Elder, George Robert. "The Saṃputa Tantra: Edition and Translation, Chapters I–IV." PhD diss., Columbia University, 1978.

English, Elizabeth. *Vajrayoginī: Her Visualizations, Rituals, and Forms*. Boston: Wisdom, 2002.

Felstiner, John. *Paul Celan: Poet, Survivor, Jew*. Urbana: University of Illinois Press, 2001.

Flood, Gavin. *The Tantric Body: The Secret Tradition of Hindu Religion*. London: I. B. Tauris, 2006.

Foucault, Michel. "Nietzsche, Genealogy, History." In *Nietzsche: Critical Assessments*, ed. Daniel W. Conway and Peter S. Groff. London; New York: Routledge, 1998.

Foucault, Michel, and Alan Sheridan. *Discipline and Punish: The Birth of the Prison*. New York: Vintage, 1979.

Fournier, Lauren. *Autotheory as Feminist Practice in Art, Writing, and Criticism*. Cambridge, MA: MIT Press, 2021.

Freschi, Elisa, Cathy Cantwell, and Jowita Kramer, eds. "Reuse and Intertextuality in the Context of Buddhist Texts." Special issue, *Buddhist Studies Review* 33, no. 1–2 (2016).

Garrett, Frances. *Religion, Medicine, and the Human Embryo in Tibet*. New York: Routledge, 2008.

Gates Jr., Henry Louis. "Editor's Introduction: Writing 'Race' and the Difference It Makes." *Critical Inquiry* 12, no. 1, "Race," Writing, and Difference (Autumn 1985): 1–20.

Gayley, Holly. "Revisiting the 'Secret Consort' (*gsang yum*) in Tibetan Buddhism." *Religions* 9 no. 6 (2018): 179.

Germano, David. "Re-membering the Dismembered Body of Tibet: Contemporary Visionary Movements in the People's Republic of China." In *Buddhism in Contemporary Tibet: Religious Revival and Cultural Identity*, ed. Melvyn C. Goldstein and Matthew T. Kapstein, 53–94. Berkeley: University of California Press, 1998.

Gossett, Che. "Blackness and the Trouble of Transvisibility." In *Trap Door: Trans Cultural Production and the Politics of Visibility*, ed. Tourmaline, Eric A. Stanley, and Johanna Burton. Cambridge, MA: MIT Press, 2017.

Gray, David B. *The Cakrasamvara Tantra (the Discourse of Śrī Heruka): Editions of the Sanskrit and Tibetan Texts*. New York: American Institute of Buddhist Studies, 2007.

——. "Disclosing the Empty Secret: Textuality and Embodiment in the *Cakrasamvara Tantra*." *Numen* 52, no. 4 (2005): 417–44.

Gyatso, Janet. *Being Human in a Buddhist World: An Intellectual History of Medicine in Early Modern Tibet*. New York: Columbia University Press, 2015.

——. "Down with the Demoness: Reflections on a Feminine Ground in Tibet." In *Feminine Ground: Essays on Women and Tibet*, ed. Janet D. Willis, 33–51. Ithaca, NY: Snow Lion, 1987.

——. "Image as Presence: The Place of the Work of Art in Tibetan Religious Thinking." In *The Newark Museum Tibetan Collection III. Sculpture and Painting*, ed. Valrae Reynolds, Amy Heller, and Janet Gyatso. Newark, NJ: Newark Museum, 1986.

——. "Letter Magic: A Peircean Perspective on the Semiotics of Rdo Grub-chen's Dhāraṇī Memory." In *In the Mirror of Memory: Reflections on Mindfulness and Remembrance in Indian and Tibetan Buddhism*, ed. Janet Gyatso. Albany: State University of New York Press, 1992.

Gzhon-nu-dpal, Gos Lo-tsā-ba, George Roerich. *The Blue Annals*. Delhi: Motilal Banarsidass, 1988.

Hackett, Paul G. "Re-making, Re-marking, or Re-using? Hermeneutical Strategies and Challenges in the Guhyasamāja Commentarial Literature." In "Reuse and Intertextuality in the Context of Buddhist Texts," ed. Elisa Freschi, Cathy Cantwell, and Jowita Kramer, special issue, *Buddhist Studies Review* 33, no. 1–2 (2016): 163–179.

Hall, Stuart. "Cultural Identity and Diaspora." *Framework*, no. 36 (1989): 222–237.

Hallisey, Charles. "'It Not the Only One': Womanist Resources for Reflection in Buddhist Studies." *Buddhist-Christian Studies* 32 (2012): 73–85.

——. "Roads Taken and Not Taken in the Study of Theravāda Buddhism." In *Curators of the Buddha: The Study of Buddhism under Colonialism*, ed. Donald Lopez. Chicago: University of Chicago Press, 1995.

Hammer Museum. "Glenn Ligon, Artist. *Notes on the Margin of the 'Black Book,'* 1991–93." https://hammer.ucla.edu/take-it-or-leave-it/art/notes-on-the-margin-of-the-black-book.

Heimbel, Jörg. "Biographical Sources for Researching the Life of Ngor chen Kun dga' bzang po (1382–1456)." *Revue d'Etudes Tibétaines*, no. 22 (2011): 47–91.

——."The Dispute Between mKhas grub rJe and Ngor chen: Its Representation and Role in Tibetan Life Writing." In *Towards a History of Fifteenth-century Tibet: Cultural Blossoming, Religious Fervour, and Political Unrest*, ed. Volker Caumanns and Marta Sernisi, 249–290. Lumbini, Nepal: Lumbini International Research Institute, 2017.

——. *Vajradhara in Human Form: The Life and Times of Ngor chen Kun dga' bzang po*. Lumbini, Nepal: Lumbini International Research Institute, 2017.

Hemphill, Essex, and Joseph Beam. *Brother to Brother: Collected Writings by Black Gay Men*. Boston: Alyson, 1991.

Hollywood, Amy. "Performativity, Citationality, Ritualization." In *Bodily Citations: Religion and Judith Butler*, ed. Ellen T. Armour and Susan M. St. Ville, 261. New York: Columbia University Press, 2006.

Hopkins, Jeffrey, and Kevin Vose. *Tantric Techniques*. Ithaca, NY: Snow Lion, 2009.

Jackson, David P. *The Early Abbots of 'Phan-po Ne-len-dra: The Vicissitudes of a Great Tibetan Monastery in the Fifteenth Century*. Vienna: Arbeitskreis für Tibetische und Buddhistische Studien, Universität Wien, 1989.

——. *Enlightenment by a Single Means: Tibetan Controversies on the "Self-Sufficient White Remedy" (dkar po chig thub)*. Vienna: Verlag der Österreichischen Akademie der Wissenschaften, 1994.

——. *The Mollas of Mustang: Historical, Religious, and Oratorical Traditions of the Nepalese-Tibetan Borderland*. Dharamsala: Library of Tibetan Works and Archives, 1984.

——. *The Nepalese Legacy in Tibetan Painting*. New York: Rubin Museum of Art, 2010.

Jackson, R. R., and Rgyal-tshab Dar-ma-rin-chen. *Is Enlightenment Possible?: Dharmakīrti and rGyal tshab rje on Knowledge, Rebirth, No-self, and Liberation*. Ithaca, NY: Snow Lion, 1993.

Jacoby, Sarah. *Love and Liberation: Autobiographical Writings of the Tibetan Buddhist Visionary Sera Khandro.* New York: Columbia University Press, 2014.

Kalff, Martin. "Selected Chapters from the Abhidhānottara-Tantra: The Union of Female and Male Deities." PhD diss., Columbia University, 1979. Ann Arbor: University Microfilms International, 1982.

Kalupahana, David J. *Nāgārjuna: The Philosophy of the Middle Way. Mūlamadhyamakakārikā. Introduction, Sanskrit Text, English Translation and Annotation.* Albany: State University of New York Press, 1986.

Kapstein, Matthew. *The 'Dzam-thang Edition of the Collected Works of Kun mkhyen Dol-po-pa Shes-rab rgyal-mtshan.* Delhi: Shedrup, 1992.

——. *The Tibetans.* Oxford: Blackwell, 2006.

Kardon, Janet, David Joselit, and Kay Larson. *Robert Mapplethorpe: The Perfect Moment.* Philadelphia: Institute of Contemporary Art, University of Pennsylvania, 1988.

Kittay, David. "Interpreting the Vajra Rosary: Truth and Method Meets Wisdom and Method." PhD diss., Columbia University, 2011.

——. *The Vajra Rosary Tantra (Vajramalatantra).* New York: American Institute of Buddhist Studies, 2013.

Klein, Anne C. *Meeting the Great Bliss Queen: Buddhists, Feminists, and the Art of the Self.* Boston: Beacon, 1994.

Kramer, Jowita. *A Noble Abbot from Mustang: Life and Works of Glo-bo mKhan-chen (1456–1532).* Vienna: Arbeitskreis für Tibetische und Buddhistische Studien, 2008.

Kramer, Ralf. *The Great Tibetan Translator: Life and Works of rNgog Blo ldan shes rab (1059–1109).* Munich: Indus Verlag, 2007.

Lee, Yong-Hyun. *The Niṣpannayogāvalī by Abhayākāragupta: A New Critical Edition of the Sanskrit Text,* rev. ed. Seoul: Baegun, 2004.

——. "Synthesizing a Liturgical Heritage: Abhayākaragupta's 'Vajrāvalii' and the Kālacakramaṇḍala." PhD diss., University of Wisconsin, Madison. UMI Dissertation information Service, 2003.

Lessing, Ferdinand, and Alex Wayman, trans. *mKhas grub rJe's Fundamentals of Buddhist Tantra, Indo-Iranian Monographs v. 8.* The Hague: Mouton, 1968.

L'Official, Pete. "Words, Words, Words: On Glenn Ligon." https://lareviewofbooks.org/article/words-words-words-on-glenn-ligon/.

Lomax, Tamura A. *Jezebel Unhinged: Loosing the Black Female Body in Religion and Culture.* Durham: Duke University Press, 2018.

Lopez, Donald. "Burnouf and the Birth of Buddhist Studies." *Eastern Buddhist* 43, nos. 1/2 (2012): 25–34.

——. "Polemical Literature [dGag lan]." In *Tibetan Literature: Studies in Genre,* ed. J. I. Cabezón and R. R. Jackson, 217–228. Ithaca, NY: Snow Lion, 1996.

——. *Prisoners of Shangri-La: Tibetan Buddhism and the West.* Chicago: University of Chicago Press, 1998.

Lubow, Arthur. "Has Robert Mapplethorpe's Moment Passed?" https://www.nytimes.com/2019/07/25/arts/design/robert-mapplethorpe-guggenheim.html.

Luczanits, Christian. "On the Earliest Mandalas in a Buddhist Context." In *Mahāyāna Buddhism: History and Culture,* ed. Darrol Bryant and Susan Bryant, 111–136. New Delhi: Tibet House, 2008.

——. "Ritual, Instruction and Experiment: Esoteric Drawings from Dunhuang." In *The Art of Central Asia and the Indian Subcontinent in Cross Culture Perspective,* ed. Anupa Pande and Mandira Sharma, 140–49. New Delhi: National Museum Institute–Aryan Books International, 2009.

——. "Siddhas, Hierarchs, and Lineages: Three Examples for Dating Tibetan Art." In *Mirror of the Buddha: Early Portraits from Tibet,* ed. D. P. Jackson and Christian Luczanits, 170–197. New York: Rubin Museum of Art, 2011.

Luke, Ben. "America is both a shining beacon and the Death Star': Glenn Ligon on Andy Warhol, Ambivalence, and His Stevie Wonder Obsession." *The Art Newspaper,* August 19, 2021. https://www.theartnewspaper.com/interview/glenn-ligon-interview-black-artist-hauser-wirth-conceptual-art-podcast.

Mahmood, Saba. "Agency, Performativity, and the Feminist Subject." In *Bodily Citations: Religion and Judith Butler*, edited by Ellen T. Armour and Susan M. St. Ville, 261. New York: Columbia University Press, 2006.

Mallinson, James. "The *Amṛtasiddhi*: Haṭhayoga's Tantric Buddhist Source Text." In *Śaivism and the Tantric Traditions: Essays in Honour of Alexis G. J. S. Sanderson*, ed. Dominick Goodall, Shaman Hatley, Harunaga Isaacson, and Srilata Raman, 409–425. Leiden: Brill, 2020.

Mallinson, James, and Mark Singleton. *Roots of Yoga*. London: Penguin, 2017.

Mapplethorpe, Robert. *Black Book*. New York: St. Martin's, 1986.

Martin, Dan. "Tibeto-Logic." https://tibeto-logic.blogspot.com.

Mathes, Klaus-Dieter. *A Direct Path to the Buddha Within: Gö Lotsāwa's Mahāmūdrā Interpretation of the Ratnagotravibhāga*. Boston: Wisdom, 2008.

Matsunaga, Yukei. *The Guhyasamāja Tantra: A New Critical Edition*. Osaka: Toho Shuppan, 1978.

McKeown, Arthur. *Guardian of a Dying Flame. Śāriputra (c. 1335–1426) and the End of Late Indian Buddhism*. Cambridge, MA: Harvard University Press, 2018.

Meisezahl, Richard O. *Hastapūjāvidhi-Texte: Der Handritus im anuttarayogischen Kult Götterpaares Cakrasambhara und Vajravārahī*. Sankt Augustin, Germany: VGH Wissenschaftsverlag, 1985.

Miller, Willa Blythe. "Secrets of the Vajra Body: *Dngos po'i gnas lugs* and the Apotheosis of the Body in the Work of Rgyal ba Yang dgon pa." PhD diss., Harvard University, 2013.

Mori, Masahide, ed. *Vajrāvalī of Abhayākaragupta: An Edition of Sanskrit and Tibetan Versions*. Tring: Institute of Buddhist Studies, 2009.

Morrison, Toni. *Playing in the Dark: Whiteness and the Literary Imagination*. Cambridge, MA: Harvard University Press, 1992.

Nag-dbang-blo-bzang-rgya-mtsho and Zahiruddin Ahmad. *The History of Tibet*. Bloomington, Indiana: Indiana University, Research Institute for Inner Asian Studies, 1995.

Nāgārjuna and David J. Kalupahana. *Mūlamadhyamakakārikā of Nāgārjuna: The Philosophy of the Middle Way: Introduction, Sanskrit Text, English Translation and Annotation*. Delhi, India: Motilal Banarsidass, 1996.

Palmer, Alex. "When Art Fought the Law and the Art Won." *Smithsonian Magazine*, October 2, 2015. https://www.smithsonianmag.com/history/when-art-fought-law-and-art-won-180956810/.

Patton, Laurie. *Myth as Argument: The Brhaddevata as Canonical Commentary*. Berlin: de Gruyter, 1996.

Radich, Michael David. "The Somatics of Liberation: Ideas about Embodiment in Buddhism from Its Origins to the Fifth Century C.E." PhD diss., Harvard University, 2007.

Rockhill, William Woodville. *The Land of the Lamas: Notes of a Journey through China, Mongolia and Tibet with Maps and Illustrations*. New York: Century, 1891.

Roesler, Ulrike. "'As it is said in a Sutra': Freedom and Variation in Quotations from the Buddhist Scriptures in Early Bka'-gdams-pa Literature." *Journal of Indian Philosophy* 43, nos. 4/5 (November 2015): 493–510.

Ross, Alex. "Neitzsche's Eternal Return." *New Yorker*, October 14, 2019.

Said, Edward W. *Humanism and Democratic Criticism*. New York: Columbia University Press, 2004.

Sakurai, Munenobu. "Another Version Prajñārakṣita's Balividhi." In *Three Mountains and Seven Rivers: Musashi Tachikawa's Felicitation Volume*, ed. Musashi Tachikawa, Shoun Ino, and Toshihiro Wada, 815–828. Delhi: Motilal Banarsidas, 2004.

Sa-skya Paṇḍi-ta Kun-dga-rgyal-mtshan, Jared Rhoton, and Victoria R. M. Scott. *A Clear Differentiation of the Three Codes: Essential Distinctions Among the Individual Liberation, Great Vehicle, and Tantric Systems . . . ; Six Letters*. New York: State University of New York Press, 2002.

Samuel, Geoffrey, and Jay Johnston. *Religion and the Subtle Body in Asia and the West: Between Mind and Body*. Abingdon, Oxon: Routledge, 2013.

Sanderson, Alexis. "Mandala and Āgamic Identity in the Trika of Kashmir." In *Mantras et Diagrammes Rituelles dans l'Hindouisme*, ed. Andre Padoux. *Équipe no. 249 'L'hindouisme: Textes, Doctrines, Pratiques.'* Paris: CNRS, 1986.

——. "The Śaiva Age: The Rise and Dominance of Śaivism During the Early Medieval Period." In *Genesis and Development of Tantrism*, ed. Shingo Einoo, 23:41–349. Tokyo: Institute of Oriental Culture, 2009.

——. "Vajrayāna: Origin and Function." In *Buddhism Into the Year 2000: International Conference Proceedings*. Bangkok: Dhammakaya Foundation, 1994.

Sayer, Rhonwen. "The Guhyasamāja Piṇḍikṛta-Sādhana and Its Context." Masters thesis, School of Oriental and African Studies, 2010.

Schaeffer, Kurtis R. *The Culture of the Book in Tibet*. New York: Columbia University Press. 2014.

Schweiker, William, and José Ignacio Cabezón. "The Discipline(s) and Its (Their) Other(s): A Response to José Ignacio Cabezón." *Journal of the American Academy of Religion* 74, no. 1 (2006): 39–46.

Schwieger, Peter. "Significance of Ming Titles Conferred Upon the Phag mo gru rulers: A Reevaluation of Chinese-Tibetan Relations During the Ming Dynasty." *Tibet Journal* 34, nos. 2/3 (2009): 313–328.

Sharf, Robert H. "Buddhist Modernism and the Rhetoric of Meditative Experience," *Numen* 42, no. 3 (1995): 228–283. Republished in *Buddhism: Critical Concepts in Buddhist Studies*, ed. Paul Williams, 2:255–298. London: Routledge, 2005.

——. "Visualization and Maṇḍala in Shingon Buddhism." *Living Images: Japanese Buddhist Icons in Context*, no. 2 (2001): 151–197.

Sheets, Hilarie. "The Writing on the Wall: Glenn Ligon on Borrowing Text to Expose American Racism, in 2011." https://www.artnews.com/art-news/retrospective/the-writing-on-the-wall-glenn-ligon-on-borrowing-text-to-expose-american-racism-in-2011-5658/.

Shen, Weirong. "On the History of Gling tshang Principality mDo khams During the Yuan and Ming Dynasties: Study on Sources Concerning Tibet in the Ming Shilu (I)." In *Tibetstudien: Festschrift für Dieter Schuh zum 65.* Geburtstag, ed. D. Schuh, P. H. Maurer, and P. Schwieger, 227–265. Bonn: Bier'sche Verlagsanstalt, 2007.

Sischy, Ingrid. "White and Black." *New Yorker*, November 5, 1989 (November 13, 1989 issue). https://www.newyorker.com/magazine/1989/11/13/white-and-black.

Smith, Gene E. and Kurtis R. Schaeffer. "Buddhist Literary and Practical Arts According to Bo dong Pan chen Phygs las rnam rgyal." In *Among Tibetan Texts: History and Literature of the Himalayan Plateau*, 179–208. Boston: Wisdom, 2001.

Smith, Jonathan Z. *Imagining Religion: From Babylon to Jonestown*. Chicago: University of Chicago Press, 1982.

——. "Religion, Religions, Religious." In *Critical Terms for Religious Studies*, ed. Mark C. Taylor, 179–195. Chicago: University of Chicago Press, 1998.

——. "Sacred Persistence: Toward a Redescription of Canon." In *Imagining Religion: From Babylon to Jonestown*. Chicago: University of Chicago Press, 1982.

Snellgrove, David. *The Hevajra Tantra: a Critical Study*. Bangkok: Orchid, 2010.

——. *Indo-Tibetan Buddhiosm: Indian Buddhists and Their Tibetan Successors*. Boston: Shambhala, 1992.

Snorton, C. Riley. *Black on Both Sides: A Racial History of Trans Identity*. Minneapolis: University of Minnesota Press, 2017.

Sobisch, Jan-Ulrich. *Hevajra and Lam 'bras Literature of India and Tibet as Seen Through the Eyes of A-mes-zhabs*. Wiesbaden: Reichert, 2008.

——. "Tibetan Interpretations of Authenticity." In *The Illuminating Mirror: Tibetan Studies in Honour of Per K. Sørensen on the Occasion of His Sixty-fifth Birthday*, ed. Per K. Sørensen, Olaf Czaja, and Guntram Hazod. Wiesbaden: Dr. Ludwig Reichert Verlag, 2015.

Sokolowski, Thomas W. "Iconophobics Anonymous," Summer 1990. https://www.artforum.com/print/199006/iconophobics-anonymous-34059.

Solomon R. Guggenheim Museum. "Implicit Tensions: Mapplethorpe Now." https://www.guggenheim.org/exhibition/mapplethorpe.

Sperling, Eliot. "The Fifth Karmapa and Some Aspects of the Relationship Between Tibet and the Early Ming." In *The History of Tibet*, ed. Alex McKay. London: Routledge Curzon, 2003.

Stanley, Phillip. "The Tibetan Buddhist Canon." In *The Wiley Blackwell Companion to East and Inner Asian Buddhism*, ed. Mario Poceski, 383–407. Oxford: Wiley, 2014.

Stearns, Cyrus. *Luminous Lives: The Story of the Early Masters of the Lam'bras Tradition in Tibet.* Boston: Wisdom, 2001.

——, trans. *Taking the Result as the Path: Core Teachings of the Sakya Lamdré Tradition.* Boston: Wisdom, 2006.

Steinkellner, Ernst. "Tshad ma'i skyes bu. Meaning and Historical Significance of the Term." *Contributions on Tibetan and Buddhist Religion and Philosophy,* no. 2 (1995): 259–274.

Stryker, Susan. "My Words to Victor Frankenstein Above the Village of Chamounix." *GLQ: A Journal of Lesbian and Gay Studies* 1, no. 3 (June 1994): 237–254.

Sugiki, Tsunehiko. "Five Types of Internal Mandala Described in the Cakrasamvara Buddhist Literature: Somatic Representations of One's Innate Sacredness." *Memoirs of the Institute of Oriental Culture* 144 (2003): 156–231.

——. "The Structure and Traditions of the Systems of Holy Sites in the Buddhist Saṃvara Cycle and Its Related Scriptural Cycles in Early Medieval South Asia: The Geography of Esoteric Buddhism in the Eyes of the Compilers of the Scriptures." In *Genesis and Development of Tantrism, Institute of Oriental Culture Special Series,* ed. Shingo Einoo, 23:515–562. Tokyo: Institute of Oriental Culture, 2009.

Szántó, Péter-Dániel. "Before a Critical Edition of the *Saṃputa.*" *Zentralasiatische Studien* 45 (2016): 397–422.

Tanaka, Kimiaki. "Nāgabodhi's Śrī-guhyasamāja-maṇḍalopāyikā-viṃśati-vidhi, 8 akasasutrapatanavidhi." *Journal of Indian and Buddhist Studies* 50, no. 1 (2001): 315–320.

——. "Nāgabodhi's Śrī-guhyasamāja-maṇḍalopāyikā-viṃśati-vidhi: The Sanskrit Text Restored from the Vajrācārānayotttam." In *Genesis and Development of Tantrism, Institute of Oriental Culture Special Series,* ed. Shingo Einoo, 425–34. Tokyo: Institute of Oriental Culture, 2009.

——. "Nāgabodhi's Śrī-guhyasamāja-maṇḍalopāyikā-viṃśati-vidhi: The Tibetan Translation and Sanskrit Text of Chapters 5 and 6." In *Three Mountains and Seven Rivers: Prof. Musashi Tachikawa's Felicitation Volume,* 857–869. Delhi: Motilal Banarsidass, 2004.

Thub-bstan-ye-shes, Jonathan Landaw, and Philip Glass. *Introduction to Tantra: The Transformation of Desire.* Boston: Wisdom, 2014.

Thurman, Robert, trans. *Brilliant Illumination of the Lamp of the Five Stages (Rim lnga rab tu gsal ba'i sgron me): Practical Instruction in the King of Tantras, the Glorious Esoteric Community.* Ed. Thomas F. Yarnall. New York: American Institute of Buddhist Studies, 2010.

Thurman, Robert A. F. *The Central Philosophy of Tibet: A Study and Translation of Jey Tsong Khapa's Essence of True Eloquence.* Princeton: Princeton University Press, 1984.

The Tibetan and Himalayan Library. http://thlib.org.

Tomabechi, Toru. "Vitapāda, Śākyamitra, and Āryadeva: On a Transitional Stage in the History of Guhyasamāja Exexgesis." In *Esoteric Buddhist Studies: Identity in Diversity,* 171–177. Koyasan University: Proceedings of the International Conference on Esoteric Buddhist Studies, 2008.

Tourmaline, Eric A. Stanley, and Johanna Burton, eds. *Trap Door: Trans Cultural Production and the Politics of Visibility.* Cambridge, MA: MIT Press, 2017.

Tsemo, Sonam. *The Yogini's Eye: Comprehensive Introduction to Buddhist Tantra Volume 1: Systematization and Interpretation.* Trans. Sonam Gyatso and Wayne Verrill. Bloomington: Xlibris Corporation, 2012.

Tsong-kha-pa Blo-bzang-grags-pa, and G. Kilty, *A Lamp to Illuminate the Five Stages Teachings on Guhyasamāja Tantra.* Boston: Wisdom, 2013.

Tsuda, Shiníchi. *The Saṃvarodaya Tantra: Selected Chapters.* Tokyo: Hokuseido, 1974.

van der Kuijp, Leonard W. J. "Apropos of a Recent Contribution to the History of Central Way Philosophy in Tibet: Tsong kha pa's Speech of Gold," *Berliner Indologische Studien* 1 (1985): 47–74.

——. "Miscellanea Apropos of the Philosophy of Mind in Tibet: Mind in Tibetan Buddhism." *Tibet Journal* 10 (1985): 32–43.

——. "Studies in Btsun pa Ston gzhon's *Pramāṇavārttika* Commentary of ?1297. Part One: Preliminary Observations and the Import of Its Title." *Revue d'Etudes Tibétaines,* no. 30 (October 2014): 111–198.

——. "Studies in the Life and Thought of mKhas grub rje I: mKhas grub rje's Epistemological Oeuvre and His Philological Remarks on Dignaga's *Pramāṇasamuccaya* I." *Berliner Indologische Studien,* no. 1 (1985): 75–105.

——. "A Text-Historical Note on *Hevajratantra* II: v:1–2." *Journal of the International Association for Buddhist Studies* 8, no. 1 (1985): 83–89.

von Rospatt, Alexander. "Remarks on the Consecration Ceremony in Kuladatta's *Kriyāsaṃgrahapañjikā* and its Development in Newar Buddhism." In *Hindu and Buddhist Initiations in Nepal and India*, ed. Astrid Zotter and Christof Zotter. Wiesbaden: Harrassowitz, 2010.

Wang, Michelle C. *Maṇḍalas in the Making: The Visual Culture of Esoteric Buddhism at Dunhuang.* Leiden: Brill, 2018.

Wangchuk, Jamyang Khyentse. "Summarizing Notes of the Outer Creation Stage from the Expansion of the Great Secret Doctrine: Summarizing Notes of Guidance for the Precious Teaching of the 'Path with the Result.'" In *Taking the Result as the Path: Core Teachings of the Sakya Lamdré Tradition,* trans. Cyrus Stearns, 477–527. Boston: Wisdom, 2006.

Wedemeyer, Christian. *Making Sense of Tantric Buddhism: History, Semiology, and Transgression in the Indian Traditions.* New York: Columbia University Press, 2012.

——. "Tantalising Traces of the Labours of the Lotsawas: Alternative Translations of Sanskrit Sources in the Writings of Rje Tsong Kha Pa." In *Tibetan Buddhist Literature and Praxis: Studies in Its Formative Period, 900–1400*, ed. Ronald Davidson and Christian Wedemeyer, 149–182. Leiden: Brill, 2006.

Wedemeyer, Christian, and Āryadeva. *Lamp That Integrates the Practices (Caryāmelāpakapradīpa): The Gradual Path of Vajrayāna Buddhism According to the Esoteric Community Noble Tradition.* New York: Columbia University Press, 2007.

Wu, Jiang, and Lucille Chia. *Spreading Buddha's Word in East Asia: The Formation and Transformation of the Chinese Buddhist Canon.* New York: Columbia University Press, 2016.

Wylie, Turrell V. "Lama Tribute in the Ming Dynasty." In *Tibetan Studies in Honour of Hugh Richardson,* 335–340. Warminster: Aris and Phillips, 1980.

——. "Monastic Patronage in Fifteenth-Century Tibet." In *The History of Tibet,* ed. Alex McKay, 319–328. London: Routledge Curzon, 2003.

Index

CPSIA information can be obtained
at www.ICGtesting.com
Printed in the USA
LVHW041416120123
736945LV00005B/368

9 780231 206099